Praise for Girls' Sexualities
and the Media

"This edited collection is a refreshing look at research that embraces the basic tenets of cultural studies work. It boldly explores the context (history) within which representations emerge, emphasizes the importance of audiences, and offers a feisty review of ways girls can talk back to the culture through resistance."

—Deb Merskin, Associate Professor, School of Journalism & Communication, University of Oregon; Co-Editor, *Critical Thinking About Sex, Love, and Romance in the Mass Media*

"This truly outstanding collection of essays—by pioneers as well as rising stars in the fields of girls, gender, sexuality, and media studies—sheds new light on the interaction of innumerable forces at work in regulating and resisting girls' sexuality in popular media. The tripartite arrangement of the essays, which critically consider the intersection of girls' age, class, race, ethnicities, nationalities, and sexualities, frames this comprehensive examination of popular representations of girls' sexuality, girls' reception and self re/presentations, as well as girls' media literacy endeavors.

"The nuanced explorations of competing fears and fantasies about female adolescent sexuality in *Twilight*, *Harry Potter*, MTV's *16 and Pregnant*, and other discursive texts are sure to resonate with students who—along with the fictional and real girls whose voices are included in this collection— already reflect, resist, and/or reclaim media sexualization in their everyday lives.

"Instructors will find that, in addition to providing essential content, context, and concepts that scrutinize social anxieties and sexual agency, the variety of methods and theories reframing current debates in these essays will inform the research of the next generation of girls' studies scholars."

—Miriam Forman-Brunell, Professor of History, Women, and Gender Studies, University of Missouri-Kansas City; Author, *Babysitters: An American History;* Editor, *The Girls' History and Culture Readers*

"This vibrant collection of essays makes a valuable contribution to girlhood studies and sexualities studies and helps to open up an important space for debate between them. Interdisciplinary, international, and attentive to the way power works intersectionally, *Girls' Sexualities and the Media* is an exciting addition to the field."

—Rosalind Gill, King's College London; Author, *Gender and the Media;* Co-Editor, *New Femininities: Postfeminism, Neoliberalism, and Subjectivity*

Girls' Sexualities
and the Media

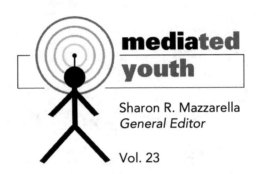

mediated youth

Sharon R. Mazzarella
General Editor

Vol. 23

The Mediated Youth series is part of the Peter Lang
Media and Communication list.
Every volume is peer reviewed and meets
the highest quality standards for content and production.

PETER LANG
New York • Washington, D.C./Baltimore • Bern
Frankfurt • Berlin • Brussels • Vienna • Oxford

Girls' Sexualities and the Media

EDITED BY Kate Harper, Yasmina Katsulis, Vera Lopez, & Georganne Scheiner Gillis

PETER LANG
New York • Washington, D.C./Baltimore • Bern
Frankfurt • Berlin • Brussels • Vienna • Oxford

Library of Congress Cataloging-in-Publication Data

Girls' sexualities and the media / edited by
Kate Harper, Yasmina Katsulis, Vera Lopez, Georganne Scheiner Gillis.
pages cm. — (Mediated youth; vol. 23)
Includes bibliographical references and index.
1. Girls—Sexual behavior—United States—History.
2. Mass media—United States—History. I. Harper, Kate.
HQ27.5.G57   306.760835—dc23   2013005251
ISBN 978-1-4331-2276-7 (hardcover)
ISBN 978-1-4331-2275-0 (paperback)
ISBN 978-1-4539-1091-7 (e-book)
ISSN 1555-1814

Bibliographic information published by **Die Deutsche Nationalbibliothek**.
Die Deutsche Nationalbibliothek lists this publication in the "Deutsche
Nationalbibliografie"; detailed bibliographic data is available
on the Internet at http://dnb.d-nb.de/.

Cover artwork: Joel Deal

The paper in this book meets the guidelines for permanence and durability
of the Committee on Production Guidelines for Book Longevity
of the Council of Library Resources.

© 2013 Peter Lang Publishing, Inc., New York
29 Broadway, 18th floor, New York, NY 10006
www.peterlang.com

Printed in the United States of America

Contents

Acknowledgments ix

Foreword xi
Catherine Driscoll

Girls' Sexualities and the Media: The Power of the Media 1
Yasmina Katsulis, Vera Lopez, Kate Harper, and Georganne Scheiner Gillis

PART ONE: HISTORICAL AND CONTEMPORARY MEDIA

1 The Girls of Carvel: Adolescent Desire in *Andy Hardy* Films 29
   Georganne Scheiner Gillis

2 "Sensible Safety Rules": Class, Race, and Girls' Sexual Vulnerability
   in the U.S. Print Media, 1950–1970 45
   Jennifer Helgren

3 Snogging, Stereotypes, and Subversion: Girls' Sexuality
   in the *Harry Potter* Series 61
   Kate Harper

4   The Pleasures of Danger and the Dangers of Pleasure:
    The Inversion of Gender Relations in the *Twilight* Series...................77
    Suzan Walters and Michael Kimmel

5   "She's All That": Girl Sexuality and Teen Film...................93
    Catherine Driscoll

6   Wrecked and Redeemed: Religio-Political Pedagogy
    and MTV's *16 and Pregnant*...................109
    Amanda Rossie

7   Just Say Me? (Mis)representing Female Adolescent Sexual
    Agency on *The Secret Life of the American Teenager*...................123
    Elena Frank

8   Producing Girl Citizens as Agents of Health: An Analysis
    of HPV Media Campaigns in the United States...................139
    Kellie Burns and Cristyn Davies

PART TWO: MEDIA USE AND SELF-REPRESENTATION

9   "Hyperfeminine" Subcultures: Rethinking Gender Subjectivity
    and the Discourse of Sexuality Among Adolescent Girls
    in Contemporary Japan...................157
    Isaac Gagné

10 Favela Models: Sexual Virtue and Hopeful Narratives
    of Beauty in Brazil...................173
    Alvaro Jarrín

11 "Chongas" in the Media: The Ethno-Sexual Politics of
    Latina Girls' Hypervisibility...................187
    Jillian Hernandez

12 Heteroflexibility: Female Performance and Pleasure...................211
    Jennifer Apple

PART THREE: MEDIA CAMPAIGNS AND LITERACY PROJECTS

13 "Hey Media, Back Off and Get Off My Body":
SPARK is Taking Sexy Back 227
Deborah L. Tolman, Lyn Mikel Brown, and Christin P. Bowman

14 From Media Propaganda to De-Stigmatizing Sex: Exploring
a Teen Magazine By, For, and About Girls 245
Linda Charmaraman and Brittany Low

15 "We're All Straight Here": Using Girls' Groups and Critical
Media Literacy to Explore Identity with Middle School Girls 263
*Amy Rutstein-Riley, Jenn Walker, Alice Diamond, Bonnie Bryant, and Marie
LaFlemme*

Contributors 285

Index 291

Acknowledgments

Our aim in developing this anthology was to begin the kind of dialogue necessary for a transformation of scholarship that transcends disciplinary boundaries, including scholars from the humanities and social sciences, anthropology, sociology, history, cultural studies, and gender studies. This collection of essays represents a culmination of those efforts.

The concept for this book began in the spring of 2010 with a seminar on girls' sexuality at Arizona State University. The seminar culminated in a symposium, "Girls' Sexualities: A Transdisciplinary Perspective," in April 2010, featuring guest speakers Dr. Meda Chesney-Lind, Dr. Deborah Tolman, and Dr. Mary Odem. Our sincerest thanks to these scholars for not only making the symposium a success, but for breaking ground in girls' research and making our own research possible. The Institute for Humanities Research provided funding for the symposium and this anthology, and we thank its director, Regents' Professor Sally L. Kitch, for her gracious support. Funding and support were also provided by the School of Social Transformation and its director, Dr. Mary Margaret Fonow.

Our appreciation to Sharon R. Mazzarella, who saw great promise in the collection as an addition to the Mediated Youths series. Thanks to Mary, Sarah, and Jackie at Peter Lang for diligently working with us through every step of the process. We would like to thank our colleagues and friends in Gender Studies and Justice Studies at Arizona State University, whose support, encouragement, and commitment to social justice makes such intellectual work possible. Our gratitude and congratulations go to all the contributors of the volume. Their enthusiasm for girls and their mediated experiences, not to mention their exceptional scholarship, kept the project moving forward.

Foreword

Catherine Driscoll

Throughout her childhood, the little girl was bullied and mutilated; but she nonetheless grasped herself as an autonomous individual; in her relations with her family and friends, in her studies and games, she saw herself in the present as a transcendence: her future passivity was something she only imagined. Once she enters puberty, the future not only moves closer: it settles into her body; it becomes the most concrete reality. It retains the fateful quality it always had; while the adolescent boy is actively routed towards adulthood, the girl looks forward to the opening of this new and unforeseeable period where the plot is already hatched and towards which time is drawing her. As she is already detached from her childhood past, the present is for her only a transition; she sees no valid ends in it, only occupations. In a more or less disguised way, her youth is consumed by waiting. She is waiting for Man.
—Simone de Beauvoir, *The Second Sex*

Simone de Beauvoir's justly famous and influential feminist text, *The Second Sex*, first published in 1949, moves from the subject of "childhood" to that of "girlhood" with the passage cited above. A great deal has clearly changed for girls in the industrialized societies that Beauvoir is accounting for in this text. It is now generally presumed that girls will move from "childhood" into "girlhood" with expectations of social independence. At the very least they expect to, and are expected to, articulate life goals beyond simply "waiting for Man."[1]

Nevertheless, I think we can take three important cues from Beauvoir when considering the continuing importance of research into girls' sexualities. The first is her distinguishing girlhood at all. Although I don't think it has ever been much foregrounded, one of the influential elements of Beauvoir's account of how one becomes, rather than being born, "woman" is its delineation of girlhood as a discrete stage of lived experience.[2] Discussing their new translation of *The Second Sex*, Constance Borde and Sheila Malovany-Chevalier single out as "a notable change" their decision to translate *la juene fille* as "girl" rather than as "the young girl."[3] That the previous translation (by Parshley) clearly left room for an older "girl" experience makes this indeed a notable change for a reader versed in girls studies.

In Beauvoir's account "the girl" clearly arrives with puberty and girlhood encompasses adolescence as a newly inflected period of embodied social identity formation. Of course Beauvoir recognized that childhood also involves embodied social identity formation—indeed, philosophers like Iris Marion Young have drawn heavily on Beauvoir's thinking about the girl's lived bodily experience.[4] The difference *girlhood* introduces here is key and Beauvoir is thus raising an important question for what we now call girls studies: how should we define "a girl"? We might well take gender as a starting premise and say, with some implicit reference to puberty as a psycho-sexual break if not to psychoanalytic stories about "latency,"[5] that this girlhood is a newly sexualized phase of learning gender roles. Or, taking Young's cautions about "gender" seriously,[6] and recognizing as well that Beauvoir never used the term, we might take some account of the "lived body" as a starting premise and say that the social interpretation of puberty opens expectations of sexuality—of an identity grounded in orientation toward sex. This, rather than age or any precise physical or psychological change, brings about the *girl* formation. And this is clearly the second cue contemporary analysis of girlhood and sexuality might take from this passage. Both the transient occupations that Beauvoir understands to characterize girlhood as a period of "waiting," and also the "plot" toward which time and anticipation are drawing her, are centrally about sex. Certainly in Beauvoir's account it seems this girl is not (yet) sexually active but in fact sex alone does not, in this narrative or in popular narratives about girlhood around us, produce a transition from girl to woman and the most important point here remains relevant— the girl's value centers on her as yet unresolved possibilities.

Beauvoir's girl is clearly an agent in her own subjection to something that looks like destiny and yet appeals to her own desires: she "looks forward" to a "plot...already hatched."[7] The chapter with the title "La Juene Fille" that begins this way is crucial to Beauvoir's account of how one both willingly takes up and is interpellated by the situational identity of woman.[8] Beauvoir doesn't slight the complexity of this situation, and this is the third cue I think we might take from Beauvoir in thinking about the analyses of girls relations with, and representation by, popular media collected in this volume. A core appeal of "the girl," for girls as well as others, is her constitution as an object of desire, a constitution Beauvoir famously argues involves the girl subordinating her own subjectivity to that object role. Yet clearly this becoming object involves a powerful validation of the girl's cultural significance and requires her own identification with that significance, and thus it compromises rather than erases her agency. Girls are constantly faced with this offer/promise of objectification rather than it being something entirely chosen for them or a choice that could ever be made once and for all.

To open a collection of essays on girls' sexualities and the media with an excursion back into Beauvoir may seem a little perverse. To begin with, discussions of girls and media have an understandable tendency to focus on the contemporary, although one of the strengths of this collection is that it recognizes there's a history behind the conversations about girl sexuality and the media carefully overviewed in the introduction to this volume. Beauvoir's foregrounding of the importance of sex to the girl experience itself also helps raises these important historicizing questions about the urgent panic sometimes generated around the sexualization of girls. A more compelling reason for setting Beauvoir aside in this context would be that she is just not up-to-date on the forms or consequences of girls' engagement with sexuality in and through the media. *The Second Sex* is outdated not so much in its theorization of the imperative to become woman as by the media industries within which girls find themselves both placed and circulated. Certainly in 1949 there was no internet or YouTube, no smart phones or sexting, and no popular discourse on girl empowerment through commodities. Except, in fact, that last claim would be quite wrong. The context into which Beauvoir wrote *The Second Sex* was rife with representations of becoming the best girl you could be through consumer culture, and of exceeding the expectations of previous generations of women with the can-do attitude of modern girls. The image of girlhood now hotly debated by feminists, scholars, and otherwise, using concepts like "girl power" and "postfeminism," was already well established and indeed forms one of the conditions for separating "girls" from girl children. While there are real differences to be acknowledged between 1949 and today, including the very important fact that it would be enormously difficult in the present tense to use girl sexuality as a sales pitch that was not about freedom and choice, the power of representations over who girls and women believe they can and should be is crucial to Beauvoir's critique.

There are, I am suggesting, still many things to be learned from even the most familiar feminist theory for the debates about the "sexualization" of girls in the media today. And new scholarship that engages such critical thinking about the meaning and experience of girl sexuality with the material conditions of girls' media practice and girls' mediated lives today is of vital importance. It is particularly important that such scholarship be critically self-reflexive considering the extent to which feminism itself has been incorporated into these dynamics. As Angela McRobbie suggests in *The Aftermath of Feminism,* in the early twenty-first century mass media representations of the social life of women are dominated by figures of liberated girlhood—a rhetoric of "freedom" constantly being "revitalized" and kept "up-to-date" by a "*faux*-feminism" dependent on girls' right and power to consume.⁹ Feminism, she argues, has been "taken into account" by a social field of institutions and industries that can use feminist rhetoric to both obscure and justify systemic inequality.

McRobbie's diagnosis of the trap laid for girls by their own pleasure in anticipating a future in which perfect heterosexual fulfilment will complete them resonates strongly with Beauvoir's despite the sixty intervening years. For both, the promises of such perfection, and their sexualization of success, make it "difficult to function as a female subject without subjecting oneself to those technologies of self that are constitutive of the spectacularly feminine" and thus without commitment to an endless, and endlessly commodified, process of self-interrogation.¹⁰ In a transnational mediasphere tied to a global political scene, McRobbie suggests, feminist politics is vilified and made unintelligible because it criticizes what offers girls this potential fulfilment. At the same time, however, feminism is incorporated into the promises made to girls and young women through the stress laid on achieving this fulfilment through their own agency. What McRobbie calls for at this juncture is insistence on "a theory of sexual power" within "feminist media and cultural studies," including a critique of "'gender aware' forms of governmentality."¹¹ This is the context in which this book appears and the project toward which these essays collectively work. If the definition of girlhood by sexuality and the sexualization of the experience of girlhood are not new, as reading Beauvoir suggests they are not, they are newly tied to institutional political monitoring of girl sexuality. An array of government inquiries into the sexualization of girlhood across the world is producing a codification of the proper representation of girl sexuality. Critical and self-conscious feminist research is urgently needed in this situation, and especially research that is both historically minded and attentive to the lived experience of girls today.

Notes

1. Simone de Beauvoir, *The Second Sex* (London: Vintage, 2009), 359.
2. Beavoir, *The Second Sex,* 283.
3. Beauvoir, *The Second Sex,* xviii.
4. Marion Iris Young, *On Female Body Experience: "Throwing Like a Girl" and Other Essays* (Oxford: Oxford University Press, 2005).
5. Sigmund Freud, *Introductory Lectures on Psychoanalysis* (Hardmondsworth: Penguin, 1953).
6. Young, *On Female Body,* 15–19.
7. Beauvoir, *The Second Sex,* 359.
8. I will leave the implicit reference to Louis Althusser undiscussed here (see Althusser, 1971). However, girls studies would do well to more closely consider the Althusserian argument about interpellation as one way of approaching the difficult questions around agency so important to the field discussed below (see Butler, 1997).

9. Angela McRobbie, *The Aftermath of Feminism: Gender, Culture, and Social Change* (London: Sage, 2008), 1.
10. Ibid., 60.
11. Ibid., 3; 2.

Works Cited

Althusser, Louis. "Ideology and Ideological State Apparatuses (Notes Towards an Investigation)." In *Lenin and Philosophy and Other Essays*, 121–173. London: NLB, 1971.

Beauvoir, Simone. *The Second Sex*. London: Vintage, 2009.

Butler, Judith. *The Psychic Life of Power: Essays in Subjection*. Los Angeles: Stanford University Press, 1997.

Freud, Sigmund. *Introductory Lectures on Psychoanalysis*. Hardmondsworth: Penguin, 1953.

McRobbie, Angela. *The Aftermath of Feminism: Gender, Culture and Social Change*. London: Sage, 2008.

Young, Iris Marion. *On Female Body Experience: "Throwing Like a Girl" and Other Essays*. Oxford: Oxford University Press, 2005.

Girls' Sexualities and the Media: The Power of the Media

Yasmina Katsulis, Vera Lopez, Kate Harper, and Georganne Scheiner Gillis

Analyses of representations of girls in the media have a long, if scattered, history. While Girls Studies has only recently been recognized as an academic subfield, its establishment is the culmination of the efforts of a number of scholars in various disciplines who have focused on girls in their research.[1] The fields of history, literature, and media studies have produced a number of studies on representations of girls, resisting the tendency to ignore girls and their experiences as significant sites of inquiry. These studies challenged the omission of girls in their traditional disciplines and set the foundations for the rapidly growing body of work on girls in the past two decades. Historical scholars have engaged in recuperative work on girls' lives, while simultaneously examining the constructed and negotiated meanings in both official documents and girls' own accounts.[2] Bringing this historical focus into a contemporary context, media and literary scholars continue to examine representations of girls in popular media, as well as girls' interactions with such media.[3] A number of recent anthologies explore the complex relationship between popular media and girls' identity construction.[4] The past twenty years have seen an explosion of new academic inquiry on the role of popular media in constructing our understanding of girls' lives and the potential for popular media to simultaneously restrict and expand cultural meanings of girlhood. Reflecting on this history, Jackson and Westrupp note, "Although the troubling of teenage girls' sexuality is historical, it has now expanded to include pre-teen and younger girls, to whom postmodern sexual proliferation has delivered, via popular culture, possibilities of being sexually knowing, aware and desiring subjects."[5]

Contemporary popular media provide girls with multiple, conflicting, and often highly idealized models of gender and sexuality. As has been noted by many scholars in gender and media studies, popular media often characterize only a narrow set of stereotypes, "tend[ing] to focus on women as sexual objects and as subordinates, who are valued primarily for their physical appearance and who willingly suppress their own needs and desires to preserve their relationships with others."[6] Teen magazines, for example, have been critiqued for reinscribing traditional gender scripts (for both males and females), the idealization of heterosexuality and romance, and the association of sex (for women and girls) with risk and danger.[7]

Central to feminist concerns around girls' sexualities and the media is "the idea that 'texts' of various kinds construct our world rather than merely report it."[8] The *power* of the media, then, as recently noted by Gill (2007), lies in the fact that "power works in and through subjects, not in terms of crude manipulation, but by structuring our sense of self, by constructing particular kinds of subjectivity."[9] What is clear from these debates is that popular media, although they may often reinforce stereotypical views of gendered sexualities, are far from monolithic. Thus, our volume seeks to enter this line of inquiry by further developing our understanding of both how girls' sexualities have been represented within the media, as well as how girls have utilized the media to represent themselves.

Sexual Subjectivity and Empowerment

There is a contentious split between those who focus on the power/empowerment end of the spectrum (the impact of girls on culture) and those who emphasize impact of culture on girls. On the one hand, some scholars have been criticized for portraying scholarship about girls' sense of empowerment as that of "naive neoliberals mutely supporting…a false discourse of free choice and individual autonomy."[10] On the other hand are scholars who seek "to counter such denial of voice and agency, and insert girls' voices into the debate."[11] Lamb suggests that the past few decades of feminist scholarship in this area have revolved around attempts to define and advocate for "a sexuality based on desire, subjectivity, and pleasure…[this] appears to be a response to three historically problematic areas for women and girls: objectification; abuse and victimization; and stereotypes of female passivity."[12] Theorists in this area of the literature explore the positive psychosocial impact of sexual subjectivity as it relates to female agency, embodiment, and an entitlement to pleasure and sexual desire, in direct contrast to portrayals of female sexual desire as largely absent or dangerous.[13] Tolman's work on the potential harms of girls' inability to feel, recognize, or experience sexual desire (as a result of these cultural narratives) was particularly critical in this area.[14]

Lamb, however, warns against defining healthy sexuality in terms of subjectivity, pleasure, and desire, arguing:

> [this] may reify the dichotomy between subject and object; [that] notions of desire, pleasure, and subjectivity may have different historical meanings and context for girls

of color; using pleasure as a gauge for whether sex is "good" has moral implications that may undermine other important goals of feminism; a healthy sexuality that includes all these elements may be unrealistic to achieve; and the kind of sexual person who feels pleasure, desire, and subjectivity may be ironically similar to the commodified, sexualized, marketed teen girl that is also problematic for feminism.[15]

Further interrogating the notion of empowerment, with special attention to how girl power has been portrayed in the popular media, Bae suggests that the postfeminist, consumer-oriented view of power as independent and pleasure-oriented is flawed in several ways.[16] Specifically, this concept of power more accurately reflects a fascination with consumerism and the marketplace more so than a change in relationships and gender inequality. Additionally, Bae argues that representations of girl power are relatively homogenous, tending to focus on white, Western girls to the exclusion of girls from a range of diverse backgrounds. We return to this tension more explicitly in discussing the debates around sexualization, girls' media use, and medial literacy.

Sexualization

A historical approach to the concept of sexualization provides a broader social context for debates around the utility of the sexualization concept, as well as how sexualization might be approached differently within the field of media and gender studies. Wouters provides such a historical approach to sexualization, defined as:

> a long-term social process that was preceded by a long-term process of desexualization, in which taboos on sexuality gained strength...[Whereas] desexualization was part of the formalization of manners and the disciplining of people, which occurred from the Renaissance to the last quarter of the 19th century...informalization occurred from then onwards, when the regime of manners and emotions allowed for more lenient and informal manners, and for an 'emancipation of emotions': emotions that had been denied and repressed, including all those related to sexuality, regained access to consciousness and wider acceptance in more informal social codes.[17]

Some authors have criticized the sexualization of culture hypotheses for being rather generic and undifferentiated.[18] However, many authors push even further than this, arguing that the examination of sexual imagery must acknowledge not only the influence of gender, but also other forms of difference. Gill (2009), for example, incorporates an intersectional analysis of media representations, showing how the range of sexualized media representations varies by race, gender, class, and age.

Cross-cultural and historical examples show that like representations about female sexuality, more generally, media portrayals of girls' sexuality is highly gendered, racialized, and classed. That is, not only is age seen as an important signifier of difference with respect to youth vs. adult sexualities,[19] but different groups of youth are thought of and treated differently depending on their social characteristics and place within the social hierarchy.[20] Thus, the sexuality of low-income girls and girls of color has been portrayed as particularly threatening, dangerous, and disruptive,[21] whereas the sexuality of white middle and upper-class girls is either ignored altogether or portrayed as something fragile that needs to be protected.[22] These distinctions have also applied with respect to the hypersexualization of girls and women from immigrant groups, native/indigenous communities, enslaved, and colonialized populations.[23] Fears about early pregnancy and reproductive control dominate this discourse, and figure prominently in the larger projects of social containment and control directed at subordinate groups.[24]

Sexualization, and the related concept of *pornofication*, have become defining concepts in the fields of media and gender studies, particularly within the U.S. and some parts of Europe (see Attwood, 2006, for an excellent review of emerging academic approaches to the study of "sexualized culture," pornofication, democratization, taste formations, postmodern sex and intimacy, and sexual citizenship).[25] Although some scholars define the term in relatively objective terms (i.e., Attwood's 2009 definition of sexualization refers to the increased visibility of sex in contemporary Western cultures), most authors typically characterize the sexualization of girls as wholly negative, unwanted, and relatively homogenous—that is, a single process whereby all girls are sexualized in the same ways and with the same (negative) consequences.[26]

The primary culprit of sexualization in the contemporary era is seen as the commodification of sexuality via popular media, advertising, and pornography, as well as the emergence of new markets related to sexuality, such as stripper cardio and pole dancing classes, and new technologies of the self that have increased the popularity of pubic hair removal and/or adornment, cosmetic vaginal surgery, and the like.[27] This latter approach, along with the panic and moral outrage it inspires, was both reinscribed and popularized by the 2007 *Report of the APA Task Force on the Sexualization of Girls*, which outlined the potentially negative impact of the media's sexualization of girls in terms of self-image, self-worth, sexuality, and other aspects of psychosocial and health and wellbeing. The central social process involved in media's presumed impact on girls is that of self-objectification, in that through media, girls learn to "internalize an observer's perspective on their physical selves and learn to treat themselves as objects to be looked at and evaluated for their appearance."[28] However, this conceptualization of sexualization is not uncontested.

Among others, Egan (2012) argues that concerns about the sexualization of girls in the media is hype-driven, stating:

Throughout history, girls—and especially "sexual" girls—have often been a scapegoat or site of transference for cultural anxiety. There is a scapegoating logic present in the current sexualization discourse that works to protect one group (white, middle class, and heterosexual girls) while marginalizing working class girls and girls of color...These distinctions promote a pecking order within girl culture, but more than this, adults use them to decide who is acceptable, who should be sanctioned, and who is in need of psychological, medical or spiritual intervention. When sexualization is cast as "pathology," it ultimately makes girls the problem. It also creates a dangerous binary between innocence and sexualization, casting the over-sexualized girl as damaged and pathological. The sexualization thesis dominating contemporary media eclipses the evidence that girls and boys in the United States today are more sexually responsible than in previous generations, and perpetuates the myth that people engage with media uncritically and uniformly. Perhaps more significantly, this emphasis on hyper-sexualization may actually create new problems for girls by vilifying their sexuality rather than interrogating the sexism, racism and classism embedded in the media message.[29]

Lerum and Dworkin (2009) have argued that the APA report reflects socially conservative values, based in the U.S., U.K., and elsewhere, that "have long been concerned with keeping girls' and women's sexuality confined within racialized, classed, and patriarchal boundaries, resulting in campaigns to keep girls and women (hence, family, race, and nation) pure of sexual corruption."[30] As such, they argue:

The APA task force report may actually interfere with some contemporary feminist goals—in particular, the goals of facilitating sexual agency and pleasure, sexual rights, and sexual health for girls and women...[by providing]: (a) an over-determined, negative impact of sexualization on girls and women; (b) a negation of a large and important feminist literature on media, consumer culture, gender, and the body; (c) a lack of integration with earlier pro-desire feminist psychology scholarship; (d) a conflation of objectification, sexual objectification, and sexualization; (e) an under-emphasis on girls' and women's sexual agency and resistance; and (f) an under-emphasis on sexual health and rights.[31]

Lerum and Dworkin paint the APA report as overly simplified, ignoring situational complexities and meanings attached to sexual imagery, as well as conflating the existence of sexualized imagery with the impact of such imagery in the everyday lives of girls. An overreliance on quantitative methods may explain why the complexities of interpretation, social context, and praxis were relatively ignored in this report. Attwood has argued that sexually explicit representations:

are experienced and understood in a variety of ways and evoke strong and often contradictory reactions...these texts function in a range of different ways, depending on context; as a source of knowledge, a resource for intimate practices, a site for identity construction, and an occasion for performing gender and sexuality.[32]

Other scholars have also criticized the report for containing no scientific evidence of a causal link between sexualized portrayals in the media and negative psychosocial outcomes,[33] or for being overly deterministic by depicting girls as passive consumers with a limited ability to construct and define their own identities.[34]

Some of the panic and anxiety around girls' sexualities and the media involve girls' use of new media technologies (such as the internet, or smart phones). As Pascoe (2011) rightly points out, as with the study of sexuality and the media more generally, there are two schools of thought regarding young people and their use of new media technologies:

> Boosters tend to hype the educational (and economic) possibilities of increased media literacy, claiming that new media helps youth learn, makes them responsible citizens, and augments their social lives (Holloway and Valentine 2003; Livingstone 2002). Detractors are usually concerned about the same level of knowledge and use, arguing that new media renders young people more vulnerable to predators, (Holloway and Valentine 2003; Thurlow and McKay 2003) leads to social isolation, ruins concentration, and exposes youth to adult themes at early ages (Holloway and Valentine 2003; Livingstone 2002; Osgerby 2004; Thurlow and McKay 2003). Both factions highlight very real possibilities of new media.[35]

Thus, like the 'sex war' debates around pornography stemming from the 1980s onward, some scholars focus almost exclusively on how culture and media shape and impact women and girls, or "what media do to people," while others focus on the social context of media *use*, or "what people do with media."[36] These latter studies examine how girls engage with media in a more critical way, and how they incorporate and/or transform such imagery into their everyday lives. In addition, this area of scholarship examines girls as media producers, particularly their production of home pages, e-zines, and blogs.[37] The availability and popularity of new media technologies has facilitated this trend, democratizing (at least to some extent) the social imaginary around girls' sexualities and the media. However, as Jackson and Westrupp have argued, "while postfeminist popular culture may open up possibilities to be sexually savvy girls, the 'price' may be intensification of (hetero)sexual self-surveillance and responsibility."[38]

Media Use

Scholarship on girls' use of media generally examines culture as a *participatory* process, and media users and producers as participants within the production of culture. As noted by Howe, "attempts to understand the particularities of media production as well as relations of consumption have attempted to comprehend "media" and "culture" not as distinct entities, one operating on the other in an instrumental way, but, rather, as ongoing reciprocal processes of mediation."[39] As with other forms of media, insight into this realm of activity requires that we recognize girls' creative roles as media users and producers, rather than simply passive consumers. Girls may play an even more significant role in democratizing how they are represented in that they can, to an even greater extent than was possible before, utilize new media technologies as a medium for self-expression and agency.

This work includes the study of what Wolhwend terms "productive consumption," illustrating how girls engaged with familiar media narratives around Disney Princess characters, how they negotiated the social limitations embedded within the gendered identities that animate these narratives, and then improvised or substantially revised story lines to generate counternarratives of their own making.[40] This approach seeks to evidence girls' creativity in creating or adapting existing media, particularly in regards to gender roles within social relationships (including those that might be defined as sexual or romantic).

Although focused on adults, Attwood's examination of "altporn'" or "smart smut" websites such as Nerve and the Suicide Girls suggests that girls might utilize media to establish what she defines as a "collaborative eroticism"—where a more artistic and stylized display is favored over highly explicit activities, what they see as a more ethical framework for sexual representation.[41] Both sites "present their commercial and community elements as part of a shared taste and aesthetic," representing a new form of pornography that constructs "sexual display as a form of recreation."[42] These types of sites represent burgeoning communities, where viewers are invited to express themselves by submitting their own erotic art and stories in ways that might defy conventional standards for beauty found in mainstream media (including mainstream pornography). Although Attwood focuses on adult women as co-producers of pornographic materials, this strategy can also be extended to the area of girls as co-producers, creators, and consumers of media to try on different sexual identities.

In a review of fifteen years of research on sexuality and the internet, Doring argues that while most existing research focuses on the potentially negative aspects of this relationship, there is a significant need for research that examines the positive impacts, such as the impact on sexual development, sexual self-determination, and self-expression.[43] Stokes examines how girls, in this case African American adolescents, engage with internet media to explore, construct, and self-define their emerging sexualities. As Stokes notes:

> The Web provides girls with a potentially anonymous space to experiment with their sexuality without the potential embarrassment or risks of face-to-face encounters. Many of the girls reproduced gender inequality and stereotypical representations of Black female sexuality in their home pages but they also claimed space on the Web to

try on identities and resist dominant sexual script discourses and sexual double standards.[44]

These girls often simultaneously incorporated and resisted various combina-
tions of multiple black sexual scripts, indicating that girls might "try on" particular sexual identities in different social settings, as well as blend them in
unique ways (see also Eklund's [2011] examination of gender performance
among female online gamers). Importantly, this scholarship also reminds us that
sexualization is not necessarily a top-down process, that multiple sexual scripts
are at play in the social universe, and that girls play a role in constructing that
universe. Stokes' work suggests empowerment for girls means more than simply
giving them the tools to critically evaluate the mediated world around them, and
requires that we engage in such activities with girls, such as training in leadership development, web design, and media production, an idea we return to in
the next section on media literacy.

Media Literacy

Media literacy is a hotly contested term that has been variously defined to
refer to how people interact with all forms of media including texts, music, tele-
vision/film, and the internet. However, most media scholars agree that at the
very minimum, media literacy empowers young people to critically assess existing media and create alternative media that can transform society by challenging
existing paradigms.[45] Other scholars argue that media literacy should also involve some degree of activism that pushes back against prevailing media images
that serve to maintain social inequalities related to gender, race, and sexual orientation.[46]

In practice, most media literacy programs—particularly in the U.S.—
continue to focus on "teaching" people how to be critical consumers of media
(see Hobbs, 1998, for discussion of limitations of this approach). This is especially true for media literacy programs focused on the sexualization of girls in
the media where the primary goal is to "teach" girls how to identify examples of
sexualization. The assumption is that once girls are "taught" to recognize and
critique such representations, they will be able to avoid the negative effects of
media sexualization on their physical, emotional, and intellectual development.[47]
Bazalgette describes this "media literacy as a panacea" view as follows:

> If children can be taught to deconstruct media texts, the magic mantra goes, then they
> won't be taken in by the fantasy, seduced by the violence, or manipulated by commer-
> cial ploys. Media education, in this scenario, is the pedagogic equivalent of a tetanus
> shot.[48]

This line of reasoning is based on the assumption that increased media literacy as defined by increased critical thinking skills will translate into better outcomes for young people. However, existing research challenges this assumption. Gill, for example, found that while girls appreciate and even enjoy identifying instances of sexualization in the media, doing so did not always translate into them feeling "better" or more "empowered" in their everyday lives.[49]

Traditional media literacy approaches also assume that young people are passive recipients of media representations, rather than active, critical consumers and creators of media.[50] Media scholars, including Jackson and Gilbertson, challenge this assumption and argue that young people are "sensemakers" who are able to differentiate between, for example, the performance of lesbianism for a male audience, and the central role of authentic, female sexual pleasure and desire as part of what it means to have a lesbian identity.[51] Other researchers argue that how young people make sense of media is largely dependent on their social positions as mediated by gender, age, race/ethnicity, class, and sexual orientation.[52] Or, as Milkie argues, "[media] images are not simply accepted or interpreted individually. Rather, the media are understood in everyday experience to be part of the collectivity of individuals' social worlds, in and beyond their local context."[53]

Finally, many youth-based media literacy efforts operate on the premise that the individual should be the target of change. Such approaches place the onus of change on girls as individual actors as opposed to tackling the larger issue of media sexualization at a societal level. Gill summarizes this position as follows:

> Media literacy thus becomes an individual obligation; we are made responsible for our own engagements with media—both what we use and how we engage. To champion media literacy, then, may be implicitly to endorse this shift in power and to make individuals responsible for the work of thinking critically and desconstructing media content. But it is also surely to espouse a kind of defeatism, for it seems to suggest that media cannot be changed; all that can be changed is how we engage with them.[54]

In the current anthology, we argue that media literacy interventions should challenge the status quo when it means directly confronting social inequalities. Girls should be active and equal partners in this process, and when possible, they should be encouraged and supported in their own efforts to develop alternative media formats (e.g., online magazines) that challenge problematic representations of girls as identified not only by white girls, but all girls irrespective of sexual orientation or sociocultural background.

Overall Structure of This Volume

The fifteen selections in this anthology examine the historical and contemporary construction of adolescent girls' sexuality in the media, drawing upon original papers specifically developed for the volume. The collection is comprised of original research submissions which focus on how adolescent girls' sexualities are presented in the media, how girls interpret and make meaning of these representations, and how media functions to shape girls' attitudes and behaviors. The volume includes a variety of theoretical and methodological perspectives from both the humanities and the social sciences, addressing not only how girls and others respond to, work with, and even resist prevailing media representations of girls' sexualities, but also how they use contemporary media as a form of sexual expression. We rely upon a broad conception of sexualities that goes beyond public health literature on sexual risk-taking behaviors and its consequences (e.g., teen pregnancy, STIs), and considers a wide array of sexual attitudes, behaviors, and expressions not commonly seen in the sexualities literature. The use of ethnographic data, in conjunction with media analysis techniques, provides a unique approach to the media studies genre, which tends to highlight an analysis of media content, as opposed to the ways in which media is used in everyday life. Additionally, the cross-cultural and historical perspectives highlighted in this anthology contribute to the broad scope and use value of this text, which can be used as an advanced reader at an undergraduate level, as well as an example of cutting edge research for graduate seminars. As editors, we recognize the importance of sociocultural, historical, and contemporary contexts as they relate to media representations of girls' sexualities and strongly encouraged our contributors to take these unique contextual factors into account. This includes presenting the voices of "Other" girls whose voices are often ignored, particularly racial/ethnic minority and indigenous girls, sexual minorities, and girls from non-U.S. settings.

We intend for this anthology to facilitate a dialogue between scholars that focus on particular areas within the literature, including scholars from the humanities and social sciences, anthropology, sociology, history, cultural studies, and gender studies. Building upon a seminar on girls' sexuality and the media in the spring of 2010, our aim in developing this project was to begin the kind of dialogue necessary for a transformation of scholarship that transcends disciplinary boundaries. This collection of essays represents a culmination of those efforts. The book is divided into three sections: Historical and Contemporary Media; Media Use and Self-Representation; and Media Campaigns and Literacy Projects.

Chapter Outlines

Section One: Historical and Contemporary Media Representations

The authors in the Historical and Contemporary Media section of *Girls' Sexualities and the Media* build on the existing body of scholarship on girls' sexuality. Although most of the seminal works discussed previously acknowledge the significance of sexuality as an aspect of girls' identities, the pieces in this section examine more explicitly the role of sexuality in popular media representations of girls. Given the persistent history of contestation over girls' sexuality, the contributors interrogate the many ways in which media representations (or the intentional absence of such representations) construct, manage, and manipulate how we imagine girls' sexual identities, as well as the implications for girls themselves. Two historical pieces begin the section, an important reminder that seemingly new representations often rely on images and associations from the past. Keeping in mind that representations in literature, television, film, and advertising are not simple reflections, but actively constructive elements, of reality, the authors here pay particular attention to the explicit and implicit messages conveyed through popular media, whether aimed specifically at girls or the broader public. Each of the pieces in this section reflects a heritage of history, literary criticism, and media analysis in the use of close readings of various mediated texts. All of the pieces also incorporate feminist and gender studies theories of intersectionality to consider the ways in which representations of girls' sexualities are inextricably linked to gender, race and ethnicity, and class.

This section includes chapters by Scheiner Gillis, Helgren, Harper, Walters and Kimmel, Driscoll, Rossie, Frank, and Burns and Davies. The section begins with chapters by Scheiner Gillis and Helgren, which examine historical constructions of girlhood and girls' interpretations of those constructions. Chapters by Harper and Walters and Kimmel focus on contemporary serial film and literature. Driscoll's chapter considers the historical trajectory of girls' sexuality in film, while Rossie and Frank both explore contemporary television portrayals. Finally, the selection by Burns and Davies illustrates the ways in which media can be (mis)used to in order to shape girls' behaviors, when such campaigns are developed without interrogating how such media might (in spite of good intentions) reinforce stereotypes about the everyday sexual lives of girls.

Media depictions provide us with a window into the cultural meanings of girlhood and how those meaning have changed over time. For the most part, girls have been represented as signaling generational change and societal instability in times of flux or crisis. While the subject of sexuality in contemporary media representations has proliferated in recent years, there is a dearth of studies that consider this subject from an historical perspective. Georganne Scheiner Gillis' "The Girls of Carvel: Adolescent Desire in *Andy Hardy* Films," looks at representations of female adolescence in the pre-World War II period. The Andy Hardy films of the 1930s and 1940s remain one of the only coherent series about teens in American history, spanning over twenty years and sixteen films. Even though the films centered on the concerns of an adolescent boy, there was a host of ancillary female characters who were clear signifiers of the female adolescent experience. While it might seem counterintuitive to use films that have been criticized for offering up a sanitized, unrealistic, and idealized vision of white girlhood to explore sexuality in the pre-WWII era, this chapter argues that it is the recurring and often conflicting tropes of heterosexual desire that make these films a useful window into historical perspectives on sexuality in the period. The 1930s and early 1940s offered competing discourses of adolescent sexuality. Teens in the period increasingly began to carve out cultural space and to create new public conventions and practices around dating. The parent culture, however, continued to articulate outdated codes of sexual behavior and appropriate desire. The *Hardy* films began to reconcile the discourse of the parent culture with the reality of teen sexual desire by recognizing the "naturalness" of that desire, but prescribing limits to it. Thus the series both underscores and assuages social anxieties about girls' sexual desire.

Although the dominant media tropes of girlhood can be grounded in the historical and material conditions of the culture that produced them, we see a clear difference between girls as discursive subjects in cultural texts and their lived experiences. Perhaps this discrepancy can be attributed to both the hopes and the fears of the dominant culture. Yet girls themselves are hardly passive consumers of images and they chose how to respond to the images that pervaded the culture. Girls have used the same tropes in turn as sites of résistance to allow them to create a social identity and to affirm cultural authority. This is underscored by Jennifer Helgren's "'Sensible Safety Rules': Class, Race, and Girls' Sexual Vulnerability in the U.S. Print Media, 1950–1970," which uses oral histories, an analysis of Girls Scouts and Camp Fire publications, and a content analysis of national magazines and newspapers to examine media portrayals of sex crimes against girls (especially stranger kidnapping and sexual assault) in 1950s and 1960s newspapers and magazines. Media coverage emphasized the danger from strangers despite evidence that young people faced equal risk from people that they knew. While most adults adopted a protective stance when it came to girls, the leaders of Girl Scouts and Camp Fire Girls, however, claimed a right for girls' access to public spaces, offering guidelines on how to stay safe instead of confining girls to domestic spaces. Girls themselves expressed fear, but also resisted adults' attempts to restrict their access.

Kate Harper continues the examination of popular film with an analysis of girls' sexuality in *Harry Potter*. Using examples from the sixth book and film,

Harry Potter and the Half-Blood Prince, she examines how sexuality functions in the series and intersects with other identities, particularly race, gender, and class. The film's heteronormative depictions of sexual desire stabilize the series, allowing a critique of racist ideology, unequal gender expectations, socioeconomic class hierarchies, and traditional notions of family. However, when one examines the ways in which representations of sexuality (or the absence of sexuality) intersect with other identity categories, the façade of progressivism becomes less convincing, revealing raced, classed, and gendered stereotypes. Harper argues that because all aspects of identity are mutually constructed and co-constitutive, the insistence upon heterosexuality and employment of stereotypes in the filmic adaptations severely limits the transgressive potential of the series.

In the next selection, Walters and Kimmel examine the popular book and film series *Twilight*, from several different angles, shedding new light on how popular media is interpreted in rather unique and unexpected ways by youth in different social and cultural contexts. Walters and Kimmel emphasize the inversion of normative gender relations within the series and the ways in which this is interpreted by U.S. girls as a key component of its popularity. They argue that in contrast to many mainstream media depictions of adolescent girls' sexualities, the best-selling *Twilight* series inverts common gender-based stereotypes, and that this inversion is one of the "sustaining pleasures" provided by the series films and books. Based on interviews with young *Twilight* fans, Walters and Kimmel explore this reversal of gender relations. Using interview data, the authors argue that amidst all the sexualization of young girls, the *Twilight* series resonates so profoundly because it turns the tables, sexualizing the boys and desexualizing the girls—and thus provides a moment's respite in an otherwise sexualized world.

In "She's All That: Girl Sexuality and Teen Film," Catherine Driscoll argues that adolescent heterosexuality and the repetition, monitoring, and disruption of gender roles have been intrinsic elements of the narrative conventions and cinematic strategies that have helped to define the teen film genre. In fact, it often seems impossible to disentangle the workings of gender and heterosexuality in teen film, which is why "queer" teen film continues to be a slippery generic mutation. Driscoll examines the dominant teen film story about heterosexual coming-of-age through the central trope of virginity and the marginal trope of the "queer" teen. She argues that the coming-of-age and rite-of-passage tropes that constitute the narrative of girl sexuality in teen film can be best understood by considering them in relation to gendered citizenship narratives.

We move from popular film and literature to television with Amanda Rossie's "Wrecked and Redeemed: Religio-Political Pedagogy and MTV's *16 and Pregnant*." Rossie challenges the tendency to see this popular pseudo-reality show as simple entertainment; instead, she argues that *16 and Pregnant* employs evangelical discourses that link extramarital sex to fear, pain, and social ills. Relying on conservative ideologies of female sexuality, reproductive choice, and the nuclear family, the series perpetuates the framing of female adolescent sexuality and insubordinate reproduction as a problem. The series also maintains the invisibility of institutional and systemic obstacles that produce conditions conducive to teenage pregnancy while expressing anxiety over the relationship between reproduction and citizenship. Rossie reveals the political and ideological work of the television series and discusses discursive tools for producing ruptures and new ways for viewers to "talk back" to representations.

Elena Frank considers the possibilities of "talking back" and girls' sexual agency in her chapter, which focuses on ABC Family's popular adolescent drama *The Secret Life of the American Teenager*. Given the centrality of sex and reproduction to the show's plot development, the series provides ample representations of the possibilities and limits of female sexual agency. The author first addresses the nuances and complexities of "agency" as a theoretical concept, particularly in terms of popular media. Frank then explores the role of gender, power, and agency in three issues on the show—abortion, birth control, and masturbation—as well as how these depictions might be simultaneously liberatory and constrictive for the series' adolescent female viewers.

Finally, in a unique study of public health media campaigns, Kellie Burns and Cristyn Davies' "Producing Girl Citizens As Agents of Health: An Analysis of HPV Campaigns in the United States" offers a critical reading of the media cultures around the U.S. HPV/cervical cancer vaccination campaign from 2007 to 2009. The authors explore girls' and young women's understandings about the vaccination, and analyze the ways in which they produce knowledge that both upholds and disrupts contemporary notions of risk, responsibility. and self-management. As the chapter illustrates, the HPV/cervical cancer vaccination was promoted by mobilizing discourses of sexual health risk and danger alongside rhetoric about women's new sexual freedoms and choice. The campaign urged young women to take control of their sexual and reproductive wellbeing—aspects of their health from which they have historically been detached. Getting vaccinated was mediated as a right and a choice that women have gained around their sexual health. At the same time, however, these new modes of accessing "better sexual health" were produced in a broader, neoliberal climate of risk management underpinned by discourses of economic pragmatism. Throughout these campaigns, girls and young women were asked to manage their (sexual) health in order to lower their collective burden of disease on the nation-state. The authors argue that this discourse upholds the ideals of dutiful female citizenship and continues to erase boys and men from public pedagogies of sexual and reproductive health.

Section Two: Media Use and Self-Representation

This section includes chapters by Gagné, Jarrin, Hernandez, and Apple, and considers how adolescent girls use, respond to, and challenge media representations of girls' sexualities in a variety of settings, including Japan, Brazil, and the United States. Utilizing qualitative methodologies, all contributors for this section examine how adolescent girls in their natural environments accommodate, reflect, and/or resist media sexualization. While Gagné and Jarrin provide an understanding of media use in non-Western settings, Hernandez, and Apple focus on culturally diverse settings in the United States. Taken as a whole, these chapters provide unique perspectives on the multiplicity of ways that mainstream media is incorporated into localized experiences and sexual expressions. These compelling examples indicate that youth interpret and use media in a diverse range of ways, reflecting localized values around gender and sexuality that may challenge those conveyed through popular culture.

Combining media analysis with ethnographic research on the linguistic practices of young women in Japan, Isaac Gagné explores how adolescent girls in Japan see themselves in relation to a number of sexualizing and infantilizing images, as well as how they incorporate such images to create their own space of adolescence and sexual fantasy. This chapter explores the young girls of one such media-infused youth subculture, "Lolita," who strive to embody an idealized "young princess" through their fashion and mannerisms, and describes how Lolitas craft their identity through gender play, performing what might be characterized as hyperfemininity. In Japan, as much as purity and modesty are important concepts, aestheticization and consumption are also well-embedded practices and are often encouraged as a part of socialization. Specifically, by revealing their gendered subjectivity in creating their version of a fantasy space vis-à-vis other subcultural groups, Gagneé explores two broad analytical issues: 1) Lolita as identity within changing dominant media representations of young girls in Japan, and 2) Lolita as subcultural activity within the context of the discourses of sexuality in Japan. Moreover, Gagné illustrates that real girls themselves are simultaneously both objects of media representations and subjects who actively respond to such mediatized images to manipulate or emulate such representations in return.

In "Favela Models: Sexual Virtue and Hopeful Narratives of Beauty in Brazil," Alvaro Jarrin looks at the connection between representations of sexual virtue and upward mobility within the modeling industry in Brazil, tracing a widespread discourse in the Brazilian media that promises upward mobility through beauty to working-class women and girls. These narratives of upward mobility—from journalistic accounts of recently "discovered" models, to the carefully crafted storylines of soap operas and televised beauty pageants—are compared with accounts from teenaged girls who attend modeling schools in Brazilian favelas. Jarrin argues that these girls, their teachers, and their parents put their hopes on performances of beauty because they understand the female body itself as a form of capital that can serve as a gateway to citizenship. However, because the idealized image of the poor young woman who achieves upward mobility through beauty is sexualized and racialized in very particular ways, those beauty pageants and modeling contests that are supposed to bring about social inclusion actually reinforce a preference for whiteness and "appropriate" feminine behavior that excludes most poor women of color from the outset. Jarrin concludes his examination by looking at an alternative beauty contest that celebrates a working-class aesthetic associated with an unruly sexuality rather than sexual constraint, and racial pluralism rather than whiteness, allowing participants to reject the bourgeois disciplining of the body associated with producing beauty for others, and to reclaim a localized aesthetic that exists for its own sake.

In the next chapter, Jillian Hernandez examines the sexual politics of visual representations of "chongas" across media such as contemporary art, YouTube, and print/broadcast outlets. Often described by Latinas in South Florida as a low-class, slutty, tough, and crass young woman, the hypervisible figure disparagingly labeled as a "chonga" is practically invisible in queer theory, media studies, and feminist scholarship. Portrayals of chonga girls represent varying forms of production, circulation, and reception, reflecting larger discourses about Latina girls' sexuality, and coming to signify and embody tropes regarding Latina girls' hypersexuality. Hernandez argues that the non-normative sexual-aesthetic excesses of chonga bodies signify a queer politics that undermines sexual policing and conveys indifference toward portraying an assimilated white bourgeois subjectivity. Offering a sexual-aesthetic excess as a concept in order to theorize this mode of dress and comportment, Hernandez suggests that the chonga girl's de-naturalized visibility is a citation of gender, class, and racial/ethnic signifiers, from her faux-gold jewelry, gelled-straight hair, and synthetic nails to the imitation designer clothes she buys at the flea market.

In the final chapter of this section, Jennifer Apple examines heteroflexibility, which refers to same-sex experimentation by those who identify as primarily heterosexual, as a source of female-centered performance and pleasure among girls. In "Heteroflexibility: Female Performance and Pleasure," Apple compares the multiple meanings and possibilities found in heteroflexibility among young women (as an act, performance, or identity) with those depicted in the media.

While existing research has primarily focused on media depictions of same-sex female sexuality, this chapter emphasizes the nature of lived experiences and meaning-making that occurs among young women and girls who identify themselves as heteroflexible. Apple suggests that heteroflexibility is both a contemporary representation of the neoliberal sexual subject and an act that queers heteronormative scripts and notions of female sexuality and sexual pleasure. Ultimately, the concept of heteroflexibility may create a productive fissure in the regime of compulsory heterosexuality, expose current categories of sexual subjectivity as insufficient, and enable exploration of distinctly female-centered pleasure.

Section Three: Media Campaigns and Literacy Projects

The third section of this volume includes innovative examples of formally established media literacy projects aimed at encouraging girls to resist hypersexualized media images. Core questions for this section are: How can media literacy projects encourage girls to think critically about popular representations of sexuality? What are the salient characteristics of media literacy projects? How do participatory approaches facilitate the development of project goals and outcomes? And finally, in what ways do these media literacy efforts help girls challenge prevailing stereotypes about sexuality, race, class, and gender? These three selections indicate that a different, more participatory, approach—one which involves girls as key stakeholders in the process—might achieve the kind of changes needed to help improve the lives (and opportunities) of girls.

In the first chapter of this section, Deborah L. Tolman, Lyn Mikel Brown, and Christin P. Bowman describe SPARK—Sexualization Pushback: Action, Resistance, Knowledge—an intergenerational social movement designed to inspire girls to "take sexy back" from the media and marketers. To illustrate SPARK in action, they describe a 2010 Summit designed to get girls and women talking about how media sexualization makes them feel, how it reinforces limited views of sexuality (e.g., illusion of sexual availability, heterosexuality), and what they can do to challenge such representations. A major contribution of this chapter is that it illustrates how girls and women can work together to create real-world solutions to combat pervasive images of sexualization (photos included in this chapter).

In "From Media Propaganda to De-Stigmatizing Sex: Exploring a Teen Magazine By, For, and About Girls," Linda Charmaraman and Brittany Low evaluate an innovative magazine internship program designed to empower teen girls of color to critically challenge prevailing images of sexuality. Program content included: 1) mentoring; 2) workshops on media literacy, identity, and health promotion, and; 3) the creation of *Teen Voices*—a magazine created by, for, and about girls. The program evaluation involved uncovering what teen participants believe about the media and how it depicts girls' sexuality, understanding how the program facilitated girls' involvement, and determining both the volume and content of sexuality articles in Teen Voices. To address these questions, Charmaraman and Low conducted sixty-plus hours of ethnographic observations, interviewed twenty-two participants, and completed a content analysis of *Teen Voices*. Findings revealed that teen girls deeply resented sexualized images that portray women in sexually degrading positions to sell products, and they expressed this anger and frustration via written articles for *Teen Voices*. The authors cite this program as an excellent example of how media-based literacy and production programs can encourage teen girls to fight back against media sexualization.

In the final chapter, Amy Rutstein-Riley, Jenn Walker, Alice Diamond, Bonnie Bryant, and Marie LaFlemme discuss the Girlhood Project, an innovative, service-learning media literacy program that partners twenty college women with twenty-five urban middle school girls. Using principles of feminist pedagogy and feminist group process, the women and girls meet on a weekly basis to critically evaluate how social institutions—including the media—shape girls' experiences and identities. Rutstein-Riley and her colleagues rely upon the college women's reflections and the middle school students' art-based media projects to examine how they collaboratively addressed sexuality, gender stereotypes, body image, and relationship issues within the context of their weekly group discussions. Findings suggest that girls-only, critical media literacy groups represent a powerful way "to harness girls' strength and resilience in the face of social pressures to conform to gender-based stereotypes consistently communicated by the media."

Notes

1. Mary Celeste Kearney, "Coalescing: The Development of Girls' Studies," *NWSA Journal*
2. Ruth Alexander, The *"Girl Problem": Female Sexual Delinquency in New York, 1900–1930* (Ithaca, NY: Cornell University Press, 1995); Paula Fass, *The Damned and the Beautiful: American Youth in the 1920s* (New York: Oxford University Press, 1977); Miriam Forman-Brunell, *Babysitter: An American History* (New York: New York University Press, 2009); Jane Hunter, *How Young Ladies Became Girls: The Victorian Origins of American Girlhood* (New Haven, CT: Yale University Press, 2002); Mary Odem, *Delinquent Daughters: Protecting and Policing Adolescent Female Sexuality in the United States, 1885–1920* (Chapel Hill, NC: University of North Carolina Press, 1995).
3. Susan Douglas, Where the Girls Are: Growing Up Female with the Mass Media (New York: Random House, 1994); Ilana Nash, American Sweethearts: Teenage Girls in Twentieth-Century Popular Culture (Bloomington, IN: Indiana University Press, 2006); Kelly Schrum, Some Wore Bobby Sox: The Emergence of Teenage Girls' Culture, 1920–1945

(New York: Palgrave, 2006); Georganne Scheiner, Signifying Female Adolescence: Film Representations and Fans, 1920–1950 (Westport, CT: Praeger. 2000).

4. Catherine Driscoll, *Girls: Feminine Adolescence in Popular Culture and Cultural Theory* (New York: Columbia University Press, 2002); Anita Harris, *All About the Girl: Culture, Power and Identity* (New York: Routledge, 2004); Sherrie Inness, *Nancy Drew and Company: Culture, Gender, and Girls' Series* (Bowling Green, OH: Bowling Green University Press, 1997); Sherrie Inness, *Delinquents and Debutantes: Twentieth-Century American Girls' Cultures* (New York: New York University Press, 1998); Mary Celeste Kearney, *Mediated Girlhoods: New Explorations of Girls' Media Culture* (New York: Peter Lang, 2011); Sharon Mazzarella and Norma Pecora, *Growing Up Girls: Popular Culture and the Construction of Identity* (New York: Peter Lang, 2001).

5. Sue Jackson and Elizabeth Westrupp, "Sex, Postfeminist Culture, and the Pre-Teen Girl," *Sexualities* 13, no. 3 (2010): 357–376, 357. See also Angela McRobbie, "More! New Sexualities in Girls' and Women's Magazines," in *Cultural Studies and Communications*, edited by J. Curran, D. Morley, and V. Walkerdine, 172–194 (London: Arnold, 2006).

6. Janna L. Kim and L. Monica Ward, "Pleasure Readings: Associations Between Young Women's Sexual Attitudes and Their Reading of Contemporary Women's Magazines," *Psychology of Women Quarterly* 28 (2004): 48–58, 48; See also M. Gigi Durham, *The Lolita Effect: The Media Sexualization of Young Girls and What We Can Do About It* (New York: The Overlook Press, 2008); Angela McRobbie, *Feminism and Youth Culture* (New York: Routledge, 2000); Lynn M. Phillips, *Flirting with Danger: Young Women's Reflections on Sexuality and Domination* (New York: New York University Press, 2000).

7. Laura M. Carpenter, "From Girls into Women: Scripts for Sexuality and Romance in Seventeen Magazine, 1974-1994," *The Journal of Sex Research* 35 (1998): 158–168; M. Gigi Durham, "Dilemmas of Desire: Representations of Adolescent Sexuality in Two Teen Magazines," *Youth and Society* 29 (1998): 369–389; Evans et al., "Content Analysis of Contemporary Teen Magazines for Adolescent Females," *Youth and Society* 23, no. 1 (1991): 99–120; Majorie Ferguson, *Forever Feminine: Women's Magazines and the Cult of Femininity* (London: Heinemann Educational Books Ltd., 1983); Kim and Ward, "Pleasure Readings," 2004; Ellen McCracken, *Decoding Women's Magazines: From Mademoiselle to Ms.* (London: Macmillan, 1993); Kate Peirce, "A Feminist Theoretical Perspective on the Socialization of Teenage Girls through Seventeen Magazines," *Sex Roles* 23 (1990): 491–500.

8. Frederick T. Attenborough, "Complicating the Sexualization Thesis: The Media, Gender, and 'Sci-candy," *Discourse & Society* 22 (2011): 659–676, 662. See also Judith Butler, *Excitable Speech: A Politics of the Performative* (New York: Routledge, 1997); Michel Foucault, *The Archaeology of Knowledge*, translated by A.M. Sheridan Smith (New York: Pantheon Books, 1972); Rosalind Gill, *Gender and the Media* (Cambridge: Polity Press, 2007).

9. Gill, Gender and the Media, 276.

10. Linda Duits, "Headscarves and Porno Chic: Disciplining Girls' Bodies in the European Multicultural Society," *European Journal of Women's Studies* 13, no. 2 (2007), 163.

11. Ibid., 162.

12. Sharon Lamb, "Feminist Ideals for a Healthy Female Adolescent Sexuality: A Critique," *Sex Roles* 62 (2009): 294–306, 294.

13. E.g., see Michelle Fine's seminal work on the missing discourse of desire found within sexuality education in the U.S.: Michelle Fine, "Sexuality, schooling, and adolescent females:

the missing discourse of desire," *Harvard Education Review* 58 (1988): 29–53; Michelle Fine, "X. Desire: the morning (and 15 years) after," *Feminism & Psychology* 15 (2005): 54–50.

14.   Deborah Tolman, "Femininity as a Barrier to Positive Sexual Health for Girls," *Journal of the American Medical Women's Association* 54 (1999): 133–138; Deborah Tolman, *Dilemmas of Desire: Teenage Girls Talk about Sexuality* (Cambridge: Harvard University Press, 2002).

15.   Lamb, "Feminist Ideals," 296.

16.   Michelle Bae, "Interrogating Girl Power: Girlhood, Popular Media, and Postfeminism," *Visual Arts Research* 37 (2011): 28–40.

17.   Cas Wouters, "Sexualization: Have Sexualization Processes Changed Direction?" *Sexualities* 13, no. 6 (2010): 723–741, 723.

18.   Attenborough, "Complicating the Sexualization Thesis," 670.

19.   Marjorie Heins, Not in Front of the Children: Indecency, Censorship, and the Innocence of Youth (New Brunswick, NJ: Rutgers University Press, 2007); Jeffrey P. Moran, Teaching Sex: The Shaping of Adolescence in the 20th Century (Cambridge: Harvard University Press, 2002); Mary Louise Rassmussen, Youth and Sexualities: Pleasure, Subversion, and Insubordination In and Out of Schools (New York: Palgrave Macmillan, 2004); Deborah L. Tolman, "Daring to Desire: Culture and the Bodies of Adolescent Girls," in Sexual Cultures and the Construction of Adolescent Identities, edited by Janice M. Irvine, (Philadelphia: Temple University Press, 1994).

20.   Janice M. Irvine, *Sexual Cultures and the Construction of Adolescent Identities,* (Philadelphia: Temple University Press, 1994).

21.   Kathryn Edin and Maria Kefalas, Promises I Can Keep: Why Poor Women Put Motherhood Before Marriage (Berkeley, CA: University of California Press, 2007); Patricia Hill Collins, Black Sexual Politics: African Americans, Gender, and the New Racism (New York: Routledge, 2005); Dorothy Roberts, Killing the Black Body: Race, Reproduction, and the Meaning of Liberty (New York: Vintage, 1998); Christine Stansell, City of Women: Sex and Class in New York, 1789–1860 (Champaign, IL: University of Illinois Press, 1987).

22.   Beth Bailey, *From Front Porch to Back Seat: Courtship in Twentieth-Century America* (Baltimore: Johns Hopkins University Press, 1989); John D'Emilio and Estelle Freedman, *Intimate Matters: A History of Sexuality in America* (Chicago: University of Chicago Press, 1998).

23.   Kirsten Fischer, Suspect Relations: Sex, Race, and Resistance in Colonial North Carolina (Ithaca, NY: Cornell University Press, 2001); Albert L. Hurtado, Intimate Frontiers: Sex, Gender, and Culture in Old California (Albuquerque, NM: University of New Mexico Press, 1999); Joane Nagel, Race, Ethnicity, and Sexuality: Intimate Intersections, Forbidden Frontiers (New York: Oxford University Press, 2003).

24.   Matthew Connelly, Fatal Misconception: The Struggle to Control World Population (Cambridge: Harvard University Press, 2008); Fischer, Suspect Relations, 2001; Betsy Hartmann, Reproductive Rights and Wrongs: The Global Politics of Population Control (Boston: South End Press, 1995); Joanna Schoen, Choice and Coercion: Birth Control, Sterilization and Abortion in Public Health and Welfare (Chapel Hill, NC: University of North Carolina Press, 2005); Alexandra Stern, Eugenic Nation: Faults and Frontiers of Better Breeding in Modern America (Berkeley, CA: University of California Press, 2005).

25.   See Ariel Levy, *Female Chauvinist Pigs: Women and the Rise of Raunch Culture* (New York: Free Press, 2006); Susanna Paasonen, Kaarina Nikunen, and Laura Saarenmaa, *Pornification: Sex*

and Sexuality in Media Culture (Oxford: Bergham Press, 2007); Durham, *The Lolita Effect,* 2008; Feona Attwood, *Mainstreaming Sex: The Sexualization of Western Culture* (New York: Palgrave Macmillan, 2009).

26. Rosalind Gill, "Beyond the Sexualization of Culture Thesis: An Intersectional Analysis of 'Sixpacks,' 'Midriffs' and 'Hot Lesbians' in Advertising," *Sexualities* 12 (2009): 137–160; Wouters, "Sexualization," 2010.

27. Attwood, "Sexed Up," 2006; Levy, *Female Chauvinist Pigs,* 2006; Brian McNair, *Striptease Culture: Sex, Media and the Democratization of Desire* (London and New York: Routledge, 2002).

28. "Report of the APA Task Force on the Sexualization of Girls," *APA (2007) Task Force on the Sexualization of Girls.* (American Psychological Association, February 2007), 18.

29. R. Danielle Egan, "Sexualizing Girls' Troubles," *Contexts* 11 (2012): 56–57, 57.

30. Kari Lerum and Shari L. Dworkin, "Bad Girls Rule: An Interdisciplinary Feminist Commentary on the Report of the APA Task Force on the Sexualization of Girls," *Journal of Sex Research* 46, no. 4 (2009): 250–263, 257. See also Patricia Hill Collins, *Black Feminist Thought: Knowledge, Consciousness, and the Politics of Empowerment* (Boston: Unwin Hyman, 1990); bell hooks, *Feminist Theory: From Margin to Center* (Boston: South End Press, 1984).

31. Lerum and Dworkin, "Bad Girls Rule," 251.

32. Feona Attwood, "What do People do with Porn? Qualitative Research into the Consumption, Use, and Experience of Pornography and Other Sexually Explicit Media," *Sexuality & Culture* 9 (2005): 65–86, 65.

33. Melissa Milkie, "Social Comparisons, Reflected Appraisals, and Mass Media: The Impact of Pervasive Beauty Images on Black and White Girls' Self-Concepts," *Social Psychology Quarterly* 62, no. 2 (1999): 190–210; Lamb, "Feminist Ideals," 2009; Arnold Veraa, "Critique: Report of the APA Task Force on the Sexualization of Girls (2007)," *Institute for Psychological Therapies Journal* 18, no. 1 (2009).

34. Carla E. Stokes, "Representin' in Cyberspace: Sexual Scripts, Self-Definition, and Hip Hop Culture in Black American Adolescent Girls' Home Pages," *Culture, Health & Sexuality* 9, no. 2 (2007): 169–184.

35. C.J. Pascoe, "Resource and Risk: Youth Sexuality and New Media Use." *Sexuality Research and Social Policy* 8 (2011): 5–17, 6.

36. Jack M. McLeod, Gerald M. Kosicki, and Zhongdang Pan, "On Understanding and Misunderstanding Media Effects," in *Mass Media and Society,* eds. J. Curran and M. Gurevitch (London: Edward Arnold, 1991): 250, as cited by Milkie, 1999.

37. Rana A. Emerson, "'Where My Girls At?' Negotiating Black Womanhood in Music Videos," *Gender and Society* 16 (2002): 115–135; Stern, *Eugenic Nation,* 2002; Mary Celeste Kearney, *Girls Make Media* (New York: Routledge, 2006).

38. Jackson and Westrupp, "Sex, Postfeminist Popular," 357.

39. Cymene Howe, "Spectacles of Sexuality: Televisionary Activism in Nicaragua," *Cultural Anthropology* 23, no. 1 (2008): 48–84, 53.

40. Karen E. Wohlwend, "Damsels in Discourse: Girls Consuming and Producing Identity Texts through Disney Princess Play," *Reading Research Quarterly* 44, no. 1 (2009): 57–83.

41. Feona Attwood, "No Money Shot? Commerce, Pornography and New Sex Taste Cultures," *Sexualities* 10 (2007): 441–446, 441.

42. Ibid.

43. Nicole M. Doring, "The Internet's Impact on Sexuality: A Critical Review of 15 Years of Research," *Computers in Human Behavior* 25 (2009): 1089–1101.

44. Stokes, "Representin' in Cyberspace," 171.

45. Sonia Livingstone, Young People and New Media: Childhood and the Changing Media Environment (London: Sage, 2004).

46. Rosalind Gill, "Media Empowerment and the 'Sexualization of Culture' Debates," *Sex Roles* 66 (2012): 736–745.

47. APA, "Report," 2007.

48. Cary Bazelgette, "An Agenda for the Second Phase of Media Literacy Development," in *Media Literacy in the Information Age*, eds. R. Kubey (New Brunswick, NJ: Transaction, 2001), 72.

49. Gill, "Media Empowerment," 2012.

50. R. Danielle Egan and Gail Hawkes, "Endangered Girls and Incendiary Objects: Unpacking the Discourse on Sexualization," *Sexuality and Culture* 12, no. 4 (2008): 291–311; Renee Hobbs, "The Seven Great Debates in the Media Literacy Movement," *Journal of Communication* 48 (1998): 16–32.

51. Sue Jackson and Tamsyn Gilbertson, "'Hot Lesbians': Young People's Talk about Representations of Lesbianism," *Sexualities* 12 (2009): 199–224, 203.

52. Gill, "Media Empowerment," 2012.

53. Milkie, "Social Comparisons," 208.

54. Gill, "Media Empowerment," 741.

Works Cited

Alexander, Ruth M. *The "Girl Problem": Female Sexual Delinquency in New York, 1900–1930*. Ithaca, NY: Cornell University Press, 1995.

American Psychological Association. "Report of the APA Task Force on the Sexualization of Girls." *APA (2007) Task Force on the Sexualization of Girls*. February 2007. URL: http://www.apa.org/pi/wpo/Sexualization.html.

Attenborough, Frederick T. "Complicating the Sexualization Thesis: The Media, Gender, and 'Sci-candy.'" *Discourse & Society* 22 (2011): 659–76.

Attwood, Feona. "What do People do with Porn? Qualitative Research into the Consumption, Use, and Experience of Pornography and Other Sexually Explicit Media." *Sexuality & Culture* 9 (2005): 65–86.

———. "Sexed Up: Theorizing the Sexualization of Culture." *Sexualities* 9 (2006): 77–94.

———. "No Money Shot? Commerce, Pornography and New Sex Taste Cultures." *Sexualities* 10 (2007): 441–46.

———. ed. *Mainstreaming Sex: The Sexualization of Western Culture*. New York: Palgrave Macmillan, 2009.

Bae, Michelle S. "Interrogating Girl Power: Girlhood, Popular Media, and Postfeminism." *Visual Arts Research* 37 (2011): 28–40.

Bailey, Beth L. *From Front Porch to Back Seat: Courtship in Twentieth-Century America*. Baltimore: Johns Hopkins University Press, 1989.

Bazalgette, Cary. "An Agenda for the Second Phase of Media Literacy Development." In *Media*

Literacy in the Information Age, ed. Robert Kubey, 69–78. New Brunswick, NJ: Transaction, 2001.

Butler, Judith. *Excitable Speech: A Politics of the Performative.* New York: Routledge, 1997.

Carpenter, Laura M. "From Girls into Women: Scripts for Sexuality and Romance in Seventeen Magazine, 1974–1994." *The Journal of Sex Research* 35 (1998): 158–168.

Collins, Patricia Hill. *Black Feminist Thought: Knowledge, Consciousness, and the Politics of Empowerment.* Boston, MA: Unwin Hyman, 1990.

———. *Black Sexual Politics: African Americans, Gender, and the New Racism.* New York: Routledge, 2005.

Connelly, Matthew. *Fatal Misconception: The Struggle to Control World Population.* Cambridge: Harvard University Press, 2008.

D'Emilio, John and Estelle B. Freedman. *Intimate Matters: A History of Sexuality in America.* Chicago: University of Chicago Press, 1998.

Doring, Nicola M. "The Internet's Impact on Sexuality: A Critical Review of 15 Years of Research." *Computers in Human Behavior* 25 (2009): 1089–1101.

Douglas, Susan. *Where the Girls Are: Growing Up Female with the Mass Media.* New York: Random House, 1994.

Driscoll, Catherine. *Girls: Feminine Adolescence in Popular Culture and Cultural Theory.* New York: Columbia University Press, 2002.

Duits, Linda. "Headscarves and Porno Chic: Disciplining Girls' Bodies in the European Multicultural Society," *European Journal of Women's Studies* 13, no. 2 (2007): 103–17.

Durham, M. Gigi. "Dilemmas of Desire: Representations of Adolescent Sexuality in Two Teen Magazines." *Youth and Society* 29 (1998): 369–389.

———. *The Lolita Effect: The Media Sexualization of Young Girls and What We Can Do About It.* New York: The Overlook Press, 2008.

Edin, Kathryn and Maria Kafalas. *Promises I Can Keep: Why Poor Women Put Motherhood Before Marriage.* Berkeley: University of California Press, 2007.

Egan, R. Danielle. "Sexualizing Girls' Troubles." *Contexts* 11 (2012): 56–7.

Egan, R. Danielle and Gail Hawkes. "Endangered Girls and Incendiary Objects: Unpacking the Discourse on Sexualization." *Sexuality and Culture* 12, no. 4 (2008): 291–311.

Eklund, Lina. "Doing Gender in Cyberspace: The Performance of Gender by Female World of Warcraft Players." *Convergence: The International Journal of Research into New Media Technologies* 17 (2011): 323–42.

Emerson, Rana. A. "'Where My Girls At?' Negotiating Black Womanhood in Music Videos." *Gender and Society* 16 (2002): 115–35.

Evans, Ellis D., Judith Rutberg, Carmela Sather, and Charli Turner. "Content Analysis of Contemporary Teen Magazines for Adolescent Females." *Youth and Society* 23, no. 1 (1991): 99–120.

Fass, Paula. *The Damned and the Beautiful: American Youth in the 1920s.* New York: Oxford University Press, 1977.

Ferguson, Marjorie. *Forever Feminine: Women's Magazines and the Cult of Femininity.* London: Heinemann Educational Books Ltd., 1983.

Fine, Michelle. "Sexuality, Schooling, and Adolescent Females: The Missing Discourse of Desire." *Harvard Education Review* 58 (1988): 29–53.

———. "X. Desire: the morning (and 15 years) after." *Feminism & Psychology* 15 (2005): 54–50.

Fischer, Kirsten. *Suspect Relations: Sex, Race, and Resistance in Colonial North Carolina.* Ithaca: Cornell University Press, 2001.

Fisher, Kate. *Birth Control, Sex, and Marriage in Britain, 1918–1960.* Oxford: Oxford University Press, 2006.

Forman-Brunell, Miriam. *Babysitter: An American History.* New York: New York University Press, 2009.

Foucault, Michel. *The Archaeology of Knowledge.* Translated by A.M. Sheridan Smith. New York: Pantheon Books, 1972.

Gill, Rosalind. *Gender and the Media.* Cambridge: Polity Press, 2007.

———. "Beyond the Sexualization of Culture Thesis: An Intersectional Analysis of 'Sixpacks,' 'Midriffs' and 'Hot Lesbians' in Advertising." *Sexualities* 12 (2009): 137–60.

———. "Media Empowerment and the "Sexualization of Culture" Debates." *Sex Roles* 66 (2012): 736–45.

Harris, Anita. *All About the Girl: Culture, Power and Identity.* New York: Routledge, 2004.

Hartmann, Betsy. *Reproductive Rights and Wrongs: The Global Politics of Population Control.* Boston: South End Press, 1995.

Heins, Marjorie. *Not in Front of the Children: Indecency, Censorship, and the Innocence of Youth.* New Brunswick, NJ: Rutgers University Press, 2007.

Hobbs, Renee. "The Seven Great Debates in the Media Literacy Movement." *Journal of Communication* 48 (1998): 16–32.

Holloway, Sarah. L. and Gill Valentine. *Cyberkids.* New York: Routledge, 2003.

hooks, bell. *Feminist Theory: From Margin to Center.* Boston: South End Press, 1984.

Howe, Cymene. "Spectacles of Sexuality: Televisionary Activism in Nicaragua," *Cultural Anthropology* 23, no. 1 (2008): 48–84.

Hunter, Jane. *How Young Ladies Became Girls: The Victorian Origins of American Girlhood.* New Haven, CT: Yale University Press, 2002.

Hurtado, Albert L. *Intimate Frontiers: Sex, Gender, and Culture in Old California.* Albuquerque, NM: University of New Mexico Press, 1999.

Inness, Sherrie, ed. *Nancy Drew and Company: Culture, Gender, and Girls' Series.* Bowling Green, OH: Bowling Green University Press, 1997.

———. ed. *Delinquents and Debutantes: Twentieth-Century American Girls' Cultures.* New York: New York University Press, 1998.

Irvine, Janice M., ed. *Sexual Cultures and the Construction of Adolescent Identities.* Philadelphia: Temple University Press, 1994.

Jackson, Sue and Elizabeth Westrupp. "Sex, Postfeminist Culture, and the Pre-Teen Girl." *Sexualities* 13, no. 3 (2010): 357–76.

Jackson, Sue and Tamsyn Gilbertson. "Hot Lesbians": Young People's Talk about Representations of Lesbianism. *Sexualities* 12 (2009): 199–224.

Kearney, Mary Celeste. *Girls Make Media.* New York: Routledge, 2006.

———. "Coalescing: The Development of Girls' Studies." *NWSA Journal* 21, no. 1 (2009): 1–28.

———. *Mediated Girlhoods: New Explorations of Girls' Media Culture.* New York: Peter Lang, 2011.

Kim, Janna L. and L. Monique Ward. "Pleasure Readings: Associations Between Young Women's Sexual Attitudes and Their Reading of Contemporary Women's Magazines." *Psychology of Women Quarterly* 28 (2004): 48–58.

Lamb, Sharon. "Feminist Ideals for a Healthy Female Adolescent Sexuality: A Critique." *Sex Roles* 62 (2009): 294–306.

Lerum, Kari and Shari L. Dworkin. "Bad Girls Rule: An Interdisciplinary Feminist Commentary on the Report of the APA Task Force on the Sexualization of Girls." *Journal of Sex Research* 46, no. 4 (2009): 250–63.

Levy, Ariel. *Female Chauvinist Pigs: Women and the Rise of Raunch Culture.* New York: Free Press, 2006.

Livingstone, Sonia. *Young People and New Media: Childhood and the Changing Media Environment.* London: Sage, 2002.

———. "Media Literacy and the Challenge of New Information and Communication Technologies." *The Communication Review* 7 (2004): 3–14.

Mazzarella, Sharon R. and Norma Pecora, eds. *Growing Up Girls: Popular Culture and the Construction of Identity.* New York: Peter Lang, 2001.

McCracken, Ellen. *Decoding Women's Magazines: From Mademoiselle to Ms.* London: Macmillan, 1993.

McLeod, Jack M., Gerald M. Kosicki, and Zhongdang Pan. "On Understanding and Misunderstanding Media Effects." In *Mass Media and Society*, eds. J. Curran and M. Gurevitch, 235–66. London: Edward Arnold, 1991.

McNair, Brian. *Striptease Culture: Sex, Media and the Democratization of Desire.* London and New York: Routledge, 2002.

McRobbie, Angela. *Feminism and Youth Culture.* New York: Routledge, 2000.

———. "More! New Sexualities in Girls' and Women's Magazines." In *Cultural Studies and Communications*, eds. J. Curran, D. Morley and V. Walkerdine, 172–94. London: Arnold, 2006.

Milkie, Melissa A. "Social Comparisons, Reflected Appraisals, and Mass Media: The Impact of Pervasive Beauty Images on Black and White Girls' Self-Concepts." *Social Psychology Quarterly* 62, no. 2 (1999): 190–210.

Moran, Jeffrey P. *Teaching Sex: The Shaping of Adolescence in the 20th Century.* Cambridge: Harvard University Press, 2002.

Nagel, Joane. *Race, Ethnicity, and Sexuality: Intimate Intersections, Forbidden Frontiers.* New York: Oxford University Press, 2003.

Nash, Ilana. *American Sweethearts: Teenage Girls in Twentieth-Century Popular Culture.* Bloomington, IN: Indiana University Press, 2006.

Odem, Mary E. *Delinquent Daughters: Protecting and Policing Adolescent Female Sexuality in the United States, 1885–1920.* Chapel Hill, NC: University of North Carolina Press, 1995.

Osgerby, Bill. *Youth Media.* New York: Routledge, 2004.

Paasonen, Susanna, Kaarina Nikunen, and Laura Saarenmaa. *Pornification: Sex and Sexuality in Media Culture.* Oxford: Bergham, 2007.

Pascoe, C.J. "Resource and Risk: Youth Sexuality and New Media Use." *Sexuality Research and Social Policy* 8 (2011): 5–17.

Peirce, Kate. "A Feminist Theoretical Perspective on the Socialization of Teenage Girls Through *Seventeen* Magazines." *Sex Roles* 23 (1990): 491–500.

Phillips, Lynn M. *Flirting with Danger: Young Women's Reflections on Sexuality and Domination.* New

York: New York University Press, 2000.

Rassmussen, Mary Louise. *Youth and Sexualities: Pleasure, Subversion, and Insubordination In and Out of Schools.* New York: Palgrave Macmillan, 2004.

Roberts, Dorothy. *Killing the Black Body: Race, Reproduction, and the Meaning of Liberty.* New York: Vintage, 1998.

Scheiner, Georganne. *Signifying Female Adolescence: Film Representations and Fans, 1920–1950.* Westport, CT: Praeger, 2000.

Schoen, Joanna. *Choice and Coercion: Birth Control, Sterilization and Abortion in Public Health and Welfare.* Chapel Hill, NC: University of North Carolina Press, 2005.

Schrum, Kelly. *Some Wore Bobby Sox: The Emergence of Teenage Girls' Culture, 1920–1945.* New York: Palgrave, 2006.

Stansell, Christine. *City of Women: Sex and Class in New York, 1789–1860.* Champaign, IL: University of Illinois Press, 1987.

Stern, Alexandra. *Eugenic Nation: Faults and Frontiers of Better Breeding in Modern America.* Berkeley: University of California Press, 2005.

Stokes, Carla E. "Representin' in Cyberspace: Sexual Scripts, Self-Definition, and Hip Hop Culture in Black American Adolescent Girls' Home Pages." *Culture, Health & Sexuality* 9, no. 2 (2007): 169-184.

Thurlow, Crispin and Susan McKay. "Profiling 'New' Communication Technologies in Adolescence." *Journal of Language and Social Psychology,* 22, no. 1 (2003): 94–103.

Tolman, Deboarah L. "Daring to Desire: Culture and the Bodies of Adolescent Girls." In *Sexual Cultures and the Construction of Adolescent Identities,* ed. Janice M. Irvine. Philadelphia: Temple University Press, 1994.

———. "Femininity as a Barrier to Positive Sexual Health for Girls." *Journal of the American Medical Women's Association* 54 (1999): 133–38.

———. *Dilemmas of Desire: Teenage Girls Talk about Sexuality.* Cambridge: Harvard University Press, 2002.

Veraa, Arnold. "Critique: Report of the APA Task Force on the Sexualization of Girls (2007)." *Institute for Psychological Therapies Journal* 18, no. 1 (2009).

Wohlwend, Karen E. "Damsels in Discourse: Girls Consuming and Producing Identity Texts through Disney Princess Play." *Reading Research Quarterly* 44, no. 1 (2009): 57–83.

Wouters, Cas. "Sexualization: Have Sexualization Processes Changed Direction?" *Sexualities* 13, no. 6 (2010): 723–741.

PART ONE

HISTORICAL AND CONTEMPORARY MEDIA

The Girls of Carvel: Adolescent Desire in *Andy Hardy* Films

Georganne Scheiner Gillis

In the third *Andy Hardy* film, *Love Finds Andy Hardy* (1938), Andy complains about girls during his obligatory man-to-man with his father the judge:

> Sometimes I don't understand these modern girls. Polly for instance. Sometimes she won't let you kiss her at all, but that Cynthia she'll let you kiss her whenever you want. She doesn't want to swim, play tennis, all she wants to do is kiss you. I'm a nervous wreck!…Why is it when you want to kiss a girl and she won't let you, you want to kiss her all the time.

This scene underscores competing paradigms and discourses about female adolescent sexuality in the 1930s filtered through the perspective of a fictional adolescent male. On the one hand, there is a recognition of new dating behaviors among teens, but on the other is the implicit critique of it. Although Polly is a prude, Andy respects her for playing hard to get, while Cynthia is suspect because of her desire. Girls' desire operated as a site of frustration and confusion both for Andy and for the parent culture in the 1930s and 1940s.

The *Andy Hardy* films remain one of the only coherent series about teens in American history, spanning over ten years and fifteen films. As Timothy Shary has noted the series offers "the most significant depiction of adolescent life in America until the mid-1950s."[1] Much like series fiction, there were recurring characters, formulaic plots and themes, and each film was a continuation of the narrative of the previous film. Even though the films centered on the concerns of an adolescent boy played by Mickey Rooney, there were a host of ancillary female characters who were clear signifiers of the female adolescent experience. In fact, the series is credited with launching the careers of Judy Garland, Lana Turner, Donna Reed, and Esther Williams. This chapter will explore heterosexual desire and practice through the lens of the female characters. While it might seem counterintuitive to use films that have been criticized for offering up a sanitized, unrealistic, and idealized vision of white girlhood and adolescence to explore sexuality in the pre-World War II era, I will argue that it is the recurring and often conflicting tropes of heterosexual desire that make these films a useful window into historical perspectives on girlhood, dating, and sexuality in the period. The 1930s and early 1940s offered competing discourses of adolescent sexuality. Teens in the period increasingly began to carve out cultural space and to create new public conventions and practices around dating. The parent culture, however, continued to articulate outdated codes of sexual behavior and appropriate desire. The *Hardy* films began to reconcile the discourse of the parent culture with the reality of teen sexual desire by recognizing the "naturalness" of that desire, but prescribing limits to it. Thus the series both underscores and assuages social anxieties about girls' sexual desire.

Like the syndicates that created some of the most popular series books of the era, the *Hardy* films offer a coherent and legible depiction of adolescent desire. There were several factors that contributed to the cohesiveness of the films. Perhaps the most important was the creative vision of its producer, Carey Wilson. Wilson was also a writer and he based many events in the films on his own boyhood in Rutherford, New Jersey. [2] In addition, all but two of the films were directed by George Seitz, who also collaborated on several of the screenplays. The stable of writers was also fairly consistent and included Agnes Christine Johnson, Kay Van Ripper, William Ludwig, and Harry Ruskin. The films create a seamless narrative as each film in the series unfolds months, weeks, and even minutes after the previous one. The formulaic nature of the series was clearly a factor in its longevity and success.

Contemporary sociologist Margaret Thorp in her study of America's movie going habits extolled the series as an accurate reflection of white, middle-class domesticity:

> The Hardy pictures are based on research as intelligent and thorough as that which goes into the making of the most elaborate film…the things that happen to the Hardy's are the sort of things that might happen to almost anyone…Because they are so genuine an American norm, families in the various brackets, far above or below them, see themselves mirrored in the Hardy's.[3]

The appeal of the franchise was further underscored by commendation from the film industry. Rooney along with Deanna Durbin were awarded a special Oscar in 1938 for their "significant contribution in bringing to the screen the spirit and personification of youth and as juvenile players setting a high standard of ability and achievement." MGM was honored by the Academy in 1942 for "its achievement in representing the American way of life in the production of the Andy Hardy series."[4] When Pearl Buck's East and West Association asked motion picture critics in 1942 to name the films that they believed were most suitable to convey an "authentic reflection" of life in the United

States to Asian audiences, the entire *Hardy* series, "in whole or in part," topped the list.[5]

While the series was honored for its wholesome depictions of American teens, historian Kelly Schrum argues that teens themselves were not attracted to the *Andy Hardy* films. She cites a study of film preferences in the late 1930s and early 1940s that found that the series ranked third for white girls and was not included in the top six rankings for white or African American boys. The chief adolescent demographic for *Hardy* films was high school freshman girls.[6] Schrum notes that older teens, however, "did not take the characters or actresses seriously as role models of teenage life," instead they were attracted to more "glamorous" adult actors and actresses.[7] Yet in a 1938 national survey of 4-Star Clubs conducted by the National Board of Review to discover film preferences among youth, *Love Finds Andy Hardy* ranked third in preference among both boys and girls.[8] While the appeal of the Hardys probably was mainly to adults because of the films' comforting, optimistic depictions of family life, the resonance of the series for children and teens cannot be discounted.

The cycle began in 1937 with the low-budget film *A Family Affair*, based on an obscure 1928 play *Skidding* by Aurania Rouverol. Lionel Barrymore and Spring Byington were cast as the parents, Cecilia Parker and Julie Hayden as the older sisters, Sara Hayden as the spinster Aunt Millie, Mickey Rooney as the girl crazy Andy Hardy, and Ann Rutherford as his girlfriend Polly Benedict. Although the series began as a "B" picture, the first film was an enormous success. The series had a particular appeal for MGM studio head Louis B. Mayer, who had a penchant for sentimentality. He immediately ordered a sequel and then a series. Mayer believed that the function of motion pictures was to entertain and MGM was noted for films that idealized the American home. As film historian Norman Zierod notes, Mayer "believed in sacred motherhood and omnipotent fatherhood, the sanctity of the family over all...good, heartwarming stories won out over grim dramas. A happy ending was decidedly necessary."[9] The *Hardy* series seemed to fit that bill perfectly. Mayer took a personal interest in the *Andy Hardy* franchise and has been described as its "foremost fan," micromanaging every detail of production.[10] While Mayer subscribed to a Victorian morality in the idealized America of his films, his own behavior underscored his hypocrisy as he was a notorious womanizer and the stories of his extensive use of the casting couch circulated widely in Hollywood.[11]

After the success of *A Family Affair*, Mayer rushed production of its sequel, *You're Only Young Once* (1938). Louis Stone and Fay Holden took over as the Judge and Mrs. Hardy, roles they would continue for the duration of the series. The older, married sister played by Julie Hayden was dropped, but Mickey Rooney, Cecilia Parker, and Sara Hayden would reprise their roles. *The New York Times* was enthusiastic in its praise of this fictional family:

> The average American family (if indeed, there is such a thing) has been so frequently li-
> beled by the average film, it is a surprising experience and an occasion for relief to
> come upon a fictional group which can reasonably be accepted as such…and in which
> individual members react like human beings instead of third rate vaudevillians.[12]

The *Andy Hardy* films must be contextualized in the material conditions of
the culture that produced them. By 1930, sixty percent of American teens of
school age were attending high school. Many teens were forced to stay in school
because of the high unemployment rates caused by the Depression. In many
ways, the Depression actually served to reinforce adolescent subcultures because of the universality of high school enrollment. Sociologists Robert Lynd
and Helen Merrell Lynd investigated the changing attitudes of teens during the
1930s in their second study of Muncie, Indiana in *Middletown in Transition* in
1937. The youth culture of Muncie as detailed by the Lynds differed markedly
from the fictional mid-western town of Carvel, Idaho, the fictional town of the
Hardy family. They noted the "increased sophistication" of teens and the pro-
nounced increase in teenage drinking. "They know everything and do everything openly—and they aren't afraid to talk about it." School authorities in
Muncie were so concerned that the high school brought in clergy and other
youth workers to confront the "drinking and immorality."[13] By the 1930s, many
adolescents themselves thought that adolescence itself should be a time of increased freedom and they began to challenge traditional ideas of parental authority and respect. Historian Grace Palladino has chronicled the efforts of
adolescents to demand an increased degree of autonomy and to assert their
right to behave the way they wanted to behave. Teenagers in the 1930s claimed
the right "to choose their own friends, and run their own social lives, based on
teenage notions of propriety and style, not on adult rules of appropriate conduct." This response prompted "professional character builders" and other
youth organizations to find acceptable ways to channel adolescent energy.[14] By
the 1930s adolescence had become a contested terrain on which the parent culture tried to inscribe prescriptive values about adulthood and sexuality.[15] Teens
themselves, however, had very different ideas.

The *Hardy* series reflects the burgeoning youth culture of the 1930s and
marks changes in dating behavior. As historian Beth Bailey points out, unlike
courting, dating rituals of the 1930s were not about marriage, family, or even
love. Instead, the purpose of dating was a way to signal "a promiscuous popularity" which measured success for teens "through the variety of dates they
commanded."[16] In 1937, sociologist Willard Waller conducted a major study of
dating and described the competitive nature of dates as the "dating and rating
system," which became a feature of teen dating in the pre-World War II years.[17]
The "dating and rating system" would also be a prominent feature of the *Hardy*
series. A major part of dating among the middle class according to Bailey was

"necking" and "petting." As she notes, both were "public conventions, expected elements in any romantic relationship between a boy and a girl."[18] While not condoning such behavior, Floyd Dell writing in *Parents Magazine* in 1931, noted that when "a girl engages in petting, she is acting according to the code of her own adolescent world."[19] Dell's comment suggests the normalization of petting practices among teens. The Lynds also documented a more permissive attitude toward sex among white teens in Muncie. One high school boy said of teenaged girls: "They've been getting more and more knowing and bold. The fellows regard necking as a taken for granted part of a date. We fellows used to get slapped for doing things, but the girls don't do much of that anymore."[20]

Historians John D'Emilio and Estelle Freedman also point to an expansion of permissible codes of sexual behavior among teens in the 1930s. They cite one study of teens in St Louis that showed that teens were more tolerant about sexual matters than about smoking and drinking. Freed from parental supervision and expectations, teens believed that petting was a natural part of a date.[21] This is not to suggest that the new customs of dating translated into public acceptance by parents and other authority figures. Teens in the 1930s were faced with competing discourses about sex from both the parent culture and the peer culture. While peer culture reified new dating customs, national media and popular discourse still tried to control and regulate sexual experimentation among teens, and this discourse was underscored by the *Hardy* series, particularly through the recurring character of Polly Benedict. The constant affirmation of traditional morality in the series might indicate that such attitudes were increasingly passé with 1930s teens.

You're Only Young Once established the character of Polly (Ann Rutherford). Polly is supposed to be fifteen, but she seems more like an affected adult, addressing Andy as "Mr. Hardy." She is prissy and demanding, shaking her head and stomping her feet when she is upset with Andy (which is always). Polly gives out ambivalent messages about sex. On the one hand, she acts frustrated with Andy's awkward, fumbling efforts to kiss her. She repeats the same admonition to Andy in several films, "Don't you think of anything else besides grabbing people in dark corners!"[22] Yet, for Polly "necking" also functions as a form of currency, and she doles out her kisses to get what she wants from Andy. As Beth Bailey points out, dating often fostered a "sense of obligation" among girls. That is, girls were expected to "put out" in proportion to the amount of money spent on her. It was the girl's responsibility to define the sexual limits of a relationship, however.[23] Polly has to draw the line for Andy in film after film. Bailey might have been describing Polly when she says, "In trying to live up to society's expectations of 'virtue,' girls were likely to build up strong barriers against sexuality. The more virtuous, the woman, the stronger her resistance."[24] Because of her disdainful attitude toward sex, Polly is continually positioned in the *Hardy* series as the nice girl. Andy often strays, but he always comes back to Polly. Rarely is Polly an integral part of the plots of the *Hardy* films, however. Instead her leaving town or generally being unavailable serves as an opportunity for Andy to be involved with another girl. That "other girl" is usually in direction opposition to Polly's virtue.

Such is the case with *You're Only Young Once* (1938). The Hardy family is vacationing on Catalina Island, where Andy meets a precocious older woman (she's sixteen), Jerry Lane (Eleanor Lynn). Jerry is far more sophisticated than both Andy and the girls of Carvel, a classic "poor little rich girl," whose mother has been divorced four times. As the product of a broken home, Jerry is well on her way to delinquency as she drinks, smokes, and encourages kissing as opposed to the virtuous Polly Benedict. Judge Hardy, concerned about her growing influence over Andy, tries to talk privately to Jerry, but she mistakes his intention as a pass. While this might indicate that Jerry has been victimized by older men in the past, Judge Hardy is outraged by her assumptions about his character. The judge functions as the moral compass of the series and the voice of the parent culture. He warns Andy, "This girl isn't good...I suppose she's a product of the bad features of the age we live in, but that doesn't keep her from being rotten proof. She'd poison whatever she came into contact with mentally, morally and spiritually."[25] This is an uncharacteristically harsh and judgmental condemnation for the judge, who would be more apt to blame the parents for their children's behavior. In fact, in a later film, *The Courtship of Andy Hardy* (1942), Judge Hardy chides the divorced, feuding parents of a young teen, Melody (Donna Reed's screen debut), for her behavior, and holds them totally responsible for their daughter's unhappiness. While Melody would be a sympathetic character, Jerry is not. Andy defies his father and calls him "old-fashioned" as he angrily goes to meet Jerry. She has arranged a seductive evening for Andy and plies him with liquor in an effort to get him to have sex. With the judge's words echoing in his head, Andy resists Jerry's advances and admits he would rather be playing football. Jerry's desire is not constructed as either normal or even as transgressive, but as deviant and the product of a dysfunctional upbringing. Andy returns chaste to Polly, whom he would rather have to beg for a kiss than be given one free. This film would begin a trend that would play out throughout the course of the series. That is, girls as the sexual aggressors and Andy as their often unwilling target.

Andy himself was both ambivalent and conflicted about his desire. In fact, Jeffrey Dennis has argued that there is a homo-erotic subtext embedded in a number of *Hardy* films.[26] While I believe Dennis overstates his case, it is clear that Andy was both attracted to and terrified of the girls and women in his life. Andy talks a good game, but faced with the real thing, his inclination is to flee. Such was the case with Jerry in the second *Hardy* offering and this pattern would be repeated throughout the series. For example, in *The Hardy's Ride High* (1939) Andy is set up with a chorus girl by an unscrupulous young man in an effort to compromise Andy. When she tries to make love to him, Andy feigns illness and literally runs away from her when faced with the reality of a sexual performance. In *Life Begins for Andy Hardy*, a beautiful Latina, Isobel Gonzales, throws herself at him repeatedly, but he is immune to her charms. Andy fends off the sexual advances of an older woman in *Life Begins for Andy Hardy* (1941) after she disparages the character of Judge Hardy. In *The Courtship of Andy Hardy* (1942), Andy underscores his ambivalence to girls as he laments to his father, "I'm a healthy normal fella, yet I can't fall in love with a girl who's dripping zip from every pore." Judge Hardy reassures him that it's only a sign of his immaturity. Yet his classmate Susie might well have been speaking of Andy himself when she says of Andy's jalopy, "As soon as a girl gets in it, it runs out of gas." Andy is all talk and no action, and seems more enamored of the idea of sex than the reality of it. Dennis notes that Andy's "girl-craziness" presented a problem for MGM in that they were depicting a teen with a sexual desire who was "five to ten years from the possibility of consummating that desire in the socially respectable institution of marriage." Instead, the films suggested that Andy's desire was simply a "childish affectation to be overcome in manhood."[27] Throughout the series, adults advised Andy that desire was both natural and immature and posited a single standard of sexual behavior for both boys and girls.

Dennis argues that Andy's "girl-craziness" was not initially a "requisite of adolescent masculinity" in the 1930s, instead it signified a "feminizing trait" of Andy. In fact, "heterosexual desire never becomes an essential characteristic of Andy's teenaged masculinity. It is always contradictory, problematized, sometimes adulated, but sometimes signifying effeminacy and even perversion." According to Dennis, it was not until the 1940s that girl-craziness would become a hegemonic characteristic of male adolescent masculinity.[28]

Conversely, "boy-craziness" was not a feature of female adolescence in either prescriptions of femininity or in popular perceptions of girlhood. Grace Palladino notes that advice dispensed from "Aunt Cherry" in *Everygirls Magazine* in the 1930s encouraged her readers to "steer clear of crushes," and while telling them that falling in love with many boys was "natural" because it was "nature's way of getting a girl interested in mating," she warned, "you can't marry them all."[29] Girls were expected to be interested in love and romance, but because the expected end game was marriage, they were encouraged to protect their reputations.

In the sexual marketplace, a girls' value was tied not only to her virtue, but to her popularity. Boys also felt the pressure to be popular and a boy's status often was gauged by whom he dated. Such was the case in the fourth *Hardy* film

Love Finds Andy Hardy (1938). The film introduced two new ingénues, Judy Garland and Lana Turner, to the series. Garland plays an awkward, sweet twelve-year-old, Betsy Booth, caught in the throes of an unrequited crush on Andy. Early on, Betsy realizes neither her age nor her looks provide her with any kind of social currency. "I'll never be able to catch a man, much less keep him," she laments, "no glamour, no glamour at all." Betsy has a bad case of puppy love, and she functions as Andy's surrogate mother, providing nurturing support and smoothing things out for the ungrateful Andy. Polly is gone for the Christmas vacation and Andy's friend Beezie pays Andy to "entertain" his girlfriend Cynthia Potter (Turner) while he is away for the holiday as well. Although Andy does not particularly like Cynthia, the money he will earn to pay off his jalopy, and Cynthia's good looks, override any compunction he might have about keeping company with her. In the "dating and rating" system, Cynthia confers a certain status on Andy and he is happy to have a "sensational girl on [his] arm." Cynthia is vapid, possessive, demanding, flirty, and a little too easy by Carvel standards. She eschews sports, but one thing she will do is to "neck." Andy differentiates between his necking with Cynthia and with Polly, referring to the latter as "good clean fun." There is something predatory about Cynthia's sexual desire. In fact, Andy refers to her at one point as a "vampire," harkening back to the 1920s term for the femme fatale. As in *You're Only Young Once*, Andy is intimidated by Cynthia's sexual aggression and he realizes that he prefers the prudish Polly because he will not be required to perform. At one point in the film, Polly suggests to Andy that they are "much too old for that sort of thing—hugging and kissing." Andy replies in a baby voice that he "ain't ever gonna get too old for huggin' and kissin'" and as Dennis notes, his "flirtations with girls his own age are often conducted in an oddly infantile manner."[30] Although his childish looks and demeanor neutralize his budding sexuality, the girls of Carvel are much more mature physically and emotionally.

Judge Hardy and Son (1939) would offer the most coherent philosophy about adolescent sexuality. Kissing a pawing Andy is still distasteful to Polly, but she reluctantly gives in occasionally to get what she wants, saying, "I guess if you're going to take me to the fireworks, I owe you a kiss." When he complains to Marion about Polly's lack of affection, she responds, "Polly will be glad when you get out of the adolescent habit of kissing." A bewildered Andy can't understand her meaning, and he defends his desire as "fun, good clean fun." Marion persists, "If you were married to Polly would you still want to kiss her all the time?" The implication throughout the film and later films of the series is that the desire to kiss and to "neck" are immature expressions of sexuality, just a stage to be successfully navigated and replaced by a more mature relationship within a marriage devoid of public displays of affection. Andy is convinced that he would never want to give up kissing until he meets a giggly flirt, who talks baby talk and wants to kiss all the time. Once again, there is such a thing as too much of a good thing for Andy. When he learns that Polly is taking cooking lessons with his mother because Andy's parents have told her that a good wife is one who "cooks well," Andy believes that Polly wants to marry him. It turns out to be a hoax, however, concocted by Polly and Andy's parents to tease Andy. In fact, as Polly asserts in the final scene, she does not believe in early marriage and will be going east the following year to go to college. It is only her declaration of independence that allows Andy to feel amorous once again as he grabs Polly, plants a messy kiss on her face, and squeals "Woo-woo!"

Garland and Rooney made two more *Hardy* films together. In *Andy Hardy Meets a Debutante* (1940), Andy has a crush on Daphne Fowler, "Deb of the Year." He brags to his friends in Carvel that he knows her; making Polly jealous enough that she calls his bluff by publishing the details of his "romance" in the school newspaper. Coincidentally, the Hardy family is about to leave for New York, so Andy must get proof of his fictional relationship with Daphne. Garland as Betsy Booth is once again the awkward, flustered adolescent. Time and distance have not lessened her affection for Andy, but he continues to treat her like a kid sister. Mrs. Hardy holds Betsy up as a paradigm to Andy extolling her as a "nice, old fashioned girl." She says to him, "Even in New York, a nice girl grows up thinking more about being a housewife than doing the rumble [sic]."[31] Once again, Betsy functions as his faithful helpmate and solves his problem when she introduces him to Daphne, who turns out to be her good friend. By the end of the film, Andy seems to take his mother's advice to heart, when he declares, "I want a nice, old fashioned girl—a girl who will look up to a man." For the first time, he seems to notice Betsy, and he bestows her first kiss.

The last pairing between Garland and Rooney in the series was *Life Begins for Andy Hardy* (1941). This film offers a decidedly darker mood than earlier offerings. After graduating from high school, Andy decides to head back to New York with visions of fame, fortune, and chorus girls. Before he leaves, he and Polly share their good-byes as they have decided they should no longer be going together. As he shakes her hand, he says seriously, "My wife will be glad that I went around with a certain kind of girl, the kind of girl with whom they were no regrets." Their dual celibacy is celebrated in their farewell. They have successfully navigated the sexual terrain of adolescence and have emerged with their virtue intact. Once in New York, Andy finds that Betsy has grown into a beautiful, self-possessed woman, telling him, that she has "lost six pounds for him," but Andy hardly seems to notice. Instead, he gets involved with an older, divorced gold-digger, Miss Hicks. This was the only *Hardy* film to be found objectionable by the Legion of Decency. The censor objected to the fact that a divorcee invited Andy to "have fun" in her apartment, even though Andy dashed out almost immediately by saying, "I don't feel much like making love to anybody." Surprisingly, the censors also objected to the film's man-to-man talk. Judge Hardy comes to town and suspects the nature of Andy's relationship with Miss Hicks. He counsels Andy, "marriage is one institution that can be spoiled by anticipating it." Andy thinks he is talking about "morality," but Judge Hardy tells him he is referring to "fidelity, fidelity to the girl that you're someday going to marry. The habit of transferring affections from one girl to another indiscriminately is very likely to spoil your ability to bestow those affections on your wife." This advice underscores the ways in which boys were held to the same standard as girls. Ironically, the Legion objected to this frank advice on celibacy even though the judge was parroting the discourse of the parent culture.[32] By the end of the film, Andy has once again successfully avoided falling prey to another young woman of desire.

The Courtship of Andy Hardy (1942) offers the most trenchant commentary on the "rating and dating" system. Before leaving for college, Judge Hardy asks Andy to be nice to the lonely daughter of divorced parents, Melody Nesbitt (Donna Reed). Andy complains that he would "rather listen to a bunch of opera records than smooch" with that "sad apple, barb." Melody is shy, bookish, and unpopular by the standards of Carvel. Despite his resistance, Andy asks her to the summer dance. Beth Bailey argues that one of the greatest sites of the dating system was on the dance floor. Since the system was reinforced by the fact that "men like girls that other men want," a girl's popularity was underscored by the number of boys who "cut-in" during dances.[33] When Andy arrives at the dance with Melody, his friends ask Andy if "she is a gag." No one will cut in on the unpopular Melody. She is conscious of her status as a wallflower and apologizes to him for being "stuck" with her. Andy must pay the boys on the stag line to cut in. On the way home, Melody asks Andy what makes a girl popular. He responds that she must be "attractive, have poise…she mustn't be too dull, she must make a fella think he has something, and she has to make other fellas want her." Thus being popular had nothing to do with the actual person, but rather "public perceptions of success in the popularity competition."[34] By the end of the film, Andy has played Pygmalion to Melody's Galatea, yet despite her becoming the popular girl he described earlier, he finds he is not attracted to her. Nonetheless, Melody has learned how to flirt with boys and wastes no time using her new skills to find a new beau.

There is a subtle change in the girls of Carvel in the latter half of the series. Even Polly Benedict seems to get the upper hand in *Andy Hardy's Double Life* (1942) as she and her visiting friend Sheila (Esther Williams) decide to teach the fickle, flirtatious Andy a lesson. Sheila is very sexy and sexually aggressive. She makes a pass at Andy, kisses him passionately, and then tells him that she kissed him because she's a psychology major doing research on reflexes. Andy has no game against this beautiful, voluptuous young woman. His youth and inexperience are underscored by his flirtation with Sheila. Polly and Sheila trick Andy into thinking he is engaged to both of them. The two girls are not dichotomized as good girl and bad girl vying for Andy's affections as in past films. Instead, they are friends united against his indiscriminate flirtations.

This theme continues in the next film, *Andy Hardy's Blonde Trouble* (1942), as Andy heads for Wainwright College, his father's alma mater. On the train he meets Kay (Bonita Granville) and he is instantly smitten. Kay is unlike any other girl he has ever met. Her maturity stands in sharp contrast to Andy's recklessness, vanity, naiveté, and immaturity. She rebuffs his clumsy attempt to kiss her, saying, "I've outgrown casual necking. When I was sixteen, I was afraid to let anyone kiss me. Then I let a nice boy kiss me, then another, then another. Now I just don't think there's any percentage in it." Kay is the personification of advice his parents have given him in earlier films. That is, she is past the adolescent stage of casual necking. She is not without desire; she has simply mastered it and now will channel it into a future marriage.

In the final film of the series, *Love Laughs at Andy Hardy* (1946), Andy returns from war to Wainwright. He seems no older and no more mature for his stint in the army and reverts back to college "frosh," complete with freshman beanie. His love for Kay has sustained him through his absence, and he believes that he and Kay will get engaged, only to find that Kay is in love with her much older guardian. For the first time in the series, Andy's heart is broken, and also for the first time he has a platonic friendship with a young woman, a wise, jive-talking, and very tall Coffy Smith. They meet when they are set up on a blind date for the frosh dance, and the imbalance in their heights becomes a running gag in the film. Coffy serves as a surrogate for Judge Hardy as she gets to dispense the final advice of the series. Her freakish height (she is 6'2") has made her sanguine about life and love. She reminds him that boys mature more slowly than girls and offers him comfort by saying, "It's not the right girl or right boy, it's the right kind of girl and the right kind of boy." As the series ends, however, Andy does not seem the wiser as he proclaims, "my past is behind me." However, a picture of Washington hanging behind him drops assuring the audience that nothing has changed.

What of Andy's long-suffering sister, Marion? She is the perpetual adolescent and problem child, which is hardly surprising in light of the centrality of Andy in the family. In fact in *Judge Hardy and Son*, she admits to being jealous of Andy because "it's more thrilling to be a boy than a girl." Marion and Andy are contentious siblings, constantly fighting or teasing one another. Marion has just graduated from college when the series begins, but she seems doomed to spinsterhood. Poor Marion simply wants to get married, but she is only allowed a number of temporary relationships, usually to the wrong man. At one point she proclaims, "I'm never going to marry. I'll be a settlement worker!" Marion falls for a married lifeguard in *You're Only Young Once* (1938) and in *Judge Hardy's Children* (1938), she becomes the pawn of a crooked lobbyist, who uses her to blackmail the judge. Her judgment is no better in *Andy Hardy's Double Life* (1942), where her boyfriend has lost his license for three months because he has a drinking problem and a penchant for driving under the influence.[35]

Although Marion is afforded two paradigms of womanhood in the figures of her domestic, nurturing mother and the competent, intelligent Aunt Milly, she is unlike either of them. Her incompetence in being a homemaker is underscored in *Love Finds Andy Hardy*, when she must run the house while her mother is out of town. Marion is officious and bossy, yet she can't even make coffee and manages to alienate the housekeeper. Marion is just as incompetent in the work force. In *Andy Hardy Gets Spring Fever* (1939), Marion decides that it is time for her to earn her own living. Judge Hardy, articulating the conventional sentiment of the Depression, counters that he would hate to see her "taking a paycheck away from a man," so he hires her himself as his personal secretary. Yet Marion fails at that role as well. By the last three films, Marion is hardly mentioned except to say that she is "away." Instead, she appears sentenced to a life of living on an allowance from her father.[36]

If the Judge infantilizes Marion, he tries to offer Andy advice that will lead to Andy's autonomy through his man-to-man talks with Andy. Judge Hardy functions as the voice of the parent culture and in many ways the discursive construction of the morality and sentimentalism of studio head Louis B. Mayer. Yet the judge seems to be more like Andy's grandfather than his father. In fact, Lewis Stone was born in 1879 and was fifty-eight when the series began and sixty-seven by the time it ended. The judge stands in sharp contrast to his vibrant children. As Jeffery Dennis notes, Stone played the judge "as thoughtful, slow-moving, crotchety [and] lacking in the robustness of youth." Although the Judge is often a "font of wisdom," he also easily "falls prey to con-artists and get-rich quick schemes."[37] Thus although the judge parrots conventional morality about teenage desire, his age and frailty subvert his message. By the end of the series, even the studio head seemed to recognize that the judge was out of touch with a generation impacted by the Depression and war, and substituted a statuesque coed to dispense platitudes in the final offering of the 1940s *Love Laughs at Andy Hardy*. This woman whom most men found too tall to date seems the perfect person to offer guidance to this small man-child.

The most consistent female presence in the series is Polly Benedict. She seems so much older and mature than the gnomish Andy, a fact illustrated by his tendency to refer to not only Polly but all girls his own age as Ma'am. While Polly starts the series as a kind of cartoon character and trope of self-righteousness, she evolves by the end of the series into a lovely, self-assured young woman. Perhaps Polly's prudishness is more attributable to Andy himself than to a lack of desire on her part. His awkward passes and his staccato style of kissing are hardly conducive to arousal. In *The Hardy's Ride High* Polly laments to Andy, "Can't you approach a girl with more finesse? Can't you be more subtle?" For the most part, Polly is one of the few girls immune to Andy's charms. Polly likes Andy more in theory than in reality and is only attracted to him when she thinks she is losing him or when he is playing hard to get. Thus Polly's desire is effectively rendered neutral by the childish Mr. Hardy.

Many of the fears and anxieties about adolescent girls of the dominant culture have been scripted into Hollywood's vision of the teenager and these concerns were especially discernable for girls. While the films promote a single standard of sexual behavior, girls are constructed as being more sexually aggressive than boys and their desire is often the source of confusion and anxiety by adolescent boys. Nonetheless, in the series, the sexual tensions of boys and girls are resolved in a safe, non-threatening manner. While there were competing discourses of female adolescent desire in the culture, these conflicting discourses are reconciled in the *Hardy* series. While desire among teens is acknowledged as natural in the *Hardy* series, it is tightly proscribed. It is still only marriage that will legitimize the sexuality of boys and girls.

Notes

1. Timothy Schary, *Teen Movie: American Youth on Screen* (London and New York: Wallflower, 2005), 11.

2. Gladwin Hill, "Andy Worries 'Daddy,'" *The Atlanta Constitution*, July 27, 1941, 9.

3. Margaret Thorpe, *America at the Movies* (New Haven, CT: Yale University Press, 1939), 131.

4. Robert Osborne, *Academy Awards Illustrated* (La Habra, CA: ESE California, 1977), 81, 113.

5. Nelson Bell, "Ten Pictures are Chosen for the Asiatic Audiences," *The Washington Post*, October 27, 1942, B8.

6. Kelly Schrum, *Some Wore Bobby Sox: The Emergence of Teenage Girls' Culture 1920–1945* (NY: Palgrave, 2004), 137. Black film historian Thomas Cripps remembers watching the series as a teen: "The teens in Andy Hardy were so off the mark that we howled and made rude noises." See "Courtship and Movies: Not at All an Odd Couple," *Reviews in American History* 17, no. 3 (September 1989): 459–463, 460.

7. Schrum, *Some Wore Bobby Socks,* 137.

8. Catherine MacKenzie, "Children and Parents," *The New York Times,* December 18, 1938, 59.

9. Norman Zierod, *The Moguls* (New York: Avon Books, 1969), 315.

10. John Douglas Eames, *The MGM Story* (New York: Crown Publishers, 1974), 138. When Mickey Rooney started to get a little too much publicity for his womanizing, Mayer reportedly took him aside and gave him the Mayer version of a Judge Hardy lecture: "You're Andy Hardy! You're the United States! You're Stars and Stripes! You're a symbol! Behave yourself!"

11. See Bosley Crowther's *Hollywood Rajah: The Life and Times of Louis B. Mayer.* (New York: Dell Books, 1961).

12. Georganne Scheiner, *Signifying Female Adolescence: Film Representations and Fans 1920–1950* (Westport, CT: Praeger, 2000), 83. "You're Only Young Once," *New York Times,* January 3, 1938, 16. After seeing this film, Louis B. Mayer reportedly said to the writers, "Don't make them any better!"

13. Scheiner, *Signifying Female Adolescence,* 58. Robert S. Lynd and Helen Merrill Lynd, *Middletown in Transition* (New York: Harcourt, Brace and World, 1937), 140–141, 170.

14. Grace Palladino, *Teenagers: An American History* (New York: Basic Books, 1996), 7–8.

15. Nancy Lesko, *Act Your Age! A Cultural Construction of Adolescence* (New York: Routledge, 2001), 50.

16. Beth Bailey, *From Front Porch to Back Seat: Courtship in 20th Century America* (Baltimore and London: John Hopkins Press, 1989), 25–26.

17. Willard Waller, "The Rating and Dating Complex," *American Sociological Review* 2 (1937): 727–34; see Bailey, 26.

18. Bailey, *From Front Porch,* 81.

19. Cited by Bailey, 81.

20. Robert S. Lynd and Helen Merrill Lynd, *Middletown in Transition,* 170–71.

21. John D'Emilio and Estelle Freedman, *Intimate Matters: A History of Sexuality in America* (New York: Harper and Row, 1988), 258.

22. Scheiner, *Signifying Female Adolescence,* 81.

23. Bailey, *From Front Porch,* 81.

24. Ibid,, 93.

25. Scheiner, *Signifying Female Adolescence,* 81.

26. Jeffrey Dennis, "Love Laughs at Andy Hardy: The Rise of the Heterosexual Male Adolescent." *Genders: On-line Journal* 41 (2005).

27. Ibid., 9.

28. Ibid., 10, 12. If there are examples of a homo-erotic subtext, there are also many examples of homophobia as well. Andy is often positioned in opposition to less masculine figures. Many of the films contain a number of euphemisms for gay men including "fancy pants," "panty waist," and "velvet britches." Andy, on the other hand, often describes himself as an "all-American male" or as a "healthy, normal fella." Part of Dennis' argument is based on the film *Life Begins for Andy Hardy* in which he posits that a young man, Jimmy, Andy meets at a YMCA-like male boarding house is coded as gay, based on the fact that he is a dancer and lounges around Andy's room in his underwear. He also argues that Jimmy works as a male prostitute based on his living in the park. In fact, his homelessness is based on an incident in the life of producer Carey Wilson. Dennis overlooks that Jimmy is more of a "hoofer" than a formally trained dancer, in the style of Gene Kelley or Buddy Ebsom. Moreover, Dennis exaggerates the weight Jimmy's story carries in the film, arguing that Andy "rejects the kiddie crush of Betsy Booth and the salacious advances of the gold-digging Miss Hicks for a plot involving a relationship with Jimmy, a flamboyantly, feminine young man"(8). My reading of the text differs substantially as the Jimmy storyline is actually a very small part of the film and used to underscore the ways in which the city can kill youthful dreams.

29. Palladino, *Teenagers,* 23.

30. Dennis, "Love Laughs," 9.

31. Scheiner, *Signifying Female Adolescence,* 83.
32. See "Hardy Film Scored by Legion of Decency," *The New York Times,* August 18, 1941, 16.
33. Bailey, *From Front Porch,* 31.
34. Ibid, 28–29.
35. Scheiner, 83.
36. Ibid.
37. Dennis, 12, 7.

Works Cited

A Family Affair, directed by George B. Seitz (1937; Culver City, CA: MGM Studies, 1937).

Andy Hardy Gets Spring Fever, directed by George B. Seitz (1939; Culver City, CA: MGM Studies, 1939).

Andy Hardy Meets a Debutante, directed by George B. Seitz (1940; Culver City, CA: MGM Studies, 1940).

Andy Hardy's Blonde Trouble, directed by George B. Seitz (1942; Culver City, CA: MGM Studies, 1942).

Andy Hardy's Double Life, directed by George B. Seitz (1942; Culver City, CA: MGM Studies, 1942).

Bailey, Beth. *From Front Porch to Back Seat: Courtship in 20th Century America.* Baltimore and London: John Hopkins Press, 1989.

Bell, Nelson. "Ten Pictures are Chosen for the Asiatic Audiences." *The Washington Post,* October 27, 1942.

The Courtship of Andy Hardy, directed by George B. Seitz (1942; Culver City, CA: MGM Studies, 1942).

Cripps, Thomas. "Courtship and Movies: Not at All an Odd Couple." *Reviews in American History* 17, no. 3 (September 1989): 459–63.

Crowther, Bosley. *Hollywood Rajah: The Life and Times of Louis B. Mayer.* New York: Dell Books, 1961.

D'Emilio, John and Estelle Freedman. *Intimate Matters: A History of Sexuality in America.* New York: Harper and Row, 1988.

Dennis, Jeffrey. "Love Laughs at Andy Hardy: The Rise of the Heterosexual Male Adolescent." *Genders: On-line Journal* 41 (2005).

Eames, John Douglas. *The MGM Story.* New York: Crown Publishers, 1974.

"Hardy Film Scored by Legion of Decency." *The New York Times,* August 18, 1941.

The Hardy's Ride High, directed by George B. Seitz (1939; Culver City, CA: MGM Studies, 1939).

Hill, Gladwin. "Andy Worries 'Daddy.'" *The Atlanta Constitution,* July 27, 1941.

Judge Hardy and Son, directed by George B. Seitz (1939; Culver City, CA: MGM Studies, 1939).

Judge Hardy's Children, directed by George B. Seitz (1938; Culver City, CA: MGM Studies, 1938).

Lesko, Nancy. *Act Your Age! A Cultural Construction of Adolescence.* New York: Routledge, 2001.

Love Finds Andy Hardy, directed by George B. Seitz (1938; Culver City, CA: MGM Studies, 1938).

Love Laughs at Andy Hardy, directed by George B. Seitz (1946; Culver City, CA: MGM Studies, 1946).

Lynd, Robert S. and Helen Merrill Lynd. *Middletown in Transition*. New York: Harcourt, Brace and World, 1937.

MacKenzie, Catherine. "Children and Parents." *The New York Times,* December 18, 1938.

Osborne, Robert. *Academy Awards Illustrated*. La Habra, CA: ESE California, 1977.

Palladino, Grace. *Teenagers: An American History*. New York: Basic Books, 1996.

Schary, Timothy. *Teen Movie: American Youth on Screen*. London and New York: Wallflower, 2005.

Scheiner, Georganne. *Signifying Female Adolescence: Film Representations and Fans 1920–1950*. Westport, CT: Praeger, 2000.

Schrum, Kelly. *Some Wore Bobby Sox: The Emergence of Teenage Girls' Culture 1920–1945*. New York: Palgrave, 2004.

Thorpe, Margaret. *America at the Movies*. New Haven: Yale University Press, 1939.

Waller, Willard. "The Rating and Dating Complex." *American Sociological Review* 2 (1937): 727–34.

You're Only Young Once, directed by George B. Seitz (1938; Culver City, CA: MGM Studies, 1938).

"You're Only Young Once." *The New York Times*, January 3, 1938.

Zierod, Norman. *The Moguls*. New York: Avon Books, 1969.

2

"Sensible Safety Rules": Class, Race, and Girls' Sexual Vulnerability in the U.S. Print Media, 1950–1970

Jennifer Helgren

In March of 1959, parents near Spokane, Washington would have read an alarming report in their local newspapers about the disappearance of nine-year-old Candy Rogers. References to the child "selling Campfire Girl mints" in her uniform when she was abducted signaled her membership in a predominantly white, middle-class national girls' organization that with its 530,000 members in 1958, served along with the Girl Scouts, to train girls to blend public service and homemaking skills.[1] When Candy's "ravished body" was found two weeks later in a remote area northwest of the city, news reports invoked girls' sexual vulnerability with details of how she had been bound "with parts of her own slip," raped, and strangled.[2] Reporters further warned parents by highlighting ways that Candy's routine diverged from the idealized girlhood that her Campfire Girl uniform symbolized.

The reports of Candy's abduction, rape, and murder form part of a larger discourse on girls' safety and their access to public spaces in the 1950s and 1960s. This article analyzes how the media reported on missing girls—especially those who were victims of crimes by strangers—in racially specific ways, and describes girls' responses to the increasing coverage of stranger violence in the 1950s. I argue that the print press offered class specific, racialized messages about girls' safety. The prevalence of stories about violence toward girls warned all girls and their parents to be on the alert, but by describing the circumstances of girls' victimization in ways that pointed to the supposed dangers to which racialized and poor "others" subjected their daughters, the mainstream media provided some assurance that "good girls" from "good neighborhoods" could avoid exploitation. The mainstream press created what *Parents* magazine referred to as "sensible" parameters that were actually difficult, especially for girls outside white, middle-class, two-parent families to maintain. Similarly, women's memories of their safety as girls diverged along lines of race and class and had very little to do with direct media exposure to stories of violence toward girls. Girls heard stories of sexual violations through friends and loved ones and through local gossip channels, and they tended to accept the lesson that girls would modify their behaviors as part of growing up female.

The postwar years are important for understanding girls' fears and racialized perceptions of their safety. As historians Estelle Freedman and Paula Fass point out, the 1950s saw an increase in popular attention to sex crime "panics," and coverage of stranger abductions became more lurid and voluminous.[3] Fass argues that the emphasis on the sexual depravities of male perpetrators and the budding sexuality of girl victims led fearful parents to privatize their parental duties, carefully monitoring and protecting their own children. By the 1960s and 1970s, as historian Miriam Forman-Brunell shows, urban legends, fiction, and films regularly featured maniacal rapists who subjected girl babysitters to horrific violence.[4] The threat of physical violence to girls was a growing and pervasive theme in the media.

Vulnerability to crime was superadded to other fears that were connected to girls' emerging sexuality, leading to restrictions on girls' access to public spaces. Journalist Brett Harvey explains that in the 1950s, girls fears included not only atomic bombs and communism, but also that feminine hygiene lapses, "getting a reputation" or "being a cock-tease," or getting pregnant would disrupt their marriage hopes.[5] Elaine Tyler May has written that "containment" was as much a postwar domestic policy to tame "potentially dangerous social forces of the new age" as it was a foreign policy approach to the Soviet Union.[6] As Americans worried about the threats posed by women's changing roles, specifically about rising divorce rates, working mothers, sexual precocity among teens, and juvenile delinquency, American public policy and media discourses urged girls toward marriage and women toward domesticity as a way to contain the menace.[7] Media messages intimated that girls whose parents did not adopt prescribed domestic norms were especially vulnerable to sex crime dangers. Whereas African American and Latina girls felt pressure toward dominant modes of respectability, they also confronted racial violence, often as a result of involvement in the civil rights movement.[8]

In the early twentieth century, media presented the city as the site where girls' virtue and safety were imperiled.[9] In the postwar era, however, media and crime experts began to associate suburban spaces with crime as well. Prompted by the dislocations of World War II and by promises of privacy, likeminded neighbors, and safety from the perils of urban life, white middle- and working-class Americans bought suburban homes, often far away from relatives and their own childhood homes.[10] Largely barring black families from buying homes in the suburbs through race-restrictive covenants, whites could imagine suburbs as places where their daughters would be safe from crime and race-mixing at a time when the civil rights movement challenged segregation.[11] But with highway systems connecting urban and suburban areas, small towns and suburbs were increasingly constructed as dangerous spaces too. In March of 1959, just four days before Candy went missing, FBI director J. Edgar Hoover announced an eight percent increase in U.S. crime with the largest increases among medium-sized communities such as suburbs.[12] Strangers in suburban spaces joined those in urban spaces as part of the mid-twentieth-century landscape of fear.

My research examined reports in the print press of girls who had gone missing or who were victims of stranger abduction or rape as well as how mainstream publications such as *Time, Parents,* and those of the Camp Fire Girls and the Girl Scouts framed issues of safety in the postwar era. To understand girls' perceptions of their safety and the ways that they accepted and sometimes resisted the limits adults placed on their movements, I interviewed eighteen women born between 1935 and 1965 about their sense of safety, awareness of crime reports, and the restrictions they encountered as girls.[13] Two of the women identify as African American, one as Hispanic, and fifteen as white. All came from upper working-class and middle-class backgrounds.

Press coverage of missing girls included "girls" ranging in age from infants to twenty-one-year-old college students. Inclusion of young women as girls served to highlight female vulnerability beyond childhood. The mainstream and national press created a false universal category of girlhood as reporters assumed a white readership and identified the race and ethnicity only of immigrant girls or girls of color. Conversely, headlines in the black press tended to mark the race of white attackers and white girl victims, leaving readers to assume their "girls" were African American.[14] The black press also emphasized that racial violence was a primary cause of black girls' vulnerability.

Ethnic, local, and national papers detailed girl victims' hair color, clothing, and other distinctive physical features. If she were found murdered, mainstream media reports objectified the victim with references to injuries to "the body" and stirred fear by documenting girls discovered in ravines, under brush, and in other deserted spots. Reports almost always mentioned sexual assault as if it were expected, even when no signs were present, but press coverage was more likely to assume a sexual motive for abductions of white girls than for African American girls.[15] Readers learned that dangerous places included their local parks, the sidewalks outside their homes, the stretch that led to their mail boxes (especially in rural and suburban areas), the bus ride or walk home from school, and the trip home from any evening or late night activity such as a dance. The locations from which girls disappeared reminded girls and their parents of a girl's constant vulnerability, and served as implicit indictments of parents who let especially young children play unsupervised and of adolescent girls who accepted rides from strangers when returning from shopping, or from movie or swimming pool trips. Finally, news of investigations alerted readers when local "sex perverts" were hauled in for questioning because they had sex crime histories, warning readers that dangerous strangers lived in their midst.[16] Although the message was that all girls were vulnerable, such stories implied standards of supervision that would be easiest for two-parent families in "good neighborhoods" to adopt, standards that, due to segregated housing codes and class status, immigrant girls and girls of color had less access to.

In *The New York Times*, stories about missing girls offered sympathy but promoted the idea that "good girls" from "good neighborhoods" were usually safe. For example, a report about a black girl who was kidnapped and murdered simultaneously humanized the family by quoting the father in his anguish but distanced the family's experience from middle-class readers as it highlighted the ways her experience diverged from that of the idealized middle-class standard. The report emphasized the father's concern for the girl's safety, telling how the family left Jamaica to get away from a "bad neighborhood." Still, by pointing attention to the family's residence in a Queens housing project and the parents' decision to leave the girl with a sitter while they worked nights, the story alerted white suburban readers that crime was a problem of the poor and of working mothers.[17] Such stories were sympathetic but white readers could filter them as bad things that happened to poor ethnic others.

Moreover, the mainstream press depicted black girls as putting themselves in danger's way as runaways or as activists. When sixteen-year-old Rose Marie Jordan of Florence, Alabama went missing, for example, newspapers emphasized that she had run away to escape a punishment for staying out shopping too late.[18] Moreover, some reports characterized black girls as aggressors in public spaces. *The New York Times* reported with flair incidents such as the Montgomery teen who hit a white girl when she refused to share a bus seat.[19] The bus incident brought to readers' attention how the civil rights movement ushered girls into public spaces in new and dangerous ways.

Indeed when the northern press covered assaults on black girls, it regularly cast stories in terms of the civil rights movement; stories either implied that girls were in danger because of their activism or portrayed the South as lacking racial justice. *The New York Times* ran stories about white southern men raping black girls but such stories were unlikely to create a sense of shared vulnerability. The high-profile 1959 case of an African American Florida college student who was taken at gunpoint and raped by four young white men illustrates how media could support civil rights themes by condemning interracial sex crimes. The Florida A&M student was parked on campus with her boyfriend and another couple after a dance when she was forcibly taken and attacked. From its first mention, *The New York Times* framed the case as part of the civil rights movement, noting that it was the "latest in a series of inter-racial incidents across the South." In follow-up articles over the next month, readers were reminded of the civil rights context as students at Florida A&M held a strike to demand charges be brought immediately in the case and read that black onlookers packed the segregated courtroom in solidarity. Repeatedly *The New York Times* explained that the death penalty was a possibility in the case, but pointing to racial injustice, documented that "no white man has ever been executed in Florida for attacking a Negro." When the all-white jury found the four men guilty but proscribed the death penalty in the case, *The New York Times* printed a letter to the editor from NAACP leader Allan Knight Chalmers. He simultaneously hailed the ruling as showing that "equal justice...is attainable in our country" but decried the ongoing sentencing disparity for black and white men in the South.[20] The coverage positioned the paper as progressive and was likely to elicit sympathy from moderate white readers, but the civil rights framework, like the association of crime with poverty areas, precluded a sense of shared vulnerability as white parents were likely to view the rape as separate from their own daughters' likely experience.

When black girls were attacked by whites, civil rights was the predominant discourse, but when white girls were victims of black men, newspapers had a tough time maintaining journalistic distance and not lapsing into "lynch" narratives that presumed the guilt of black men in any sexual attack against white women.[21] In 1967, when the six- and seven-year-old white Barili sisters were found sexually molested and murdered in an African American neighborhood in Los Angeles, *The New York Times* noted the race of the girls in the headline and the text, juxtaposing their innocence and whiteness to the "weed-grown vacant lot in the Negro district of Watts" where the girls were found. At the same time, the reporter seemed to recognize the bias and countered it by quoting Los Angeles Homicide Sergeant Walt Thornton who assured readers that there was "certainly no racial implication whatsoever in the fact that the bodies were found in Watts."[22]

Although not a sex crime, the most thoroughly covered act of public violence against black girls during this period was the 1963 bombing of the 16th Street Baptist Church in Birmingham where four African American girls, Addie

Mae Collins, Carole Robertson, Cynthia Wesley, and Denise McNair, all just a little older than Candy, were murdered. Still this act of violence, like the Florida A&M rape before it, was not one that threatened "girlhood" for most white Americans. Mainstream news services were sympathetic, humanizing the victims through descriptions of girlhood innocence and respectability, but the press saw the Birmingham bombing as primarily a crime about race relations, not about girlhood.

In a sympathetic article, *Time* emphasized the senselessness of the deaths and painted a picture of girls who were respectable: Christian, well-dressed, and cared for by loving families. *Time* quoted a weeping man: "My grandbaby was one of those killed! Eleven years old! I helped pull the rocks off her!" Descriptions of "mangled" bodies in feminine "white lace choir robes" humanized the victims and fostered outrage.[23] Although mainstream media emphasized the deaths of innocent girls to show what was wrong with vicious racists and how society failed to protect girls, the civil rights context opened the door for attacks on the girls and their families by opponents.

Letters to the editor at *Time* magazine blamed the African American community for the deaths, arguing that despite efforts toward respectability, black families put their daughters in harm's way. One Kerman, California man wrote:

> To think that an individual or individuals could do this to a church gathering is shocking to say the least; however, it is not any more shocking than the fact that a group could go to a church and mix pep talks for integration with a form of worship. It is sad that this had to happen to children, but it is war; and when the Negroes encourage their own children to lie in front of cement trucks, disregarding the laws of safety just to get arrested, it doesn't appear they care too much whether the children are killed or not.[24]

Like the runaways who courted the violence they might encounter in public spaces, civil rights activists could be seen as complicit in their fates. Whites might feel enraged, but they did not need to identify these types of dangers with anything their children might face.

Conversely, for African American families, stories about race violence invoked a profound sense of danger. A woman I interviewed from Shreveport, Louisiana had been involved in the civil rights movement as an adolescent in the 1950s and had been arrested after attending a meeting at her local church. After spending the night in jail and receiving threats that her father would be kicked out of the home that the family was renting, she drastically reduced her involvement in the movement. Furthermore, although most of the women I interviewed knew stories of bad things happening to people they knew, this woman alone spoke of the racial violence that marked her growing years. She had been abducted by a white man when she was about four years old, an experience of which she has only a vague memory. As a child she was keenly aware of people who were taken from their homes and beaten because of their race, and her own father and uncle had had urine thrown on them from a passing car as they walked home from work.

Although white suburban parents avoided these horrors, popular magazines such as *Time, American Magazine,* and *Parents* magazine ran stories about stranger danger and the vulnerabilities of middle-class girls in good neighborhoods. The mass media commonly linked sex crimes to strangers and to public spaces even though data on sex crimes showed that perpetrators most commonly knew victims and that most crimes occurred within the homes of victims or perpetrators. Stories depicted crime as increasing and thereby contributed to a sense of unease, but they offered parents advice that suggested that with "sensible" supervision parents could keep girls safe, veiling the degree to which sensible supervision was a matter of class and race privilege. In 1947 and 1953, articles titled "How Safe Is Your Daughter?" and "How Safe Is Your Youngster?" by J. Edgar Hoover appeared in *American Magazine* calling sex offenses "the most rapidly increasing type of crime."[25] Hoover used fear to dislodge parents' proclivity to dissociate from these crimes: "It can happen—and does happen—to children in every strata of society, and citizens everywhere must arouse themselves to the menace of the growing army of criminals who violate and oftentimes slay defenseless boys and girls." His article was filled with horrifying examples of unsuspecting children who were attacked in public spaces. Hoover called on parents to redress what he called their "flagrant failure to train and safeguard their own children properly." Particularly alarming to Hoover were children who were unsupervised at nightfall and youth who hitchhiked, went to "lovers' lanes," or frequented other "lonely places."[26]

Simultaneously media voices tempered these calls for obsessive public vigilance, affirming the idea that good girls from good neighborhoods would be all right. Most important among them were the popular reports of Alfred Kinsey's studies. In a 1954 article in the popular *Parents* magazine, Edith Stern used Kinsey's research to address the issue of sex offenses against children with reassuring tones. She reminded parents that the number of offenses was still very small and argued that the perception that these crimes were everywhere was a result of how shocking they were and of publicity.[27] While Stearns noted that eighty percent of adults said that during childhood they had some experience with a sex offense—usually verbal, fondling, or exhibition, to lessen parents' fears, Stearns pointed out that less than one percent of subjects reported "actual relations" with an adult. Oddly, this reassurance tempered panic but masked the harm that results from crimes that do not include sexual intercourse. Stern painted a picture of sex offenders as emasculated and relatively non-threatening. Rather than "a powerful...brute who hid[es] behind bushes and pounc[es] out at passing children," exhibitionists, peeping toms, and "childlike seniles" were the majority of perpetrators. Finally, the article portrayed the long-term effect on child victims as minimal, citing Kinsey's statistics that showed few children became "seriously disturbed."[28]

Moreover, popular media and popular psychology pathologized both girl victims and male attackers by painting girls' involvement in sex acts, regardless of age, as complicit, and by employing the symbol of the broken home. Stern cited the case of a twelve-year-old statutory rape victim who had apparently seduced a twenty-seven-year-old man as evidence that he did "not constitute a hazard to children not already showing behavioral difficulties." By marking some girl victims as sexual deviants, this line of reasoning could ease middle-class parents' fears since most of them were unlikely to see their own children as "deviants."[29]

Psychologists and crime experts connected victims and criminals to broken homes. Hoover described how a boy who "had little parental attention since the age of 10" because his father worked days and his mother worked nights became a sex criminal and a murderer by the age of seventeen.[30] Victims' home lives were similarly pathologized. Their behaviors were attributed to the very problems that newspapers associated with Candy Rogers's home: "serious marital conflicts" and children who "felt deprived of their mothers." This could distance readers from the thought that they would become victims and warn against lapses in the idealized middle-class family structure. Newspapers described Candy's home life, for example, in ways that suggested a disrupted home life. Without overt condemnation, but assuming relevance, newspapers explained that Candy's mother was divorced and worked full time, and that Candy's father lived in another state. Although Candy left her home to sell mints at 4 o'clock, newspapers described her as being out in the evening, blurring her afternoon outing into a night-time one when girls were supposed to be home. Moreover, by repeating that the last sighting of Candy was 6:30 pm, when middle-class families could expect to be having dinner together, news stories called attention to a disrupted family life. Indeed such a reading is consistent with 1950s popular and scientific research that reassured readers that sex criminals and victims came from broken homes. Although such stories likely left even white, middle-class families with lingering fears, the message was that if girls were home with parental supervision after dark, a privilege of a dual parent, non-working-class, and often white family, that they would be safe.

Girls' organizations echoed Stern's advice in *Parents* magazine to "set up sensible safety rules" regarding where and when children played by themselves, teaching "safety from sexual offenders…unobtrusively…along with other lessons in safety."[31] Camp Fire and Girl Scout officials walked a careful line. They avoided sensationalizing the threats to girls' safety from strangers in public spaces to maintain access to public activities such as fundraising even as they sought to maintain girls' safety and respectability. Rejecting the demands of some community members to end the use of girls as "solicitors," national organizations urged leaders against "mak[ing] a girl overcautious about dangers."[32] Still, using language that invoked universal girlhood, but that almost always presumed a suburban neighborhood, girls' organizations set out safety guidelines most accessible for their typical middle-class members.

The Camp Fire Girl, a monthly magazine for girls' leaders, never mentioned the Candy Rogers case directly, but subtle changes in the reporting on safety and national fundraising sales in the months after her murder showed growing awareness of abduction and sexual assault. An article called "Child Safety: Our Responsibility" warned, "no community, no matter how placid seeming and 'safe,' is entirely immune."[33] Officials urged group leaders to teach stranger danger as they would familiar forms of safety awareness such as traffic safety and how to properly handle a pocketknife. This approach deflected fear by making dangers seem ordinary but also had the effect of normalizing the precautions girls were expected to take. A list of rules included "politely" declining strangers' invitations to go anywhere, staying clear of strangers' cars, and not talking to strangers at the movies. Girls were implored to contact adult authorities immediately if they felt uncomfortable: "Report at once to a police officer or to the first older person you see, any stranger who talks to you, offers you candy or toys, invites you into a car, or bothers you in any way."[34] Although the rules still permitted girls to play outside their homes, attend movies, and generally move about in public, they sent stern warnings to be on guard and maintain feminine standards of politeness. Such advice, directed through predominantly white, middle-class youth organizations promoted a concept of respectable middle-class girlhood as consistent with sensible safety measures, measures that many women came to see as common sense choices that were just part of being female.

Some girls were deeply impacted by specific missing-girl cases. In the 1980s, Spokane Girl Scout leader Jeannie Lyonnais still had vivid memories of what Candy's murder had meant to her as a six-year-old. She recalled a day when she heard footsteps coming up behind her. She was sure it was "the man who had killed Candy…You expected strangers to be lurking behind trees waiting to jump." In the 1980s, then a leader of her own Scout troop, Lyonnais carefully prepared her girls for the annual cookie sale with strict rules about never selling alone and never walking alone from school to meetings. Her girls even role-played interactions with strangers. They knew, as one ten-year-old told a reporter, "You could get abducted."[35]

In the interviews that I conducted, however, most women remembered their childhoods as safe. They described playing outdoors and told of parents who limited their mobility in ways that the women regarded as reasonable. Specific stories they recalled, however, belied their assurances of security and reflected that the safety they felt was often a result of circumscribed movements or what they now consider naivety. Few racial differences emerged in how women remembered their feelings of safety. Still, although my sample was small, despite (or because of) the media message of dangers in communities of color, the African American women reported more restrictive mothers and black communities that looked after children more collectively.

Most of the women I interviewed felt that as children they were sheltered from media coverage of crimes against women and children. They said that they did not read newspapers, although their parents did, and that television was relatively new. A few noted that they watched news in the 1950s and 1960s with their parents, recalling international and national events such as Kennedy's assassination and Patty Hearst's kidnapping, but they rarely recalled learning about crimes against girls directly through the news. A Mexican-American girl growing up in a rural part of San Bernardino County, who described herself as a latch-key kid, however, remembered sitting at home with her siblings watching scary shows in the evenings as they waited for their parents to return from work. *The Twilight Zone* and a show re-enacting crimes and asking for viewer tips (probably CBS's *Wanted,* a mid-1950s precursor to *America's Most Wanted*) aroused deep fears. When an episode featured an escapee from the nearby Chino prison, she and her siblings hid, certain that every noise was the escaped killer in their isolated home. Her experience of being home alone was a class-based experience that likely would have found disapproval in mainstream media like *Parents* magazine.

More commonly, girls were exposed to crime stories through word of mouth and local gossip. One Bakersfield woman recalled that through local rumor she learned that an older boy had forced several girls in a vacant lot to perform oral sex. Her memories of how she learned about the events were vague and she was sure that at the time she did not know what a "blow job" was. Still, her sense of vulnerability led her to avoid walking home from school. As a middle-class child, she had a bicycle and access to adult drivers to make it home without crossing the lot. Thus, she remembers the 1950s and 1960s as "an innocent time" and feels "privileged to have grown up in that era." Her sense of safety derived from resources, parental and community protections, and from her acceptance that women and girls would modify their lives to minimize dangers.

Parents worked quietly and diligently to keep girls safe. Although they still allowed girls to play outside, go to the movies or roller skating rinks, and fundraise for youth organizations, they also put restrictions in place to maintain respectability and to keep girls safe. An African American girl in the San Francis-Francisco Bay Area was forbidden to go to sleepovers. A white Santa Cruz girl was forbidden to visit the Boardwalk because of its association with Hippies and Hell's Angels. She was forbidden to date until she was sixteen and continued to experience close surveillance even after that. Restrictions were not always effective. The mother of the Shreveport girl who was kidnapped had assigned a slightly older brother to chaperone the girl, but his presence had not prevented her from being taken. Unlike the Bakersfield girl who had the means to avoid the vacant lot, the family of the Shreveport girl could not congratulate themselves that they had taken "sensible" measures to protect her, despite the similarity of the kinds of restrictions that they put in place.

Not recognizing dangers in the same way that their parents did, girls sometimes resisted parental rules. In letters to the advice columnist in *American Girl,* the Girl Scout magazine, girls voiced their displeasure about their limited access to public space and their concerns about interactions with strangers. Editors used the space to mediate conflicts between girls and their parents and to explain parental decisions to girls in cautionary ways. One twelve-year-old girl was distressed because her parents would not allow her to attend movies by herself. Davies responded that "anything can arise—from illness to accident," thereby implying, but skirting, the issue of sexual assault in a youth-oriented magazine.[36] Other letters hinted that there was more to fear that a sudden attack of the flu. One girl, who was allowed to go to the movies with friends, was asked by a young man to sit with him. The thirteen-tear-old girl explained to Davies that he was well dressed and seemed nice but she had turned down his offer. Now she wondered if it would have been acceptable to sit with him. Davies assured her she did "exactly the right thing." Implying danger in meeting strangers, Davies oversimplified that a nice boy would not "try to pick up a girl."[37]

Other letters reveal girls' resistance to parental restrictions and Girl Scouts' cautious, though evasive, approach to mediating between girl–parent relationships. A thirteen-year-old Connecticut girl wrote that her father did not trust her because he would not let her ride the bus alone. Davies replied, "It's not you that your father distrusts, but some of the people and situations you might encounter when out alone…In a big city there are people abroad who might easily take advantage of a young girl like you." She told the girl to be glad she had such a caring father.[38] Such letters tell a story of girls who wanted greater access to public spaces but were denied them due to threats from strangers.

Still, the overwhelming majority of the women I interviewed felt like they were relatively free compared to today's girls, responding that they played outside with little supervision. A 1956 national survey of nearly 2000 U.S. girls ages eleven to eighteen corroborates the interviews, showing that girls felt relatively free to engage in a variety of activities even as their lives were shaped by adults' and their own fears about vulnerability. In response to an open-ended question about what they worried about most, girls focused on personal appearance, popularity, and success in school. A small number listed "other," which may have included concerns about health and violence.[39]

Moreover, although a sizable number of girls chafed against parental restrictions, most did not see restrictions as overly burdensome. Regarding the disputes girls had with their parents, only thirty-five percent said parents tried to control their movements such as how often they went out and where they went. Restrictions eased as girls grew. Fifty-one percent of girls earned at least some of their own money outside the home through babysitting and clerking in stores and offices. They also engaged in a range of social activities such as attending parties and dances, going to the movies, and meeting friends at the drug store. But girls still spent much of their time engaged in home-based activities such as cooking, sewing, listening to the radio, and reading.[40] Thus, although some girls actively sought more freedom, the interviews and the survey demonstrate that the media images of endangered girls only indirectly affected girls' sense of safety and their access to public spaces. Whereas the African American and Latina women I interviewed were more likely to experience fear for their physical safety as a result of racism and spending time in the house while parents worked, the white women felt they were protected as girls and that those protections, though restrictive, were appropriate to growing up female.

In the postwar era, news stories about missing girls and stranger abductions presented different messages to girls based on race. For white, middle-class girls—constructed as good girls from good neighborhoods—the media, youth organizations, families, and youth experts established a set of parameters within which girls could feel relatively safe. The "sensible" guidelines, however, were the privileges of an idealized white, middle-class girlhood, and not accessible to all girls. Girls with divorced parents, those with parents who had to work and leave them home alone, and girls from black families struggling for civil rights did not have access to the carefully supervised and psychologically idealized girlhoods that the media suggested would ensure safety. A race- and class-based image of girlhood emerged that allowed whites to distance themselves from the stories of crime against girls. While all families may have felt unsettled by the increasing attention to stranger danger, sensible guidelines were a privilege of middle-class girlhood.

Notes

1. Camp Fire Girls, Annual Report of the Camp Fire Girls, 1958, at Camp Fire USA, Missouri.
2. "Girl's Body Discovered near Spokane," *The Bend Bulletin* 90, March 23, 1959, 1.
3. Estelle B. Freedman, "'Uncontrolled Desires': The Response to the Sexual Psychopath, 1920–1960," *The Journal of American History* 74, no. 1 (June 1987): 83–106; Paula Fass, *Kidnapped: Child Abduction in America* (New York: Oxford University Press, 1997).
4. Miriam Forman Brunell, *Babysitter: An American History* (New York: New York University Press, 2009). For a discussion of the way women today regulate their behaviors due to fear of physical violence, see Colette Dowling, *The Frailty Myth: Redefining the Physical Potential of Women and Girls* (New York: Random House, 2000). See James R. Kincaid, *Erotic Innocence: The Culture of Child Molesting* (Durham, NC: Duke University Press, 1998) for a discussion of the cultural role sex crime stories play in both demonstrating and denying the erotic possibilities of children.
5. Brett Harvey, *The Fifties: A Women's Oral History* (New York: Harper Perennial, 1993), xv. On girlhood in the 1950s and 1960s, see also Beth Bailey, *Sex in the Heartland* (Cambridge: Harvard University Press, 2002); Wini Breines, *Young, White and Miserable: Growing Up Female in the Fifties* (Chicago: University of Chicago Press, 2001); and Rachel Devlin, *Relative Intimacy: Fathers, Adolescent Daughters and Postwar American Culture* (Chapel Hill, NC: University of North Carolina Press, 2006).
6. Elaine Tyler May, *Homeward Bound: American Families in the Cold War Era* (New York: Basic Books, 1999), xxiv–xxv.
7. Ibid.
8. See Rickie Solinger, *Wake Up Little Susie* (New York: Routledge, 1992).
9. See Kathy Peiss, *Cheap Amusements* (Philadelphia: Temple University Press, 1986); Ruth Alexander, *The "Girl Problem": Female Sexual Delinquency in New York, 1900–1930* (Ithaca, NY: Cornell University Press, 1998); and Mary Odem, *Delinquent Daughters: Protecting and Policing Adolescent Female Sexuality in the United States, 1885–1920* (Chapel Hill, NC: University of North Carolina Press, 1995).
10. May, *Homeward Bound*, 18–20.
11. On restrictive housing covenants, see Andrew Wiese, *Places of their Own: African American Suburbanization in the Twentieth Century* (Chicago: University of Chicago Press, 2004).
12. "Crime Increase Noted by Hoover," *The Bend Bulletin* 72, March 2, 1959, 7.
13. All interviews were completed under University of the Pacific IRB approval and are in the personal collection of the author. Narrators' names have been withheld in compliance with IRB recommendations. Recordings of the interviews are in the possession of the author.
14. See, for example, "Rape of 9-Year-Old Girl Gets White Grocer Sentence," *Arkansas State Press*, July 10, 1953, 1.
15. Fass, *Kidnapped*, 259.
16. As Freedman and Neil Miller, *Sex-Crime Panic: A Journey to the Paranoid Heart of the 1950s* (Los Angeles: Alyson Books, 2002) show, "sex perverts" was a catch-all term for sex deviants and included many homosexuals in consensual relationships.

17. "Boy is Questioned in Death of Girl, 6," *The New York Times*, July 13, 1966, 6.

18. "Florence Negro Girl Missing since Thursday," *Times Daily*, July 8, 1958, 5.

19. "Negro Girl is Fined," *The New York Times*, November 30, 1957, 12.

20. "4 Whites Seized in Rape of Negro," *The New York Times*, May 3, 1959, 45; "Grand Jury Called in Co-Ed Rape Case," May 5, 1959, 23; Claude Sitton, "4 Whites on Trial in Rape of Negro," June 11, 1959, 67; "4 Begin Defense in Trial on Rape," June 13, 1959, 13; Allan Knight Chalmers, "Florida Verdict Praised," July 5, 1959, E6. The white men's working-class status (all but one had a court-appointed attorney) and the use of a weapon in the commission of the crime weighed against the men's defense that the sex had been consensual.

21. On lynch narratives, see Kristina DuRocher, *Raising Racists: The Socialization of White Children in the Jim Crow South* (Lexington: University Press of Kentucky, 2011) and Crystal Feimster, *Southern Horrors: Women and the Politics of Rape and Lynching* (Cambridge: Harvard University Press, 2009).

22. "2 Slain Children Found In Watts: Bodies of White Sisters in Lot 25 Miles From Home," *The New York Times*, August 11, 1967. Despite the long history of black men being associated with the rape of white women, they were not especially demonized in the sociological and psychological literature on sex crimes against children. A 1955 study claimed, however, that black men were more likely to commit "rape and adult sexual assault." Johann Mohr, Robert Turner, and Marian Bernice Jerry, *Pedophilia and Exhibitionism: A Handbook* (Toronto: University of Toronto Press, 1964), 55.

23. "Civil Rights: The Sunday School Bombing," *Time*, September 27, 1963.

24. "Letter to the editor," *Time*, October 4, 1963.

25. J. Edgar Hoover, quoted in Wayne A. Logan, *Knowledge as Power: Criminal Registration and Community Notification Laws in America* (Stanford, CA: Stanford University Press, 2009).

26. J. Edgar Hoover, "How Safe Is Your Youngster?" *American Magazine* (March 1955): 19, 99–103.

27. Edith M. Stern, "The Facts on Sex Offences Against Children," *Parents* 29 (October 1954), 43. On Kinsey Institute findings, see Seth S. King, "Dr. Kinsey Doubts Rise in Sex Crimes," *The New York Times*, September 28, 1955, 26; and Eric Pace, "New Kinsey Report Challenges Popular Concept of Sex Crimes," *The New York Times*, July 18, 1965, 1.

28. Ibid., 43, 138.

29. Ibid., 137. See also Vincent De Francis, "Protecting the Child Victim of Sex Crimes," (Denver: American Human Society, Children's Division, 1969), vii, viii, 57; Mohr, Turner, and Jerry, *Pedophilia and Exhibitionism*, 34; and Fass, *Kidnapped*, 222–25.

30. Hoover, "How Safe," 103.

31. Stern, "The Facts," 138.

32. For an example of a community call to stop girls from fundraising, see "Time to Look at Yakima's Use of Children as Solicitors," clipping from Yakima Valley Mirror in Roganunda Council Scrapbook, Yakima, 1959. Girl Scouts, Leadership of Girl Scout Troops: Intermediate Program (New York: Girl Scouts, 1943), 98.

33. "Child Safety: Our Responsibility," *Camp Fire Girl* 39, no. 1 (September 1959): 5.

34. Ibid.

35. Rebecca Nappi, "Selling Safely," *Spokane Chronicle* 130, February 20, 1985, 10, 16.

36. "What's On Your Mind," *American Girl* 39, no. 11 (November 1956), 31.
37   "What's On Your Mind," *American Girl* 44, no. 4 (April 1961), 40.
38. "What's On Your Mind," *American Girl* 43, no. 9 (September 1960), 64.
39. Elizabeth Ann Duvan, "Adolescent Girls: A Nation-Wide Study of Girls between Eleven and Eighteen Years of Age," (New York: Girl Scouts, 1956), 16, A8. The Girl Scouts commissioned the study, but it surveyed a sampling of girls and was not limited to Girl Scout members.
40. Ibid., 66, 126, 141, 142, 143.

Works Cited

"2 Slain Children Found In Watts: Bodies of White Sisters in Lot 25 Miles From Home." *The New York Times*, August 11, 1967.

"4 Begin Defense in Trial on Rape." *The New York Times*, June 13, 1959.

"4 Whites Seized in Rape of Negro." *The New York Times*, May 3, 1959.

Alexander, Ruth. *The "Girl Problem": Female Sexual Delinquency in New York, 1900–1930*. Ithaca, NY: Cornell University Press, 1998.

"Annual Report of the Camp Fire Girls." *Camp Fire Girls*. Camp Fire USA, Missouri, 1958.

Bailey, Beth. *Sex in the Heartland*. Cambridge: Harvard University Press, 2002.

"Boy is Questioned in Death of Girl, 6." *The New York Times*, July 13, 1966.

Breines, Wini. *Young, White and Miserable: Growing Up Female in the Fifties*. Chicago: University of Chicago Press, 2001.

Brunell, Miriam Forman. *Babysitter: An American History*. New York: New York University Press, 2009.

Chalmers, Allan Knight. "Florida Verdict Praised," *New York Times*, July 5, 1959.

"Child Safety: Our Responsibility," *Camp Fire Girl* 39, no. 1 (September 1959): 5.

"Civil Rights: The Sunday School Bombing." *Time*. September 27, 1963.

"Crime Increase Noted by Hoover." *The Bend Bulletin* 72. March 2, 1959.

De Francis, Vincent. "Protecting the Child Victim of Sex Crimes." Denver: American Human Society, Children's Division, 1969.

Devlin, Rachel. *Relative Intimacy: Fathers, Adolescent Daughters and Postwar American Culture*. Chapel Hill, NC: University of North Carolina Press, 2006.

Dowling, Colette. *The Frailty Myth: Redefining the Physical Potential of Women and Girls*. New York: Random House, 2000.

DuRocher, Kristina. *Raising Racists: The Socialization of White Children in the Jim Crow South*, Lexington, KY: University Press of Kentucky, 2011.

Duvan, Elizabeth Ann. "Adolescent Girls: A Nation-Wide Study of Girls between Eleven and Eighteen Years of Age." New York: Girl Scouts, 1956.

Fass, Paula. *Kidnapped: Child Abduction in America*. New York: Oxford University Press, 1997.

Feimster, Crystal. *Southern Horrors: Women and the Politics of Rape and Lynching*. Cambridge: Harvard University Press, 2009.

"Florence Negro Girl Missing since Thursday." *Times Daily*. July 8, 1958.

Freedman, Estelle B. "'Uncontrolled Desires': The Response to the Sexual Psychopath, 1920–1960." *The Journal of American History* 74, no. 1 (June 1987): 83-106.

Girl Scouts, *Leadership of Girl Scout Troops: Intermediate Program*. New York: Girl Scouts, 1943.

"Girl's Body Discovered near Spokane." *The Bend Bulletin*. March 23, 1959.

"Grand Jury Called in Co-Ed Rape Case." May 5, 1959.

Harvey, Brett. *The Fifties: A Women's Oral History*. New York: Harper Perennial, 1993.

Hoover, J. Edgar. "How Safe Is Your Youngster?" *American Magazine*. March 1955.

Kincaid, James R. *Erotic Innocence: The Culture of Child Molesting*. Durham, NC: Duke University Press, 1998.

King, Seth S. "Dr. Kinsey Doubts Rise in Sex Crimes." *The New York Times*, September 28, 1955.

"Letter to the editor." *Time*. October 4, 1963.

Logan, Wayne. *Knowledge as Power: Criminal Registration and Community Notification Laws in America*. Stanford, CA: Stanford University Press, 2009.

May, Elaine Tyler. *Homeward Bound: American Families in the Cold War Era*. New York: Basic Books, 1999.

Miller, Neil. *Sex-Crime Panic: A Journey to the Paranoid Heart of the 1950s*. Los Angeles: Alyson Books, 2002.

Mohr, Johann, Robert Turner, and Marian Bernice Jerry. *Pedophilia and Exhibitionism: A Handbook*. Toronto: University of Toronto Press, 1964.

Nappi, Rebecca. "Selling Safely." *Spokane Chronicle* 130, February 20, 1985.

"Negro Girl is Fined," *The New York Times*. November 30, 1957.

Odem, Mary. *Delinquent Daughters: Protecting and Policing Adolescent Female Sexuality in the United States, 1885–1920*. Chapel Hill, NC: University of North Carolina Press, 1995.

Pace, Eric. "New Kinsey Report Challenges Popular Concept of Sex Crimes." *The New York Times*. July 18, 1965.

Peiss, Kathy. *Cheap Amusements. Working Women and Leisure in Turn of the Century New York*. Philadelphia: Temple University Press, 1986.

"Rape of 9-Year-Old Girl Gets White Grocer Sentence." *Arkansas State Press*. July 10, 1953.

Sitton, Claude. "4 Whites on Trial in Rape of Negro." *The New York Times*. June 11, 1959.

Solinger, Rickie. *Wake Up Little Susie*. New York: Routledge, 1992.

Stern, Edith. "The Facts on Sex Offences Against Children." *Parents* 29 (October 1954): 43.

"Time to Look at Yakima's Use of Children as Solicitors." *Yakima Valley Mirror*. 1959.

"What's On Your Mind." *American Girl* 39, no. 11 (November 1956): 31.

"What's On Your Mind." *American Girl* 43, no. 9 (September 1960): 64.

"What's On Your Mind." *American Girl* 44, no. 4 (April 1961): 40.

Wiese, Andrew. *Places of their Own: African American Suburbanization in the Twentieth Century*. Chicago: University of Chicago Press, 2004.

3

Snogging, Stereotypes, and Subversion: Girls' Sexuality in the *Harry Potter* Series

Kate Harper

When J.K. Rowling casually announced in a Q&A session following a reading of *Harry Potter and the Deathly Hallows* in October 2007, "Dumbledore is gay, actually," it seems unlikely that she did not suspect the level of excitement and debate that would follow. Conservative groups campaigning against the wildly popular series since the first book's initial release saw this as another example of its danger to children, while members of the GLBTQ community hailed Dumbledore as a new addition to the family. The "gay Dumbledore" conversation that continued in the following months provides only one example of the various controversies surrounding the books and the films, but it illustrates a longstanding moral panic around children's literature and popular culture, as well as the ways in which concerns over "our children" often stand in for other ideological agendas.

This chapter begins with the cultural significance of the *Harry Potter* phenomenon, recognizes its potential social and ideological impact, and has several goals. First, using the existing body of critical work on the *Harry Potter* series as an example, I briefly consider the ways in which the category of children often operates as a monolithic identity that supersedes all others in the field of children's literary and cultural criticism. Second, I demonstrate how the feminist theory of intersectionality provides a framework for disrupting this category and revealing children's identities as multiple, interrelated, and complex. Finally, building on this intersectional approach, I enter sexuality into the existing academic conversation, considering what depictions of sexuality and its intersections with other identities reveal about race, class, and gender ideology in the series. Rather than considering sexuality as simply another aspect of identity, I want to investigate the ways in which heterosexuality operates as a normalizing force in the books and the films.[1] Using examples from *Harry Potter and the Half-Blood Prince*, I argue that the unchallenged, pervasive depiction of heterosexual desire stabilizes the series, functioning as the axle of a wheel. This 'centering' effect allows the series to superficially critique racist ideology, unequal gender expectations, socioeconomic class hierarchies, and traditional notions of family. The naturalization of heterosexual desire and the insistence upon heterosexuality actually limits the transgressive potential of the series. Furthermore, when one examines the ways in which representations of sexuality (or the absence of sexuality) intersect with other identity categories, the façade of progressivism becomes less convincing, revealing reductive stereotypes of race, class, and gender.

Literature Review

When considering the construction of sexuality in the *Harry Potter* series, three bodies of literature are particularly relevant. Mary Pipher's foundational text, *Reviving Ophelia* (1991), is largely representative of the "moral panic" camp. Pipher's book began a new wave of scholarly literature concerned with "saving the selves" of America's girls who were in dire need of attention and intervention. Pipher describes American culture as "girl poisoning," writing, "Girls today are much more oppressed. They are coming of age in a more dangerous, sexualized and media-saturated culture…as they navigate a more dangerous world, girls are less protected."[2] Pipher's language of danger, crisis, and vulnerability illustrates her intent to "raise the alarm" about American girls' new crisis. William Pollack's *Real Boys* responded to Pipher's work, arguing that girls are in fact doing much better than boys, and boys are falling behind because of the overwhelming attention paid to girls. Both Pipher and Pollack draw on their experiences and expertise as psychologists and therapists working with young people to suggest that the crises they see in their offices are much more widespread than we might think.[3]

The language of impending disaster, fragility, self-destruction, and vulnerability used throughout both Pipher's and Pollack's work is not new, nor has it diminished since their publications.[4] The current proliferation of work on the sexualization of American culture and its harmful effects demonstrates one strand of the continuing focus on young people, particularly girls. Sexualization critics focus on the ways in which sexual imagery saturates American culture, and argue that such blatant representations are causing an epidemic of sexual behavior that is "increasingly outrageous" at increasingly younger ages.[5] Within this discourse, young girls are the target of media sexualization, and are constructed as victims who lack sexual agency and desire. The sexual activities of boys are relatively absent from the discussion, reinforcing the idea that boys are always sexual, and that girls' sexual activity must be the result of some form of coercion. Overwhelmingly, these critics consider the sexualization of culture as fundamentally negative and destructive, and argue that the sexual behavior of young girls and boys can be directly attributed to the representations they see in the media.

This wholesale condemnation of sexual imagery has sparked two counter-critiques. First, some feminist scholars argue that the increased visibility of sexuality in the media is not inherently damaging, as no discourse can be categorized as entirely positive or negative. As Stuart Hall points out, "Popular culture is neither, in a 'pure' sense, the popular traditions of resistance...nor is it the forms which are superimposed on and over them. It is the ground which the transformations are worked."[6] Different individuals respond to and interact with representations of sexuality in different ways; these interactions are always contextual, situational, and dependent upon the intersectional identities of the individual, leaving room for interpretation and subversion. The proliferation of sexual imagery and open discussions of sexual activity and desire may signal a progression toward sexual plurality, acceptability, and equality.[7] As individuals are exposed to more sexual activity and desires, they may be more likely to explore their own desires and behaviors, as well as be more accepting and understanding of those whose desires differ from their own. In this way, the "sexualization of culture" could be an avenue for the democratization of sexuality in the United States.

Other scholars agree that it is inaccurate (and not useful) to label all sexualization as negative, but argue that the positive potential of increasing public discussions of sexuality has limits, since the representations of positive sexuality are confined to particular "acceptable" bodies.[8] While the sheer amount of sexual imagery in the media has increased in the last two decades, the range of bodies, desires, and behaviors has remained closely aligned to traditional standards of beauty, sexual desirability, and acceptable behaviors. Importantly, the representations of desire are raced, classed, and gendered in specific ways, as are the resulting moral panics about young people's potential susceptibility to those images.[9] Adults seem particularly anxious about the impending dangers to girls (i.e., white, middle-class girls from "good" families), and place literature and popular culture targeted at girls under intense scrutiny. In many cases, it becomes evident that anxiety around innocent, impressionable children, especially girls, actually conceals broader ideological concerns.

The incredible range of criticism directed at the *Harry Potter* series since the publication of the first book demonstrates the ways in which the discourse of "protecting our children" disguises other ideological agendas.[10] Concerns about gender roles, racial and ethnic identities, class representations, religion, and family formations have been raised, and critics and defenders continue to debate the appropriateness of the series for its young target audience. Several edited collections of scholarly work on the *Harry Potter* series are currently available, and the contributing authors engage with numerous themes, from various disciplines and perspectives. Three dominant themes are education, psychology and development of children and adolescents, and the series' various performances of literary genres.[11] Religion and morality, the good/bad dichotomy, and "Harry-as-hero" are other popular topics of inquiry. Several authors deal with broader social issues: authority, the social roles of technology, law and justice, love and resistance, and animal stewardship. The series' development into popular culture and the dilemmas of consumerism are also addressed. Issues of race, class, and gender are dealt with briefly, but primarily as isolated categories of analysis.[12] A smattering of other academic articles exist outside these edited volumes, as well as countless popular press articles.[13] A brief glance at the topics in these collections suggests an engagement with a broadening academic audience, as more scholars realize the cultural impact of the series.

Surprisingly, little has been said regarding sexuality in the *Harry Potter* series. The existing academic literature remains primarily classified as "kiddie lit crit," focusing on its role as a fantasy text.[14] More often than not, children (as an audience and as characters) tend to be treated as a monolithic category, untouched by race, class, gender, sexuality, disability, and other identity categories.[15] I hope to complicate the discussion by considering the representations of sexuality in the *Harry Potter* series. Which characters are constructed as sexual beings? Whose sexuality is questioned, sanctioned, ignored, or denied? Do these representations match a shared cultural understanding of developing adolescent sexuality? Does the series function as a normalizing discourse by providing illustrations of acceptable and/or unacceptable sexualities? Because race, class, gender, sexuality, and other identities are not experienced in isolation from one another, we must consider the ways in which these various identities are represented in the series. An intersectional framework allows us to take into account the complex ways in which various identities are mutually and simultaneously constitutive and constructive.

Why Intersectionality?

Put simply, intersectionality is a theoretical framework and analytical approach based on an understanding that social identities are historically situated "organizing features of social relations" which "mutually constitute, reinforce, and naturalize one another."[16] An intersectional approach, as employed here, proceeds from the understanding that identities are interrelated, integrated, and co-constitutive. In other words, identities such as race, ethnicity, class, gender, sexuality, disability, and other social identities do not exist separately or in a vacuum, but depend upon each other in their construction. An intersectional approach insists that one cannot understand representations of sexuality in *Harry Potter* without interrogating the ways in which gender is constructed in relation to race, class, and gender. Intersectionality proves particularly useful for the analysis of popular culture, as the "contents" of popular culture are always fluid, unstable, and changing.[17]

In considering points of difference as multiple and mutually constructing identities, rather than simply additive, intersectionality recognizes that identities are always interrelational; they do not exist in isolation, nor are they static. An intersectional perspective insists on recognizing the interrelationality of these relationships, which brings to light power dynamics that might otherwise appear natural or neutral. Paying attention to the constructions of these identities through representation in children's literature and film have sociocultural and material implications. I argue here that the very existence of the controversies over the *Harry Potter* series, as well as its widespread availability and popularity, illustrate the social power of discourses made salient through literature and film.

Is There Sex in *Harry Potter*?

I begin with the opening credits and the first scene in which we re-encounter Harry in *Harry Potter and the Half-Blood Prince*. The film is rated PG for "mild sensuality," a warning not previously applied to the first four films (two of which are rated PG-13 for "sequences of fantasy violence and frightening images"). After a brief glance at the trouble the Death Eaters are causing in the Muggle world, we find ourselves in a diner at the train station, watching Harry read *The Daily Prophet* and catch the attention of one of the waitresses. A tall, thin, light-skinned Black girl, the waitress shyly approaches Harry and asks, "Who is Harry Potter?" Harry quickly puts the paper down, as his name features prominently on the front page. Harry brushes off the question ("No one. Bit of a tosser, really"), and then begins to ask the girl when her shift ends. She interrupts, telling him, "Eleven. That's when I get off. You can tell me all about that tosser Harry Potter, then, if you'd like." Harry smiles and nods, then quickly checks his breath and pops a breath mint in his mouth as the girl heads back to the kitchen.

Dumbledore interrupts Harry's potential late-night date. The elderly wizard appears outside the diner and Harry joins him on the platform. The two stand gazing at a large fragrance advertisement as they discuss Harry's new pastime of riding the trains around London. The advertisement boasts a stereotypically attractive, white young woman with brunette hair in an evening gown, gazing seductively at the viewer. The sign reads, "Tonight, Make a Little Magic With Your Man" in bold script. Dumbledore informs Harry that he needs assistance in an errand, and the scene ends with Harry glancing over his shoulder as the girl leaves the diner, clearly looking for him. Dumbledore apporates with Harry to "the charming village of Budleigh Babberton."

This scene, although not as explicitly sexual as others in the film, establishes several notable characteristics of sexuality in the film. It establishes Harry (at least superficially) as a sexual being. More specifically, through Harry's interactions with the waitress, the scene affirms the audience's presumption of Harry's heterosexuality. Finally, Harry's willingness to follow Dumbledore with little hesitation reminds the viewer that magic remains Harry's number one priority (although, of course, Harry assumes at the point of apporation that he will return to the diner tomorrow and "make some excuse"). These factors may seem relatively mundane until we consider that this opening scene was created specifically for the film. In the book, Harry awaits Dumbledore's arrival in his room at Privet Drive, and the pair apporate from this location after a conversation between Dumbledore and Harry's aunt and uncle. By creating an opening scene in which Harry demonstrates interest in a girl who reciprocates his attention, the filmmakers establish Harry's (hetero)sexual maturation and set the stage for the heightened level of (hetero)sexuality throughout the remainder of the film.[18]

The brief, unfruitful exchange between Harry and the waitress hints at the series' depictions of interracial relationships: they simply do not work out.[19] The film's depiction of the waitress approaching Harry simultaneously utilizes racial and gendered stereotypes: because she is black, she must therefore be the sexual aggressor and make the first move. However, her coyness and flirtation in the exchange demonstrate her ability to sufficiently adhere to hegemonic expectations of femininity. The scene's linkage of race and class is similarly predictable: Harry (a white male) is a patron at the diner, riding trains for entertainment, while the waitress (a black female) works late hours in a menial job. Finally, Harry's departure with Dumbledore reminds the audience that Harry possesses a fundamental characteristic of hegemonic masculinity: the ability to postpone or reject sexual desire for a more vital and noble cause or project.

The "love potion" scenes from the film offer additional insight into the construction of sexuality. The first of this series occurs as the Weasley family, Harry, and Hermione visit Fred and George's magic shop on their yearly shopping trip for school supplies to Diagon Alley. We find Hermione and Ginny amid numerous others girls, looking over an array of pink products under a "Wonder Witch" sign. Fred and George explain that the bestsellers are love potions, but joke with Ginny, "you, sister, seem to be doing fine on your own!" Ginny blushes and responds, "It's none of your business," while Hermione looks around anxiously. As she catches the eye of Cormac McLaggan, she hastily returns the love potion to its spot and hurries off after the others. As the group moves off, we catch our first glimpse of Lavender Brown, crowded with other giggling girls around another display of love potions. She says hello to Ron, who waves and turns around with a huge grin on his face.

The second "love potion" scene takes place in the first day of Potions class, as Professor Slughorn has produced several potions as an example of the types of potions they will be learning throughout the year. One of these is Amortentia, "the most powerful love potion in the world," as Hermione explains to the class. The love potion smells differently to each individual; Hermione smells "freshly mown grass and new parchment." As Hermione appears almost overwhelmed by the scents rising from the cauldron, the other girls in the room hover close by, including Lavender Brown and Romilda Vane. The boys in the room seem relatively uninterested in the potion, but the girls appear on the brink of losing control as Slughorn reminds the class that the love potion does not create real love, only "powerful infatuation." Hermione pulls back slightly, seemingly embarrassed and disturbed by her strong reaction to the potion.

The final "love potion" scene occurs when Harry returns from a lesson with Dumbledore to find Ron sitting cross-legged on the floor, surrounded by chocolate wrappers and gazing out the window into the moonlight. As Harry sits on the edge of his bed, Ron climbs up next to him and insists, "I'm in love with her." Harry assumes that Ron is referring to Lavender until he realizes the half-eaten box of chocolates is addressed to himself, from Romilda Vane.[20] Ron stumbles down the hallways with Harry to Slughorn's office, where Slughorn stirs up an antidote. He looks dopey-eyed, hugs Harry and Slughorn repeatedly, and clutches the throw pillow that Harry shoves in his arms. As soon as Ron takes the tonic, the look of euphoria slides off his face, and he stutters, "I feel really bad!" Slughorn offers Harry and Ron each a glass of oak-matured mead. Ron drinks first, then falls quickly to the floor. After Harry revives him, Ron sinks back and gasps, "These girls. They're gonna kill me."

The "love potion" scenes emphasize specific stereotypical assumptions about boys' and girls' behaviors regarding love and affection. As demonstrated by Fred and George's marketing strategies in the first scene, the love potions are designed with girls in mind, as their packaging in pink under the sign "Wonder Witch" makes clear. We can deduct that such design and placement not only draw groups of girls, but also repel boys in the shop. The different reactions to Amortentia in Potions class also emphasize a distinction between genders. The boys in the room appear unaffected in the love potion, while the girls seem magnetically drawn, as a group, toward the cauldron containing the love potion. They move closer and closer to the cauldron as if in a daze, and retreat as if waking from a dream when Slughorn places the lid on the cauldron. Ron's later encounter with the potioned chocolates proves that boys are not immune. However, the scene in the classroom leads the audience to believe that the girls are not only more interested in love (or infatuation, in this case), but are more susceptible to the effects of the potion.

The next grouping of scenes all center around "snogging," the (British) wizarding world's term for kissing. The scene begins with Ron, Hermione, and Harry entering Honeydukes for some butterbeer. As the three sit down, Ron spies Ginny and Dean in the corner and seems visibly disturbed. Hermione laughs, telling Ron: "they're only holding hands…and snogging." Ron announces, "I'd like to leave," to which Hermione responds, "You can't be serious…What if she looked over here and saw you snogging me, would you expect her to get up and leave?" Ron looks taken aback and Hermione blushes. Luckily, Professor Slughorn approaches their table and changes the subject. As the trio leaves Hogsmeade, Ron asks Harry if he "heard what she said, about me and her snogging?" Later, Ron returns to the conversation as he and Harry lay in their beds, asking Harry what he thinks Dean sees in Ginny. Harry responds:

> "I don't know. She's smart, funny, attractive…"
> "Attractive?"
> "You know…she's got nice skin."
> "Skin… Are you saying Dean's dating my sister because of her skin?"
> "Well, no…I mean, I'm just saying it could be a contributing factor."
> "…Hermione's got nice skin. Wouldn't you say? As skin goes, I mean?"
> "I've never really thought about it. But, I suppose, yeah. Very nice."

This rather humorous conversation highlights Ron's growing awareness of Hermione as a potential romantic interest.[21] Harry ends the conversation by announcing his intentions to sleep, but both he and Ron stare off into space. We are to assume that they are puzzling over Ginny and Hermione, respectively, as they drift off.[22]

Lavender Brown quickly interrupts Ron's seeming interest in Hermione, as she showers Ron with attention before the first Quiddich match. During a post-game celebration in the Griffindor common room, Lavender wraps her arms around Ron and pulls him in for a kiss, as Hermione flees the room. The next thirty minutes of the film are peppered with Lavender's constant appearance alongside Ron; more often than not, the pair are snogging or cuddling in some fashion. Ron tells Harry after the post-Quiddich party, "I can't help it if she's

[Hermione] got her knickers in a twist! What Lav and I have, well, let's just say, there's no stopping it. It's chemical. Will it last? Who knows? The point is, I'm a free agent!" Despite this proclamation, Lavender soon appears to wear on Ron's nerves, with her excessive displays of affection, clinginess, and constant snogging.

This series of scenes (and indeed, the full film), demonstrates a particular preoccupation with physical intimacy, something that has been glaringly absent in the previous films.[23] In addition to these explicit depictions of sexual desire, there are numerous sexual innuendos added to the film: Cormac McLaggan licks his fingers suggestively at Hermione during one of Slughorn's "Slug Club" parties; and Ron asks Harry (referring to hiding the Half-Blood Prince's book) if he and Ginny "did it," for example. The focus on burgeoning sexual expression may simply be an attempt by the filmmakers to cater to an adolescent audience. However, these depictions are both stereotypical and subversive, a topic to which I will return.

Three relatively brief but important scenes comprise the final series I want to discuss, and each depicts the growing attraction between Harry and Ginny. In the first scene, the Weasley kids and Harry have traveled to the Weasley home for holiday break, and everyone is getting ready for bed. Harry stands looking out a window as Ginny climbs the stairs, wearing a robe, her hair wet. She kneels down to tie Harry's shoe, and as she stands she steps closer to him. "Merry Christmas, Harry," she says, and Harry begins to respond, "Merry Christmas" as the two lean in for a kiss. The Death Eaters' arrival interrupts the moment and Ginny and Harry rush outside to fight. The second scene shows Ginny and Harry hiding the Half-Blood Prince's book after his attack on Draco Malfoy. The camera focuses on their hands as Ginny offers hers to Harry and leads him into the Room of Requirement. She instructs Harry to close his eyes, "That way you can't be tempted." As Ginny hides the book, the camera remains on Harry, standing with his eyes closed. Ginny moves back into the shot and kisses Harry, whispering, "That can stay hidden up here, too, if you like." The next shot shows Harry walking down the empty corridor with a dreamy smile on his face, as Ron catches up to him. The third scene capturing Ginny and Harry's growing relationship follows Dumbledore's death. As Harry cries over Dumbledore's broken body, Ginny leaves the surrounding crowd of students and kneels at his side, holding him. Although the development of Ginny and Harry's romantic relationship features heavily in this film, the film ends in a way that reasserts Harry's focus from the beginning scene: Harry must complete Dumbledore's task. Although Hermione insists, "Ron's okay with it, you know—you and Ginny," Harry responds that he will not be returning to Hogwarts.[24] As in the opening scene, Harry's (sexual) desire comes second to his loyalty to Dumbledore.

Who is Sexual, and Why Does it Matter?

When examining the representation of sexuality in the film *Harry Potter and the Half-Blood Prince*, we can begin by noting which characters are granted sexual desire or agency, and how sexuality intersects with the characters' other identities. The intersection of race and ethnicity with sexuality lacks complexity in the film; every character constructed as a sexual actor in this film is white, with the exception of Dean and the nameless waitress in the opening scene. In fact, Dean and Cho are the only two non-white sexual actors throughout the films, and as we already know, the relationships between both Dean and Ginny and Cho and Harry are destined for failure. In this sense, Dean and Cho represent people of color as sexually attractive but not romantically viable. Several other characters illustrate another stereotypical construction: non-white Others as hypersexual or the sexual aggressor. The nameless waitress who approaches Harry in the train station diner falls into this category, as does Romilda Vane, the girl who sends Harry the love-potioned chocolates. Although the book does not give a physical description, the film casts a (albeit light-skinned) girl with stereotypically black features—very curly black hair, dark eyes, full lips—to play the role of Romilda, who is so obsessed with catching Harry's attention that she uses a forbidden love potion. Bellatrix, despite her claim to a pure blood family of wizards, appears darker than her fair sister, with heavy-lidded eyes and wild, untamed hair. Her presumed degeneracy due to her stint in Azkaban combines with her physical description to construct Bellatrix as a sexual Other. Similarly, Fennir Grayback, the werewolf granted Death Eater status, embodies the animalistic "Other" and threat of sexual violence.[25]

Certainly, one could argue that since most of the students (and the lead characters) in the film are white, it only makes sense that white students are more frequently depicted as sexual actors. While this may be true, depicting only two students of color as having or being the objects of sexual desire could serve to further emphasize their tokenism in the series.[26] On the other hand, being white does not guarantee granting of sexual agency in the series, as Luna Lovegood and Neville Longbottom illustrate. Although both play significant roles from *Harry Potter and the Order of the Phoenix* to the end of the series, neither is depicted as having or being the object of sexual desire. Luna is too quirky and Neville too nerdy and unathletic to be considered stereotypically attractive or sexually desirable.

The film's depictions of sexuality also rely on stereotypical expectations of gender, as Hermione and Ginny appear more relationship- and romance-savvy than Harry or Ron. The movie features two groups of girls: those focused on infatuation (the 'love potion' girls, like Romilda Vane), and the 'mature' relationship girls (Hermione and Ginny). Both groups of girls are concerned with love and the acquisition of an acceptable boyfriend, and physical intimacy is not their first concern. Hermione makes this clear when she tells Harry about Romilda Vane's crush on him: "She only likes you because she thinks you're the chosen one!" Lavender Brown provides an interesting exception to this pattern; she is both sexually aggressive (she kisses Ron first and initiates most of the snogging—so much that Ron begins to avoid her) and overwhelmed with infatuation. Lavender dresses in very "girly" fashion—skirts, frilly blouses, knee socks, flowered headbands, all in pink and purple—and always wears makeup and her hair in ringlets. Lavender embodies the threat of girls' sexuality. She exudes immature emotion and sexual desire. The film contrasts the overly aggressive, girly Lavender with Hermione and Ginny, who both perform a more subdued, intellectual form of femininity. Hermione, although portrayed in the films (much more than the books) as highly emotional, appropriately keeps her love for Ron to herself and always maintains a certain level of decorum. The hospital scene following Ron's poisoning exemplifies the contrast between Hermione and Lavender.[27] Similarly, the distinction between Ginny and Lavender can be seen in the two kissing scenes: Lavender and Ron's first kiss in the common room, and Ginny and Harry's first kiss in the Room of Requirement. The film constructs Lavender's affection as out of control, immature, and inappropriate.

I want to turn finally to a brief discussion of the film's pervasive construction of sexuality as strictly heteronormative. To avoid being cumbersome, I have avoided inserting 'hetero' alongside 'sexuality' in most places. This analysis aims to demonstrate the level to which the film naturalizes heterosexuality as the 'normal' development of sexuality by depicting heterosexuality as the only expression of sexuality available. The film not so subtly reinforces Ron and Harry's strict heterosexuality (as if their sexual interactions with Lavender and Ginny are not sufficient) through two scenes that display distaste and disapproval for same-sex desires. During the train ride home for Christmas break, Harry and Ron are in one of the boxcars alone, since Hermione and Ron are not speaking. As Harry and Ron discuss a secretive conversation between Draco and Snape, Lavender passes by, stopping to draw a heart with her and Ron's initials on the window. Ron smiles faintly, then complains to Harry that he cannot escape her: "She won't stop snogging me! My lips are chapped—See?!" As Ron leans in closely to Harry, presumably to display his poor, worn-out lips, Harry hastily pulls back and pushes Ron away, replying, "I'll take your word for it."[28] Later, in the third 'love potion' scene (when Ron eats the love-potioned

chocolates), Harry is visibly disturbed when Ron crawls onto the twin bed close
to him, and quickly slides off the bed and away from Ron.[29] In both scenes,
Harry, the supposedly sensitive, open male, rejects any close physical contact
between himself and Ron. The physical nearness only seems to garner a negative reaction when it occurs without Hermione or some other female nearby.
Throughout the film, Harry and Ron are in physical contact when they are in
others' presence, but these scenes suggest that without Hermione, they require
more distance to maintain their heterosexual identities. Interestingly enough,
these scenes that rely on homophobia to secure Harry and Ron's heterosexuality actually provide subtle ruptures in an otherwise seamless depiction of heterosexuality as natural, and alert the viewer to the instability and constructedness of
heteronormativity. These tiny fissures also clue us in to the possibility for other
subversive readings and re-constructions.

Concluding Thoughts and Implications

This chapter has briefly considered the construction of girls' sexuality within the *Harry Potter* series, as well as how heterosexuality acts as a stabilizing
force. The film's narrow representation of sexuality as explicitly gendered and
exclusively heterosexual functions in at least two ways. First, it creates a sexual
world that is culturally legible and comfortable, one in which all girls (and boys)
develop heterosexual interest at an appropriate age and follow prescribed gendered sexual scripts. Second, the normative script of heterosexual desire provides a certain level of stability, allowing for what appears to be a greater
flexibility in representations of race, class, and gender. However, this elasticity
only stretches so far; what appears transgressive may only be superficial. An
intersectional interrogation of sexuality alongside other aspects of identity reveals that seemingly progressive depictions of race, class, and gender are frequently exploded, revealing familiar and troubling stereotypes.

Although this chapter focuses on a set of popular culture texts, the aim is
"fundamentally sociological," concerned with the ways in which discourses of
progressivism are frequently 'carriers' of reworked conservatives ideologies.
When we consider the connections between advertising agencies, film production companies, publishing franchises like Scholastic, political groups (both
conservative and liberal), etc., it becomes clear that these discourses have
broader social implications. I do not want to suggest, however, that hegemony
operates without resistance. The subversive co-optation of these texts—re-
readings, re-writings, and re-signification—can be seen in the vast array of fan
and slash fiction sparked by the *Harry Potter* series, and overwhelmingly produced by girls. These slippages provide space for transformation and, as Hall
reminds us, "that is why 'popular culture' matters."[30] Young girls taking up the

Harry Potter stories and rewriting them may not seem revolutionary, but it opens opportunities for negotiating sexual identities and resisting hegemonic norms.

Notes

1. Following Corbin and Strauss, I use open coding to examine the various depictions of characters and cull themes and patterns for further analysis. As a preliminary investigation of the discourse of adolescent sexuality in the *Harry Potter* films, the information gathered may provide guidance for a comprehensive study of the other films and books in the series, as well as subversive readings. I will return to the implications of such work at the end of the chapter.
2. Mary Pipher, *Reviving Ophelia: Saving the Selves of Adolescent Girls* (New York: Penguin Group, 1994).
3. See Pipher, *Reviving Ophelia* 1994; William Pollack, *Real Boys: Rescuing our Sons from the Myths of Boyhood* (New York: Henry Holt and Co, 1998); Pipher and Pollack's work, along with others, demonstrate a tendency to discuss "crisis" or anxiety over girls in terms of their sexuality and/or bodies, while concern over boys' progress and/or "decline" focuses on academic achievement and potential as future wage earners.
4. Scholars, parents, policymakers, and reformers have expressed concern over boys and girls since the creation of the category of "adolescence" in the early twentieth century. See Ruth A. Alexander, *The "Girl Problem:" Female Sexual Delinquency in New York, 1900–1930* (Ithaca, NY: Cornell University Press, 1995); Elizabeth A. Clement, *Love for Sale: Courting, Treating and Prostitution in New York City, 1900–1945* (Chapel Hill, NC: University of North Carolina Press, 2006); Nancy Lesko, *Act Your Age! A Cultural Construction of Adolescence* (New York: Routledge, 2001); Ilana Nash, *American Sweethearts: Teenage Girls in Twentieth Century Popular Culture* (Bloomington, IN: Indiana University Press, 2006); and Mary Odem, *Delinquent Daughters: Protecting and Policing Adolescent Female Sexuality in the United States, 1885–1920* (Chapel Hill, NC: University of North Carolina Press, 1995).
5. See Patrice. Oppliger, *Girls Gone Skank: The Sexualization of Girls in American Culture* (Jefferson, NC: McFarland & Co, 2008)
6. Stuart Hall, "Notes on Deconstructing 'the Popular," in *Popular Culture: A Reader*, eds. Raiford A. Guins and Omayra Zaragoza Cruz, 64–71 (London: Sage Publications, 2005), 68.
7. Feona Attwood. "Sexed Up: Theorizing the Sexualization of Culture," *Sexualities* 9 no. 1(2006): 77–94.
8. See Rosalind Gill, "Beyond the 'Sexualization of Culture': An Intersectional Analysis of 'Sixpacks', 'Midriffs' and 'Hot Lesbians' in Advertising," *Sexualities* 12 no. 2 (2009): 137–60.
9. Pipher and Pollack, along with the more contemporary 'moral panic' authors mentioned here, have been critiqued for only expressing concern about certain children: the "prettiest girls from the most successful families." For example, see Sharlene Azam, *Oral Sex is the New Goodnight Kiss: The Sexual Bullying of Girls* (Bollywood Filmed Entertainment, 2009).
10. Scott Thomas catalogs many of the controversies over the series; see Scott Thomas, *The Making of the Potter-verse: A Month-By-Month Look at Harry's First Ten Years* (Chicago: Independent Publishers Group, 2007).
11. I have avoided citing each chapter from the edited volumes here, for brevity's sake. Citations for the collections can be found in the works cited.
12. Karin E. Westman, "Specters of Thatcherism: Contemporary British Culture in J.K. Rowling's Harry Potter Series," in *The Ivory Tower and Harry Potter: Perspectives on a Literary Phenomenon,* edited by Lana A. Whited (Columbia: University of Missouri Press, 2002). Westman

examines the intersections of race, class, and consumerism, as well as the general public's interpretations of realism in the series.

13. Jeffrey Michael Rudski, Carli Segal, and Eli Kallen, "Harry Potter and the End of the Road: Parallels with Addiction," *Addiction Research and Theory*, 17 no. 3 (2009): 260–77; David Nylund, "Reading Harry Potter: Popular Culture, Queer Theory and the Fashioning of Youth Identity," *Journal of Systemic Therapies*, 26 no. 2 (2007): 13–24.

14. Two more recent edited volumes, *The Ultimate Harry Potter and Philosophy* and *Harry Potter and History*, examine the series in disciplinary terms.

15. I am not arguing that scholars have not critiqued the series for perpetuating racist and sexist ideology; this work certainly exists. I am suggesting that these arguments often discuss race, for example, as a broader social phenomenon and not as an aspect of identity for the characters.

16. Stephanie A. Shields, "Gender: An Intersectionality Perspective," *Sex Roles* 59 no. 1 (2008): 301–11, 308.

17. Stuart Hall, "Notes," 68.

18. The film's framing of Harry and Dumbledore's initial conversation in the train station as they both look at the perfume advertisement portrays the male gaze in a way that reestablishes Dumbledore as presumably heterosexual, a rejection of J.K. Rowling's announcement in October 2007 that "Dumbledore is gay, actually." The advertisement's recommendation to the (presumably straight) female purchaser for her evening plans with her "man" is certainly meant as word play, but also prioritizes male (heterosexual) desire and pleasure.

19. There are several examples of this failed interracial relationship trend: Cho and Cedric and Hermione and Victor Krum in *Harry Potter and the Goblet of Fire*; Cho and Harry in *Harry Potter and the Order of the Phoenix*; Ginny and Dean in *Harry Potter and the Half-Blood Prince*.

20. In a previous scene, Hermione warns Harry that Romilda Vane has a crush on him and has been trying to slip him a love potion.

21. This scene is one of several in which Ron is depicted as seemingly clueless and rather thickheaded when it comes to Hermione. His sudden recognition of Hermione as "a girl" under pressure to find a date for the Christmas ball in Harry Potter and the Goblet of Fire is perhaps the best example.

22. One could argue that Harry's focus here is on Malfoy's mysterious activities rather than Ginny.

23. Two minor exceptions include Hermione's brief mention of Victor Krum as "a physical being" in *Harry Potter and the Goblet of Fire*, and Harry and Cho's brief kiss in *Harry Potter and the Order of the Phoenix*.

24. The book further highlights Harry's sacrifice of his burgeoning romance with Ginny, as Harry notes that a relationship with Ginny could place her in further danger, even if she remains at Hogwarts.

25. The Christmas scene in which Ginny follows Harry into the swamp to fight the Death Eaters suggests Grayback's role as sexual predator well.

26. A perfect example of this tokenism: Blaise is the only non-white student in the film's depiction of Slughorn's Christmas party.

27. In this scene, Lavender flurries into the room and suggests that Hermione only wants to be with Ron "now that he's all interesting," to which Hermione responds, "He's been poisoned, you daft bimbo!" As Ron murmurs Hermione's name, Lavender runs from the room, crying. Throughout the scene, Hermione remains calmly seated by Ron's bed, seemingly unflustered. Although the film clearly prefers Hermione's version of femininity to Lavender's, it also confirms an assumption that girls play games and are manipulative. Even Hermione

participates to a certain degree, specifically inviting Cormac to Slughorn's Christmas party to annoy Ron.

28. This is another scene that was created for the film; in the book, Harry and Ron discuss the significance of the Unbreakable Vow in the Weasley's kitchen. As with the opening scene of the film discussed earlier, this scene operates as a way of stabilizing heterosexual desire.

29. This scene does occur in the book, although with a slight variation: rather than climbing onto Harry's bed, Ron responds to Harry's dismissal of his 'love' for Romilda Vane by punching him in the head. The film replaces Ron's belligerent display of masculine anger with 'girly' antics, hence the homoerotic tension between him and Harry.

30. Hall "Notes," 71.

Works Cited

Alcoff, Linda M. *Visible Identities: Race, Gender, and the Self.* Oxford: Oxford University Press, 2006.

Alexander, Ruth M. *The "Girl Problem:" Female Sexual Delinquency in New York, 1900–1930.* Ithaca, NY: Cornell University Press, 1995.

Anatol, Giselle Liza, ed. *Reading Harry Potter: Critical Essays.* Westport, CT: Praeger Publishers, 2003.

———. ed. *Reading Harry Potter Again: New Critical Essays.* Santa Barbara, CA: ABC-CLIO, 2009.

Attwood, Feona. "Sexed Up: Theorizing the Sexualization of Culture." *Sexualities* 9, no. 1 (2006): 77–94.

Azam, Sharlene. *Oral Sex is the New Goodnight Kiss: The Sexual Bullying of Girls.* Bollywood Filmed Entertainment, 2009.

Bassam, Gregory, ed. *The Ultimate Harry Potter and Philosophy.* Hoboken, NJ: John Wiley & Sons, 2010.

Brown, Elsa Barley. "'What Has Happened Here': The Politics of Difference in Women's History and Feminist Politics." *Feminist Studies* 18, no. 2 (1992): 295–312.

Brumberg, Joan Jacob. *The Body Project: An Intimate History of American Girls.* New York: Random House, 1997.

Clement, Elizabeth A. *Love for Sale: Courting, Treating and Prostitution in New York City, 1900–1945.* Chapel Hill, NC: University of North Carolina Press, 2006.

Corbin, Julie and Anselm Strauss. *Basics of Qualitative Research.* 3rd ed. Los Angeles: Sage Publications, 2008.

Corliss, Richard. "Why 'Harry Potter' Did a Harry Houdini." CNN.com. CNN, 21 July 2000. Web. 3 May 2 2010.

Crenshaw, Kimberlé. "Demarginalizing the Intersection of Race and Sex." *The University of Chicago Legal Forum,* 1 (1989): 139-167.

Downs, Douglas. "Harry Potter: Witchcraft Repackaged (Movie Review)." ChristianAnswers.Net. Web. May 8, 2010.

Gill, Rosalind. "Beyond the 'Sexualization of Culture': An Intersectional Analysis of 'Sixpacks,' 'Midriffs' and 'Hot Lesbians' in Advertising." *Sexualities* 12, no. 2 (2009): 137–60.

Hall, Stuart. "Notes on Deconstructing 'the Popular.'" In *Popular Culture: A Reader,* eds. Raiford A. Guins and Omayra Zaragoza Cruz, 64–71. London: Sage Publications, 2005.

Hann, Amy Teegan. *Memory and Material Culture in Harry Potter.* Tempe, AZ: Arizona State University, 2007.

Harry Potter and the Goblet of Fire, directed by Mike Newell (2005; Burbank, CA: Warner Home Video, 2006). DVD.

Harry Potter and the Half-Blood Prince, directed by David Yates (2009; Burbank, CA: Warner Home Video, 2009). DVD.

Harry Potter and the Order of the Phoenix, directed by David Yates (2007: Burbank, CA: Warner Home Video, 2007). DVD.

Heilman, Elizabeth E., ed. *Critical Perspectives on Harry Potter.* New York: Routledge, 2009.

Lesko, Nancy. *Act Your Age! A Cultural Construction of Adolescence.* New York: Routledge, 2001.

Levin, Diane E. and Jean Kilbourne. *So Sexy So Soon: The New Sexualized Childhood and What Parents Can Do To Protect Their Kids.* New York: Ballantine Books, 2009.

McCallum, Robyn. *Ideologies of Identity in Adolescent Fiction.* New York: Garland Publishing, 1999.

Nash, Ilana. *American Sweethearts: Teenage Girls in Twentieth Century Popular Culture.* Bloomington, IN: Indiana University Press, 2006.

Nylund, David. "Reading Harry Potter: Popular Culture, Queer Theory and the Fashioning of Youth Identity." *Journal of Systemic Therapies* 26, no. 2 (2007): 13–24.

Odem, Mary E. *Delinquent Daughters: Protecting and Policing Adolescent Female Sexuality in the United States, 1885–1920.* Chapel Hill, NC: University of North Carolina Press, 1995.

Oppliger, Patrice. *Girls Gone Skank: The Sexualization of Girls in American Culture.* Jefferson, NC: McFarland & Co, 2008.

Pipher, Mary. *Reviving Ophelia: Saving the Selves of Adolescent Girls.* New York: Penguin Group, 1994.

Pollack, William. *Real Boys: Rescuing our Sons from the Myths of Boyhood.* New York: Henry Holt and Co, 1998.

Reagan, Nancy R., ed. *Harry Potter and History.* Hoboken, NJ: John Wiley & Sons, 2011.

Rowling, J.K. *Harry Potter and the Half-Blood Prince.* New York: Scholastic, 2005.

"Rowling Says Dumbledore is Gay." Newsweek.com. *Newsweek.* October 16, 2007. Web. March 14, 2010.

Rudski, Jeffrey Michael, Carli Segal, and Eli Kallen. "Harry Potter and the End of the Road: Parallels with Addiction." *Addiction Research and Theory* 17, no. 3 (2009): 260–77.

Saad, Chris. "The Gender of Chronically Ill Characters in Children's Realistic Fiction, 1970–1994." *Sexuality & Disability* 17, no. 1 (1999): 79–93.

Shields, Stephanie A. "Gender: An Intersectionality Perspective." *Sex Roles* 59, no. 1 (2008): 301–311.

Thomas, Scott. *The Making of the Potter-verse: A Month-By-Month Look at Harry's First Ten Years.* Chicago: Independent Publishers Group, 2007.

Weeks, Jeffrey. "Discourse, Desire and Sexual Deviance." In *Culture, Society and Sexuality: A Reader,* eds. Richard Parker and Peter Aggleton. New York: Routledge, 2007.

Whited, Lana A., ed. *The Ivory Tower and Harry Potter: Perspectives on a Literary Phenomenon.* Columbia: University of Missouri Press, 2002.

4

The Pleasures of Danger and the Dangers of Pleasure: The Inversion of Gender Relations in the *Twilight* Series

Suzan Walters and Michael Kimmel

Introduction

The *Twilight* series has become a touchstone text for a generation of young Americans. Suddenly, Americans—young and old—can't get enough of vampires and werewolves. We thrill to the pleasures of danger, the dangers of romance. Women swoon over the exposed male bodies, choosing whether they are members of Team Jacob or Team Edward. Set in the context of a culture in which the sexualization of young girls has become a serious social issue, *Twilight* offers a fascinating set of literary and cinematic texts in which to explore the meaning of that sexualization for young women.

Historically, of course, the vampire trope offered a narrative of sexual seduction and loss of innocence: the worldly older man, the vampire, would bite the neck of the beautiful, virginal, young damsel, and, in drawing her blood, initiate her into the world of the undead. Deflowered, she was now eternally carnal. Vampires were sexual predators, their victims were hapless virgins.

Not so in *Twilight*. In fact, we will argue in this essay that the *Twilight* series offers a desexualized female protagonist and revels in the sexualization of men. It inverts traditional gender relations—as a way to give young girls, weary from their constant sexualization in the media and in real life, a short mental vacation. It's the guys who are sexualized—whether it's Edward, gazing longingly and pale, at the girl he loves, or Jacob, stripped to the waist, buff and sinewy.

Edward refuses to have sex with Bella—even though she wants to! Imagine a guy who is so caring that he won't have sex with the girl.

And Bella, whom they both love? She's utterly un-sexualized in her flannel shirts, shapeless jeans, and sensible shoes.

Twilight has given women the opportunity to view men on display, as men have so frequently viewed women. In this series the men are the sexual objects. For once, that sensible shoe is on the other foot. We argue that this inversion of stereotypes—both the sexualization of men and the desexualization of women—is one of the sustaining pleasures of the films and books. Indeed, we argue that the entire vampire genre is fueled in part by the desexualization of girls and the sexualization of boys. However, we do not simply assert this. We demonstrate it empirically. Based on in-depth interviews with twenty-one young women, all of whom claim to be fans of the *Twilight* series, we will explore this reversal of gender relations. We use these interview data to make a case that amidst all the sexualization of young girls, the *Twilight* series has resonated so profoundly because it turns the tables, sexualizes the boys and desexualizes the girls—and thus provides a moment's respite in an otherwise sexualized world.

Traditional Tropes

In its original telling, *Dracula* encapsulates a variety of men's anxieties about female sexuality. The vampire is, himself, the archetypal sexual predator—insatiable, his thirst for blood is a thirst for sex with virgins. Each time he drinks the blood of a young woman, we read of a blood-stained nightgown—a definitive sign of her deflowering. Dracula's seductions are epigrammatically sexual. He comes to her bedroom, where she lies, innocent and full of life. He penetrates her with his teeth; she bleeds, deflowered. The Count is aristocratic in his bearing; Stoker's language suggests an aging fop, more lugubrious than predatory. Mina describes him as "a tall, thin man, with a beaky nose and black moustache and pointed beard."[1] Jonathan Harker describes him as

> very strong, aquiline, with high bridge of the thin nose and peculiarly arched nostrils, with lofty domed forehead, and hair growing scantily round the temples but profusely elsewhere. His eyebrows were very massive, almost meeting over the nose, and with bushy hair that seemed to curl in its own profusion. The mouth, so far as I could see it under the heavy moustache, was fixed and rather cruel-looking, with peculiarly sharp white teeth. These protruded over the lips, whose remarkable ruddiness showed astonishing vitality in a man of his years. For the rest, his ears were pale, and at the tops extremely pointed. The chin was broad and strong, and the cheeks firm though thin. The general effect was one of extraordinary pallor.[2]

The Count's eyes are deep and bright, his mouth cruel, and his teeth extraordinarily white and his lips equally extraordinarily red. The characters are as drawn to him as they are repulsed by him. He is surely not sexualized; predators rarely are.

It is his prey who are sexualized. The women—Lucy and Mina—are described as voluptuous, arousing sexual desire in pretty much all the male characters (even Van Helsing, who is older, feels affection if not carnal lust). Mina is "so true, so sweet, so noble, so little an egoist."[3] She's a "pearl among women" and "precious."[4] She is pale and wan, which is desirable in a woman. "Mina is sleeping now, calmly and sweetly like a little child," writes Jonathan. "Her lips are curved and her face beams with happiness. Thank God, there are such moments still for her."[5]

For her own part, Mina sees herself as a soft and sweet damsel, whose "years teaching etiquette and decorum to other girls" have left her utterly prim and proper.[6] Lucy, too, is "looking sweetly pretty in her white lawn frock," with "a beautiful colour."[7] Writes Mina:

> I noticed that the old men did not lose any time in coming and sitting near her when we sat down. She is so sweet with old people, I think they all fell in love with her on the spot. Even my old man succumbed.[8]

Their white nightgowns imply sexual modesty and virginity. Once bitten, drops of blood on these nightgowns indicate their fall from innocent purity into animality and lust. "The sweetness was turned to adamantine, heartless cruelty, and the purity to voluptuous wantonness" and once unleashed, once deflowered, the most voraciously carnal of the vampires are the transformed women.[9] They are insatiable, lustful, and unrepentant. Lucy, especially, exacts her revenge for her own initiation into sexuality by destroying children.

> She seemed like a nightmare of Lucy as she lay there, the pointed teeth, the blood stained, voluptuous mouth, which made one shudder to see, the whole carnal and unspirited appearance, seeming like a devilish mockery of Lucy's sweet purity (Stoker 1912, 690).

Sexually voracious, she herself must now be destroyed.

In this model, women are either virgins or whores, Madonnas or, more like Madonna. Virginal and pure, she is the embodiment of virtue. When sexually aroused, she is the living incarnation of omnivorous desire, literally the vagina dentata, that will seduce and destroy men who do not destroy her first.

The Desexualization of Bella

Young women and girls are constantly sexualized in the media. From what they wear, how they move, and how they interact, they are constructed as minivixens who use their bodies and affect to arouse interest from boys and men. Indeed, some research suggests that. In this hypersexualized media context,

Bella Swan is quite a contrast. She is utterly desexualized, able to inhabit her girlhood without premature salacious femininity.

Let's start with her name. A swan is a most adult bird, long a symbol of graceful and elegant femininity. Bella, though, is less swan and more Ugly Duckling, a tripe with which young women would instantly identify. She is not yet the swan—but she will be, if she is permitted the metamorphosis on her own terms, in her own time. As a swan, Bella embodies graceful potentiality. If young girls are sexualized through their bodies, then Bella's body—always clothed, indeed, always "over-clothed," is another element of her desexualization. She doesn't wear any makeup.

In the first film of the series, *Twilight*, the viewer is introduced to Bella in Phoenix, Arizona where her mother lives. Bella is wearing a long sleeve blue shirt with a brown short sleeve flannel over it. She is wearing jeans and converse shoes. She stands in contrast to her mother who is wearing a tank top. Bella is pale, despite the sun. She wears her hair down in an unstyled fashion and she appears to have no makeup on. Not your typical adolescent female movie star. As the films progresses, we see that this is the norm for Bella. She is always clothed and maintains a simple appearance, right down to her expressions. Bella rarely smiles and her character is largely emotionless. The exception is in the second movie, *New Moon*, when there are scenes of Bella crying and screaming in her sleep (although consciously, she remains inexpressive). Even when she is devastated about Edward, the love of her life leaving her, she remains emotionless.

To add to her simple façade and non-girl-like character Bella drives an old red pick up truck that is rusted, a truck that Jacob rebuilt. In the book, Bella describes the truck as being "a faded red color, with big rounded fenders and a bulbous cab," and she says that she loves it.[10] She also works at a sporting goods store, not that she likes sports. In fact she is terrible at sports. Bella is extremely clumsy and accident prone but perhaps sporting goods is much more pleasant than women's retail for Bella. Bella hates shopping with the girls and absolutely hates dresses.

In the book we are introduced to the person Bella is through her eyes. When talking about her move from Arizona to Forks, Washington and her plans to attend a new school Bella's internal dialogue says:

> Maybe if I looked like a girl from Phoenix should, I could use this to my advantage. But physically, I'd never fit in anywhere. I *should* be tan, sporty, blond—a volleyball player, or a cheerleader, perhaps—all the things that go with living in the valley of the sun.
>
> Instead, I was ivory-skinned, without even the excuse of blue eyes or red hair, despite the constant sunshine. I had always been slender, but soft somehow, obviously not an

athlete; I didn't have the necessary eye hand coordination to play sports without humiliating myself—and harming both myself and anyone else who stood close.[11]

In almost all of the descriptions in the book of Bella's attire, Bella is wearing a hooded sweatshirt. She does not describe the typical adolescent girl routine of applying makeup before school or styling her hair. She merely throws on some clothes, eats breakfast, then jumps in her truck and drives to school. This is replicated in the films with the deviation of a few long sleeve shirts in replacement of sweatshirts. At any rate, she is always over-clothed and minimally groomed. Bella is not someone who you would label as sexy.

The young women in our study definitely notice Bella's desexualization. Fully twenty of the twenty-one respondents mentioned Bella's "plain" appearance and nineteen of them mentioned how she was dressed. And all did so approvingly. Says Keira:

> I think it's actually really funny that he is like the sex icon in the film and is not the girl. Its like Jacob, Taylor Lautner. He's like the sexy person in the film where as Kristin Stuart is never shown as sexy.

"To me she seems pretty normal in that she is your average teenager they kind of make her well I think um she looks like a plain Jane," adds Shanta. Katherine notes that Bella "is very laid back in a way and doesn't care about her looks too much as other girls really do. She didn't really stand out in high school."

The young women were particularly attentive to how Bella dresses: "From what I remember she usually is wearing like a hoodie, dark colors and I guess jeans," observed Tara. Alexia recalls that Bella is "always bundled up, has hoodies on and stuff. Rarely do you see her with like a shirt that's open that shows her chest." J'vel also notes that she wears "jeans, sweatshirts, t-shirts, nothing special," and that "she doesn't care that everything matches. It doesn't have to be fancy or of the high end." Not only her clothes, but also her natural hairstyle and the fact that Bella doesn't wear makeup are all noticed by the women in our interviews.

"I liked that she doesn't really wear makeup," says Corynna. "She kind of wears her hair natural…It's definitely different from most of the mainstream TV shows like *Gossip Girls*, which is all about the fashion." Ogechi likes the fact that Bella "doesn't try to stand out, she doesn't put on makeup, she doesn't do anything to herself." Magon summarizes these observations:

> I feel like she doesn't wear anything too crazy, you know? She wears things that are generic like jeans and sweaters, and like she doesn't wear makeup, and her hair was like you know. It kind of was similar to me, you know? Like I'm not too eccentric.

An extract of the interview with Jasmine delves further into this:

Jasmine: What I thought in the film which was different from other films is that I don't think that they over sexualized her. I mean she was thin, which is like what all actors are, but she wasn't wearing dresses. Like she was wearing normal clothes like a typical high schooler would dress.

SW: Is this appealing to you?

Jasmine: Yes because she dressed normally and she wasn't wearing makeup and was not all like done like how you would typically see. So I guess that would appeal to me more and the fact that she was not always sexy all the time and she still got a like a guy that would work for her and constantly be there and stuff.

Twelve respondents explicitly contrasted Bella's depiction to other media depictions of young women and girls, in which, respondents claimed, women and girls were "sluttier" and their clothes "skimpy." Contrasts ranged from *iCarly* and other Nickelodeon television shows to this comment from Katherine about *Mean Girls:*

I do I like that because movies like *Mean Girls* it all about like the weird clothes and the sluttly clothes, whatever, and she is more conservative in how she dresses and I think its better as a role model, I'd say for girls, because they see *Mean Girls* and they think we have to dress like this but in *Twilight* she's saying "Hey you can wear jeans sneakers and a sweatshirt," so I think it's a good thing.

Although she didn't refer to a specific film, Ansley contrasted Bella to a genre of sexualized young women when she said:

I guess she is a lot less sexualized, which is nice that she doesn't, you know. I feel like whenever women are in movies they pop up and it's like big boobs. At least the leading character that the really cute guy falls in love with it's kind of like, I don't know, they never look they are covering themselves up and she definitely looks like that. Like she is always wearing long sleeves, probably because they are in Washington but, and I like that I like that she is not over sexed.

Several of the respondents developed a theory about Bella's desexualization as a deliberate Hollywood ploy to entice female viewers. Keira, for example, says:

I think the reason why they do that now that I think about it is so that more girls can relate to her because ff she was Angelina Jolie or something people are gonna be like well I'm not Angelina Jolie. I could never be Angelina Jolie. It has to be someone the girls can identify with in terms of being an average girl.

Perhaps the most telling element in Bella's desexualization is her self-identification as desexualized. She does not see herself as attractive, but rather as a plain and normal high school girl. Her very plainness, of course, is what enables millions of young women and girls to identify with her. When asked if Bella sees herself as sexually attractive, Sarah replies:

Not really because I don't think she thinks that she is. She goes on about how she's very plain looking and um she goes on about how there is nothing extraordinary about her so no I don't think she presents herself that way because I don't think she sees herself that way.

Bella's desexualization renders her simultaneously atypical and familiar. On the one hand, it feels entirely dissimilar to the depictions of femininity in the media, the hyper-sexualization of girls and women. On the other hand, it feels familiar, comfortable, and in that lies her attraction to young women. As Arielle puts it: "She doesn't care how she looks. She is normal." And Crystal completes the identification: "I am totally like her." To be "totally like her" means to be normal, desexualized, a plain Jane. But it also enables an identification that is non-competitive: Bella's plainness means that Edward and Jacob could fall for any "plain Jane" and that Bella doesn't possess anything particularly special. That means that all readers and viewers are potential partners for Edward and Jacob. Bella may be, as young girls consider themselves, an Ugly Duckling. But when loved by the right man, we know she—and we—will be swans.

The Sexualization of Jacob and Edward

On the other hand, the young men in the series are already swans. Perhaps "swans" is not the right word. Closer to stallions. First, there is Jacob Black, the tan, buff, Native American/werewolf, whose bare chest reveals a taut, lean, and muscular body, and a barely contained animalistic passion and energy. And then there's Edward Cullen, the pallid, brooding, sensitive vampire/man, morose under the weight of his secret, which handcuffs him with an enormous sense of guilt and responsibility. Two contrasting visions of romantic masculinity: on the one hand, the distant sensitive brooder, who can be reached emotionally only by a woman who cares so deeply as to enable him to shed his terrible burden and trust again, and, on the other hand, the tensile strength of the passionate animal, who can be tamed only by the love of a good woman.

In the books, Edward and Jacob are described in traditionally gendered terms. Indeed, they represent the two most persistent tropes in representations of masculinity: animalistic power and passion vs. rational control. Jacob is the former: an exotic Native American werewolf who is tall, dark, and handsome, to say the least. In *Eclipse*, Bella says:

The laughter in his deep-set black eyes, the feverish heat of his big hand around mine, the flash of his white teeth against his dark skin, his face stretching into a wide smile that had always been like a key to a secret door where only the kindred spirits could enter. (Meyer, 2007, 71)

Later in the book we get to see a different side of Jacob when Bella describes a scene where Jacob arrives at her school to talk to her and Edward. She says she notices Jacob's face as Edward and she walk toward Jacob. She further states that she:

> Notices other faces too—the faces of my classmates. I noticed how their eyes widened as they took in all six foot seven inches of Jacob's long body, muscled up the way no normal sixteen-and-a-half-year-old ever had been. I saw those eyes rake over his tight black t-shirt—short-sleeved, though the day was unseasonable cool—his ragged, grease-smeared jeans, and the glossy black bike he leaned against. Their eyes didn't linger on his face—something about his expression had them glancing quickly away. And I noticed the wide berth everyone gave him, the bubble of space that no one dared to encroach on.[12]

While Jacob is the safe friend that Bella can always count on and confide in, he is also rugged, strong, dangerous. Jacob is unpredictable, reckless even. He is wild and exotic. He is nature, natural manhood.

Edward, on the other hand, is culture to Jacob's nature. He is always in control. Edward never looses his temper like Jacob does. He is always rational and calculating, never emotional and volatile. This is because Edward is so strong and powerful that he must not lose control. He controls his animal passions, his blood lust. And he resists Bella's sensuality. Edward has been alive for over a hundred years and has had plenty of time to practice his self-control. He has reined in his carnal instincts and lust for blood. He is now a "good" vampire, a vampire with a soul. Edward and his family never drink the blood of humans. Instead they are "vegetarian"; they only eat animals. Edward compares this to a human only eating tofu.

When Bella describes Edward it is generally in reference to his perfection and often she contrasts him to her. Bella sees Edward as perfect and herself as undeserving, since she is far from perfect. This can be seen when Bella describes Edward with his shirt unbuttoned. She says,

> His white shirt was sleeveless and he wore it unbuttoned, so that the smooth white skin of his throat flowed uninterrupted over the marble contours of his chest, his perfect musculature no longer merely hinted at behind concealing clothes. He was too perfect, I realized with a piercing stab of despair. There was no way this godlike creature could be meant for me.[13]

Edward is Bella's true love. She swoons at his every move. He is flawless in her eyes. In the third book she describes Edward again. She had not seen Edward for some time and he is finally back to be with her. She says,

> Time had not made me immune to the perfection of his face, and I was sure that I would never take any aspect of him for granted. My eyes traced over his pale white features; the hard square of his jaw, the soft curve of his full lips—twisted up into a smile, the straight line of his nose, the sharp angle of his cheekbones, the smooth marble span of his forehead—partially obscured by a tangle of rain-darkened bronze hair...

I saved his eyes for last, knowing that when I looked into them I was likely to lose my train of thought. They were wide, warm with liquid gold, and framed by a thick fringe of black lashes. Staring into his eyes always made me feel extraordinary—sort of like my bones were turning spongy. I was also a little lightheaded, but that could have been because I'd forgotten to keep breathing. Again.[14]

The real contrast between the two men is highlighted in the movies. Jacob spends most of his time shirtless. The other males in the wolf pack never have their shirts on either. In fact, they are clothed less than Jacob is. The wolves are completely sexualized. They even eat dinner, at the table, shirtless. When the food gets placed on the table they frantically grab for it. They are savage and ravenous.[15] Conversely, Edward is pristine. Edward is perfectly dressed. His skin is usually covered but the clothes fit tightly. His hair is never out of place and his eyebrows are perfectly shaped. When Edward sits or stands he has flawless posture. He is well-mannered and polite.

Of course their beings describe all of their mannerisms. Jacob is a werewolf and werewolves are "naturally" hot. As Jacob says, he "run[s] at a toasty one-oh-eight point nine these days" when discussing his body temperature.[16] Jacob is hot like fire, literally. Thus, he encompasses everything that fire does. He is passionate, warm, powerful, wild, and uncontrollable. Edward on the other hand is a vampire and his body is cold as ice. He is frozen, still, and piercing. The two men encompass very different images of masculinity, both images are eroticized by young women.

It is not coincidental that Edward's origins are in the European aristocracy: the man of rational control, prim and flawless, and ageless. Jacob's origins are in nature: Native Americans are perceived as closer to the earth, closer to its primal rhythms, more sensual, more animated by naturalistic passions. In western literature, this contrast has been the backbone of countless historical novels—and, indeed, the historical narratives of British textbooks—for generations, re-telling the story of how civilization tamed nature through the application of rational self-control over animalistic passions. Indeed, it is the Freudian take of how each individual must use the rational ego to tame the impulsive, sexual libido.

"Team Edward" and "Team Jacob" Spell Team/Teen Lust

In cyberspace, young women square off into "Team Edward" and "Team Jacob" as they define their somatic soul mate. But our respondents were more attuned visually to the cinematographic representations. And the overwhelming majority expressed a smoldering desire for Jacob. "Edward is so pale to me. He's a handsome boy, but he is just so pale," explains Tara. "Now Jacob, he is, oh, he is so sexy. Jacob, ya!" Maggie says she prefers Jacob as well:

He is very, very muscular. I like that and his face is just very, his face is nicer. He is manlier than Edward is to me. More masculine. Edward seemed a little on the feminine side.

In her preference for Jacob, Maggie feminizes Edward, to further draw out the contrast. And what about Jacob that makes him so desirable is his sexualization. While Bella remains fully clothed—indeed, she wears more clothes than most high school girls these days, hiding beneath her hoodie and baggy jeans—Jacob takes his shirt off. Indeed, half of our respondents pointed directly to the scenes in which Jacob has his shirt off. As Magon put it, "Yes because I guess really what it was, was when he had his shirt off 'cus that was crazy. Because his abs it's really muscular and stuff." And Sam recalled a scene in which Jacob resembles a female porn star:

SW: Are there particular parts of the film you find to be more inciting?

Sam: Like every time he takes off his shirt to like switch into like wolf mode. Like I remember the time when he came out the water I was like "Oh ya, you're dripping with water" like that was cool.

A few of our respondents pointed to other elements that made Jacob stand out—his hair, his smile, his face, for example. "I don't know if it was his tan or what but his hair was beautiful in the first film," noted Katherine. "I mean ya he has a nice body," says Ogechi. "He has a good face on that body." Tiffany points to these other features: "Definitely his physique, insane, his smile, insane (sighs) he is just so hot and I guess his character in the movie is very like manly and like kind of rugged," she says. But eventually, she, too, circles back to his shirtless body:

SW: Are there particular scenes that you prefer or like in terms of Jacob being sexy?

Tiffany: When his shirt is off when he is turning into a werewolf.

Jen explained that it was precisely Jacob's sexualization—and Bella's desexualization—that brought her into the theater in the first place. "I prefer Jacob because he's like tan, muscular."

SW: Is that part of why you watch the film?

Jen: Ya I actually watched the film to see him. That was the only reason why I saw *New Moon* because, like in the [coming] attractions he looked so hot, I was, like, I have to see it. I want Bella to get with him even though I think he should be with someone a little cuter like me.

The De-Erotics of Male Sexualization

The visceral pleasures of male sexual objectification and the emotional relief of female desexualized subjectification is a central component in the success of the *Twilight* series. But that sexual objectification of men must also be accompanied by the same dynamic that accompanies female sexual objectification: by being turned into a sexual object, an object of desire, women are stripped of sexual agency and can act, sexually, only in response to the initiation of desire from a man. Being the object means forgoing being a subject.

With the reversal augured by the *Twilight* series, though, this runs afoul of traditional gender arrangements. Men are the sexual actors. Indeed, in the traditional vampire stories, males are voracious sexual predators, wanton seducers, and women, while enticing sexual objects, have no sexual agency of their own. (Of course, this trope has been an effective way to enable women to experience their desire and not have to take responsibility for it—that is to enable them to be both carnal and innocent, to have their sexual cake and eat it too—even if it's someone else who is drinking their blood.)

Unlike most of our respondents, of course, Bella falls for Edward (though it is certainly nice to have a hunk like Jacob around just in case she either wants a FWB or a booty call). And Edward—sexualized, and, by literary tradition, a bloodthirsty, carnal, predator—does not try to have sex with Bella. Indeed, he resists it. He rebuffs her efforts at seduction, and parries her entreaties for sex. Desexualized, Bella can claim her sexual agency. Sexualized, Edward cannot reciprocate corporeally. In a media-dominated world saturated with hypersexualized images of women-as-sexual object and in their day-to-day interactions with young men who seem to be constantly on the make, the sexualization of the body of Edward and Jacob is coupled with—and, we argue, *necessarily* coupled with—their behavioral desexualization. They are the sexual objects; they cannot act sexually.

And, of course, this makes them even *more* exciting to female viewers. All but two of our respondents commented on how much they appreciated that Edward did not take advantage of Bella's attraction to him, that he remained a gentleman, that he didn't want to have sex *because he cared so much about her*. As Corynna explains, it was because "he had strength over her he didn't want to hurt her and even though she pushed for it which shows that in a way she really did love her because he didn't want to hurt her." "I think that's good," says Sam. "You don't see most guys like that like if you're not doing anything they are like 'oh well can't talk to you anymore.' They disappear." Natasha agrees:

> No man should really rush a girl to have sex because it's really a decision between the two of you. It's not like 'oh well, I say so, let's go' it's like if I am not ready then I am not ready. You can wait till I am ready. If you love me you will wait and because Edward can show that it shows that he really does really love her he doesn't you know just like her for now 'cus like you know at one point in the book she feels like well that he was just there because like you know just like using her. But he does love her more

than anything in the world. He loves her more than himself. He would like kill himself for her.

"It's usually the other way around it's the woman trying to hold off not the man," notes Alexia. "Since it's him I guess it's attractive."

In texts, too, as Arielle explains, the man is more predatory. "When I read that in the book it shocked me a bit," Maggie recalls. "Because you know the stereotypical guy wouldn't really turn down a sure thing with his girlfriend so it was very off kilter when I read that I was like oh, that's a little different." "In most books you wouldn't even see that or anything. You would see a girl wanting to have sex and a guy jumping on it. But also it's like the fact that he thought he would hurt her, I don't know, I think that because he is older and because he is a vampire and everything he has those manners, like old-fashioned manners, and I like that."

Ironically, it is the utterly unscrupulous predator—Edward *is* a vampire, remember?—who has the manners, Arielle tells us; Edward is the bearer of morality in the topsy-turvy world of the *Twilight* series. J'vel notes that "the average guy that you meet isn't like that and then growing up with the morals and the backgrounds in the church, you know? You would want that in a guy. Yes there are other guys that you could find out there but the majority of them aren't, so it's sort of respectable."

Respectable—and completely different from the more common sexual arrangements in these young women's lives—both in the movies they watch and in the interactions they have with young men in their lives. It's so different, that Tara labels Edward "alternative" as if he were some alt-rock band.

> SW: What do you think about Edward not having sex with Bella when she asks to have sex with him?
>
> Tara: I think that's very alternative because usually I would think he would try to force it upon her that's the one movie that I think I've seen where a guy is telling her to wait. I think it's very different she is pushing herself on him.
>
> SW: Is that sexy for you?
>
> Tara: That is actually very, I think it's very cute, ya that's sexy.
>
> SW: Is that something that you would look for in a partner and why?
>
> Tara: Ya because I'm a virgin and usually when you like talk to guys, especially the guys like around our age, it's like they chase after you because you're a virgin so they can kind of like de-flower you I guess if you want to call it. I only had one guy in my life that wanted me to wait so it's very different when a guy is kind of on the same level that you are knowing that you want to wait till I guess you find that love or get married, whatever, so it's very attractive to find someone on the same level as you.
>
> SW: So generally you don't find that with men here?

> Tara: Men here no matter what nationality or race or anything. Guys is like if you're a virgin they either will put up with you for like a bit of time thinking they can kind of like persuade you. When they know they can't get anything out of you they are totally over you so the fact that he's in love with and hasn't really had any physical contact with her, I think that's so cute. That's one reason why I also watch the movie.

What is crucial for Tara is that, as a virgin, she requires that respect, that commitment. Sex for these young women is serious, loving, and committed. For men, in their eyes, sex is spontaneous, random, and physical. Edward's feminine sexuality is coupled with his sexual objectification to make a truly compelling romantic character.

"I like that he made that decision," explains Crystal. "It makes me feel like he is not in it for that like I feel like it's a lot deeper where he comes from where she is like yearning for it and she wants it but he's just like don't rush this I am here because I love you like genuinely I feel like that's when Bella was, like, oh, when she figured that out from him. I like that." If it's "a lot deeper" where Edward comes from, then women, as the consumers of textual pleasures, can be more "like, Oh."

Conclusion

In contemporary social life, the male is the pursuer, the women the pursued. In the original vampire stories, this contemporary reality is exaggerated to the point of hysterical hyperbole: Dracula is pure predator, defiling as he deflowers swooningly luscious virginal damsels. They are alive, their bosoms heaving with smoldering desire. Through sex, he brings them death. In the original story, Mina writes in her journal what she imagines may be the future of gender relations. She imagines women having more power; she writes about Lucy, seemingly returned to the flock:

> Lucy is asleep and breathing softly. She has more colour in her cheeks than usual, and looks, oh so sweet. If Mr. Holmwood fell in love with her seeing her only in the drawing room, I wonder what he would say if he saw her now. Some of the 'New Women' writers will some day start an idea that men and women should be allowed to see each other asleep before proposing or accepting. But I suppose the 'New Woman' won't condescend in future to accept. She will do the proposing herself. And a nice job she will make of it too! There's some consolation in that.[17]

Mina anticipates the *Twilight* series in that prescient paragraph. Yes, those New Women writers enable women to do the proposing themselves. Indeed, women can ask for it, beg for it, and take it. But women's agency comes with both benefits and costs. The benefits are obvious—and continue to delight its millions of female consumers. In this new world of greater female agency, neither male nor female is predatory, their love is mutual—and pure. Bella retains her subjectivity through desexualization; Edward and Jacob become corporeal through their sexualization. But their sexualization allows them also to rise above it, to be moral, to resist sex. Through resisting sex, Edward can actually remain alive.

The *Twilight* series, we argue, thus represents a contradictory experience for female viewers, a midpoint in a centuries-long process of female sexual emancipation. In one sense, it turns the tables on the traditional notions of female sexual objectification, rendering the female protagonist desexualized—as a point of entry for identification by young women. Bella is in possession of her subjectivity. Part of that subjectivity is the capacity to objectify, to experience the visceral pleasure of seeing the other as a sexual object. And in this case, both Edward and Jacob are sexualized so that they may be the object of the female gaze.

But there are costs to this reversal of subjectivities and sexualizations. And one of those costs is that nobody gets laid. Bella is desexualized but wants sex; Edward and Jacob are sexualized but don't want sex. Or, more precisely, they do want it, but they are far too gallant to actually have it. In the *Twilight* world, you can look, but you can't touch—no matter how much you actually might want it.

Notes

1.   Bram Stoker, *Dracula* (London: Archibald Constable & Co., 1897), 556.
2.   Ibid., 59-60.
3.   Ibid., 608.
4.   Ibid., 352, 780.
5.   Ibid., 1051.
6.   Ibid., 555.
7.   Ibid., 210.
8.   Ibid., 210.
9.   Ibid., 680.
10.   Meyer, *Twilight*, 8.
11.   Ibid., 10.
12.   Meyer, *Eclipse*, 77.
13.   Meyer, *Twilight*, 246.
14.   Meyer, *Eclipse*, 17.
15.   Chris Weitz, *The Twilight Sage: New Moon*, eds. Wyck Goofrey and Karen Rosenfelt (California: Summit Entertainment, 2009).
16.   Meyer, *Eclipse*, 490.
17.   Stoker, *Dracula*, 294.

Works Cited

Meyer, Stephanie. *Twilight*. First ed. New York: Hachette Book Group USA, 2005.
———. *New Moon*. First ed. New York: Hachette Book Group USA, 2006.
———. *Eclipse*. First ed. New York: Hachette Book Group USA, 2007.
———. *Breaking Dawn*. First ed. New York: Hachette Book Group USA, 2008.

Stoker, Bram. *Dracula*. London: Archibald Constable & Co., 1897.

Twilight, directed by Catherine Hardwicke (2008; California: Summit Entertainment, 2009). DVD.

The Twilight Saga: New Moon, directed by Chris Weitz (2009; California: Summit Entertainment, 2010). DVD.

The Twilight Saga: Eclipse, directed by (2010; California: Summit Entertainment, 2010). DVD.

5

"She's All That": Girl Sexuality and Teen Film

Catherine Driscoll

Sex as a social function, as a developmental proposition, and as an idea about pleasure and desire, is undeniably pivotal to modern adolescence. Few things seem more central than sexuality to the disciplines, images, and rhetorics that elaborate the importance of adolescence to modern subjectivity. And the emergence of modern adolescence can be mapped by changing ideas about sex as new distinctions between minority and children and between physical and social maturity emerged in legislation, political philosophy, psychology, and popular genres. These distinctions formed a duration ripe for narrative.[1] While an older but newly ambivalent marker of puberty continued to distinguish childhood, the "age of sexual consent" emerged to locate "sexual maturity" in late puberty and situate various forms of "mature" education not only as *before* sex but in important respects as *about* sex. This is the history within which I want to locate teen film, but my aim in this essay is not only to closely consider how sex defined by sexuality works in teen film but also to argue that the sex characterizing teen film operates, both as psychological drama and as pedagogy of citizenship, on particular premises about girl sexuality. Thus, this essay aims not only to contribute to how we understand teen film but also to challenge the ways we think about the continually fraught public subject of girl sexuality.

Sex in Teen Film

There is no such thing as a teen film that does not include sex, even if there is no sex on screen. At this level, the sex of teen film is a field of possible identi-

ties defined by gendered attitudes toward sex. The genre's unfolding history has
been closely tied to the repetition, monitoring, and entertaining disruption of
gendered sex roles presumed to be integral to the production of viable social
identity. A cluster of questions about the sex of girls dominate the earliest forms
of teen film, including the flapper films of the 1920s, such as the Clara Bow
vehicles *The Plastic Age* (1925) and *The Wild Party* (1929), and the later 'bobby-
soxer' movies, such as the teen Shirley Temple vehicles *Kiss and Tell* (1945) and
The Bachelor and the Bobby-Soxer (1947). These are not only questions concerning
whether or not X girl is having sex but also questions about what sex means
that the genre presumes are particularly weighty for girls. Teen film plays out
the questionable sex of girls in relation to a developmental narrative for which
sex names multiple possible but not predetermined markers.

My selection of the U.S. film *She's All That* (1999) as a central example for
this discussion is fairly arbitrary. Nothing about this film especially singles it
out. The style and narrative are generic teen film. Popular boy Zac is dumped
by his popular girlfriend and bets a manipulative friend that he can easily make
another popular girl out of geek Laney. While Zac grooms Laney for the prom
they fall in love. The manipulative friend reveals the bet, Laney rejects Zac, and
before they can be reunited Zac must admit to the lessons in self-respect she
has taught him and Laney must learn to trust him again. The film opens with
heroine Laney's social protest art, singling her out as the "scary inaccessible"
girl and thus as the kind of school-hall "freak" to which 1980s U.S. teen film
had given new narrative credibility. As *Not Another Teen Movie* (2001) would
mockingly have it two years later, Laney is one of those "pretty ugly" heroines
whose make-over is coming from the very first shot and, just as generically, that
makeover both produces and reflects the awakening of her sexuality at Zac's
attention. Like most mainstream teen films across the genre's history, *She's All
That* both fulfills and laughs at the clichés on which its plot depends. This use,
rather than repetition, of generic cliché is most obvious in the scene where
Laney's "pretty ugly" status is affirmed. Removing her glasses and cutting her
hair transforms her from unattractive loser to prom queen material, but her
dramatic staircase entrance to Zac's/the camera's admiring gaze is undercut
when she falls down the stairs because she is not wearing her glasses. *Not Another Teen Movie* emphasizes the cliché in just this undercutting and has Janey fall
through the floor and destroy the house. The central plot of *Not Another Teen
Movie* is in fact taken from *She's All That*, attesting to the latter film's representing the state of the genre at the end of the twentieth century. What I want to
highlight here, however, is the centrality to this use of one convention teen film
routinely cites but rarely fulfills—sex as a transformative rite of passage.

Teen films focus on rites of passage that mark the achievement of a limited independence that, at the same time, does not produce adulthood. They offer no transition to adulthood because the protagonists of teen film must remain adolescent even at the end of the film. While the most obvious examples are institutional ones, like high school graduation or learning to drive, many explicitly revolve around sex, itself determined by a kind of licensing system in the age of consent. Virginity is a particularly important narrative device of this type in teen film, tracing the sexualized form of a supposedly linear trajectory even while operating as an in no way inevitable point of adolescent transformation. Virginity represents both the expert licensing of maturity—a transformation officially permitted only at a certain point—and that licensing system's representational sleight of hand. Virginity and the age of consent circle one another in teen film—distinct but not opposed, attached but not complementary. This tension also exemplifies the ways in which rites of passage are central to coming-of-age in teen film as a narrative that cannot be completed. As Greg Tuck puts it, "the virgin/nonvirgin boundary is not traversed in a single moment through a single act."[2] Many critics have noticed the importance of virginity plots in teen film. Timothy Shary claims losing virginity was "The most common plot of youth sex films throughout the early 1980s."[3] And the gendering of the virginity trope is also often discussed. But this is all too quickly reduced to that famous "double standard" in which sex adds value to boys and removes it from girls. The relation between virginity and consent in teen film needs another frame of reference than historical and generic associations with protecting the virginity of girls by questioning their capacity to consent. To begin with, passing the age of consent in a teen film signifies neither maturity nor any other version of readiness for sex. Culturally established prohibited activities defining virginity differ from legal limits that restrict sexual activity but it is never literally virginity or the age of consent that is at stake in teen film, but instead they together sketch a set of opportunities for negotiating what sex is wanted, available, and means.

For Shary, the dominant themes of teen film are either 'sex, school and delinquency' or 'delinquency, romance and schooling.'[4] He does not discuss this slippage between sex and romance but it reveals something important, especially in dialogue with those other more stable categories that describe how youth functions as public problem. As Shary's slippage suggests, the sex of teen film turns on a dialectical relation between sex and romance—terms tied together as opposing but complementary social forces that together expose a fraught contradiction in the meaning of both for adolescent development. Gender is a way of naming this contradiction but not because girls want romance and boys want sex, although this is another cliché teen film both embraces and ridicules. The relation between sex and romance in teen film is primarily an ethical distinction. *She's All That* turns on a sexual wager plot. Such narratives usually begin with a bet as to who can "lose it" first or win sex with someone in particular. Across the long history of sexual wager films as varied as *G.I. Blues* (1960) and *Cruel Intentions* (1999), those making such wagers are routinely taught that sex should have emotional content, presuming an audience that will feel the same. These films are generally comedies that downplay the ethical problem of what can be traded for sex by staging the wager as one between peers too immature to realize their mistake at first. Critics like Shary and Roz Kaveney suggest that comedy is thus used to avoid exposing something too telling about the gendered system of power in which adolescent sex appears.[5] But the sexual wager films overwhelmingly insist on the cost of treating relationships like tradeable objects.

In Ronald Maxwell's *Little Darlings* (1980), rich girl Ferris and poor girl Angel join girls from diverse backgrounds at summer camp. Ferris and Angel, both fifteen and thus importantly below the age of sexual consent for the film's main audience, stake their peer group credibility on a competition to see who can lose their virginity first. As Lisa Dresner notes, *Little Darlings* distinguishes between male and female relations to sex but it also suggests that sex has a negotiable and thus unstable meaning for adolescent girls.[6] The other girls at camp, some of whom claim to be sexually active (but are later revealed to be lying) and some of whom declare themselves virgins, form support teams. As this is a girls' camp the options for male sexual partners are few (the possibility that the girls—at least Angel—could be lesbian is raised early and vigorously dismissed). Ferris decides on one of the camp counsellors and Angel on a boy from a neighboring camp. Ferris is rejected but for a while allows the other girls to think she had sex anyway. Angel, after a series of tense experimental scenes, does have sex, but finds it an emotionally affecting experience and tells the other girls it never happened. The bet is cancelled, camp ends, and Ferris and Angel return to their lives apparently more mature, but certainly still not adults. While Ferris and Angel learn that sex does not make them women it is clearly suggested that sex makes Angel more mature: she chastises her mother for saying sex is "nothing," insisting she must have been "hanging around creeps." This contradictory relation between sex and maturity is not only typical of teen film but gestures toward the important role played by sex in negotiating the meaning of modern adolescence. In the end, while Ferris merely seems embarrassed by her own immaturity, Angel now has sufficient wisdom to correct her mother's negative attitude to sex. This contradictory closing scene is crucial because maturity is never resolved for teen film—that is, in a teen film it is never entirely clear what constitutes maturity or who has it. And no teen film resolves the problem of where and how sexuality arrives either. Both are problems cast into sharp relief by adolescence but not presumed to be inevitably parts of growing older.

None of this complexity explains why teen film's representation of sexuality has such a bad reputation. Thomas Doherty, Shary, and Kaveney all attack the genre as generically sexist and homophobic.[7] As *Little Darlings* suggests, the heterosexuality of teen film is tightly bound to its simultaneously generational and developmental presumptions. It seems impossible to disentangle the workings of gender and heterosexuality in teen film so that "queer" teen film continues to be a slippery generic mutation. Alternatives to heterosexuality are widely confined to secondary characters or to comic or tragic dead ends. While the field of scholarship on teen film is relatively small, within it considerable attention has recently been paid to the possibility of queer teen film.[8] But these "queer" narratives remain relative to, even reinforcing, the dominant teen film story about heterosexual coming-of-age. This is in no way to devalue the importance of coming-of-age and coming-out stories to their audiences or even to the teen film genre. Susan Driver may well be right to stress the power of fiction to make non-normative sexuality comprehensible, if not permissible, and film has the added impact of putting these representations into a popular public domain.[9] But a pivotal difference between coming-out and coming-of-age intervenes in the queer teen film. In teen film heterosexual sex is a statement about identity in process where no sexual statement or position is the last word—the closure of adolescence that teen film avoids. The coming-out statement instead wagers that sex is *identity* rather than adolescence. The tension between the queer coming-out story and teen film coming-of-age stories is also grounded in the importance of heterosexual development and sociality to mainstream teen film representations of sex relative to film classification, but the impossibility of exchanging this "queer" sex for any *unclosed* knowledge about maturity also means that queer sex is very difficult to center in teen film narrative. In this context it is important that lesbian identity or sex are less common in teen films than the gay male equivalents. If sex in teen film is transformative but never finally so this is most crucially true of girls.

It is tempting here, perhaps via gender theorist Judith Butler's account of gender as radically exclusionary, to push this discussion back to the psychoanalytic theories of development that directly shaped teen film.[10] For Sigmund Freud, adolescence was not a passage into adult roles for which childhood had been a training ground. Instead it was a complicated clash between new sexual capacity, already conflicting and often inexpressible fears, ideals, and desires built up and elaborated in childhood, and new social expectations built into immanent adulthood. At the same time, Freud's narrative about the production of sexuality through processes of identification especially associated the lateral sharing of identification which does not produce individual unique identity with girls.[11] *The Bachelor and the Bobby-soxer*'s citation of Freud would be an explicit example of this influence, but *She's All That* certainly continues loosely psychoanalytic accounts of development and identification in relation to parents and groups. Kaveney both rejects such "easy" Freudian readings of teen film and yet explicates teen film sex through the Freudian concept of "polymorphous perversity."[12] In teen film, Kaveney argues, anyone can *potentially* be paired with anyone else. This does not deny the privileging of heterosexuality in teen film because Kaveney excludes from the genre any films which are not centrally about heterosexuality. While emphasizing the importance of homoerotic possibilities in teen film she argues that the "queer" film about adolescence is insufficiently "polymorphous," by which she means not *subtextually* perverse. Regardless of how useful this is or isn't as a reading of Freud, teen film's presumption that heterosexual closure is a norm does not categorically preclude queer teen film. To also work as queer a teen film, as with *Saved!* (2004), must allow queer sexuality to be incomplete and thus available to teen film stories about (im)maturity.

Visible Articulations; Articulating Visibility

The sex of teen film is a question concerning visibility, which means more than assessing what representations are available—of sexual desire for girls or adolescence for kids who aren't straight. Many teen film narratives can be paraphrased as a series of lessons concerning what can be known through and about sex. What can be seen and what can be said of sex are not just questions one can ask of teen film, they are questions teen films repeatedly ask. Here I'm employing two key terms from Gilles Deleuze's reading of Michel Foucault: the visible and the articulable.[13] On the one hand these seem tailor-made for talking about how any film meets an audience, allowing consideration of the documentary and speculative possibilities of film through analysis of the relations between what is seen to be said and said to be seen. But these terms are especially apt for considering the sex of teen film because of the simultaneously internal and external forms of regulation and disruption it involves. Perhaps such an approach seems too tightly tied to semiotics to disrupt the primacy of the statement—in this case, what counts as good/permissible sex.[14] The relation between what can be seen and what can be said about adolescent sexuality is brought into sharp relief by teen film, where what's *visible* as the possible sex of teen film is a field of uncloseable questions even if what's *articulable* as the sex of teen film is a story about development. There's no denying the authority of the developmental statement over teen film. It operates at textual and meta-textual, cinematic and post-cinematic, levels. In all these registers if the sex of teen film is pedagogical it teaches less normative sexuality than the problematic relations to normative sexuality that good citizens should have.

I want to trouble any teleological historical understanding of this problematic normativity by stepping back to the teen film of another generation. Histories of teen film dominate scholarship on the genre, often presuming that they reflect, in a naively mimetic sense, the forms of teenage life around them. *Gidget* (1959) is not only an important milestone in the representation of girls in teen film but also surprisingly explicit about the good girl's sex life. The components of Gidget's story—the tomboy who discovers her femininity, the geek whose prettiness is revealed by a makeover, the outsider girl whose sporting rather than sophisticated attitude wins the boy's heart—remain key motifs representing girl sexuality in teen film. They both establish and disrupt the equation between ideal gender performance and successful sexuality. Doherty and many others position *Gidget* as a typical middle-class "clean teen" narrative,[15] but the clean-ness of Gidget is easily exaggerated. Frances is a sixteen-year-old tomboy whose friends have discovered sex (which means flirting, dating, "making out" and "going steady," and, as risky but explicitly possible behavior, intercourse). They want her to join in chasing boys, but Frances is a girl geek who thinks catching waves seems more fun. But she simultaneously determines to learn to surf and falls in love. Alison Whitney describes Gidget as "free of drugs, alcohol, and other vices, sexually inhibited and respectful of [her] parents."[16] But interest in sex turns out to be a good idea for *Gidget* even while apparently innate virtue protects her from the ramifications of all the moments where she actually chooses sex.

Reflecting on *Gidget*, or *Where the Boys Are* (1960), raises many questions about the sexual liberation story characterizing teen film histories.[17] The equally prevalent critical story about teen film of the 1990s closing down comedic sexual narratives seems equally dubious in this historical frame. For both Doherty and Shary, the disappearance of the crude sex face from teen film reflects the impact of AIDS awareness, which led to "a marked shift in the [late 1980s] teen sex film from promiscuity to romance."[18] In fact, while public discourse on sex consistently impacts on teen film, in the '90s as always it worked with and on existing generic tendencies.

She's All That typically represents a shift in attitudes toward sex as having already happened and clarifies this shift as centrally gendered. In every film I've cited thus far an already established change that is nevertheless meant to surprise is represented by girls who manipulate and bully as openly as boys and boys who are no more consistently instrumental in their use of sex than girls. In *She's All That*, the villainess, Taylor, is the only girl we know has sex. The title "she's all that" appears in the film as a description of what Taylor thinks about

herself; explaining why she is cruel and sexually manipulative. That it also describes Zac's romantic idealization of Laney establishes the importance of an
opposition less between Taylor and Laney than between Taylor's and Zac's ideas about sex. It remains remarkable that the hit U.S. sexual wager films of
1999—*She's All That*, *American Pie*, and *Cruel Intentions*—tell similar stories about
the recent arrival of girls' sexual authority and aggressivity and the hidden truth
of any worthwhile boy's willingness to put feeling first as do *The Plastic Age*,
Gidget, *Where the Boys Are*, and *Little Darlings*. In fact, girls' "new" access to sex is
a dominant motif across the history of teen film. Certainly films like *American
Pie* or *Porky's* (1982) tell different stories about sex than *Gidget* or *She's All That*.
They luxuriate in what Jonathan Bernstein calls "grossout" comedy especially
focused on sex.[19] But the focus on learning sex for citizenship remains even
here and proceeds through the same twists on gender expectations the genre
suggests are expected to be twisted.[20]

   If it seems too obvious to be worth closer consideration that citizenship is
mapped onto maturity, teen film's representation of this educational process for
adolescents places considerable weight on sex in the impossible task of marking
progress toward this goal. Of course there are markers of citizenship—
checkpoints and permits like the age of consent and graduation—but modern
adolescence is fragmented rather than cohered by these markers and the con-
tingency and multiplicity of milestones for sexual citizenship don't merely ex-
emplify this liminality but are its rationale.[21] This brings me to the interplay
between the way sex centrally positions films in a classification system and the
way classificatory systems depend on ideas about adolescence as a gendered
account of sex. Classification brings the training and citizenship narratives of
teen film into a new sort of visibility. The clean-ness of certain teen films is not
so much established by their sale-ability, as Doherty argues, as by teen film elements packaged to invoke a "general audience" defined as a symbolic family
centered on the monitoring of adolescence.[22] Sex is crucial to this idea of adolescence. To be cleanly teen the genre's characteristic reference to sex must not
include realistic expectations of sex, even if these expectations are set aside only
by a fantasy setting.

   Sixteen Candles (1984) is an interesting case, in part because it foregrounds a
line between adolescents who need "parental guidance" and those who might
not. In *Sixteen Candles*, a series of accidents make the heroine Sam's sixteenth
birthday a turning point despite it having been forgotten by her family under
the shadow of her sister's wedding. The day brings her into new proximity with
two boys from school—The Geek, who desires her, or at least desires a girl;
and the popular Jake on whom she has a crush—invoking although never directly broaching the significance of sixteen as the age of consent. This is the

first of three John Hughes films to star Molly Ringwald as a teen ideal that Ann deVaney argues is overwhelmingly invested in heterosexual romance, offering girl viewers "the promise of insight but giving them only the smallest kinds of rebellions within safe geographies of school and home."[23] In fact, *Sixteen Candles'* story about girl sexuality is conflicted, and Jake, like Zac in *She's All That*, seems ideal partly because he expresses romantic but not explicitly sexual interest in the heroine, in counterpoint to a field of on-screen sexual relations that are either exploitative or stagnant. It is not, however, as has often been suggested with reference to girls' consumption of music and film stars,[24] that teen film represents sex positively only as ideal rather than in practice. Jake and Zac are boy ideals in comprehending the dialectical relation between sex and romance associated with girls in teen films. But if teen film represents sex as potentially harmful whenever it is not romantic this doesn't mean harmful or questionable sex isn't represented—quite the contrary. No sex and no romance escapes its opposing term in teen film and no ideal possibility for either escapes its threatening conversion into exploitation. For a film like *Porky's*, where romance is only a marginal suggestion—although its suggestion matters—the sex at its narrative center is blatantly exploitative. And in both *Revenge of the Nerds* (1984) and *Sixteen Candles* a key late scene reveals the sensitivity of the geek as a lover to the popular girl who would never have sex with him if she had a choice. In *Revenge of the Nerds* he is disguised as her boyfriend and in *Sixteen Candles* she is too drunk to choose. The fact that both boy and girl find this sex revelatory hardly cleans teen film's romantic sex and sexualized romance of dangerous self-interest.

The classification of *Sixteen Candles* involved a transnational terrain and cross-cultural negotiation of ideas about adolescence. It was subject to considerable classificatory uncertainty: initially rated R in the U.S. but re-rated PG on appeal; receiving three different ratings in different Canadian provinces and re-rated down in both Canada and the U.K. but up in Australia in order to be screened on television. The U.S. appeal claimed the film's inclusion of nudity, discussion of off-screen sex, drug use, and foul language was appropriate in context because that is how adolescents behave and because the negative consequences of such behavior are represented. But *Sixteen Candles* was never a controversial PG rating because it was released immediately *before* the introduction of a new PG-13 ratings category in 1984. Heightened debate around *Sixteen Candles* exemplifies the way the genre endlessly negotiates what can be seen/said as teen film, especially around sex. It represents one of many such historical transitions which less marks than produces new possible content. At PG, *Sixteen Candles* was situated in the middle zone of teen film, becoming shocking only as the PG-13 category transformed R from "Adult" to a more advanced form of parental guidance. Doherty rightly claims that Hughes made "a virtual franchise of PG-13-rated and G-sensibility teenpic fare," if only because the fresh slipperiness of PG-13 defines what was new about 1980s teen film.[25]

Currently, for Australian DVD release, *She's All That* is rated "M: recommended for mature audiences 15 years and older" despite the oddity in most other public or popular sphere contexts of associating maturity with fifteen. The DVD tells me "It contains coarse language, violence, sex scenes, nudity, drug use and adult themes." But in fact this apparent cornucopia of licentiousness amounts to little controversy. The language stops at asshole or bitch, explicit violence at mostly psychological bullying, the sex is implied sexual history and two scenes with a couple tangled but concealed in sheets post-sex, and the nudity is actually a few unrevealing underwear scenes. Apart from underage drinking and some villains smoking the "adult concepts" are where the action is. And apart from an early scene in which bullies taunt Laney by saying she should kill herself to become a famous artist these themes are *sex*: sexually inflected bullying; veiled references to a range of non-normative sexual activities from blow-up sex dolls, homosexuality, and prostitution; and, most explicitly, an off-screen scene of attempted coercive seduction. Importantly for a teen film there is no implication that any sex that would satisfy the demands of normative sexual citizenship is likely to happen. While this is precisely what Doherty means by "PG-13-rated and G-sensibility teenpic fare" when dismissing Hughes, such classification indicates the way teen film suspends the distinction between maturity and immaturity for narratives about sexual socialization, sexual consent, and the sex/romance dialectic. The classification system's taxonomy of adolescence is an aspiration ladder of fantasies in which girls are a narrative focus because they are presumed to be the willing subject validating any normative sex. In this taxonomy—apparently distinguishing between children, adolescents, and adults—maturity is as simultaneously ever-present and categorically unreachable as it is in teen film stories. Addressing an audience whose choices are managed by a system for which they should be both mature and immature, Laney lectures Zac that he should take control of his life because he's "eighteen and that's old enough to be making your own choices." Zac wants to know if she tells *herself* that. It's an important question. Several scenes later her father is lecturing seventeen-year-old Laney about getting on with "the business of being a kid" rather than worrying about lifelong consequences. Both Zac and Laney's fathers also separately lecture them about the future happening whether or not one is ready or paying attention, a position the film links to their own unhappy adult romantic lives.

The *difficulty* of film classification is manifest in the middle zone described by and describing teen film. In this zone, classificatory categories shift, appear, and disappear while General and Adult categories on either side remain comparatively stable (even when their content is debated). The fact that puberty, sexual consent, and voting age are the broadly shared parameters for film classification ladders across the world glosses one of the things that has been most controversial about them—their focus on sex.[26] On classification ladders, fine distinctions proliferate around and between categories that do not equate puberty with the onset of sexual maturity *or* the age of consent with access to sexual content. Instead, these proliferating rungs on often contradictory ladders constitute developmental steps within a field of guidance. In this field, maturity means being able to contextualize both un-citizenlike and expressly prohibited behavior. But this same maturity is categorically denied to adolescence as defined by classification and positioned as delusion or manipulation by the genre itself; that is, maturity and sex operate very similarly within teen film narrative. If girls are expected to achieve both sexual maturity and adult citizenship as much as boys are—in teen film as elsewhere—the difference of the experience this signifies and makes possible is evident in the gendering of sexual agency in teen film. In the case of teen film, as with girl sexuality in general, anxiety over influence is a binding force. Overviews of ratings practices support the assertion that most classification systems treat sex far more restrictively than violence for any reference to real life to underpin them. Sex is more important because of its realistic availability, which means its articulability must be managed through its visibilities.

Conclusion

Teen film sexuality is *girl* sexuality. That is—for slasher films, the noir-ish psychological dramas of *Rumblefish* (1983) or *Donnie Darko* (2001), and for grossout comedy such as *Porky's* or *American Pie* as well as for *She's All That*— teen film sexuality is openly regulated by self-reflexivity, group-identity, and changing social norms and their contestation, all at once. It depends on a well-established idea of girl sexuality as vulnerable and of this vulnerability as an asset in a pervasively dominant sexual economy. But paying close attention to teen film suggests the value of this vulnerability lies in openness to reconfiguration; or, we might say, impressionability. This idea is produced in legislation, in the more governmental sphere of film classification, and in popular unpopular public sentiment, every bit as forcefully as in teen film. For considering the constraints on representing girls' desires in teen film—operating at the level of genre and of classification and at both levels actively influenced by changing sociopolitical frames, including feminism—I think we need a theoretical account. Abstraction in this case stops us falling back on what we have all been trained to know by just this nexus of public policy and popular genre.

Deleuze's drawing out of the terms visible and articulable accounts for what we've come to call Foucauldian "discourse" is also shaped by what has been called Deleuze's "pragmatism." This is an emphasis on the *uses* made of representation. As Deleuze puts this in his work with Felix Guattari,

> the pragmatic variables of usage are internal to enunciation and constitute the implicit presuppositions of language...Linguistics is nothing without a pragmatics (semiotic or political) to define the effectuation of the *condition of possibility* of language and the *usage* of linguistic elements.[27]

This encourages us, I think, to reframe the history of teen film and its classification as *uses* of girl sexuality. If there is no way of resolving the question of when sexuality becomes relevant for girls categorically, despite the apparent necessity of treating images as if it were possible to make that judgment, then pragmatism seems the best approach. This focus on use must be taken not only to the commercial interests and audience investments in the genre but also to cultural debates circulating around girl sexuality that pervade all aspects of it. Girls are widely understood as naturally directed toward sexuality and yet categorically to be protected from it. It is not merely a paradox that a sixteen-year-old Australian girl is legally allowed to consent to sex but cannot see it on screen—it speaks, and in a way that is not true of the parallel statement for boys as teen film also explains, to the irresolvable contradiction between a developmental model of sexuality which must be progressive and border discourse on sexuality in which girls, *sui generis*, are the ones to be protected from sexualization. In its dominant narratives and their constant engagement with classification processes, teen film makes explicit the fractured liminality maintaining and organized around sexual education on behalf of future citizenship. The ways in which teen film presses on the limits of its classification seems worth closer consideration in this light.

Teen film is clearly both on the side of articulating girl sexuality and makes its ongoing constraint visible. This grounds the elaborate adjustments of classification relative to the presumed experience of its audiences and teen film's endless testing of these adjustments. If I seem to be saying nothing more than that people learn from teen film because they're carefully instructed that they should, and that what they learn is in part that girls define sexuality as a normative ethical terrain—then that is enough to stress the importance of teen film. Teen film and the classification systems defining it represent sex and maturity as interrelated fields populated by unclosed questions and contingent strategic positions, and as precisely gendered. That the form of that gendering is unstable because it is culturally contingent and endlessly under review should be indication enough that the girl sexuality in/as teen film is alive to a political history that often dismisses it.

Notes

1. I have been interested in this nexus of ideas about adolescence for some time. It is foundational to my discussion of modern girlhood in *Girls: Feminine Adolescence in Popular Culture
   and Cultural Theory* (New York: Columbia University Press, 2002)—in particular my discussion of puberty and majority (47–104)—and exemplary in my discussion of modern subjectivity in *Modernist Cultural Studies* (Miami, FL: University Press of Florida, 2010, 45–88). This
   essay draws most heavily on my book *Teen Film: A Critical Introduction* (London: Berg, 2011)
   and a forthcoming essay on the sexualization of girlhood.

2. G. Tuck, "Orgasmic (Teenage) Virgins: Masturbation and Virginity in Contemporary
   American Cinema," in *Virgin Territory: Representing Sexual Inexperience in Film*, ed. T. J.
   McDonald (Detroit: Wayne State University Press, 2010), 158.

3. T. Shary, *Generation: Multiplex: The Image of Youth in Contemporary American Cinema* (Austin,
   TX: University of Texas Press, 2002), 226.

4. T. Shary, *Teen Movies: American Youth on Screen* (New York: Wallflower Press, 2005), 56, 76.

5. R. Kaveney, *Teen Dreams: Reading Teen Film from Heathers to Veronica Mars* (London: I. B.
   Tauris, 2006).

6. Lisa Dresner, "Love's Labor's Lost? Early 1980s Representations of Girls' Sexual Decision
   Making in *Fast Times at Ridgemont High* and *Little Darlings*," in *Virgin Territory: Representing
   Sexual Inexperience in Film*, ed. T. J. McDonald (Detroit: Wayne State University Press, 2010),
   174-99, 180.

7. T. Doherty, *Teenagers and Teenpics: The Juvenilization of American Movies in the 1950s*
   (Philadelphia: Temple University Press, 2002); Shary, *Generation*, 2002; Shary, *Teen Movies*,
   2005; Kaveney, *Teen Dreams*, 2006.

8. Shary and Alexandra Seibel's collection *Youth Culture and Global Cinema* (Austin, TX: University of Texas Press, 2007) includes three essays on "Coming-of-Age Queer" focusing
   substantially on European examples. But this collection's general insistence on framing
   "global" narrative cinema about adolescence as "youth" rather than "teen" film in order to
   not compromise a definition of teen film as American also means they do not have to fully
   engage with the relation between "queer" and "teen" coming-of-age narratives.

9. Sharon Driver, *Queer Girls and Popular Culture: Reading, Resisting, and Creating Media* (New
   York: Peter Lang, 2007).

10. See Judith Butler, *Bodies That Matter: on the Discursive Limits of Sex* (New York: Routledge,
    1993). The modern idea of adolescence is often credited to sociologist G. Stanley Hall, but
    this common citation often ignores the influence of psychoanalysis on Hall's thinking. In
    1909, between the release of the two volumes of his *Adolescence* (New York: Appleton,
    1911), Hall brought Freud and Carl Jung to lecture in the United States, establishing the in-
    fluence of psychoanalysis there at the same time as his own work was propagating a story
    about adolescence as a period of sturm und drang (storm and stress) that influenced not
    only psychology and sociology but (at their intersection) also education.

11. S. Freud, *Group Psychology and the Analysis of the Ego* (London: The Hogarth Press, 1922), 64–
    5; see also Driscoll, *Girls*, 2002.

12. Kaveney, *Teen Dreams*, 5–6, 28.

13. G. Deleuze, *Foucault* (London: The Athlone Press, 1988).

14.   Ibid., 43.
15.   Doherty, *Teenagers and Teenpics,* 161, 196–97.
16.   A. Whitney, "Gidget Goes Hysterical," in *Sugar, Spice, and Everything Nice: Cinemas of Girlhood,* eds. F. K. Gateward and M. Pomerance (Detroit: Wayne State University Press, 2002), 55.
17.   See, for example, J. Bernstein, *Pretty in Pink: The Golden Age of Teenage Movies* (New York: St Martin's Press, 1997), 7–33; Shary, *Generation,* 235. It is telling that the boy-centred volume of the companion texts on teen film edited by Murray Pomerance and Frances Gateward (Detroit: Wayne State University Press, 2005) adapts *Where the Boys Are* for its title because this film is indisputably about girl sexuality. It centers on the "spring break" holiday to which, the opening voiceover tells us, "The girls come very simply because this is where the boys are." Every girl at this party is waiting impatiently, as the title song puts it, for love and marriage. It is also a text about sexual citizenship. The opening frame scenes function as an admonishing preface articulating, from the perspective of first teachers and then the police, a "war against higher education" in which "the students of America are gathering to celebrate the rites of spring."
18.   Shary, *Generation,* 142.
19.   Bernstein, *Pretty in Pink,* 7.
20.   See Kenneth Kidd, "He's Gotta Have It: Teen Film as Sex Education," in *Sexual Pedagogies: Sex Education in Britain, Australia, and America, 1879–2000,* eds. C. Nelson and M. H. Martin (New York, Palgrave Macmillan, 2004); Sharyn Pearce, "'As Wholesome As…': American Pie as a New Millennium Sex Manual," in *Youth Cultures: Texts, Images, Identities,* eds. K. Mallan and S. Pearce (Westport, CT: Praeger, 2003). Both Kidd's discussion of teen film as sex education and Pearce's more direct consideration of American Pie as a "sex manual" stress the importance of such dynamics for teen film.
21.   A. Martin, "Teen Movies: The Forgetting of Wisdom," *Phantasms* (Ringwood, VIC: McPhee Gribble, 1994).
22.   Doherty, *Teenagers and Teenpics,* 153–56, 196–97.
23.   A. deVaney, "Pretty in Pink?: John Hughes Reinscribes Daddy's Girl in Homes and Schools," in *Sugar, Spice, and Everything Nice: Cinemas of Girlhood,* eds. F. K. Gateward and M. Pomerance (Detroit: Wayne State University Press, 2002), 204.
24.   E.g. Angela McRobbie and S. Frith, "Rock and Sexuality," in *Feminism and Youth Culture: From 'Jackie' to 'Just Seventeen,'* ed. A. McRobbie (London: Unwin Hyman, 1991).
25.   Doherty, *Teenagers and Teenpics,* 201.
26.   Kirby Dick's documentary expose of the US MPAA system, *This Film Is Not Yet Rated* (2006), is especially committed to uncovering a bias in this system against sex rather than violence, and against images of female rather than male sexuality.
27.   G. Deleuze and F. Guattari, *A Thousand Plateaus* (Minneapolis: University of Minnesota Press, 1987), 94.

Works Cited

Bernstein, J. *Pretty in Pink: The Golden Age of Teenage Movies.* New York: St Martin's Press, 1997.
Butler, J. *Bodies That Matter: on the Discursive Limits of Sex.* New York: Routledge, 1993.
Cruel Intentions, directed by Roger Kumble (1999; Culver City, CA: Columbia Pictures, 1999). DVD.

Deleuze, G. *Foucault.* London: The Athlone Press, 1988.

Deleuze, G. and F. Guattari. *A Thousand Plateaus.* Minneapolis: University of Minnesota Press, 1987.

deVaney, A. "Pretty in Pink?: John Hughes Reinscribes Daddy's Girl in Homes and Schools." In *Sugar, Spice, and Everything Nice: Cinemas of Girlhood,* eds. F. K. Gateward and M. Pomerance, 201–16. Detroit: Wayne State University Press, 2002.

Doherty, T. *Teenagers and Teenpics: The Juvenilization of American Movies in the 1950s.* Philadelphia: Temple University Press, 2002.

Donnie Darko, directed by Richard Kelly (2001; Los Angeles, CA: Flower Films, 2001). DVD.

Dresner, L. M. "Love's Labor's Lost? Early 1980s Representations of Girls' Sexual Decision Making in *Fast Times at Ridgemont High* and *Little Darlings.*" In *Virgin Territory: Representing Sexual Inexperience in Film,* ed. Tamar J. McDonald, 174–200. Detroit: Wayne State University Press, 2010.

Driscoll, C. *Girls: Feminine Adolescence in Popular Culture and Cultural Theory.* New York: Columbia University Press, 2002.

———. *Modernist Cultural Studies.* Miami, FL: University Press of Florida, 2010.

———. *Teen Film: A Critical Introduction.* London: Berg, 2011.

Driver, S. *Queer Girls and Popular Culture: Reading, Resisting, and Creating Media.* New York: Peter Lang, 2007.

Freud, S. *Group Psychology and the Analysis of the Ego.* London: The Hogarth Press, 1922.

Gateward, F. K. and M. Pomerance, eds. *Where the Boys Are: Cinemas of Masculinity and Youth.* Detroit: Wayne State University Press, 2005.

Gidget, directed by Paul Wendkos (1959; Culver City, CA: Columbia Pictures).

G.I. Blues, directed by Norman Taurog (1960; Hollywood, CA: Paramount Pictures).

Hall, G. S. *Adolescence: Its Psychology and Its Relations to Physiology, Anthropology, Sociology, Sex, Crime, Religion, and Education.* New York: Appleton, 1911.

Kaveney, R. *Teen Dreams: Reading Teen Film from Heathers to Veronica Mars.* London: I. B. Tauris, 2006.

Kidd, K. "He's Gotta Have It: Teen Film as Sex Education." In *Sexual Pedagogies: Sex Education in Britain, Australia, and America, 1879–2000,* eds. C. Nelson and M. H. Martin, 95–112. New York: Palgrave Macmillan, 2004.

Kiss and Tell, directed by Richard Wallace (1945; Culver City, CA: Columbia Pictures).

Little Darlings, directed by Ronald F. Maxwell (1980; Hollywood, CA: Paramount Pictures).

Martin, A. "Teen Movies: The Forgetting of Wisdom." *Phantasms,* 63–9. Ringwood, VIC: McPhee Gribble, 1994.

McRobbie, A. and S. Frith. "Rock and Sexuality." In *Feminism and Youth Culture: From 'Jackie' to 'Just Seventeen,'* ed. Angela McRobbie, 137–58. London: Unwin Hyman, 1991.

Not Another Teen Movie, directed by Joel Gallen (2001; Culver City, CA: Columbia Pictures, 2002). DVD.

Pearce, S. "'As Wholesome As…': American Pie as a New Millennium Sex Manual." In *Youth Cultures: Texts, Images, Identities,* eds. K. Mallan and S. Pearce, 69–80. Westport, CT: Praeger, 2003.

Porky's, directed by Bob Clark (1982; Canada: Melvin Simon Productions).

Revenge of the Nerds, directed by Jeff Kanew (1984; Los Angeles, CA: Twentieth Century Fox).

Rumble Fish, directed by Frank Coppola (1983; Universal City, CA: Universal Studios).

Saved! directed by Brian Dannelly (2004; Beverly Hills, CA: United Artists, 2004). DVD.

Shary, T. *Generation: Multiplex: The Image of Youth in Contemporary American Cinema.* Austin, TX: University of Texas Press, 2002.

——. *Teen Movies: American Youth on Screen.* New York: Wallflower Press, 2005.

Shary, T. and A. Seibel. *Youth Culture in Global Cinema.* Austin, TX: University of Texas Press, 2007.

She's All That, directed by Robert Iscove (1999; New York City, NY: Miramax, 1999). DVD.

Sixteen Candles, directed by John Hughes (1984; Universal City, CA: Channel Productions/Universal Studios, 1998). DVD.

The Bachelor and the Bobby-Soxer, directed by Irving Reis (1947; New York City, NY: RKO Radio Pictures).

The Plastic Age, directed by Wesley Ruggles (1925; Claremont, CA: B.P. Schulberg Productions).

The Wild Party, directed by Dorothy Arzner (1929; Los Angeles, CA: Paramount/MCA-Universal).

This Film Is Not Yet Rated. Directed by K. Dick. U.S.A., U.K.: Independent Film Channel, 2006.

Tuck, G. "Orgasmic (Teenage) Virgins: Masturbation and Virginity in Contemporary American Cinema." In *Virgin Territory: Representing Sexual Inexperience in Film*, ed. T. J. McDonald, 157–73. Detroit: Wayne State University Press, 2010.

Where the Boys Are, directed by Henry Levin (1960; Beverley Hills, CA: Metro-Goldwyn-Mayer).

Whitney, A. "Gidget Goes Hysterical." In *Sugar, Spice, and Everything Nice: Cinemas of Girlhood*, eds. F. K. Gateward and M. Pomerance, 55–72. Detroit: Wayne State University Press, 2002.

6

Wrecked and Redeemed: Religio-Political Pedagogy and MTV's *16 and Pregnant*

Amanda Rossie

Introduction

On the heels of Diablo Cody's hit film *Juno* (2007), Judd Apatow's *Knocked Up* (2007), and Bristol Palin's public pregnancy and "choose life" PSA campaigns, MTV set out to create a show that "offers a unique look into the wide variety of challenges pregnant teens face" (MTV, 2010a). *16 and Pregnant* is a blend of documentary, reality television, *Juno*-like aesthetics, confessionals, and a hip soundtrack that is a hit among MTV's 12-34-year-old age demographic. The series provides viewers with an up-close and personal account of what unintended teenage pregnancy *looks* like.

As a visual text promoting a political project, *16 and Pregnant* (which I will forthwith call *16*) is an opportunity, as Kristin Luker suggests, to interrogate the belief that teenagers and their pregnancies are representative of "a host of other worrisome changes that are deeply rooted in American society—changes involving race, age, gender, and poverty."[1] The show attends to the public's growing fears and anxieties about young women's sexualities, desires, and reproductive capacities since the rise of the New Right's pro-family movement in the 1980s. As a response to the women's rights movements of the 1960s and 1970s, members of the New Right called for a "return to basics" that "entailed a mass-based crusade against liberal abortion" and its coded signifiers: "teenage sex, nonmarital sex, nonreproductive sex, hedonism, careerism, women's workforce participation, the denigration of 'traditional' gender identities, and the dis-

solution of the nuclear family."[2] *16* contributes to this "return to basics" by putting a youthful spin on three-decade-old rhetoric.

The series' ongoing appeal and popularity is not, however, just a facet of
this anxiety about young women's unfettered sexuality. It is also a product of
the genre of reality television. In *Reality Squared: Televisual Discourse of the Real*,
James Friedman notes the unprecedented use of "reality" by the industry "as a
promotional marketing tool."[3] Indeed, MTV has come to rely more on its
reality programming than its music content, and *16* adds to the network's lineup
of docu-reality series targeted at young adults who are drawn to the network
with the promise of catching a glimpse of a (mediated) reality that is not their
own.

My examination of *16*'s aesthetics, its representational choices, its underlying conservative politics, and its contributions to historical and contemporary
debates informing sex education policies and practices in the U.S. is built upon
an important theoretical framework: religio-political pedagogy. The term,
coined by Jason Bivins, describes "how political cultures are narrated and
taught."[4] I see MTV's work with *16* as doing exactly this: teaching a new generation about evangelical political culture and its views on reproduction. An important clarification to make here is my usage of "evangelical." I employ the
term as a style that reflects a particular set of political beliefs based on Bible-
based values and concerns.[5] This usage complicates and pushes at the relationship between conservative religious politics and secular cultural productions. It
also clarifies an understanding of the term "evangelical" as the conflation of
morality with Christianity in contemporary American culture.[6] For example,
those who speak out against social programs, same-sex marriage, abortion, and
comprehensive sex education might not be evangelical churchgoers, but their
motivations for reclaiming, as Hartouni writes it, a "morally decadent, spiritually
impoverished, and sexually debauched" America align with the New Right's call
for a return to the "basics," or a biblically-based national morality.[7] Janet Jakobsen and Ann Pellegrini (2004) argue that the result of this conflation is a turn
toward self-regulation, since morality proceeds through "self-regulation in the
form of conscience and the direct and indirect regulation of others."[8]

16 communicates conservative ideologies about women's sexuality and desires, sex education, reproductive choice, and the nuclear family through its use
of particular visual and narrative techniques. I show what cultural work these
images do as well as how the "liberal" space of MTV veils the placement and
reinforcement of conservative ideologies about sexual transgressions while policing often poor, white, feminine youth bodies. I contend that while MTV is
ostensibly trying to do the work that abstinence-only education programs fail to
do, *16* relies on evangelical discourses that link sex outside of marriage to fear,

pain, and social ills. It therefore perpetuates the invisibility of institutional obstacles and prejudices that allow for the conditions conducive to teenage pregnancy—like poverty, single-parent homes, and abstinence-only education proprograms—to remain untouched and under-theorized.

These multilayered discourses are further supported by the show's visual components. By intermixing scenes of partner violence, painful births, and tragic storylines with caricatures of these very same moments, the show gives viewers room to psychologically distance themselves from the *real* effects these problematic representations of race, class, sexuality, and gendered violence truly have. Moreover, claiming these images as "truth" removes the multiplicities of female sexuality from the series. Functioning as entertainment, observation, and pedagogy, *16* combines long-standing anti-poor and racialized fears about out-of-wedlock births in the U.S. with youthful aesthetics, old-fashioned representations, and evangelical politics to reinforce what it subtly claims to reject. Ultimately, I contend that the series teaches viewers *how* to fear by using a religio-political pedagogy that hides conservative anti-choice rhetoric behind a pro-choice façade.

This chapter is organized into three major sections—aesthetics, representation, and the politics of fear. In order to situate the series contextually, historically, and socially, I focus on circulating discourses—about teenage pregnancy, sexuality, "morality," and citizenship, for instance—while also offering a frame for examining its power, currency, and construction outside of the bounds of genre or viewer demographic. I also examine how *16*'s aesthetic techniques, particularly the documentary-stylized reality television and caricatured frames, contribute to and/or disrupt the episodic narrative flow and do a particular kind of political work.

Attentive Aesthetics, Savvy Structure

16 is not MTV's typical docu-reality series. Despite the network's success with shows like *The Real World, Road Rules, The Jersey Shore,* and *True Life,* MTV departs from this model by incorporating animation into *16*'s narrative flow. The show has three distinctive aesthetic styles: documentary, reality, and animation. While contributing to the show's general look, each aesthetic component produces varying affective responses that contribute to an overall political sensibility. Episodes are structured around the "informing logic" that Bill Nichols (1991) describes in *Representing Reality*:

> A paradigmatic structure for documentary would involve the establishment of an issue or problem, the presentation of the background to the problem, followed by an examination of its current extent or complexity, often including more than one perspective

or point of view. This would lead to a concluding section where a solution or path toward solution is introduced.[9]

In this paradigmatic structure, the producers establish the "problem" as unwed
teenage pregnancy and present the problem's background (including how each
teenage girl became pregnant and by whom) through dialogue, voice-over narra-
tion, and animation sequences. Finally, the show ends with each teen's confes-
sion, which attempts to offer a narrative conclusion as well as a future path
solving the problems in their own lives.

The network's marketing of the series as "docu-reality," however, complicates Nichols' more traditional notions of documentary. The "fly on the wall"
camera apparati create an observational mode of representation that "stresses
the nonintervention of the filmmaker" and "[cedes] 'control' over the events
that occur in front of the camera."[10] Making use of this observational mode, *16*
targets viewers' assumptions that the "sounds and images bear an indexical relation to the historical world."[11] Aside from the confessional-style conclusion
punctuating the end of each episode, the social "actors" involved in the series
do not recognize the camera's presence; instead, the teenage mothers and the
secondary players in their journeys are seen as simply living their lives, which
are then recorded, edited, and presented as a "true" reality. This heavy reliance
on visual evidence is present in the marketing and presentation of *16* as not
only *a reality* but also *the reality* about teenage pregnancy in American life.

The last and one of the most notable markers of *16* is its reliance on animation frames to infantilize, fantasize, and fetishize within the narrative structure.
These individualized and stylized graphic interventions recur throughout the
series and add affective texture in four main ways. First, by mixing of documentary and reality genres with animations, the show infantilizes the teenage mothers. Animated graphics incorporating the series' logo appear inside an open
spiral notebook, alluding to teenagers who fill notebooks with drawings and
doodles while bored at school. These graphics become visual cues to signal
youth and immaturity, and they reinscribe the "babies having babies" thematic.

Second, these graphics foreshadow, contextualize, and provide biographical
back-stories that fill the gaps in time and space created by the use of evidentiary
editing.[12] Because the camera cannot capture and represent the historical past or
the potential future, animation slides function to fill that narrative space. For
example, graphics recreate the start of the teens' relationship, show them succeeding (or failing) in the future, and are even used to condense the hours each
teen mother is in labor. Oftentimes, these animations appear as dream sequences and fantasy scenes. The use of these kinds of graphics is frequent yet unpredictable, and each episode relies upon these imaginative frames to make each
teen's story cohesive within the larger series.

Third, these graphic frames provide background knowledge often omitted from abstinence-only sex education programs. Animation slides are used to define key terms related to pregnancy and birth. For example, three of the most common vocabulary lessons presented to viewers in the second season are animated slides defining "epidural," "pitocin," and "induce labor." Important to note, however, is the series' choice to *only* define terms related to medicalized birth, rather than information about contraceptives, alternative parenting choices, and partner violence, which are themes also relevant to *16*. Although intended to be an educational component to the series, MTV is, in effect, imparting a limited range of messages about women's reproductive options and sexual agency that are only framed through the medical-industrial complex.

Fourth, the animation sequences fetishize the pregnant teenage body. For instance, at the end of each opening sequence, the camera zooms in on each teen's protruding pregnant torso and freezes the frame, replacing it with a caricatured image. These disembodied images reduce each teen mother down to body parts. By detaching each mother's head from her body, she is not only disembodied but her fetus is brought to the fore. Viewers are literally prompted to see *through* her to a different (perhaps brighter) futurity alluded to by the fetus. This fetishization of the fetus provides viewers with a moment to psychologically distance themselves from the mothers' realities and the hardships of unintended teenage pregnancy and, instead, focus on and celebrate the fetus as a subject-in-the-making. As such, the mother becomes secondary to viewer's concerns, to her own narrative, and within the visual frame.

The decision to use animation in *16* has conservative effects with larger political implications. The animation stylizes reality to the extent that it becomes cartoonish and, at times, flippant. Because cartoons have historically been considered "low art," the series' animations are linked both subtly and explicitly to assumptions about which forms of art and entertainment should be taken seriously and which are for the uneducated "masses." These assumptions about "value" then seep into mainstream perceptions about the lives of *16*'s teen mothers who are treated as cultural jokes and cautionary tales. Moreover, larger issues of sex education, pregnancy prevention, and reproductive choice are individualized rather than situated within larger structures, institutions, and policies that create these constrained choices to begin with. The production, framing, and reception of *16* provides the space for viewers and critics to blame the circumstances of each teen mother on bad decision making, poverty, lack of family support, or naïveté. And, while these factors are certainly part of a larger equation, they do not comprise the whole picture, which is also constituted by conservative religious and political ideologies that create an environment of fear that works against these teen mothers' reproductive and parenting decision-making abilities.

"Peering" Into the Politics of Fear:
Abortion, Adoption, and Fetal Citizenship

The show's visual and narrative representations of constrained reproductive choice provide a starting place for thinking more critically about how Bivins' religio-political pedagogy functions within the series. First, and perhaps most obviously, is the show's total disengagement from abortion. Viewers enter into these teen mothers' lives during the late second trimester or early third trimester, long after the decision to abort becomes a legal option. In effect, this is a visual denial of reproductive rights and the dilemmas of young womanhood in the U.S. Conversations about abortion enter the series on primarily two occasions: 1) when abortion is denounced (by the girls, their boyfriends, or their caretakers) as an unthinkable or immoral alternative to parenting; and 2) as a suggestion put to the pregnant teen by the villains in the series, including antagonistic mothers or abusive boyfriends. Through these visual and narrative denials, the series disengages from productive conversations about reproductive choice and, instead, constructs the fetus as "a privileged legal, medical, and cultural subject" at the expense of the "disenfranchisement, disembodiment, and marginalization of women."[13]

The consistent focus on the fetus centralizes it as *the* object of concern for everyone on the show and its audience. Viewers witness 3-D ultrasound appointments and see sonogram photos of the fetus, and these peering technologies—including neonatal care *and*, I argue, the docu-reality genre itself—contribute to discourses about fetal citizenship. These representations also provide yet another outlet for society to monitor the behaviors of "irresponsible" teen parents and simultaneously position the fetus (victim) and mother (villain) against one another. State control of reproductive practices alongside MTV's stake in controlling what forms of social, political, and citizenship (re)production become visible are wrapped up into anxieties about how viewers "'see' the fetus as an embodied person, [which is further] reinforced by visual images distributed by abortion opponents" and popular culture alike.[14] Furthermore, while MTV's ads for sites such as www.itsyoursexlife.org[15] appear to advocate for a pro-choice stance on reproductive rights, the series offers no choice at all. While this particular website supplies valuable information about contraception, STD and HIV testing, as well as tips for teenagers about how to start conversations with their partners about sex-related issues, abortion is only briefly mentioned once as an option, while any details about the procedure and links to resources or clinics are completely absent.

In the series, adoption is only presented as an option in one episode (out of ten) in the second season. Lori, the Catholic teen from "classic small town America," was adopted as a child and wants the chance to parent and create a biological family of her own (Season 2, Episode 5). Yet, her adoptive parents refuse to support the child or Lori financially—or even allow Lori to live in their home—should she choose to parent. Lori is coerced into adoption simply because she is forbidden to choose abortion or parenting. In spite of Lori's pleadings and fears that she would have a "psychological breakdown" should she give her son up for adoption, her parents have the last word. This episode illustrates the way *16* frames adoption: adoption is rendered the *least* desirable option for the series' teen mothers, since abortion is never an option for them *or* the series.[16]

Through these visual and narrative refusals, the series disengages from productive conversations about reproductive choice and, instead, continues to stigmatize abortion and deny teenage girls the agency to decide whether or not they want to become parents at all. In these scenes, a religio-political pedagogy emerges both within the episodes and as a by-product of the show's casting choices and televisual framing. If we are to believe that representations affect the material conditions of people's lives, then the images, decisions, or options erased from the series have effects as well. Thus, an analysis of the role(s) that these representations—and their erasures—play in a larger social, cultural, and political milieu more clearly illustrates the conservative ideologies framing *16*.

Wrecked and Redeemed

16 employs a range of conservative politics that masquerade as stylistic and casting preferences. But the series' visuality also serves another pedagogical purpose: the creation of fear. During the course of the series, these unwed teenage mothers are literally put on display to incite worry, shame, and abstinence among viewers. Instead of keeping the "sins" of pregnant teens hidden away in maternity homes historically run by evangelical women, MTV takes a "private" matter *very* public. In *16*'s after-show titled *Life After Labor*, the teen mothers gather together for a reunion hosted by Dr. Drew Pinsky. In this therapeutic talk-show model, teens and their families recollect their journeys to motherhood, confront irresponsible teen fathers, and reminisce about their lost childhoods, while Dr. Drew reminds viewers that the more disturbing, traumatic, and heart-wrenching pieces of footage are simply the challenges resulting from teens' irresponsible sexual practices. Dr. Drew then proceeds with a psychological "rehabilitation," which has historically been America's way of explaining away white teenage pregnancies.

Beginning in the 1950s, white illegitimate pregnancies moved from private stigma to social shame. Rickie Solinger writes, "While illegitimate pregnancy and babies had, in the past, been a private matter handled by family members…by mid-century, these issues had become public concerns and public business."[17] To justify "going public," white teenage pregnancies came to be viewed as psychologically explainable rather than culturally inevitable. Black teenage pregnancies, on the other hand, were always stigmatized by "cultural" hypersexuality and degeneracy. This correlation between white teenage pregnancy as a psychologically justifiable and redeemable "sin" and black teenage pregnancy as a sign of cultural deviance and biological inferiority provides important context for *16*'s overwhelmingly white cast, as well as Dr. Drew's role as both producer and psychologist. By issuing a "talking cure" for teenage pregnancy and pointing out the psychological flaws that led each teen to unwed motherhood, Dr. Drew places individual responsibility over institutional failure. In his formulation, teens' misjudgment, immaturity, and naïveté explain the causes of the cast's mostly-white teenage pregnancies.

Focusing on teenage pregnancy at the individual level also allows for the construction of sexual progress narratives, thereby making white unwed pregnancy pedagogical. Within this framework, "The white girl '[is] encouraged to look within herself for the reasons for her mistake because the white subculture stresses individual responsibility for error."[18] In other words, for young white mothers, "Learning the lesson [means] stepping on the road to real womanhood."[19] This rhetoric of maturity through motherhood is common in *Life After Labor*. The young mothers reiterate how their babies forced them to grow up sooner than they had to—or wanted to. Yet, in spite of all their hardships, they claim that their children are still the *best* things that have ever happened to them. Conversely, the progress narratives of black teenage motherhood are complicated by institutional structures and histories of racism and slavery. Perhaps this is one reason why MTV casts its minorities sparsely. Too many young women of color might draw attention to structural inequalities that create intersectional oppression, thereby disrupting the show's focus on the individual and rendering Dr. Drew's psychological approach ineffective. When compared to her white counterpart, the unwed black teenage mother is beyond grace. After all, race is one measure by which American culture distinguishes between which teenage mothers remain wrecked and which get redeemed.

Conclusions: Political Religion, Pop Culture Pedagogy, and "Productive Perversity"

16's intersecting components—aesthetic modes, visual representations of race and class, presentations of constrained reproductive choice, and representations of fetal citizenship—do particular kinds of cultural and pedagogical work. Three main sociopolitical instabilities inform the series and operate alongside its visual representations in order to produce a brand of (politically and religiously) conservative fear that seeks to regulate behavior and challenge liberal beliefs about young women's sexual freedom.

First, *16* builds upon fears of the disintegrating nuclear family. The show teaches viewers *why* they should fear insubordinate reproduction through visual representations of pain, suffering, and dysfunction. At the center of the series' concern is the failing white family, and the decision to code particular people and places as "white trash" is central to *16*'s dynamics. Whiteness and its social and cultural meanings are momentarily overturned, and, instead, "White trash becomes a term which names what seems unnamable: a race (white) which is used to code 'wealth' is coupled with an insult (trash) which means, in this instance, economic waste."[20] Because the nuclear family is capitalism's base economic unit, the show has a stake in upholding and promoting "traditional" families that produce viable citizen-subjects. According to Solinger (1992), "During times when women have few reproductive rights, their bodies have become symbols and implements of large national projects that depend on women's dependency, hence their endangerment."[21] This larger national project written on young women's bodies harkens back to the initial goals of the New Right—a "return to the basics" that includes "antiabortion, antigay, anti-ERA, profamily, prolife, pro-America rhetoric."[22]

Heightened by immigration debates and legislation, the second sociopolitical instability informing the series is the meaning and value of citizenship. Anxieties about *what* constitutes American citizenship—and *who* should qualify—are most clearly depicted in the visualization of the fetus as a "super-subject."[23] Through particular aesthetic choices and a reliance on "peering technologies," "the live fetal image of the clinic appears simply to have been transported into everyone's living room."[24] Enlarging the fetus as an emblem of public concern suggests the value of the fetus far exceeds its use-value for the nuclear family alone. Because white babies are born "classless," for example, "A poor 'white trash' teenager could have a white baby in Appalachia; it could be adopted by an upper-middle class couple in Westport, Connecticut and the baby would, in the transaction, become upper-middle class also."[25] Because the fetus of a white mother of any socio-economic bracket is both a potentiality in the womb and a blank slate onto which liberal values are inscribed at birth, carrying the baby to full term is seen as a young woman's duty as a "good" American citizen.

A third and final anxiety foundational to *16* is the effect of abortion on civic society and the effect the procedure has on women. In a 1996 "Statement of

Pro-Life Principle and Concern," a "broad spectrum of pro-life organizational leaders and scholars" gathered together to "articulate a pro-life vision of the American future."[26] Situating women as "victims" of the "abortion regime," they expressed the following concern:

> It is ever more clear...that women pay a huge price for abortion. By providing an al-leged technological 'fix' for unintended pregnancy, the [abortion] license has encour-aged widespread male irresponsibility and predatory male sexual behavior. Abortion-on-demand has given an excuse to a man who shirks his responsibilities, claiming that the child he helped to conceive ought to have been aborted, or that the woman who declined to abort may not impose on him any responsibility for her 'lifestyle choice.'[27]

Here, the focus remains on the "alarming breakdown of the American family" and assumptive (and unfair) links between male irresponsibility and women's reproductive choice. In this view, abortion—and women's choice to actualize this legal right—becomes the root cause of male irresponsibility, abuse, and neglect rather than the institutions, cultural productions, and societal factors that construct masculinity in particular ways.

These three major socio-political instabilities—the white nuclear family, cit-izenship, and abortion—are keynotes in a broader conservative evangelical po-litical sensibility. Conservative evangelical ideals like essentialized gender roles, punishment for extra-marital sex, the erasure of women's sexual pleasure, and the promotion of the fetus to first-class citizenship at the expense of the moth-er operate as "visual evidence" to support an agenda that is both politically and religiously conservative. The result is the creation of an ideological message: In Solinger's words, "teenage girls are not to be trusted with authority over their own bodies, even their own fertility."[28] Visually, the series teaches viewers what a violation of patriarchal trust and a *lack of fear* produce—unhappy, unwed teen-age mothers without money, diplomas, familial support, friend networks, or a future. *16* succeeds as a pedagogical tool because of its ability to hone in on the subjects at the center of American concern—young pregnant bodies—and turn these young women into symbols of larger political concerns. The more conse-quential implications for the series are embedded within MTV's cool aesthetics, soundtracks, and promotional marketing, making *16* a stealthy site of conserva-tive religious and political values.

Notes

1.   Kristin Luker, *Dubious Conceptions: The Politics of Teenage Pregnancy*. (Cambridge: Harvard Uni-versity Press, 1996), 12–13.
2.   Valerie Hartouni, "Containing Women: Reproductive Discourse(s) in the 1980s," in *Cultur-al Conceptions: On Reprodutive Technologies and the Remaking of Life*, ed. Valerie Hartouni, 26–50 (Minneapolis: University of Minnesota Press, 1997), 32.

3.   James Friedman, "Introduction," In *Reality Squared: Televisual Discourse on the Real,* edited by James Friendman, 1–22 (New Brunswick, NJ: Rutgers University Press, 2002), 7.

4.   Jason C. Bivens, *Religion of Fear: The Politics of Horror in Conservative Evangelicalism* (Oxford: Oxford University Press, 2008), 4.

5.   As a word with multiple meanings and connotations, I want to be clear from the beginning about what the terms "evangelical" or "conservative evangelical" mean in the context of this intellectual project. According to the Institute for the Study of American Evangelicals (ISAE), there are three contemporary usages of the term "evangelical." First, the term can be used to describe "all Christians who affirm a few key doctrines and practical emphases" such as "conversionism, the belief that lives need to be changed; activism, the expression of the gospel in effort; biblicism, a particular regard for the Bible; and crucicentrism, a stress on the sacrifice of Christ on the cross." Second, the term can be used "to look at evangelicalism as an organic group of movements and religious traditions. Within this context 'evangelical' denotes a style as much as a set of beliefs." Lastly, "evangelical" is a "self-ascribed label for a coalition that arose during the Second World War."

6.   Janet Jakobsen and Ann Pellegrini (2004) contend that Christian morality has become the nation's naturalized "common sense" version of American values. They write, "[It's] time for Americans to come to terms with the fact that Christianity, and often *conservative* Christianity, functions as the yardstick and measure of what counts as 'religion' and 'morality' in America. *To be traditionally American is to be Christian in a certain way*" (13, emphasis added). See Janet Jakobsen and Anne Pellegrini, *Love the Sin: Sexual Regulation and the Limits of Religious Tolerance* (Boston: Beacon Press, 2004).

7.   Hartouni, "Containing Women," 32.

8.   Jakobsen and Pelligrini, *Love the Sin*, 11.

9.   Bill Nichols, *Representing Reality: Issues and Concepts in Documentary* (Bloomington, IN: Indiana University Press, 1991), 18.

10.   Nichols, *Representing Reality*, 38.

11.   Ibid., 27.

12.   Nichols describes "evidentiary editing" in the following: "Instead of organizing cuts within a scene to present a sense of a single, unified time and space in which we can quickly locate the relative position of central characters, *documentary organizes cuts within a scene to present the impression of a single, convincing argument in which we can locate a logic.* Leaps in time or space and the placement of characters become relatively unimportant compared to the sense of the flow of evidence in the service of this controlling logic." See Nichols, *Representing Reality*, 19–20.

13.   Janine P. Holc, "The Purest Democrat: Fetal Citizenship and Subjectivity in the Construction of Democracy in Poland," *Signs* 29 no. 3 (2004), 755–82, 758.

14.   Joseph Boven, "Anti-Choice 'Egg-as-Person' Initiatives Threaten the Rights of Women," RHRealityCheck.org. (November 12, 2009), 760, 766.

15.   Itsyoursexlife.org is "is the official website of MTV and the Kaiser Family Foundation's Emmy Award winning It's Your (Sex) Life public information campaign." Although the site reminds teens "that having sex is a choice (not just the first time, but every time) and your decision is your own," it does not offer the full gamut of reproductive options like abortion or adoption. While the site does go into some detail about many types of contraception and

debunks some myths associated with these preventative practices, the site noticeably shies away from discussing abortion in any detail: "When you find out you are pregnant, you essentially have three options to consider: to continue the pregnancy and keep the baby, to have the baby and put it up for adoption, or to have an abortion. This is a big decision; take your time and talk with your partner, your family and other trusted advisers." http://www.itsyoursexlife.com/iysl/about.

16. The creators of *16 and Pregnant* eventually produced an abortion special titled *No Easy Decision*, which aired in December 2010. The show chronicled Markai Durham, a former *16 and Pregnant* subject from Season 2B, and her decision to have an abortion after her second unplanned pregnancy. By setting Markai's story apart, MTV created a space where abortion could be dealt with in a comprehensive way, with Dr. Drew Pinsky leading a Q&A session following the episode. However, setting abortion apart from the other teens' parenting stories reinforced cultural understandings of abortion as taboo and rare.

17. Rickie Solinger, "Race and 'Value': Black and White Illegitimate Babies, in the U.S.A., 1945–1965," *Gender & History* 4, no. 3 (1992), 343–63, 348.

18. Charles Bowerman quoted in Solinger, "Race and 'Value,'" 357.

19. Ibid.

20. Annalee Newitz and Matt Wray, "Introduction," in *White Trash: Race and Class in America*, eds. Annalee Newitz and Matt Wray, 1–12, (New York: Routledge, 1997), 8.

21. Rickie Solinger, *Pregnancy and Power: A Short History of Reproductive Politics in America* (New York: New York University Press, 2005), 251.

22. Hartouni, "Containing Women," 32.

23. "Super-subject" is a term coined by Susan Bordo in reference to the new fetal subject created by and through fetal rights discourse and its advocates.

24. Ibid., 36.

25. Solinger, "Race and 'Value,'" 349.

26. Priests for Life, "The America We Seek."

27. Ibid.

28. Solinger, *Pregnancy and Power*, 242.

Works Cited

Ashcraft, Catherine. "'Girl, You Better Go Get You a Condom': Popular Culture and Teen Sexuality As Resources for Critical Multicultural Curriculum." *Teachers College Record* 108, no. 10 (2006): 2145–86.

Benfer, Amy. "Death to the 'Juno Effect': Finally: Statistical evidence that 'glamorized,' knocked-up girls in pop culture didn't boost teen pregnancy." In *Salon.com*, April 9, 2009. http://www.salon.com/mwt/broadsheet/2010/04/09/end_of_the_juno_effect

Bivins, Jason. C. *Religion of Fear: The Politics of Horror in Conservative Evangelicalism.* Oxford: Oxford University Press, 2008.

Boven, Joseph. "Anti-Choice 'Egg-as-Person' Initiatives Threaten the Rights of Women." RHRealityCheck.org. November 12, 2009.

Caldwell, John. T. *Televisuality: Style, Crisis, and Authority in American Television.* New Brunswick, NJ: Rutgers University Press, 1995.

Fetveit, Arlid. "Reality TV in the Digital Era: A Paradox in Visual Culture?" In *Reality Squared: Televisual Discourse on the Real,* edited by James Friedman, 119-137. New Brunswick: Rutgers University Press, 2002.

Friedman, James. *Reality Squared: Televisual Discourse on the Real.* Piscataway, NJ: Rutgers University Press, 2002.

Hartouni, Valerie. "Containing Women: Reproductive Discourse(s) in the 1980s." In *Cultural Conceptions: On Reproductive Technologies and the Remaking of Life,* ed. Valerie Hartouni, 26–50. Minneapolis: University of Minnesota Press, 1997.

Holc, Janine. P. "The Purest Democrat: Fetal Citizenship and Subjectivity in the Construction of Democracy in Poland." *Signs* 29, no. 3 (2004): 755–82.

hooks, bell. "The Oppositional Gaze: Black Female Spectators." In *The Feminism and Visual Culture Reader,* ed. Amelia Jones, 107–18. London: Routledge, 2010.

Jakobsen, Janet. R., and Ann Pellegrini. *Love the Sin: Sexual Regulation and the Limits of Religious Tolerance.* Boston: Beacon Press, 2004.

Luker, Kristin. *Dubious Conceptions: The Politics of Teenage Pregnancy.* Cambridge: Harvard University Press, 1996.

MTV. "16 and Pregnant" casting now," *MTV.com.* 2010a .http://www.mtv.com/news/articles/1613577/20090609/story.jhtml

———. "Full Summary," *MTV.com.* May 20, 2010b. http://www.mtv.com/shows/16_and_pregnant/season_2/series.jhtml

Newitz, Annalee and Matt Wray. "Introduction." In *White Trash: Race and Class in America,* eds. by Annalee Newitz and Matt Wray, 1-12. New York: Routledge, 1997.

Nichols, Bill. *Representing Reality: Issues and Concepts in Documentary.* Bloomington, IN: Indiana University Press, 1991.

Ouellette, Laurie, and James Hay. "TV's Constitutions of Citizenship." In *Better Living Through Reality TV: Television and Post-welfare Citizenship,* eds. Laurie Ouellette and James Hay, 170–202. Malden, MA: Blackwell Publishing, 2008.

Priests For Life. "The America We Seek: A Statement of Pro-Life Principle and Concern." From Priests For Life (1996): http://www.priestsforlife.org/articles/americaweseek.html

Shales, Tom. "'16 and Pregnant' Deftly Plumbs The Parent Trap." *The Washington Post* (Suburban edition). Washington, DC. June 11, 2009: http://www.washingtonpost.com/wp-dyn/content/article/2009/06/10/AR2009061003833.html

Shimizu, Celine. P. *The Hypersexuality of Race: Performing Asian/American Women on Screen and Scene.* Durham: Duke University Press, 2007.

Solinger, Rickie. *Pregnancy and Power: A Short History of Reproductive Politics inAmerica.* New York: New York University Press, 2005.

———. "Race and 'Value': Black and White Illegitimate Babies, in the U.S.A., 1945–1965." *Gender & History* 4, no. 3 (1992): 343–63.

Valenti, Jessica. *The Purity Myth: How America's Obsession with Virginity is Hurting Young Women.* Berkeley, CA: Seal Press, 2009.

Weprin, Alex. "MTV's '16 and Pregnant' Draws in Demo; Teenage pregnancy docu-series top program among F12–34s." *Broadcasting & Cable.* Dow Jones Factiva, June 12, 2009.

Wheaton College. "Defining the Term in Contemporary Times." Institute for the Study of American Evangelicals, 2008. http://isae.wheaton.edu/defining-evangelicalism/defining-the-term-in-contemporary-times/

7

Just Say Me? (Mis)representing Female Adolescent Sexual Agency on *The Secret Life of the American Teenager*

Elena Frank

In recent years a large pool of popular literature that examines the sexualization of adolescent girls has emerged. Books such as *Girls Gone Skank* (2008), *So Sexy So Soon* (2008), and *Oral Sex is the New Good Night Kiss* (2009) seek to expose the many ways that present-day U.S. culture, particularly the media, sexually exploits young women and girls. All of these books are meant to serve as a wake-up call to naïve parents—to demonstrate that even "good" girls may participate in a variety of age-inappropriate or illicit sexual activities. Ultimately, all of these books demonize what they consider to be the eroticization of childhood, leaving no space for considering the existence of forms of healthy sexuality or sexual agency for young adolescent women.

Historically, teenage girls' sexuality has been defined as both dangerous and deviant.[1] As a result, girls' sexuality is often perceived as a psychological and social problem that requires intervention.[2] Consequently, many studies assume that sexually active teenage girls have a deficit or illness.[3] In addition, the majority of studies equate sexuality directly with penile–vaginal intercourse, considering only the visible consequences (e.g., pregnancy or HIV transmission) of this activity as relevant to adolescent girls' sexuality. Populations that exhibit more visible consequences than others also bear the brunt of social policies concerning sexuality, including young girls, poor and working-class youth, teenagers with disabilities, black and Latino adolescents, and LGBTQ youth.[4] The fact that so many of the studies on adolescent sexuality focus on sexual health solely in the context of sexual risk reinforces a widespread culture of fear around youth sexuality, consistently framing girls as sexual victims, rather than sexual agents.

Furthermore, little research has been conducted on the multiple meanings associated with sexual agency among adolescent girls, including the ways in which sexual agency is represented in popular media, as well as whether and how adolescent girls interpret sexual agency. As a result, the goal of this research is to shed light on the complexity of meanings associated with the sexual agency of adolescent girls in U.S. popular media. Through an exploration of the roles gender and power play in the negotiation of abortion, birth control, and masturbation on the popular primetime television drama *The Secret Life of the American Teenager,* I develop a theoretical framework that takes into account both the possibilities for the recognition of adolescent female sexual agency *and* the constraints simultaneously inherent in these depictions. The unveiling of the nuances of adolescent female sexual agency, and the complex interplay of sexuality, gender, and power for young people, are crucial steps toward understanding young women's multiple, and sometimes contradictory, paths to becoming active, embodied, desirous, pleasure-seeking sexual citizens.

Literature Review

While some theorists singularly define the *capacity* "to determine and act" as agentic, others assert that the *exercise* "of will and conscious action" is also an essential component of agency.[5] Taken a step further, agency can be conceived as a complex relational and contextual process; something one attempts to achieve or accomplish, rather than a static entity.[6] Consequently, enactment of sexual agency can be understood as a specific form of empowerment that is about taking control of sexuality; an interactive, constantly renegotiated process.[7]

Minimal research on the meaning of sexual agency has been conducted, particularly from a feminist perspective. Topics addressed include negotiating sexual consent,[8] negotiating sexual reputation,[9] negotiating safer sex,[10] agency and virginity loss,[11] and agency in relation to motherhood and childbirth.[12] Consistent within this research is the notion that gender norms may greatly influence young women's experience of and possibilities for agency.

Defined as "the pleasure we get from our bodies and the experience of living in a body," *sexual subjectivity* has been conceptualized in feminist work as a significant component of agency.[13] For example, Tolman's research on the phenomenology of teenage girls' sexual desire explores how each young woman experiences herself as a sexual being, feels a sense of entitlement to sexual pleasure and safety, makes active sexual choices, and acknowledges, experiences, and acts upon sexual desire.[14] Contrary to popular discourses about adolescent female sexuality, Tolman contends that "not feeling sexual desire may put girls in danger or 'at risk.'"[15] Furthermore, spurred on by Fine's notion of a "missing discourse of desire"—the tendency of young women to define themselves in terms of men's sexual needs and desires, rather than their own[16]—feminist research on sexual education has sought to expose the heteronormative, 'unnatural' lessons girls are often taught about their bodies and sexuality.[17] Concerned about the negative ramifications of the continuing denial and silencing of female adolescent sexual desire and agency, these researchers ultimately call for an analytic and policy framework that conceptualizes sexual subjectivity and agency as a crucial component of girls' sexual health.

On the other hand, concerns about the oppressive potential of sexual agency have also arisen within recent feminist research on the sexualization of culture. Based on the concept of a "postfeminist sensibility," Gill argues that the notion of choice, being one's authentic self, and pleasing oneself have become central for young women, with a language of empowerment and control dominating media discourse.[18] A primary component of this "postfeminist sensibility" is the performance of femininity and sexiness, with girls experimenting and "playing" with their sexual "power."[19] Lazar's notion of "power femininity" also comes into play here, as girls appear to adopt an empowered, desiring, and sexual feminine identity that supposedly operates in contrast to their previous "sex object" status.[20] In addition, the mainstreaming of "raunch feminism" and *Sex in the City's* "have sex like a man" mantra has resulted in young women adopting a male model of sexual power where participation in the pornography industry, sexual objectification, and body modification practices are constructed as a path to liberation rather than oppression.[21]

Gill contends that these young women do not possess "real" power, but rather have been endowed with a conditional agency rooted in the reinforcement of traditional gender norms.[22] Gill argues that it is the display or performance of a certain dimension of sexual knowledge, practice, and agency that has become normative.[23] This contention is reinforced by the notion that girls' sexual agency tends to be represented as legitimately "active" in the media only when linked to consumption.[24]

Ultimately, research on the sexualization of culture overwhelmingly concludes that this "postfeminist" media discourse contains a regulatory element. While "hailed through a discourse of 'can-do girl power,'" Gill contends that young women's bodies "are powerfully reinscribed as sexual objects; women are presented as active, desiring social subjects, but they are subject to a level of scrutiny and hostile surveillance which has no historical precedent."[25] Serving as a guide for girls' self-management, such popular culture representations may impose new discourses that govern subjects through the internalization of regimes of disciplinary power. Evans, Riley, and Shankar's "technologies of sexiness" framework reiterates this point by arguing that these so-called sexually "empowered" girls actually draw on existing dominant discourses of female sexuality in order to formulate these "new" sexual subjectivities, consequently reproducing hegemonic discourses rather than challenging them.[26] As a result, power can be seen in this case as not necessarily operating by "silencing or suppressing female sexual agency, but by constructing it in highly specific ways."[27] Consequently, sexual agency may be conceived as a mechanism of regulation and oppression rather than a potential tool of liberation.

Methodology

With the understanding that sexual agency is a highly complex, contextualized, and potentially contradictory process, this research seeks to explore the ways that girls' sexual agency may be enabled and disabled simultaneously, keeping in mind that representations of the enactment of sexual agency may often result in both the resistance *and* recuperation of hegemonic gender norms. By interrogating the nuances of sexual agency as represented in this context, the following analysis considers the ways that sexual agency may be presented as both a mechanism of liberation and oppression. With the Foucauldian (1976) understanding that discourse around sexuality operates as a powerful instrument for the regulation of societies and individuals,[28] this research conceives of popular media as a form of social control, a disciplinary technology that serves to delineate the boundaries between normative and non-normative sexuality, and consequently, shape the interpretations of individual behavior. As adolescents are particularly likely to learn about sex-related topics through popular media, it is apparent that *The Secret Life of the American Teenager* provides a ripe site for examining the interplay between sexuality, gender, and power as presented to young people today.[29]

In its debut season in 2008, *Secret Life* was rated television's number one program in the twelve-to-thirty-four-year-old demographic and the highest rated original series in *ABC Family's* history.[30] After three seasons, *Secret Life* continues to dominate in the television ratings for the adolescent demographic. Revolving around the relationships between families and friends as they deal with multiple unexpected teen pregnancies, issues of sex and reproduction are central to the program's plot development. However, because *ABC Family* is owned by the Disney Corporation, and creator Brenda Hampton is known for producing programs with strong religious undertones, the motivation behind the incorporation of seemingly 'liberal' topics is unclear. Given this ambiguity, as well as the program's sustained mainstream popularity and sex-focused dialogue, *Secret Life* is situated as an ideal medium for evaluating present-day discourse(s) surrounding adolescent sexuality.

The initial sample for analysis consisted of the sixty-one episodes of *Secret Life* aired as of January 2011. This included season one (twenty-three episodes), season two (twenty-four episodes), and half of season three (fourteen episodes). I conducted an initial viewing of all the episodes in order to identify those that address the three main focal points for this analysis—abortion, birth control, and masturbation. Each topic was found in at least one episode from each of the three seasons, and dialogue concerning abortion (seven episodes), birth control (four episodes), and masturbation (five episodes) were coded using purposive sampling. All of the scenes that included discussion of these topics were transcribed and coded using axial coding.[31] This resulted in the analysis of nine scenes addressing birth control, twenty-five scenes addressing abortion, and sixteen scenes addressing masturbation.

According to this theory building approach, "concepts and relationships emerge from the data," rather than the reverse.[32] The theoretical concepts outlined earlier in the literature review were used as a starting point for analyzing the dialogue from these scenes, encouraging the exploration of related topics and themes. The aim was to identify discourses around abortion, birth control, and masturbation and the representation of gender, sexuality, and power in these contexts. A line-by-line analysis of each scene was conducted, and the transcripts were read multiple times in order to continue to reflect on and reformulate working theories about the relationships that emerged within the dataset. As the transcripts were examined further, the data was grouped thematically, as is presented below.

Results

Abortion

Over the course of three seasons of *Secret Life*, two main female adolescent characters, Amy and Adrian, discover that they are pregnant. Subsequently, the storyline follows these girls' lives as they consider their "options." This topic is presented in three primary ways: 1) having an abortion is a *bad* choice; 2) having (or not having) a baby *is* a choice; and 3) choosing to have an abortion is always a *difficult* decision that comes with a lot of *uncertainty*.

While peers and parents repeatedly tell both Amy and Adrian that they have the right to make the decision about whether or not to have an abortion, abortion is simultaneously constructed as not the "right" choice. This message is communicated in a variety of ways. First, most of Amy and Adrian's friends and family refuse to help them obtain access to an abortion or accompany them to a clinic. Second, it is suggested that this decision requires parental guidance or authority because a pregnant teenager is still a "child" and not a "woman." Third, having an abortion is represented as reflecting negatively on a girl's character—as weak, or the "easy" way out. Fourth, obtaining an abortion is constructed as irresponsible if you have other "choices," such as an offer of marriage. Fifth, abortion is discussed by some characters as being a sin or crime. Finally, it is suggested that only "certain" groups of people need, advocate for, or obtain abortions. The only characters who consistently conceptualize abortion as a valid choice are African American and Latina women. Furthermore, abortion is discussed as something "messy" from which "rich kids" are protected.

Having a baby is not considered the only possible outcome of pregnancy on *Secret Life*. Some characters advocate for the girls' right to choose—to choose to follow through with the pregnancy *or* to choose to terminate it. At times, both Amy and Adrian appear to construct their choice to have an abortion as way of "taking control" and doing what is "right," "responsible," and "best" for them. Additionally, while framing the potential father's input as valuable, this choice is constructed as the girls' decision to make. Furthermore, in several instances it is insinuated that having an abortion may actually be a *more* "responsible" or "right" decision than going through with the pregnancy.

Whether represented as a valid decision to be made by the expectant adolescent, or as a "bad" choice, the message that abortion is a difficult decision accompanied with much uncertainty is clearly represented on *Secret Life*. The father of Amy's baby, Ricky, explains that he is not "for" or "against" abortion, but rather is "for" the parents making a responsible decision before the baby is born. Adrian's boyfriend, Ben, similarly acknowledges, "There is no good decision. Neither is a good choice." After we see Amy and Adrian struggle with their parents, peers, and selves about how to define the "right" choice over the course of several episodes, ultimately both go to the family planning clinic intending to obtain an abortion, but change their minds and decide to go through with the pregnancy at the last minute.

Birth Control

While discussion of contraceptive options is generally minimal on *Secret Life*, over the course of three seasons many of the female adolescent characters consider going on the birth control pill. Notably, the majority of the dialogue about "the pill" occurs between a girl and her parent(s) or friends, and not with a sexual partner. The pill is discussed in three primary ways: 1) as a prophylactic that does not protect against all sexual risks; 2) as a mechanism for girls to make a choice that allows them to feel more sexually confident and knowledgeable; and 3) as having negative associations.

The discussions of birth control on *Secret Life* frequently serve to reiterate that pregnancy is not the only risk of having sex. Parents and peers often encourage the pairing of a condom with the pill, reminding the teenage characters, "…anytime you have sex, even if you're using birth control, things can go wrong." In this context condoms tend to be constructed as the boy's responsibility, with the pill constructed as the girl's option for sexual protection.

Going on the pill is also constructed as a choice girls can make that allows them to feel more sexually confident and knowledgeable. Amy's sister Ashley's experience going to her pediatrician to obtain the pill illustrates that girls do not need parental permission to procure birth control. Grace, another main character, contends that the process required to obtain birth control—visiting a doctor, getting a prescription, going to the pharmacy—makes one more aware of the realities and potential consequences of engaging in sex. In fact, Grace even argues that having the pill is a more "real" and effective deterrent from having sex than her promise ring. Grace acts excited and happy just having the pill in her possession, expressing that she feels a certain power and pleasure in knowing "If I do want to have sex, I can have safe sex." Despite their commitment to maintaining abstinence, both Ashley and Grace indicate that they want to be "protected" and have a "back-up plan" if they are unable to stop themselves from "making a mistake."

On *Secret Life* the pill is also associated with a number of negative characteristics. First, it is suggested that the pill is associated with promiscuity—possessing the pill means that a girl is available and wants to have sex. Adrian tells Grace not to tell her romantic interest that she has the pill because "he's just going to want to have sex with you, and so is half the school." Furthermore, it is suggested that it is not "Christian" to have the pill, and that sex is solely for procreative purposes within the context of marriage.

Masturbation

Referenced in five episodes and the focus of an episode entitled "Just Say Me," female masturbation is represented in the following three ways on *Secret Life*: 1) as a substitute for partner sex and consequently a mechanism for maintaining abstinence; 2) as a display of active, autonomous female sexuality; and 3) as a healthy and normal sexual activity. The main female characters develop the notion of "just say me" as a more "positive," "practical," and "active" alternative to "just say no." They start this campaign to "take care of themselves" as a way to keep them from "having sex with guys." Grace considers "just say me" as a "substitute for sex, not a substitute for a relationship." However, the girls claim that "just say me" means more than masturbation—it is about empowerment and "taking control of your life."

Female masturbation is constructed as a tool for girls to resist sexual activity and remain abstinent. Grace's mother advocates masturbation as a way for Grace to resist her "raging hormones" and Ashley's father grants permission for her and her boyfriend's "parts...[to] work alone, but not together." Additionally, Grace sees masturbation as something that fits in with the agenda of her church's teen abstinence group. However, Amy expresses doubt that "just say me" would actually stop people from having partner sex, and Ashley and Adrian both concede that masturbation is a valid option with or without a boyfriend.

The girls' frank discussion of female masturbation and their "just say me" campaign serves as a representation of a public display of active, autonomous female sexuality. However, rather than framing masturbation in terms of girls' sexual pleasure, masturbation is primarily employed as a means for girls to resist sex, and therefore manipulate boys. The primary goal of "just say me" is to keep the boys from cheating. What emerges is a battle of the sexes, with the girls "staging a revolution," which results in "guys not hooking up" as the "collateral damage."

Masturbation is also presented as healthy and normal in *Secret Life*. Statistics indicating that adolescent boys *and* girls masturbate are presented in the dialogue. Factual information about the physical and psychological health benefits of masturbation are also presented. Furthermore, humorous commentary about masturbation and religion highlight the hypocrisy of religious taboos on masturbation. For example, characters refer to "a great way to go blind" or enjoying engaging in "eye-damaging activities." Also, when the president of the teen abstinence group kicks Grace out and states, "Jesus never said 'just say me.' He said 'just say no,'" Grace responds, "Jesus never said 'just say no.' Nancy Reagan said 'just say no.'" Some of this dialogue also serves to highlight the existence of a sexual double standard of behavior. For example, Grace tells her ex-boyfriend Jack "I'm pretty sure you break the rules all the time. Guys break the rules all the time, but for some reason nobody likes it when girls break the rules."

While it is implied that some of the girls masturbate semi-regularly, the majority are shown smiling the first few days of their week of "just say me," but are later depicted as looking bored and restless. The "just say me" episode resolves with the girls going back to their boyfriends by the end of the week, with the implication being that they no longer masturbate.

Discussion

Analysis of the representation of abortion, birth control, and masturbation on *Secret Life* clearly reflects the complex and contradictory nature of adolescent female sexual agency. The girls on *Secret Life* are primarily depicted as feeling like they have the right to make an active choice and take control of their bodies by electing to obtain an abortion. They consistently express the belief that any decision about their body is theirs to make, and not their boyfriends' or parents'. However, while represented as possessing the capacity to choose, they are ultimately unable to take action and go through with the abortion. The girls' ability to exercise their will appears to be undermined by their parents' insistence that girls lack the capacity to make decisions about their sexuality because they are not adults. Girls are also shown as having internalized the construction of abortion as a "weak" or "bad" choice by parents and peers. Presented as a choice that people with other choices do not make, abortion becomes associated solely with those individuals who fall outside a heteronormative framework or who may be considered 'deviant.' As a consequence, what it might mean to feel or act agentically for these girls becomes more complex. When there is no clear-cut "good" or "right" choice, it appears to be more difficult to feel "in control" or "empowered." Challenging prevailing sexual discourses by providing a positive example of girls feeling an entitlement to control their bodies *and* simultaneously recuperating gendered, raced, and classed stereotypes about abortion, this representation ultimately suggests that negotiating between being a teenage mother and having an abortion is a stressful and difficult process for everyone, and that neither choice will really make you feel "in control." Ultimately, this presents unintended pregnancy and reproductive "choice" as an issue that "responsible" girls should simply avoid.

The notion that girls might experience pleasure in making an active sexual choice, such as obtaining the pill, is also represented on *Secret Life*. Feeling entitled to protection from pregnancy and taking action to ensure this sexual safety appears to enhance girls' confidence and self-esteem. It is suggested that by allowing girls to assert control over their bodies and sexual lives, they might be more assertive in sexual situations, and consequently more likely to "just say no." However, the girls on *Secret Life* express a desire to go on the pill based on the concern that they might not have the ability to exercise agency in a sexual situation. Despite a commitment to abstinence, fearing that they may not always have control over their own sexuality, these girls pursue the pill as a preemptive safeguard against any future "mistakes." Consequently, the agency represented as exercised and experienced by obtaining the pill obscures the fact that these girls clearly do not feel that they possess control over their sexuality and bodies. This representation suggests that these girls are endowed with a conditional agency—one that applies only to those individuals who conform or intend to conform to traditional hegemonic norms of gender and sexuality.

On *Secret Life* girls are also depicted as discussing and participating in the ultimate safer sex behavior: masturbation. A challenge to traditional norms of femininity and double standards of sexual behavior, girls are represented as "in control" of their sexuality, displaying an active, autonomous, and even public sexuality. Presented as healthy and normative, masturbation is constructed as a way for girls to be sexually "active" and safe, without engaging in partner sex. "Just say me" is hailed as highly agentic—a mechanism for girls to control their sexuality and feel empowered. However, while one would expect sexual desire and pleasure to be a central component, these factors are largely absent. Instead, the "just say me" campaign is a sexual power play; a performance intended to manipulate the boys. While a small proportion of the girls are depicted as possessing a genuine sexual desire and interest in masturbation, the majority appear to be performing a particular version of liberated femininity as a means of shifting the balance of sexual power.

This representation of sexual agency on *Secret Life* enables the recognition of adolescent female sexual subjectivity and challenges traditional notions of femininity through the portrayal of girls making active sexual choices, feeling "in control" over their sexuality, and claiming their right to sexual safety and health. In addition, providing representations of girls negotiating controversial issues related to their sexuality challenges dominant discourses by exposing viewers to topics and perspectives generally deemed inappropriate or dangerous for girls. Consequently, adolescent viewers are potentially armed with information, however biased, that they might not necessarily receive in formal sexual education programs or at home. In addition, while conservative perspectives are rife, *Secret Life* does boldly attempt to debunk popular religious ideologies about abortion and masturbation.

Despite the liberating potential of these representations, however, adolescent female sexual agency is simultaneously disabled. Often accommodated within a heteronormative context, the sexual agency exhibited by the girls on *Secret Life* also reinforces essentialist notions about gender and a sexual double standard of behavior. Adultist assumptions about girls' sexual knowledge and behavior permeate these representations, undermining the opportunity for recognition of these girls' capacity for sexual agency. In addition, consistent with the bulk of academic, education, and policy research that examines young women and sexuality, the portrayals of sexual agency on *Secret Life* tend to revolve around the prevention of physical sexual health risks. While the negative right to engage in sex free from danger is an important component of sexual subjectivity, the positive right to embodied experience of sexuality and pleasure is also crucial. Shockingly, even in the context of masturbation, these girls are rarely, if ever, depicted as experiencing themselves as sexual beings, possessing sexual desire, or expressing entitlement to sexual pleasure. This omission serves to recuperate assumptions about sex as serving a primarily procreative and male pleasure purpose, and consequently devalues female sexual pleasure within mainstream sexuality discourse.

Thus, it is apparent how the representation of certain kinds of conditional agency within popular media discourse may at times operate in a regulatory manner, obscuring the realities and nuances of girls' sexual experiences and feelings. For example, the girls' expression of agency with regard to the birth control pill masks the fact that they do not expect to be able to control their bodies in a sexual situation. A common theme in research on girls' virginity loss, this "it just happened" rhetoric perpetuates the notion that girls often do not feel agentic with regard to intercourse.[33] An "exercise of self-determination," many of the girls on *Secret Life* also appear to enact "power femininity" as part of the "just say me" campaign.[34] Adopting a male model of sexual power, the girls perform "pleasing" themselves in the hopes of shifting the balance of sexual power. This "performance of active, confident, autoerotic sexuality"[35] presents a form of sexual agency that may challenge norms of passive femininity, but that does *not* challenge conventions of masculinity, and consequently reinscribes heteronormative gender relations.[36]

Conclusion

While popular media may call on young women to manage and discipline their own sexuality by drawing on and reinforcing dominant discourses of gender and sexuality, new elements that challenge traditional discourses are nevertheless present. For example, despite the underlying messages that mirror abstinence-only-until-marriage sexual education ideologies and reiterate that there is no "healthy" sexuality for girls, offering up masturbation as an "active" mechanism for girls to manage their sexuality is clearly a novel, and potentially more effective, approach to advocating abstinence in comparison with more traditional methods. In addition, given research indicating that disciplines of conventional femininity can inhibit young women's agency in ensuring safer sex encounters, presenting the pill as a way for girls to exercise sexual assertiveness without necessarily visibly violating norms of femininity, such as passivity and sexual innocence, may increase girls' understanding of their possibilities for exercising sexual agency.[37] This is particularly relevant considering that many young women may be less concerned about pregnancy or STI infection than with the "risk" of losing social status, being labeled as promiscuous, or losing their boyfriends.[38]

Ultimately, while the situating of these liberal ideologies within more conservative, traditional discourses may make many feminists uncomfortable, the reality is that viewers may be much more likely to consume potentially controversial ideas in an open-minded manner when embedded within the discourses with which they are already familiar. Regardless of whether the overarching messages communicated about sexuality, gender, and power on *Secret Life* can be classified as liberating or oppressive, representing a diversity of possibilities for at least partial recognition of girls' sexual agency, and its inherent complex and contradictory nature, encourages young viewers to think critically and reevaluate prevailing social norms regarding sexuality and gender roles. Examples of girls exercising (and not exercising) sexual agency in varying capacities in popular media provide an avenue for engaging adolescent girls and boys in dialogues about a range of discursive alternatives about sexuality. Ultimately, the ways in which youth (and adults) engage with these representations is more important than the specific messages produced by media conglomerates; such media may facilitate a challenge to, and a reformulation of, mainstream discursive practices.

Notes

1. Constance A. Nathanson, *Dangerous Passage: The Social Control of Sexuality in Women's Adolescence* (Philadelphia: Temple University Press, 1991), 3.
2. Deborah P. Welsh, Sharon S. Rostosky, and Myra C. Kawaguchi, "A Normative Perspective of Adolescent Girls' Developing Sexuality," in *Sexuality, Society, and Feminism*, eds. Cheryl B. Travis and Jacquelyn W. White, 111–40 (Washington, DC: American Psychological Association, 2000), 113.
3. Ibid., 115.
4. Michell Fine and Sara I. McClelland, "Sexuality Education and Desire: Still Missing after All These Years," *Harvard Educational Review* 76, no. 3 (2006): 297–338, 299.
5. Heather Powers Albanesi, *Gender and Sexual Agency: How Young People Make Choices about Sex* (Plymouth, UK: Lexington Books 2010), 10; Ellen Messer-Davidow, "Acting Otherwise," in *Provoking Agents: Gender and Agency in Theory and Practice*, ed. Judith Kegan Gardiner, 23–51 (Chicago: University of Illinois Press, 1995), 25; Rob White and Johanna Wyn, "Youth Agency and Social Context," *Journal of Sociology* 34, no. 3 (1998): 314–27, 318.
6. Carolina Overlien, "Innocent Girls or Active Young Women? Negotiating Sexual Agency at a Detention Home," *Feminism & Psychology* 13, no. 3 (2003): 345–67, 346–47; White and Wyn, "Youth Agency," 315–16, 318.
7. Albanesi, *Gender and Sexual Agency*, 148; Rosalind Gill, "Empowerment/Sexism: Figuring Female Sexual Agency in Contemporary Advertising," *Feminism & Psychology* 18, no. 1 (2008): 35–60, 37; Janet Holland and Caroline Ramazanoglu, "Risk, Power, and the Possibility of Pleasure: Young Women and Safer Sex," *AIDS Care* 4, no. 3 (1992): 273.
8. Ingrid Smette, Kari Stefansen, and Svein Mossige, "Responsible Victims? Young People's Understandings of Agency and Responsibility in Sexual Situations Involving Underage Girls," *Young* 17, no. 4 (2009): 351–73, 351; Sarah A. Vannier and Lucia F. O'Sullivan, "Sex

Without Desire: Characteristics of Occasions of Sexual Compliance in Young Adults' Committed Relationships," *Journal of Sex Research* 47, no. 5 (2010): 429–39, 429.

9. Feona Attwood, "Sluts and Riot Grrrls: Female Identity and Sexual Agency," *Journal of Gender Studies* 16, no. 3 (2007): 233–47, 233; Jenny Kitzinger, "'I'm Sexually Attractive but I'm Powerful': Young Women Negotiating Sexual Reputation," *Women's Studies International Forum* 18, no. 2 (1995): 187–96, 187.

10. Holland et al. 1998, 117; Holland and Ramazanoglu, "Risk, Power," 7; Albanesi, *Gender and Sexual Agency*, 145.

11. Laura Carpenter, *Virginity Lost: An Intimate Portrait of First Sexual Experiences* (New York: New York University Press, 2005), 195–97; Karin A. Martin, *Puberty, Sexuality, and the Self: Boys and Girls at Adolescence* (New York: Routledge, 1996), 15.

12. Saara Greene, "Becoming Responsible: Young Mothers' Decision Making Regarding Motherhood and Abortion," *Journal of Progressive Human Services* 17, no. 1 (2006): 25–43, 25; Mary Horton-Salway and Abigail Locke, "'But you might be damaging your baby': Constructing choice and risk in labour and childbirth," *Feminism & Psychology* 20, no. 4 (2010): 435–53, 435.

13. Martin, *Puberty*, 10.

14. Deborah Tolman, *Dilemmas of Desire: Teenage Girls Talk about Sexuality* (Cambridge, MA: Harvard University Press, 2002), 6.

15. Ibid., 21.

16. Michelle Fine, "Sexuality, Schooling, and Adolescent Females: The Missing Discourse of Desire," *Harvard Educational Review* 58, no. 1 (1988): 29–53, 29.

17. Jessica Fields, *Risky Lessons: Sex Education and Social Inequality* (New Brunswick, NJ: Rutgers University Press, 2008), 102.

18. Rosalind Gill, "Postfeminist Media Culture," *European Journal of Cultural Studies* 10, no. 2 (2007): 147–66, 153.

19. Ibid., 151.

20. Michelle M. Lazar, "'Discover the Power of Femininity!': Analyzing Global 'Power Femininity' in Local Advertising." *Feminist Media Studies* 6, no. 4 (2006): 505–17, 505.

21. Ariel Levy, *Female Chauvinist Pigs: Women and the Rise of Raunch Culture* (New York: Free Press, 2005), 82.

22. Rosalind Gill, "Critical Respect: The Difficulties and Dilemmas of Agency and 'Choice' for Feminism: A Reply to Duits and van Zoonen," *European Journal of Women's Studies* 14 (2007): 69–80, 72.

23. Ibid.

24. Gill, "Postfeminist Media Culture," 153; Sue Jackson and Elizabeth Westrupp, "Sex, Postfeminist Popular Culture and the Pre-Teen Girl," *Sexualities* 13, no. 3 (2010): 357–76, 372; Estella Ticknell, Deborah Chambers, Joost Van Loon, and Nichola Hudson, "Begging for It: 'New Femininities,' Social Agency, and Moral Discourse in Contemporary Teenage and Men's Magazines," *Feminist Media Studies* 3, no. 1 (2003): 47–64, 53.

25. Gill, "Postfeminist Media Culture," 163.

26. Adrienne Evans, Sarah Riley, and Avi Shankar, "Technologies of Sexiness: Theorizing Women's Engagement in the Sexualization of Culture." *Feminism & Psychology* 20, no. 1 (2010): 114–31, 127.

27. Gill, "Empowerment/Sexism," 53.
28. Michel Foucault, *The History of Sexuality: Volume 1 An Introduction,* Trans. Robert Hurley (New York: Penguin Books, 2006).
29. Michael J. Sutton, "Shaking the Tree of Knowledge for Forbidden Fruit: Where Adolescents Learn About Sexuality and Contraception," in *Sexual Teens, Sexual Media: Investigating Media's Influence on Adolescent Sexuality,* eds. Jane D. Brown, Jeanne R. Steele, and Kim Walsh-Childers, 25–56 (Mahwah, NJ: Lawrence Erlbaum Associates, Inc. 2002), 32.
30. "'The Secret is Out!' ABC Family Orders Thirteen Additional Episodes of the Hit ABC Family Series 'The Secret Life of the American Teenager,'" ABCFamily.com. Last modified July 17, 2008, 1.
31. See Strauss and Corbin's procedures for grounded theory methodology: Anselm Strauss and Juliet Corbin, *Basics of Qualitative Research: Techniques and Procedures for Developing Grounded Theory* (Thousand Oaks, CA: SAGE Publications, 1998).
32. Ibid., 33.
33. Carpenter, *Virginity Lost,* 195–97; Martin, *Puberty,* 15.
34. Lazar, "Discover the Power," 510.
35. Evans, Riley, and Shankar, "Technologies of Sexiness," 124, 126.
36. Holland et al., *The Male in the Head,* 119.
37. Ibid., 117.
38. Holland and Ramazonglu, "Risk, Power," 7; Holland et al., *The Male in the Head,* 30; White and Wyn, "Youth and Agency," 320.

Works Cited

Albanesi, Heather Powers. *Gender and Sexual Agency: How Young People Make Choices about Sex.* Plymouth, UK: Lexington Books, 2010.

Attwood, Feona. "Sluts and Riot Grrrls: Female Identity and Sexual Agency." *Journal of Gender Studies* 16, no. 3 (2007): 233–47.

Carpenter, Laura. *Virginity Lost: An Intimate Portrait of First Sexual Experiences.* New York: New York University Press, 2005.

Evans, Adrienne, Sarah Riley, and Avi Shankar. "Technologies of Sexiness: Theorizing Women's Engagement in the Sexualization of Culture." *Feminism & Psychology* 20, no. 1 (2010): 114–31.

Fields, Jessica. *Risky Lessons: Sex Education and Social Inequality.* New Brunswick, NJ: Rutgers University Press, 2008.

Fine, Michelle. "Sexuality, Schooling, and Adolescent Females: The Missing Discourse of Desire." *Harvard Educational Review* 58, no. 1 (1988): 29–53.

Fine, Michelle and Sara I. McClelland. "Sexuality Education and Desire: Still Missing after All These Years." *Harvard Educational Review* 76, no. 3 (2006): 297–338.

Foucault, Michel. *The History of Sexuality: Volume 1 An Introduction.* Trans. Robert Hurley. New York: Penguin Books, 2006.

Gill, Rosalind C. "Critical Respect: The Difficulties and Dilemmas of Agency and 'Choice' for Feminism: A Reply to Duits and van Zoonen." *European Journal of Women's Studies* 14 (2007a): 69–80.

————. "Postfeminist Media Culture." *European Journal of Cultural Studies* 10, no. 2 (2007b): 147–66.

————. "Empowerment/Sexism: Figuring Female Sexual Agency in Contemporary Advertising." *Feminism & Psychology* 18, no. 1 (2008): 35–60.

Greene, Saara. "Becoming Responsible: Young Mothers' Decision Making Regarding Motherhood and Abortion." *Journal of Progressive Human Services* 17, no. 1 (2006): 25-43.

Holland, Janet and Caroline Ramazanoglu. "Risk, Power, and the Possibility of Pleasure: Young Women and Safer Sex." *AIDS Care* 4, no. 3 (1992): 273.

Holland, Janet Caroline Ramazanoglu, Sue Sharpe, and Rachel Thompson. *The Male in the Head: Young People, Heterosexuality, and Power*. London: The Tufnell Press, 1998.

Horton-Salway, Mary and Abigail Locke. "'But You Might Be Damaging Your Baby': Constructing Choice and Risk in Labour and Childbirth." *Feminism & Psychology* 20, no. 4 (2010): 435–53.

Jackson, Sue and Elizabeth Westrupp. "Sex, Postfeminist Popular Culture and the Pre-Teen Girl." *Sexualities* 13, no. 3 (2010): 357–76.

Kitzinger, Jenny. "'I'm Sexually Attractive but I'm Powerful': Young Women Negotiating Sexual Reputation." *Women's Studies International Forum* 18, no. 2 (1995): 187–96.

Lazar, Michelle M. "'Discover the Power of Femininity!': Analyzing Global 'Power Femininity' in Local Advertising." *Feminist Media Studies* 6, no. 4 (2006): 505–17.

Levy, Ariel. *Female Chauvinist Pigs: Women and the Rise of Raunch Culture*. New York: Free Press, 2005.

Martin, Karin A. *Puberty, Sexuality, and the Self: Boys and Girls at Adolescence*. New York: Routledge, 1996.

Messer-Davidow, Ellen. "Acting Otherwise." In *Provoking Agents: Gender and Agency in Theory and Practice*, ed. Judith Kegan Gardiner. Chicago: University of Illinois Press, 1995.

Nathanson, Constance A. *Dangerous Passage: The Social Control of Sexuality in Women's Adolescence*. Philadelphia: Temple University Press, 1991.

Overlien, Carolina. "Innocent Girls or Active Young Women? Negotiating Sexual Agency at a Detention Home." *Feminism & Psychology* 13, no. 3 (2003): 345–67.

Smette, Ingrid, Kari Stefansen, and Svein Mossige. "Responsible Victims? Young People's Understandings of Agency and Responsibility in Sexual Situations Involving Underage Girls." *Young* 17, no. 4 (2009): 351–73.

Strauss, Anselm and Juliet Corbin. *Basics of Qualitative Research: Techniques and Procedures for Developing Grounded Theory*. Thousand Oaks, CA: SAGE Publications, 1998.

Sutton, Michael J., et al. "Shaking the Tree of Knowledge for Forbidden Fruit: Where Adolescents Learn About Sexuality and Contraception." In *Sexual Teens, Sexual Media: Investigating Media's Influence on Adolescent Sexuality*, eds. Jane D. Brown, Jeanne R. Steele, and Kim Walsh-Childers. Mahwah, NJ: Lawrence Erlbaum Associates, Inc., 2002.

"The Secret is Out! ABC Family Orders Thirteen Additional Episodes of the Hit ABC Family Series 'The Secret Life of the American Teenager.'" ABCFamily.com. Last modified July 17, 2008. http://www.documbase.com/ABC-Family-American-Teenager.pdf

Ticknell, Estella, Deborah Chambers, Joost Van Loon, and Nichola Hudson. "Begging for It: 'New Femininities,' Social Agency, and Moral Discourse in Contemporary Teenage and Men's Magazines." *Feminist Media Studies* 3, no. 1 (2003): 47–64.

Tolman, Deborah. *Dilemmas of Desire: Teenage Girls Talk about Sexuality.* Cambridge, MA: Harvard University Press, 2002.

Vannier, Sarah A. and Lucia F. O'Sullivan. "Sex without Desire: Characteristics of Occasions of Sexual Compliance in Young Adults' Committed Relationships." *Journal of Sex Research* 47, no. 5 (2010): 429–39.

Welsh, Deborah P., Sharon S. Rostosky, and Myra C. Kawaguchi. "A Normative Perspective of Adolescent Girls' Developing Sexuality." In *Sexuality, Society, and Feminism*, eds. Cheryl B. Travis and Jacquelyn W. White. Washington, DC: American Psychological Association, 2000.

White, Rob and Johanna Wyn. "Youth Agency and Social Context." *Journal of Sociology* 34, no. 3 (1998): 314–27.

8

Producing Girl Citizens as Agents of Health: An Analysis of HPV Media Campaigns in the United States

Kellie Burns and Cristyn Davies

Introduction

In this chapter, we offer a critical reading of the promotional campaigns for the United States (U.S.) Gardasil® HPV/cervical vaccination program communicated through heritage and new media. We argue that critical readings of health media should focus on questions of production and consumption rather than just reception and representation.[1] Health media does more than merely reflect social norms and values about bodies and health; it produces and governs them. Conducting a close reading of televisual and online promotional materials, we make three key arguments: first, that the national Gardasil® vaccination campaign reflects a new public health model that positions individuals as neoliberal consumer-citizens responsible for managing their health and wellbeing. Second, we argue that the campaign, directed primarily at young women, mobilizes neoliberal discourses of risk, choice, and self-management alongside feminist political rhetoric that values empowerment, freedom, choice, and rights. Feminist tropes are co-opted by Merck's marketing imperatives in order to produce young women as a niche market of health consumers. Third, we foreground a low-budget counter-narrative alternative media campaign produced by young women and disseminated through YouTube. This campaign demonstrates the role of new media in producing agentic female citizenship and disrupting Merck's neoliberal, economic imperatives.

Mediating Healthy Citizenship

Critical Health Studies is concerned with the ways in which knowledge about health and illness is shaped by social, political, and institutional norms, and by media in its various forms.[2] Critical analyses of health media tend to ask how discourses of healthy or unhealthy bodies and lives are *represented* or *misrepresented* through mass media. Health media is understood to reflect social values and norms and is thus considered important for understanding dominant meanings of health. In this chapter we move beyond questions of representation to focus on questions of governmentality and mediation. Nikolas Rose (1999) suggests that, unlike other critical approaches, studies of governmentality

> ...seek to interrogate the problems and problematizations through which 'being' has been shaped in a thinkable and manageable form, the sites and locales where these problems formed and the authorities responsible for enunciating upon them, the techniques and devices invented, the modes of authority and subjectification engendered, and the telos of these ambitions and strategies.[3]

Through the lens of governmentality, we are concerned with how media texts produce and govern knowledge about health and thus construct the parameters for what constitutes intelligible healthy subjectivities and citizenship. Subjectivities are never formed solely by exterior or imposing forces of power, but are, instead, assembled through the tactics of state and institutional bodies along with the strategies that individuals employ to manage and make sense of the world around them. Governmentality studies shift the analytical focus of health media from questions of representation to questions of production and consumption and acknowledge that media cultures do more than merely influence or reflect the real. Instead, discourses of health produced through media outlets function as normalizing modalities that produce, shape, and regulate the norms of healthy bodies, healthy lives, and healthy citizen-subjects.

We understand media texts as active cultural objects that produce and govern social norms.[4] Media texts are fluid and polysemic, open to a variety of meanings depending on context within which texts are produced and consumed.[5] Following Latour, we understand mediation as incorporating processes that transform, translate, distort, and modify meaning.[6] Mediation is particularly significant in an era of convergent media where communication takes place across multiple media platforms. The cooperation between multiple media industries, and the migratory behavior of media audiences across entertainment platforms encourages and constructs consumers' active participation.[7] Following Jenkins, we believe that convergent media "alters the relationship between existing technologies, industries, markets, genres and audiences."[8] Our analysis attends to the extension of health media campaigns through social and new media including online forums and various consumer items linked to health campaigns or discourses. This kind of media convergence represents more than a corporate branding opportunity for health campaigns and/or pharmaceuticals, but also offers a reconfiguration of media power, a reshaping of media aesthetics, subjectivities and economics.[9] Media convergence is central to understanding how health media functions as site of knowledge production and how it is consumed by target niche audiences.

Risk, Choice, and Discourses of New Public Health

Since the mid-1970s, with the rise of neoliberalism and its critique of the welfare state, health policy and practice have placed a greater emphasis on individualism, and are characterized by the devolution of state responsibility for health care and social services to individuals and communities.[10] This represents a mode of governance where power operates "at a distance" to "conduct the conduct" of individuals and citizen groups.[11] A broad range of technologies ensures individuals participate in the process of self governance by taking responsibility for their health and for lessening their disease burden on the state apparatus. The new public health model, which characterizes health policy in the twenty-first century, mobilizes discourses of health rights and choice alongside discourses of self-care and responsibility.[12] Health is deemed a universal right and a fundamental good for which individual citizens should take personal responsibility. Individuals are both hailed and interpolated by health policies and media campaigns to take responsibility for managing their health and minimizing health risks for the future, both of which serve to minimize the burden of disease on the national economy. Lupton argues that the discursive coupling of health as a *right*, with practices of self-management and individual advocacy, shapes the way individuals access this *right*, and invisibilize governmental agendas. Individuals are assumed to be atomistic and agentic and it is through this discourse that new public health agendas receive "broad-based support while remaining closely wedded to official objectives. [This discursive coupling] serves to mask shifting relations of power involving, in particular, a redefinition of citizenship rights and responsibilities."[13]

Risk functions as a technology of governance in a neoliberal governmental climate and is thus central to new public health discourse.[14] According to Robert Castel risk is not bound to concrete or specific dangers, but to a series of abstract factors that pose *possible* dangers or threats.[15] This shift from concrete individual risk to abstract risk factors, extends risk's regulatory effect and multiplies the possibilities for self-management and intervention. Peterson and Lupton (1996) illustrate how risk is produced through new public health discourse and how it is mobilized as a technology of governance. They understand both the origin and outcomes of health threats to be socially, culturally, and politically constituted. It is through these social processes and modalities that health dangers and threats become labelled "health risks."[16]

The body becomes the site and object for self-work and having a healthy body is central to individuals' identity within the current neoliberal era of new public health. A healthy body signifies self-control, self-entrepreneurialism and is intelligible within the parameters of Western neoliberal citizenship. In contrast, an unhealthy body marks incomplete or failed citizenship, for it has not been appropriately managed despite a range of knowledge cultures and consumer products available to *become healthier*.[17] As Lupton (2003) explains, attention to the body as a project in new public health discourse means bodies are always open to management and reconstruction and this project is bound almost entirely to the desire and drive of the individual. Consumer practices and goods are linked to the countless projects of bodily maintenance, improvement, and compliance.

Gender difference organizes discourses of health risk. Feminist scholarship has highlighted the role of science and medical discourse in reproducing gender difference as a mode of control over women's capacity to act as equal citizens, and to solidify and naturalize men's social and political power.[18] This scholarship has been significant in shifting the dominant discourses governing scientific and medical research and practice. Despite this shift, pathologies around women's reproductive capacities persist and the human subject in Western medicine is premised on the white heterosexual male subject.[19] Discourses of risk and self-management still organize approaches to women's health, though greater emphasis is placed on the freedom women have acquired to manage this themselves. The new public health approach mobilizes feminist discourses of freedom, rights, and choice in order to rearticulate women as agentic, self-directed subjects taking control of their health. As a complex regime of power and knowledge,[20] new public health policies and practices mobilize language similar to that of feminist and other equity-based movements—self-determination, access, participation, control, and empowerment—and in doing so, produce and broaden the reach and effects of self-regulation.

The use of feminist and equity discourses to promote health campaigns is a strategic rhetorical move because contemporary citizen-subjects are attuned to these discourses, associating this language with freedom, equity, and agency. The HPV campaign materials, produced by Merck, appealed to girls and young women by emphasizing young women's *right* to agency around their current and future sexual health. The specific marketing of agentic girlhood by Merck's HPV vaccination marketing campaign not only produces girls and young women as an 'at risk' population, but also constitutes healthy girlhood through postfeminist and neoliberal notions of choice, empowerment, and continual self-management.

Girlhood, Citizenship, and Sexual Health

Feminist and cultural studies scholars have widely theorized girlhood and gendered experiences of being a girl.[21] This scholarship has identified ways in which girls take up different subject positions within competing discourses of gender that are available to them. As Robinson and Davies (2008) have argued, girls' location in discourses of gender can depend on a range of issues such as one's age, class, sexuality, ethnicity, and peer group influences.

Through neoliberal discourses of postfeminism, girls' bodies, labor, power, and social interactions are subject to governance to an unprecedented degree.[22] Notions of choice, of 'being oneself,' and 'pleasing oneself,' constitute the post-feminist sensibility in contemporary Western media culture.[23] Post-feminist discourses construct women as autonomous agents no longer constrained by power inequalities or power imbalances—instead women and girls are produced through neoliberal discourses, which imply that practices are freely chosen. Girls are expected to forego basic social and civil rights in exchange for new sets of consumptive rights and freedoms. They are asked to manage the uncertain conditions of contemporary living by investing in a range of entrepreneurial, self-managing strategies in order to become "responsible self-made citizens."[24] However, responsibility and personal direction are produced to ensure young women's economic independence from the state, rather than repositioning them as more active public citizens.[25] Later we read the American HPV/cervical cancer vaccination campaigns against longstanding gendered and heteronormative narratives and emerging discourses of girls and young women as managers-of-the-self. We illustrate how the risks and dangers HPV and cervical cancer pose for girls and young women are mediated alongside postfeminist rhetoric about new knowledge, freedom, and choices concerning their sexual health. Girls and young women are encouraged through campaign messages to take control of their sexual and reproductive well-being, aspects of their health from which they have been historically detached.

Girls and young women are prescribed a clear set of interventions for the maintenance of good sexual health. Advertising campaigns around Gardasil® construct ideal girl citizens as having healthy, heterosexual futures, without yet being sexually active. Rather than being agents of their sexual desires, they are positioned as agentic health consumers who are making empowered choices to ensure a healthy future. This reinstates the norms of gendered and sexual citizenship and erases boys and men from discourses of sexual health. As Kubba has argued, excluding boys sends the wrong message that girls and women alone are responsible for sexual health.[26] Kubba points out that historically, gender-specific immunization programs have been demonstrably less effective than gender-neutral immunization programs, and refers to the success of the rubella vaccination program when boys, as well as girls, were included later in the program. In addition, HIV infection is strongly linked with persistent HPV infection, and the re-activation of latent HPV infection.[27] In a study that compared data from over a million men, using population-based cancer and AIDS registries in the U.S.A and

Puerto Rico, the incidence of anal cancer in HIV-positive men who have sex with men was found to be twice that of HIV-negative men.[28] The supposed heteronormativity of the original target audience for the Gardasil® campaigns in the U.S., that is, girls and young women, overlooks the diverse sexual practices of this population (who are presumed not to have futures that include anal sexual practices), and excludes boys and men who may engage in anal sex.[29]

Gardasil®, Cervical Cancer, and HPV

On November 23, 2006, Merck & Co. Inc. announced the launch of a national print, television, and online advertising campaign for the first cancer vaccination, Gardasil®.[30] Merck developed a campaign comprising of four phases, which started before the Food and Drug Administration (FDA) approval process. The campaign ensured that Gardasil® had the power to construct public discourse surrounding HPV, and its links to cervical cancer. The campaign was constructed through discourses of risk—primarily the risk of a cervical cancer diagnosis, rather than a diagnosis of HPV—and neoliberal discourses of responsibility, choice, and self-management. The campaign employed postfeminist discourses of empowerment in which girls and young women were positioned as active agents capable of making an informed 'choice' to be healthy, wherein discourses of health were explicitly linked to having the series of three shots comprising the Gardasil® vaccine. The vaccine followed a different advertising model to other vaccinations, which had been identified by the disease they were preventing (e.g., measles, mumps), or by their creators (Salk or Sabin), but rather, was identified by a trade name, Gardasil®.[31] In addition, the vaccine was promoted as assisting in the prevention of cervical cancer, rather than guarding against HPV viruses, avoiding the link to sexually transmitted infections. This was a strategic marketing decision; by evoking a fear of cervical cancer, the target audience was more likely to pay attention to the benefits of the vaccine, rather than to evoke unease in parents, guardians, and the general public by associating young female populations (the target audience) with sexual activity during adolescence.

The Merck advertising campaign began on September 30, 2005, featuring the slogan, "Make the Connection," which later became "Make the Commitment."[32] This campaign was designed to create awareness of HPV and its links to cervical cancer in young women and was run by the Cancer Research and Prevention Foundation (CRPF) and celebrity charity Step Up Women's Network.[33] In order to encourage the target audience to 'make the connection,' Merck released a beaded bracelet kit that could be ordered over the internet.[34] This merchandise offered girls a literal metaphor through which they could piece together facts about HPV and cervical cancer with the assistance of educational material included in the kit. In addition, Merck offered to donate $1 to the Cancer Research and Prevention Foundation for each kit ordered.[35] The Merck website featured links to personal stories from a diverse group of women explaining the risks of cervical cancer, and provided information e-cards, which could incorporate a personalized message for visitors using the site. By individualizing the target audience's relationship to the brand, Merck created a mediated environment through which girls and young women could experience a seemingly personalized relationship to cervical cancer, as well as advertising awareness in the form of jewelry, and by sending e-postcards to family, friends, and colleagues. By personalizing and individualizing the economy (political and material) of disease prevention, individuals became central actors in disease prevention. Individuals could control how and when they accessed information about cervical cancer and then insert themselves into the master-narrative being offered by Merck. Critically, the Merck logo and Gardasil® brand name were not located during phase one or phase two of the advertising campaign because FDA approval had not been obtained, but Merck was generating discussion and preparing the general public and target audience for the Gardasil® product. The advertising campaign focusing on awareness of cervical cancer produced through discourses of risk prepared women to be agentic subjects invested in their own health when the Gardasil® brand was finally advertized.

Phase two of the campaign included the first series of television advertisements designed and implemented by the Edelman public relations company, which contained the slogan "Tell Someone." The testimonial style television and magazine ad campaign employed viral marketing and encouraged young women to make the connection between HPV and cervical cancer, and let others know.[36] Viral marketing describes strategies that encourage individuals to pass on a marketing message to others creating the potential for exposure and growth of the message being communicated.[37] Not unlike the "Make the Connection" campaign, "Tell Someone" also encouraged girls to send personalized e-cards, featuring the question: "Did you know that cervical cancer is caused by certain types of a common virus?"[38] Exploiting girls' relationship to online social media to negotiate their connectedness to peer groups, online communities, and identity construction, Merck positioned girls and young women as powerful agents who could inform their networks about cervical cancer. The silencing of HPV as 'the common virus' sanitized the vaccine and dissociated girls and young women from early sexual practice. Girls and young women's agency in accessing their *right* to good health was linked to self-management and relied on their skills and individual labor to promote public health. The campaign also made available magazine pull-out information cards in English and Spanish, which could be accessed in doctor's offices.

Phase three began after Merck had received FDA approval in June 2006, and in mid-November of that year, Merck launched its direct-to-consumer campaign, featuring the slogan, "One Less," which was disseminated across television, print, and online advertising. The ads employed a documentary-style approach portray-

ing empowered, healthy, active girls and young women who were making a commitment to be one less cancer statistic. The television advertisements featured
upbeat music, and fast-paced visual editing reminiscent of a music video clip.
Many of the girls featured in the ads challenged traditional gender stereotypes by
skateboarding, playing soccer, playing the drums, and surfing, as well as engaging
in dance and shopping. These girls had attitude and were depicted as in control of
their lives and their health, with the support of their mothers. The television advertisements disclosed the possible side effects produced by having the vaccine,
but these were positioned as minor in comparison to the risk of cervical cancer.
Merck also funded public service announcements developed by the Cancer Research and Prevention Foundation, featuring celebrities including: actress Kimberly Elise; MTV's Susie Castillo; Stacy London, who is featured on cable fashion
reality show *What Not to Wear;* as well as Maria Shriver and Elisabeth Rohm. This
phase of the campaign included Merck's name, logo and the brand name, Gar-
dasil®. Merck also targeted medical practitioners, especially pediatricians, gynecologists, and family practitioners, in a print ad run in medical journals such as
American Family Physician and the *Journal of the American Medical Association,* which
included information on Gardasil® (Herskovits, 2007).[39] Knowledge about cervical cancer and its health risks and strategies for self-prevention preceded the introduction of Gardasil® as the official and authoritative preventative response.
Further, HPV remained unexplained across all stages of the campaign, despite the
vaccine's direct response to HPV 6, 11, 16, and 18.

Phase four of the campaign featured the slogan, 'I Chose,' which encouraged
girls and young women to be vaccinated, and prompted mothers to vaccinate
their daughters. Like the 'One Less' campaign, these ads were also cut like music
videos, with fast-paced editing, upbeat music, and depicted active young women
enjoying everyday activities. One of the television ads in this campaign featured
culturally diverse mothers and daughters in which mothers repeat the phrase 'I
chose to have my daughter vaccinated because…', followed by reasons, including
being 'one less' cervical cancer statistic. The reiteration and intertexuality of the
phrase 'one less' recalled Merck's previous cervical cancer awareness campaign.
Mothers also reasoned that they chose to have their daughters vaccinated following the advice of a physician. Mothers positioned doctors' authority as central to
their endorsement of the vaccine. Medical discourse directs decision-making, and
strategies of prevention are positioned to serve the best interests of girls and
young women (Lupton, 2003). Following these scenes in the television advertisement, girls and young women reiterated, 'I chose to get vaccinated,' also linking
their reasons to doctors' recommendations, not only about prevention of cervical
cancer, but also the prevention of other HPV-related diseases. The ads end with
the postfeminist, neoliberal tagline: 'You have the power to choose,' calling up

and re-articulating second wave feminism's tropes about "women's choice" within the economy of health consumption in the marketplace. In making this choice—to be a healthy agentic citizen or not—girls and young women are positioned to participate in a neoliberal, postfeminist ideology that silences the links between HPV as a sexually transmitted infection and cervical cancer. Further, girls and young women are positioned by Merck to become neoliberal managers-of-the-self by taking up the *right* to be vaccinated against cervical cancer without gaining full knowledge about HPV and its relationship to sexual health. Produced through neoliberal discourses of choice, the Gardasil® site, which was re-launched in 2008, featured interactive devices ranging from Gardasil® personalized e-mails, and 'I Chose' wallpaper for personal computers. Based on the FDA guidelines, direct-to-consumer advertisements must include seminal information about vaccination side effects, but do not give up their persuasive product messages.

HPV Boredom

An alternative campaign designed by activist, artist, and academic Giovanna Chesler was launched in October 2006 as a video series on YouTube titled, *HPV Boredom*. Unlike Merck's fast-paced, catchy Gardasil® campaign, *HPV boredom* was a low-budget, slow-paced depiction of a young woman recovering from HPV-related surgery. YouTube, famous for its directive, 'broadcast yourself,' is a platform for and aggregator of content, but is not a producer itself.[40] The platform has become known amongst producers and consumers as a vehicle for self-expression, rather than just a video storage database. Following Burgess and Green, we believe that consumer co-creation "is fundamental to YouTube's value proposition, as well as its disruptive influence on established media business models."[41] In the second YouTube video released by Chesler, a young woman (Chesler) listens to a computer-generated voice claiming to be a medical professional, and stating:

> HPV is usually contracted by direct skin-to-skin contact during intimate sexual contact with someone who is infected. Condoms do not offer complete protection from HPV. The test for women can find thirteen strains of the virus. Unfortunately, there are 100 strains of HPV. However, there is a vaccine for women. Your insurance will only cover the vaccine if you are between the ages of 9 and 26. It is our hope that if you are over the age of 26, that you no longer have sex with multiple partners. By the age of 26, you should be married, settled down, and monogamous. There is a 75% chance of contracting HPV in your lifetime. There is no treatment available for the virus itself.

In contrast to Merck's Gardasil® campaign, *HPV Boredom* explicitly provides information about HPV as a sexually transmitted infection that is invisibilized in Merck's Gardasil® campaign. *HPV Boredom* not only provides information about how HPV is contracted, but also addresses issues of limited medical insurance, and positions the pharmaceutical industry as producing young women through moral, heteronormative discourses about marriage and family life. In addition to providing a counter-discourse to Merck's Gardasil® campaign, Chesler's discursive intervention demonstrates the ways in which consumers are learning how to use technologies in order to respond to mass media market content. Chesler uses YouTube as a platform for user-created content that challenges the commercial incentives driving Merck's Gardasil® campaign.

Chesler expanded her *HPV Boredom* campaign into a larger project titled 'Tune in HPV' (www.tuneinhpv.com), which was launched in February 2008, in collaboration with web architect Zulma Aguiar and students in "Communication and Social Change" at the American University.[42] The project aimed to diversify the kinds of sexual citizens who may be affected by the virus represented in the Merck campaign, and was designed as a participatory web channel that provided information about HPV in an entertaining style.[43] The producers of the site offered a subtitle to the 'Tune In' project: 'Don't tune out what you know,' employing a media metaphor to encourage consumers of the project to actively seek knowledge about HPV, and not to disavow information they seek through the project about contracting and living with HPV. The 'Tune In' site was developed in consultation with, and supported by, the Washington, D.C. Department of Health and the Centers for Disease Control. The site contained user-generated stories about HPV, which were submitted anonymously through a story submission tool and videos made by the producers of the site. This project opened up a space with a focus on sexual practice and more direct consideration of the HPV virus than was offered in the Merck advertising campaign. The stories submitted to the site focused on HPV transmission and treatment, while the videos made available by the site's producers were concerned with HPV contraction, combined with elements of users' narratives.[44] Chesler and her colleagues represent active and critical consumers who re-imagine their relationship to consumption by producing alternative health narratives through the use of multiple media platforms.

Conclusion

The promotion of the U.S. HPV vaccination program reflects a new public health approach that is produced through discourses of neoliberalism and bound by the imperatives of health advertising campaigns. New public health discourse positions individuals as responsible for their own health and wellbeing, which relieves their financial burden on the state. Within this neoliberal framework, discourses of risk and choice are employed to sell the campaign across heritage and new media outlets. Girls and young women are produced as agentic, postfeminist actors with access and choice to a range of health services and consumer products. The use of new and social media, and media convergence, was critical in producing, communicating, and shaping health discourses around the promotion of the vaccine. The use of new and social media in the promotion of the vaccine allowed the Gardasil® brand and message to be taken up by girls and young women as a personal and political cause.

Our critical reading in this chapter does not intend to discredit the important role vaccination plays in public health prevention. Offering a reading of health media that attends to questions of governmentality and mediation deconstructs knowledge production and the management of healthy citizenship. We have argued that Merck conjoined neoliberal imperatives with feminist tropes including risk, choice, freedom, and rights. These discourses produce girls and young women as agents of their health and wellbeing and ensure their investment in the projects of self-care, self-management, and health consumerism. Ironically, however, the target audience is given limited information about HPV as a sexually transmitted infection in order to sanitize the vaccination program and enhance uptake by parents and guardians. Discourses of health, choice, and healthy living operate as technologies of government that encourage compliance with national health agendas and are positioned to create profit for pharmaceutical companies like Merck.

Notes

1. Kellie Burns and Cristyn Davies, "Producing Cosmopolitanism on The L Word," *Journal of Lesbian Studies* 13, no. 2 (2009): 174–188.

2. Virginia Berridge and Kelly Loughlin, *Medicine, the Market and the Mass Media: Producing Health in the Twentieth Century* (London: Routledge, 2005); Linda M. Harris, *Health and the New Media: Technologies Transforming Personal and Public Health* (Mahwah, NJ: Lawrence Erlbaum Associates, 1995); Samantha J. King, "Doing Good by Running Well: Breast Cancer, the Race for the Cure, and New Technologies of Ethical Citizenship," in *Foucault, Cultural Studies and Governmentality*, eds. Jack Z. Bratich, Jeremy Packer and Cameron McCarthy (Albany, NY: Suny Press, 2003); Martin King and Katherine Watson, "Introduction," in *Representing Health: Discourses of Health and Illness in the Media*, eds. Martin King and Katherine Watson (New York: Palgrave Macmillan, 2005); Deborah Lupton, *The Imperative of Health: Public Health and the Regulated Body* (Thousand Oaks, CA: Sage, 1995); Deborah Lupton, ed., *Risk and Socio-cultural Theory: New Directions and Perspectives* (Cambridge: Cambridge University Press, 1999): Deborah Lupton, *Medicine as Culture, 2nd ed* (London: SAGE Publications, 2003); Allan Peterson, "Risk, Governance and the New Public Health," in *Foucault, Health and Medicine*, eds. Robin Bunton and Allan Peterson (London: Routledge, 1997); Allan Peterson and Deborah Lupton, *The New Public Health: Health and Self in the Age of Risk* (Thousand Oaks, CA: Sage, 1996); Kane Race, *Pleasure Consuming Medicine: The Queer Politics of Drugs* (Durham, NC: Duke University Press, 2009); Clive Seale, *Media and Health* (Thousand Oaks, CA: Sage, 2002); and Clive Seale, *Health and the Media* (Malden, MA: Blackwell Publishing Ltd, 2004).

3. Nikolas Rose, *Powers of Freedom: Reframing Political Thought* (Cambridge: Cambridge University Press, 1999), 22.

4. Burns and Davies, "Producing Cosmopolitanism"; Cristyn Davies and Kellie Burns, "Imagining Queer Community In and Beyond *The L Word*," in *Loving the L Word: The Full Series in Focus*, ed. Dana Heller (London: I.B. Tauris, 2013).
5. John Fiske, *Understanding Popular Culture* (Boston: Unwin Hyman, 1989).
6. Bruno Latour, *Reassembling the Social: An Introduction to Actor Network Theory* (Oxford: Oxford University Press, 2005).
7. Henry Jenkins, *Convergence Culture: Where Old and New Media Collide* (New York: New York University Press, 2006); Davies and Burns, "Producing Cosmopolitanism."
8. Henry Jenkins, "The Cultural Logic of Media Convergence," *International Journal of Cultural Studies* 7, no. 1 (2004): 33–43, 34.
9. Jenkins, "The Cultural Logic."
10. Peterson and Lupton, *The New Public Health*.
11. Nikolas Rose, "Medicine, History and the Present," in *Reassessing Foucault: Power, Medicine and the Body*, eds. Colin Jones and Roy Porter (London: Routledge, 1994).
12. Lupton, *Medicine as Culture*.
13. Peterson and Lupton, *The New Public Health*, 10.
14. Peterson, "Risk"; Peterson and Lupton, *The New Public Health*; Rose, "Medicine"; Rose, *Powers of Freedom*.
15. Robert Castel, "From Dangerous to Risk," in *The Foucault Effect: Studies in Governmentality*, eds. Gordon Burchell, Colin Gordon, and Peter Miller (Chicago: The University of Chicago Press, 1991).
16. Peterson and Lupton, *The New Public Health*.
17. Kellie Burns and Kate Russell, "Producing the Self-managing Female-citizen in a Climate of 'Healthy' Living," in *Current issues and Controversies in School and Community Health, Sport and Physical Education*, ed. Jennifer O'Dea (New York: Nova Science Publishers, 2012).
18. Susan Bordo, *Unbearable Weight: Feminism, Western Culture and the Body* (Berkeley, CA: University of California Press, 1993); Elizabeth Grosz, *Space, Time, and Perversion: Essays on The Politics of The Body* (New York: Routledge, 1995); Donna Haraway, *Primate Visions: Gender, Race, and Nature in the World of Modern Science* (New York: Routledge, 1989); Haraway, *Simians, Cyborgs and Women: The Reinvention of Nature* (London: Free Association, 1991); Haraway, "A Cyborg Manifesto: Science, Technology, and Socialist-feminism in the Late Twentieth Century," in *The Transgender Studies Reader*, eds. Susan Stryker and Stephen Whittle (London: Routledge, 2006); Lois McNay, *Foucault and Feminism: Power, Gender, and the Self* (Cambridge: Polity Press, 1992); Jana Sawicki, *Disciplining Foucault: Feminism, Power, and the Body* (New York: Routledge, 1991).
19. Lupton, *Medicine as Culture*.
20. Michel Foucault, "Truth and Power," in *Power/Knowledge: Selected Interviews & Other Writings 1972–1977*, ed. Colin Gordon (New York: Pantheon Books, 1980).
21. Sinikka Aapola, Marnina Gonik, and Anita Harris, *Young Femininity: Girlhood, Power and Social Change* (Basingstoke: Palgrave Macmillan, 2005); Kellie Burns, "(re)Imagining the Global, Rethinking Gender in Education," in *Troubling Gender and Education*, eds. Joanne Dillabough, Julie McLeod, and Martin Mills (London: Routledge, 2009); Cristyn Davies, "Becoming Sissy," in *Judith Butler in Conversation: Analysing the Texts and Talk of Everyday Life*, ed. Bronwyn Davies (New York: Routledge, 2008); Catherine Driscoll, *Girls: Feminine Adolescence in Popular Culture and Cultural Theory* (New York: Columbia University Press, 2002); Leslie Johnson, *The Modern*

Girl: Girlhood and Growing Up (St. Leonards: Allen & Unwin, 1993); Angela McRobbie, ed., *Feminism and Youth Culture: From Jackie to Just Seventeen* (London: Macmillan, 1991); Diane Reay, "'Spice Girls', 'Nice Girls,' 'Girlies,' and 'Tomboys': Gender Discourses, Girls' Cultures and Femininities in the Primary Classroom," *Gender and Education* 13, no. 2 (2001): 153–66; Kerry H. Robinson and Cristyn Davies, "Tomboys and Sissy Girls: Power, Agency and Girls' Relationships in Early Childhood," *Australian Journal of Early Childhood* 35, no. 1 (2010): 24–31; Valerie Walkerdine, *School Girl Fictions* (London: Verso, 1990).

22. McRobbie, *Feminism and Youth Culture*; Robinson and Davies, "Tomboys."

23. Rosalind Gill, *Gender and the Media.* Cambridge: Polity, 2007.

24. Harris, *Health and the New Media,* 268.

25. Burns, "(re)Imagining the Global."

26. Tamara Kubba, "Human Papillomavirus Vaccination in the United Kingdom: What About Boys?" *Reproductive Health Matters* 16, no. 32 (2008): 97–103.

27. Ibid.

28. Ibid.; Goedert, Cote et al., "Spectrum of AIDS-associated Malignant Disorders." *The Lancet* 351, no. 9119 (1998): 1833–39.

29. From 2013, Australia will become the first country to fund a school-based vaccination program for boys aged 12 and 13 years under the National Immunisation Program. Year 9 boys will also be able to get the vaccine at school under a catch-up program for the next two years.

30. Merck, known also as Merck Sharp & Dohme (MSD), was established in 1891 as a subsidiary of the German company known now as Merck KGaA, and is one of the largest pharmaceutical companies worldwide.

31. Sheila M. Rothman and David J. Rothman, "Marketing HPV Vaccine: Implications for Adolescent Health and Medical Professionalism," *A Journal of the American Medical Association* 302, no. 7 (2009): 781–86.

32. Judith Siers-Poisson, *Research, Develop, and Sell, Sell, Sell: Part Two in a Series on the Politics and PR of Cervical Cancer.* The Center for Media and Democracy's PR Watch, 2007.

33. Ibid.

34. Beth Herskovits, "Brand of the Year," *Pharmaceutical Executive: Where Business Meets Policy* (February 1, 2007).

35. Marcee Nelson, "Direct to Consumer: Emotional Connection, Pharmaceutical Executive," *Where Business Meets Policy* (November 1, 2006).

36. Daniel J. Edelman is the founder and chairman of Daniel J. Edelman Public Relations, also known as 'Edelman.' Edelman is the largest independently owned PR company with forty-six offices and fifty affiliates around the world.

37. Justin Kirby, "Viral Marketing," in *Connected Marketing: The Viral, Buzz and Word of Mouth Revolution,* eds. Justin Kirby and Paul Marsden (Oxford: Butterworth Heinemann, 2006); Robert Payne, 'Virality 2.0,' *Cultural Studies,* iFirst (2012): 1–21. This article is available through *Cultural Studies* from July 20th, 2012 through iFirst. It will be available in hard copy in 2013, at which time volume, issue, and page numbers will be available.

38. Herskovits, "Brand of the Year."

39. In addition, unrestricted educational grants were offered to professional societies in order to assist physicians to address issues around the vaccine, such as patient forms and reimbursement (Herskovits, 2007).

40. Jean Burgess and Joshua Green, *You Tube: Digital Media and Society Series* (Cambridge: Polity, 2009).
41. Ibid., 5–6.
42. Giovanna Chesler and Bree Kessler, "Re-Presenting Choice: Tune in HPV," in *Three Shots at Prevention: The HPV Vaccine and the Politics of Medicine's Simple Solutions*, eds. Keith Wailoo, Julie Livingston, Stephen Epstein, and Robert Aronowitz (Baltimore: Johns Hopkins University Press, 2010).
43. Ibid.
44. Ibid.

Works Cited

Aapola, Sinikka, Marnina Gonick, and Anita Harris. *Young Femininity: Girlhood, Power and Social Change.* Basingstoke: Palgrave Macmillan, 2005.

Berridge, Virginia and Kelly Loughlin. *Medicine, the Market and the Mass Media: Producing Health in the Twentieth Century.* London: Routledge, 2005.

Bordo, Susan. *Unbearable Weight: Feminism, Western Culture and the Body.* Berkeley, CA: University of California Press, 1993.

Burgess, Jean and Joshua Green. *You Tube: Digital Media and Society Series.* Cambridge: Polity, 2009.

Burns, Kellie. "(re)Imagining the Global, Rethinking Gender in Education." In *Troubling Gender and Education*, eds. Joanne Dillabough, Julie McLeod, and Martin Mills, 42–56. London: Routledge, 2009.

Burns, Kellie and Cristyn Davies. "Producing Cosmopolitanism on The L Word." *Journal of Lesbian Studies* 13, no. 2 (2009): 174–88.

Burns, Kellie and Kate Russell. "Producing the Self-managing Female-citizen in a Climate of 'Healthy' Living." In *Current issues and Controversies in School and Community Health, Sport and Physical Education*, ed. Jennifer O'Dea, 45–54. New York: Nova Science Publishers, 2012.

Castel, Robert. "From Dangerous to Risk." In *The Foucault Effect: Studies in Governmentality*, eds. Gordon Burchell, Colin Gordon and Peter Miller, 281–98. Chicago: The University of Chicago Press, 1991.

Chesler, Giovanna and Bree Kessler. "Re-Presenting Choice: Tune in HPV." In *Three Shots at Prevention: The HPV Vaccine and the Politics of Medicine's Simple Solutions*, eds. Keith Wailoo, Julie Livingston, Stephen Epstein, and Robert Aronowitz, 146–64. Baltimore: Johns Hopkins University Press, 2010.

Davies, Cristyn. "Becoming Sissy." In *Judith Butler in Conversation: Analysing the Texts and Talk of Everyday Life*, edited by Bronwyn Davies, 117–33. New York: Routledge, 2008.

Davies, Cristyn and Kellie Burns. "Imagining Queer Community In and Beyond *The L Word*." In *Loving the L Word: The Full Series in Focus*, ed. Dana Heller. London: I.B. Tauris, 2013.

Driscoll, Catherine. *Girls: Feminine Adolescence in Popular Culture and Cultural Theory.* New York: Columbia University Press, 2002.

Fiske, John. *Understanding Popular Culture.* Boston: Unwin Hyman, 1989.

Foucault, Michel. "Truth and Power." In *Power/Knowledge: Selected Interviews & Other Writings 1972–1977*, ed. Colin Gordon, 109–33. New York: Pantheon Books, 1980.

Gill, Rosalind. *Gender and the Media.* Cambridge: Polity, 2007.

Goedert, James T., Timothy R. Coté, Phillip Virgo, Steven M. Scoppa, Douglas W. Kingma, Mitchell H. Gail, Elaine S. Jaffe, and Robert J Biggar. "Spectrum of AIDS-associated Malignant Disorders." *The Lancet* 351, no. 9119 (1998): 1833–39.

Grosz, Elizabeth. *Space, Time, and Perversion: Essays on The Politics of The Body.* New York: Routledge, 1995.

Haraway, Donna. *Primate Visions: Gender, Race, and Nature in the World of Modern Science.* New York: Routledge, 1989.

———. *Simians, Cyborgs and Women: The Reinvention of Nature.* London: Free Association, 1991.

———. "A Cyborg Manifesto: Science, Technology, and Socialist-feminism in the Late Twentieth Century. In *The Transgender Studies Reader*, eds. Susan Stryker and Stephen Whittle, 103–18. London: Routledge, 2006.

Harris, Linda M. *Health and the New Media: Technologies Transforming Personal and Public Health.* Mahwah, NJ: Lawrence Erlbaum Associates, 1995.

Herskovits, Beth. "Brand of the Year." *Pharmaceutical Executive: Where Business Meets Policy.* February 1, 2007. http://www.pharmexec.com/pharmexec/article/articleDetail.jsp?id=401664&pageID=1&sk=&date=

Jenkins, Henry. "The Cultural Logic of Media Convergence." *International Journal of Cultural Studies* 7, no. 1 (2004): 33–43.

———. *Convergence Culture: Where Old and New Media Collide.* New York: New York University Press, 2006.

Johnson, Leslie. *The Modern Girl: Girlhood and Growing Up.* St. Leonards: Allen & Unwin, 1993.

King, Martin and Katherine Watson. "Introduction." In *Representing Health: Discourses of Health and Illness in the Media*, eds. Martin King and Katherine Watson, 1–21. New York: Palgrave Macmillan, 2005.

King, Samantha J. "Doing Good by Running Well: Breast Cancer, the Race for the Cure, and New Technologies of Ethical Citizenship." In *Foucault, Cultural Studies and Governmentality*, eds. Jack Z. Bratich, Jeremy Packer and Cameron McCarthy, 295–316. Albany, NY: Suny Press, 2003.

Kirby, Justin. "Viral Marketing." In *Connected Marketing: the Viral, Buzz and Word of Mouth Revolution*, eds. Justin Kirby and Paul Marsden, 87–106. Oxford: Butterworth-Heinemann, 2006.

Kubba, Tamara. "Human Papillomavirus Vaccination in the United Kingdom: What About Boys?" *Reproductive Health Matters* 16, no. 32 (2008): 97–103.

Latour, Bruno. *Reassembling the Social: An Introduction to Actor Network Theory.* Oxford: Oxford University Press, 2005.

Lupton, Deborah. *The Imperative of Health: Public Health and the Regulated Body.* Thousand Oaks, CA: Sage, 1995.

———. ed. *Risk and Socio-Cultural Theory: New Directions and Perspectives.* Cambridge: Cambridge University Press, 1999.

———. *Medicine as Culture.* 2nd ed. London: SAGE Publications, 2003.

McNay, Lois. *Foucault and Feminism: Power, Gender, and the Self.* Cambridge: Polity Press, 1992.

McRobbie, Angela, ed. *Feminism and Youth Culture: From Jackie to Just Seventeen.* London: Macmillan, 1991.

Merck. *Annual Review: Driving Growth With Our Commitment to Vaccines.* 2007. http://www.merck.com/finance/annualreport/ar2007/vaccines.html

Nelson, Marcee. *Direct to Consumer: Emotional Connection, Pharmaceutical Executive: Where Business Meets Policy.* (November 1, 2006). http://www.pharmexec.com/pharmexec/

article/articleDetail.jsp?id=382541&page ID=1&sk=&date=

Payne, Robert. 'Virality 2.0.' *Cultural Studies, iFirst* (July 2012): 1–21.

Peterson, Allan. "Risk, Governance and the New Public Health." In *Foucault, Health and Medicine*, eds. Robin Bunton and Allan Peterson, 189–206. London: Routledge, 1997.

Peterson, Allan and Deborah Lupton. *The New Public Health: Health and Self in the Age of Risk.* Thousand Oaks, CA: Sage, 1996.

Reay, Diane. "'Spice Girls,' 'Nice Girls,' 'Girlies,' and 'Tomboys': Gender Discourses, Girls' Cultures and Femininities in the Primary Classroom." *Gender and Education* 13, no. 2 (2001): 153–66.

Rabinow, Paul and Nikolas Rose. "Foucault Today." In *The Essential Foucault: Selections from the Essential Works of Foucault, 1954–1984*, eds. Paul Rabinow and Nikolas Rose, vii–xxxv. New York: New Press, 2003.

Race, Kane. *Pleasure Consuming Medicine: The Queer Politics of Drugs.* Durham, NC: Duke University Press, 2009.

Robinson, Kerry H. and Cristyn Davies. "Boy Nerds, Girl Nerds: Constituting and Negotiating Computing and Information Technology and Peer Groups as Gendered Subjects in Schooling. In *Gender and IT: Ongoing Challenges for Computing and Information Technology Education in Australian Secondary Education*, ed. Julie Lynch, 97–110. Victoria, Australia: Common Ground Publishing, 2007.

———. "She's Kickin Ass, That's What She's Doing': Deconstructing Childhood Innocence in Media Representations." *Australian Feminist Studies* 23, no. 57 (2008): 343–58.

———. "Tomboys and Sissy Girls: Power, Agency and Girls' Relationships in Early Childhood." *Australian Journal of Early Childhood* 35, no. 1 (2010): 24–31.

Rose, Nikolas. "Medicine, History and the Present." In *Reassessing Foucault: Power, Medicine and the Body*, eds. Colin Jones and Roy Porter, 48–72. London: Routledge, 1994.

———. *Powers of Freedom: Reframing Political Thought.* Cambridge: Cambridge University Press, 1999.

Rothman, Sheila M. and David J. Rothman. "Marketing HPV Vaccine: Implications for Adolescent Health and Medical Professionalism." *A Journal of the American Medical Association* 302, no. 7 (2009), 781–86.

Sawicki, Jana. *Disciplining Foucault: Feminism, Power, and the Body.* New York: Routledge, 1991.

Seale, Clive. *Media and Health.* Thousand Oaks, CA: Sage, 2002.

———. *Health and the Media.* Malden, MA: Blackwell Publishing Ltd, 2004.

Siers-Poisson, Judith. *Research, Develop, and Sell, Sell, Sell: Part Two in a Series on the Politics and PR of Cervical Cancer.* The Center for Media and Democracy's PR Watch. 2007. http://prwatch.org/node/6208

Smith, Anthony, Paul Agius, Anne Mitchell, Catherine Barrett, and Marion Pitts. *Secondary Students and Sexual Health 2008: Results of the 4th National Survey of Australian Secondary Students, HIV/AIDS and Sexual Health.* Melbourne: Australian Research Centre in Sex, Health & Society, 2009.

Wailoo, Keith, Julie Livingston, Steven Epstein, and Robert Aronowitz, eds. *Three Shots at Prevention: The HPV Vaccine and the Politics of Medicine's Simple Solutions.* Baltimore: Johns Hopkins University Press, 2010.

Walkerdine, Valerie. *School Girl Fictions.* London: Verso, 1990.

———. *Daddy's Girl: Young Girls and Popular Culture.* London: Macmillan, 1997.

Watkins, Elizabeth L. *On the Pill: A Social History of Oral Contraceptives, 1950–1970.* Baltimore: John's Hopkins University, 1998.

PART TWO

MEDIA USE AND SELF-REPRESENTATION

| 9

"Hyperfeminine" Subcultures: Rethinking Gender Subjectivity and the Discourse of Sexuality Among Adolescent Girls in Contemporary Japan

Isaac Gagné

Introduction

In both Western and Japanese media, "young Japanese girls" are represented by extreme images which are internally contradictory. In particular, recent media images portray young Japanese girls at best as pure and demure, and at worst as hedonistic and materialistic. The image of the servile and innocent girl has been crafted by certain genres of comic books (*manga*) and cartoons (*anime*) that have also made deep inroads into the Western market. In contrast, the latter image of the calculative consumer of luxury goods became a social panic in Japan with the conspicuous presence of young women seen as "brand-girls" or "bad girls," generally glossed as *kogyaru*.[1]

Despite these exaggerated media representations and polarized images of young Japanese girls, neither is entirely true or false. In Japan, as much as purity and modesty are seen as important, aestheticization and consumption are also well-embedded practices and are often encouraged as a part of socialization. Moreover, real girls themselves are simultaneously both objects of media representations and subjects who actively respond to such mediatized images to manipulate or emulate such representations in return.[2]

The widespread aestheticization, commodification, and further emulation and appropriation of the image of young girls—and its importation and consumption—is neither a new phenomenon nor limited to Japan. Like the young women of the Bowery in New York City of the 1800s, the flappers of 1920s North American and European cities, and the "ladettes" of contemporary U.K. cities, the media representations and social co-optation of young female subcultures reveals the ambivalence and deep fascination of moral panics that have been a recurring phenomenon in modern societies.[3]

In studying Japanese schoolgirls' language use, Inoue (2006) traces the dynamic processes of aestheticization and commodification between the media and schoolgirls themselves to the 1920s and 1930s, when print media such as women's magazines began to circulate widely throughout the country.[4] She argues that despite intellectual critiques the media image of schoolgirls grew so overpowering that actual young women across Japan became active producers *and* consumers in emulating such images through urban speech patterns and lifestyles. In contemporary Japan as well, where media diversification has increased exponentially for young girls, there has also been an increasing self-consciousness and reappropriation of media representations by young girls themselves.

This chapter explores the young girls of one such media-infused youth subculture, "Lolita," who strive to embody an idealized "young princess" through their fashion and mannerisms. I describe how Lolitas craft their identity through a particular gender play—what might be called their performance of hyperfemininity. Based on fieldwork and interviews in Tokyo in 2003 and follow-up interviews in 2005 and 2007, I analyze the responses to and tensions within the mediatized popular culture of contemporary Japan. Specifically, by revealing their gendered subjectivity in creating their version of a fantasy space vis-à-vis other subcultural groups, I explore two broad analytical issues: 1) Lolita as identity within changing dominant media representations of young girls in Japan, and 2) Lolita as subcultural activity within the context of the discourses of sexuality in Japan. I argue that Lolita is a specific gender play that is imbricated with changing dominant media representations of women and the liminality of adolescence within the life course. Whereas all-female subcultural groups frequently invoke issues of *inter*-gender tensions between women and men and fears of enduring anti-social identities, my research reveals that their hyperfemininity is constructed through *intra*-gender subcultural tensions against other dominant representations of Japanese girls. Furthermore, I argue that while their participation enabled them to transcend everyday social roles and broader discourses of sexuality, such gender play is able to thrive relatively unproblematically within a woman's complex identity and life-course. This is because Lolita participants self-consciously manage to bracket such fantasy spaces within their larger life course.

The Path to Lolita

Lolita consists of young girls who participate in a broad subculture of fashion-based consumption and performance. The term Lolita describes a particular style of fashion, performance, and identity.[5] Lolita emerged in the mid-1990s, and cultural trends including music and fashion have contributed to the development of the Lolita style. Although the popularity of Lolita as a distinct subculture peaked in the early 2000s and they are less visible in Harajuku in the early 2010s, the aesthetics and mystique of Lolita has fed into broader mainstream fashions in Japan and into subcultural aesthetics around the world.

The origins of the Lolita motifs are debatable, but Japanese "visual rock" bands, girl's comics (*shōjo manga*), and Victorian-era European motifs are generally seen as important influences.[6] The medium of *shōjo manga* in particular has long provided readers with a particular "visualization of fantasy" which the Lolitas themselves have emulated.[7] Participating girls can draw from both Gothic and Lolita dimensions, ranging from dark clothes and makeup with aristocratic, vampire, and Christian motifs featuring angels and demons, to light clothes and distinctive doll-like makeup with elaborate frills and ribbons and demure poses. Despite the clear differences in these extremes, girls on both ends described to me that their style was "ladylike" (*shukujo*).

Despite this "ladylike" thematic, the Lolitas I spoke with were neither from aristocratic backgrounds nor from Europe, but rather they were from middle- or lower-middle-class Japanese families. Lolita subculture was born during the "Lost Decade" of the 1990s post-bubble economy, continued to evolve during the subsequent stagnation of the early 2000s, and has been boosted by increasing media representations of youth subcultures since the 1990s. While some Lolitas received economic assistance from parents to buy expensive designer brands (which cost $350 or more for a dress), others worked part-time jobs to buy materials to make their own clothes. Given this heterogeneity, socio-economic conditions alone cannot fully explain the attraction of Lolita. Furthermore, while many Japanese (including Lolitas) were affected by the post-bubble recession, it is difficult to see Lolita participants' motivation as the manifestation of particular socio-economic struggles against other classes or socio-political agendas, in contrast to the explicit motivations of many subcultural movements such as punks, mods, and riot grrrls in the U.S. and Europe.[8]

Nonetheless, for Lolitas, the desire for "aristocratic" gender play was instead enabled partly by their social circumstances and their educational consciousness, which were connected with socio-economic conditions. In interviews, some girls highlighted their lonely social situations, explaining that they felt isolated in their schools or neighborhoods, particularly because unlike many others of their age they were not pursuing studies for college entrance examinations. Without other peer groups to closely engage with, the Lolita community—virtual or actual—fueled their sense of identity and belonging.

Similar to male youth groups such as hip hop artists[9] and motorcycle gang members[10] who spend their energy on diverse subcultural activities in Japan, many did not have strong ambitions to pursue higher education other than two-year vocational or design schools. This enabled them to spend their weekends freely rather than studying at cram schools for entrance examinations. Lolitas I met generally ranged from their mid-teens to mid-twenties, lived at home, attended junior high or high school or two-year vocational schools, or were part-time workers who bought a few expensive brand items while hand-making most of their clothes and accessories. In other words, while social class in terms of *economic capital* per se did not elucidate the particularities of Lolita, social class in terms of *cultural capital*, and in particular educational aspirations, can be a revealing index of how young people choose to spend their adolescence involved with particular hobbies and subcultures.

Lolita Vis-a-Vis Shifting Dominant Media Representations of Young Girls in Japan

Every weekend, various distinctive subcultural groups come together around the open areas of Harajuku, a shopping district in western Tokyo. Since the mid-1990s, the fashion reputation and mediatized atmosphere of western Tokyo has attracted a number of youth subcultural groups. Certainly Lolita was neither the first nor the only subcultural group to habituate this space.[11] This indeed played an important role in the formation of the various groups that emerged in Tokyo.

During the heyday of Japan's "bubble economy" in the 1980s, new waves of female liberation along with a massified-scale of consumer culture gave birth to diverse male and female subcultural formations. In particular, a subcultural fashion and lifestyle trend known as *gyaru*, consisting of young working women (OLs) and college students who dressed in extremely tight or flashy clothes, came to represent young women as vibrant consumers.[12] They challenged previous images of young women as benign consumers and resurrected an awareness of them as active producers of fashion and consumer trends.[13] By the late 1990s and early 2000s, such images of *gyaru* and their consumption were further emulated by an increasingly younger generation of girls, who became known as *kogyaru*. Noting their "nonconformity" in terms of gaudy fashions and a penchant for shopping, Miller and Bardsley describe them as "brand-girls" and "bad girls."[14] Their extreme aesthetics and mannerisms included blond hair, deep tans, flashy makeup, revealing clothing, loud speech, and coarse manners.

However, these young girls' subcultures were concomitantly complicated by mass media *and* actual people during the 1990s and 2000s. As the ostentatious image of *kogyaru* took center stage in both media and scholarly attention,[15] a range of other girls' subcultures also emerged including their "opposite," the Lolita. Indeed, some Lolitas like Sasaki-san differentiated themselves by emphasizing what they were *not* in relation to other female subcultures. Sasaki-san was in her late teens and had been a Lolita for three years. By commuting two hours from Ibaragi Prefecture to Tokyo, she took being a Lolita quite seriously. For her, other young girls' groups were a source of misunderstanding about Lolita, noting that, "We [Lolitas] are not 'cosplay' and not *kogyaru.*"

As Miller explains, what was significant about *kogyaru* was their "gender-transgressing identity and language style" that "challenge longstanding norms of adolescent femininity."[16] Female subcultures like *kogyaru* accomplished this by appropriating brash and masculine forms of speech and mannerisms, and their image is often linked to "deviant" and "un-feminine" behavior by social critics and foreign analysts,[17] to the extent that they were seen as "self-centered young woman who [were] in no hurry to marry and who maintain[ed] a stable of boyfriends to serve her different needs."[18]

The *kogyaru,* or more precisely the media image of *kogyaru,* were precisely what Lolitas like Sasaki-san hoped to distance themselves from. It was not just the fashion of a "ladylike princess" but also *embodying* a "ladylike princess," which included careful attention to detail and total coordination, that marked Lolita from female groups and the new image of adolescent femaleness that had become dominated by the *kogyaru.* For my informants the key point of Lolita was their coordination of hyperfemininity, of being "ladylike," which includes dressing, acting, and speaking in a refined way, and avoiding behaviors that could be considered rude, vulgar, or un-ladylike.

Thus, given the importance of tensions with other similar age-group activities, subcultures in Japan often thrive *within* cohort tensions rather than *against* society. Indeed, some Lolitas I spoke with claimed that "*Kogyaru* are vulgar," "They are not spiritually pure," or "They are just 'middle-aged women' who happen to wear school uniforms!" From Lolitas' perspective, materializations of *kogyaru,* represented as vulgar speech and mannerisms including talking and laughing loudly, squatting on street corners, dressing loosely, smoking, and drinking in public spaces, were all considered "disruptive to others" and "unsightly."

The Hyperfemininity of "Cuteness"

When I asked Matsumoto-san, another young woman in her late teens from Tokyo, about media representations of Lolita, she explained, "Because of the way we dress and look, some people might misunderstand us. But I do Lolita because [coming to Harajuku] this is the only time I dress like this." In this sense, one can see how Lolita's gender play of hyperfemininity is consciously constructed by girls.

The concept of hyperfemininity has been described as "emphasized femininity,"[19] "hetero-feminine girly girls,"[20] or "supergirly."[21] Scholars have analyzed such extreme expressions to emphasize the non-original and non-essential nature of femininity by stressing that gendered expression is not biologically rooted. In other words, the formation of gender identities is shaped by social forces that interlink the formation of one gender with formations of other genders, as well as *within* the same gender. In this sense, to follow Butler, hyperfemininity is an imitation of an imitation that has no original, but rather is rooted in desires and meanings that are constructed by and through this social link.[22]

In her study of gender terms and their implications, Paechter nuances the social dimension of Butler's work on the non-essentialism of gender by arguing that "'doing femininity well' seems to mean enacting a hyperfemininity that many women, possibly the majority, do not themselves perform, at least much of the time."[23] For Paechter, hyperfemininity is a dramaturgical and glamorized expression of femininity that is hardly related to women's "conventional" roles of housework and childcare. She argues that those women who desire hyperfemininity "no longer feel feminine" due to the banality of their everyday lives, and thus she suggests that this form of hyperfemininity is "idle, or at least leisured, operating outside the practicalities of the lives even of those women in traditional heterosexual family relationships."[24] Similarly, Lolita's hyperfemininity offers an example of how "being a young girl" does not guarantee "feeling like a young girl" by virtue of either biology or daily social activities in late capitalist Japan. Instead, as Matsumoto-san's comments imply, some were also caught up in this consumption of hyperfemininity by idealizing and striving to perfect an idealized image of being "ladylike" because it is different from their everyday gendered subjectivity.

To some extent these girls' desire for "ladylike" hyperfemininity resonates with the discourse of respectability in behaving like "'proper' upper-middle class ladies" that Allan observed among girls at a British single-sex primary school.[25] Allan notes that "respectability," or what she calls British middle-class "girly girl" desires, comes from *actual* middle-class backgrounds. By constructing a particular intensified femininity juxtaposed *against* working class girls, these British middle-class girls promote a strong sense of heterosexuality coupled with an explicit rejection of any intimations of homosexuality that may arise due to the separation of girls and boys into single-sex schools.

In contrast, among my informants, Lolita's "respectability" was not marked by class background and was deliberately more aesthetic and (homo)social than sexual in nature. When I asked them about what participating in Lolita meant to them, they mostly answered in terms of aesthetic pursuit and social purposes. While many I met were single, one Lolita, Hirayama-san, had recently started dating, which seemed to be a source of problems. Hirayama-san told me that her new boyfriend did not like her Lolita fashion and asked her to change her style. Despite this, she told me that she had no intention of "quitting Lolita" because she was not dressing that way for him.

While Allan locates "neoliberal femininity"—being "powerful, agentive, and (hetero)sexually desirable"—as a key element of respectability among the British girls,[26] Lolita participants often rejected any sexual reading (both heterosexuality and homosexuality) of their hyperfemininity. More precisely, for these girls, (hetero)sexual desire or motivation itself could potentially undermine their premise of being a "ladylike princess." At the same time, their deliberate materialization of hyperfemininity enabled them to suspend their participation in mainstream adult gender norms and sexuality.

Although gender expression is frequently elided as a manifestation of larger gender and sexual politics and ideologies, studies of Japanese society reveal the potential for more than two genders, based not merely on sexual maturity, but also on "stage in life."[27] Moreover, one could argue that it is not just one's actual "stage in life" that enables diverse gendered experience (both in the forms of reality and reflection), but also participation in certain commodified cultural activities and fantasy spaces can *create* an individual's "stage in life."

As Nakamura and Matsuo argue in the case of fans of the all-female theater Takarazuka in Japan, participating in certain kinds of commodity culture serves to transcend women's ordinary gender identities and roles and thus is potentially "one active and dynamic way that Japanese women can control their sexuality."[28] Just as many female fans think that sexualized readings of Takarazuka might obstruct their "emotional catharsis,"[29] for many young girls who participated in Lolita, sexualized readings of their performance could be seen as potentially harmful to their self-conscious adolescent subjectivity.[30] As their demographic became more deeply embedded in media representations and mass consumer culture, these girls were also faced with decreasing opportunities for feeling like a *shōjo* or "young girl."

Furthermore, as changing socio-economic conditions for youth and changing media representations of young girls in Japan reveal, the economic future of many young girls (and boys) is not as promising as it once was. As the period of adolescence previously encapsulated by the concept of *shōjo* is no longer taken simply as a natural stage of life, the innocent and carefree image of the *shōjo* has become pure fantasy. In addition to these social conditions, the increasing media representation of "brand-girls" and "bad girls" confronted Lolitas with other identities that they must navigate around in their social lives.

Despite their ostentatious fashion and tensions with other groups, most men and women in Japan did not see actual Lolitas as transgressive. While some girls were discouraged by their family members, friends, or boyfriends, others received encouragement for their dedication to "cuteness." This Lolita "cuteness" is distinct from the "dangerous" sexuality in dominant media representations of "brand-girls" and "bad girls." Rather, their "cuteness" taps into a transcending category of "cuteness" that encompasses their "safe," "girly" subjectivity and sexuality and which reflects a certain cultural sanction for adolescence. In this way, the manner in which the majority of Japanese viewed Lolita echoes *shōjo* as a subjectivity and practice in life that can be constructed through a "cuteness" which counteracts the potential for sexual maturity.[31] As a result, their hyperfeminine mannerisms and seemingly infantilizing clothes were able to thrive, even to the extent that it offered them "autonomy" through their explicit rejection of such readings of sexuality.

Adolescence and Sexuality in Contemporary Japan

Whether *gyaru* or Lolita, adolescent girls in Japan seemed carefree despite the particular social conditions that also motivated them to join subcultural activities. Why is it that such distinctive and at times seemingly provocative activities by young girls have been able to thrive more or less unproblematically in Japanese society? In this last section, I extend my analysis of Lolita to examine the larger social implications of the place of adolescence within the discourse of sexuality in Japan.

Despite certain media and scholarly projections, Japan is not a paradise of youth gender play and sexual freedom. In the writings of Christian leaders and male intellectuals in Japan the activities of adolescent girls have been treated as potentially problematic sites of moral corruption and sexual deviance.[32] However, while some manifestations of female youth at certain historical moments were indeed ascribed with potentially problematic sexuality, particularly in regards to *"pan pan* girls," young Japanese women who associated with American soldiers during the U.S. occupation, or in the case of "compensated daters," school-age girls who went on dates (and sometimes more) with older men for money during the 1990s and 2000s, the particular moral discourse of sexuality did not emerge from an institutionally and ideologically driven "moral monopoly" of religious institutions.

While Lolita and *gyaru* as subcultural groups have diverged from the "mainstream" through their subcultural play, they maintained distinctive social circles with distinctive rules and practices of socialization, all of which were managed within particular bracketed times and spaces. Although they may have been a Lolita on weekends, they also returned to manage other aspects of their lives—i.e., their obligations within institutions of family or school. Indeed, young Japanese girls' behaviors more generally, sexual or otherwise, have rarely been subjected to the same kind of categorical *moral* denigration as in the West. As DeVos has shown how the moral weight of social obligations can be separated from the spheres of sexuality,[33] it is in this context that Japanese youth can explore gendered and subcultural expressions without being subjected to ideological or pathological readings that such practices would invoke in other cultural contexts.

Put differently, analytical approaches to entire demographics like adolescent girls or toward subcultures like Lolita are always in danger of reading into or projecting onto actual individuals a subjectivity that may or may not be present—in this case, some sort of cultural rebellion, gendered resistance, or sexual politics. In Western society, the discourse of sexuality is dominant to the extent that it often frames morality and even delinquency.[34] In contrast, Japan is not as heavily influenced by Western conceptions of sexuality, and morality and delinquency are not as directly associated with sexuality.[35] While religiously influenced and moral and legal distinctions between the sexuality of adults and children have underwritten these conceptions in the West,[36] contemporary Japanese society is the inheritor of a somewhat different discourse of sexuality.

When the categorization of sexuality within medical and juridico-legal domains of knowledge took shape in Japan during the seventeenth and eighteenth centuries, the control of sexual desire and activity was based on a "subtle series of discriminations rather than categorical imperatives" and thus avoided pathologizing internal states based on desire or actions.[37] Moreover, later psychoanalytical, medical, and legal knowledge from the West during the early twentieth century was based on Japanese interpretations of Western conceptions of "civilization" and German/Austrian models of eugenics and social health rather than local ideologies of virtue and morality.[38] Even the discourse of "dangerous sexuality" since the 1980s, related to the AIDS epidemic in the U.S. and Western incarnations of "seductive deviance," has little traction in Japan[39] and sexuality as a social discourse has not achieved the same dominance as in Europe and North America.[40]

This is not to say that sexuality is not problematized at all. Judgments about what is acceptable and unacceptable in regards to sex do exist[41] but they are based on the avoidance of "public demonstrativeness" rather than private pleasures.[42] In Japan, with the exception of certain intellectual circles, Freudian and Lacanian psychoanalysis of sexual relationships and social perversions have not been successful, and popular understanding among older and younger generations still tend to associate personal sexual desires and behaviors with "object-choice and not personal identity."[43] As a result, the source of moral panics about adolescent behavior in Japan is not necessarily *sexuality per se*. Rather, it is a social fear that these young girls will not uphold social expectations of them when they mature. It is a forward-projected anxiety of what might come to pass that reads potential degeneracy in the present.

Conclusion

Set against the backdrop of increasing media attention to "vulgar" youth cultures like *kogyaru*, Lolita was an "alternative" style that thrived in the shadow of changing dominant representations of young girls in Japan. As an ambivalent subculture that occupied a marginal position between generations and genders and between childhood and adulthood, Lolita can be understood as a liminal and alternative "safe" space not subjected to the discourse of adult (gendered) responsibility and sexuality. It also allowed participants to transcend everyday pressures and everyday gendered subjectivity.

The energy of Lolita was neither projected against broader society or mainstream norms, nor was it economic/class rebellion or sexual politics. As my research reveals, the internal dynamics of Lolita participants were much more about constructing a particular socialization of hyperfemininity and navigating intra-gender, inter-group tensions. Through gatherings and self-education on Lolita aesthetics the young girls channeled their youthful passion for social experimentation into a fantasy space as a "young princess" that emerged in tandem with contesting media representations, other peer groups, and prolonged socio-economic uncertainty.

In short, despite moral panics invoked by the media in the case of adolescent girls and youth cultures in the West, social fears in Japan do not stem from the same kind of sexual politics or identity politics. Instead of converging around issues of sexuality, gender, class, or race, Japanese girls' subcultures are formed out of desires for self-expression in terms of fashion and selective sociality with other girls who share similar aesthetics. As such, youth tensions among adolescent girls in Japan such as in Lolita are constructed *within* gendered age cohorts rather than against "mainstream" society or as a challenge to gender norms.

Ultimately, through their active gender play in the contexts of changing social conditions and media representations of young women, the young girls who participated in Lolita offer a living example of creative and self-conscious dislocation of gender and sexuality through hyperfeminine fantasy. Lolita reveals a localized example of both the malleability of gender and the construction of youthhood in the current moment of socio-economic and demographic change in Japan.

Notes

Acknowledgments: This research is based on fieldwork and interviews in Tokyo in 2003 and follow-up interviews in 2005 and 2007. All the names in this chapter are pseudonyms. I would like to thank my informants for sharing their time and experiences with me. I would also like to thank Yasmina Katsulis, Katie Harper, Vera Lopez, and Georganne Scheiner Gillis for their time and help.

1. Laura Miller and Jan Bardsley, eds. *Bad Girls of Japan* (New York: Palgrave Macmillan, 2005).
2. Western media also re-appropriate the image of young Japanese girls, such as the schoolgirl killer Yubari in Quentin Tarantino's 2003 film *Kill Bill* or singer Gwen Stefani's exoticized back-up dancers called "Harajuku Girls."
3. Christine Stansell, *City of Women: Sex and Class in New York, 1789–1860* (New York: Knopf, 1986); Carolyn Jackson and Penny Tinkler, "'Ladettes' and 'Modern Girls': 'Troublesome' Young Femininities," *Sociological Review* 55, no. 2 (2007): 251–72.
4. Miyako Inoue, *Vicarious Language: Gender and Linguistic Modernity in Japan* (Berkeley, CA: University of California Press, 2006).
5. In the West, "Lolita" connotes a man's attraction to adolescent girls (see Debra Merskin, "Reviving Lolita? A Media Literacy Examination of Sexual Portrayals of Girls in Fashion Advertising," *American Behavioral Scientist* 48, no. 1 [2004]: 119–29). In Japan, the term "Lolita Complex" known as lolikon can be associated with the word "Lolita" (Sharon Kinsella, "Minstrelized Girls: Male Performers of Japan's Lolita Complex," *Japan Forum* 18, no. 1 [2006]: 65–87; Mark McClelland, "No Climax, No Point, No Meaning? Japanese Women's Boy-Love Sites on the Internet," *Journal of Communication Inquiry* 24, no. 3 [2000]: 274–91). However, Lolita evolved independently as a fashion-driven subculture, and often Lolitas themselves refuse any connotation of lolikon.
6. Yuniya Kawamura, "Japanese Teens as Producers of Street Fashion," *Current Sociology* 54, no. 5 (2006): 784–801; Wim Lunsing, "LGBT Rights in Japan," *Peace Review: A Journal of Social Justice* 17 (2005): 143–48; Theresa Winge, "Undressing and Dressing Loli: A Search for the Identity of the Japanese Lolita," *Mechademia* 3 (2008): 47–63.
7. See Deborah Shamoon, "Situating the Shōjo in Shōjo Manga: Teenage Girls, Romance Comics, and Contemporary Japanese Culture," in *Japanese Visual Culture: Explorations in the World of Manga and Anime*, ed. Marc W. MacWilliams (Armonk, NY: M.E. Sharpe, 2008).
8. See Catherine Driscoll, "Girl Culture, Revenge, and Global Capitalism: Cybergirls, Riot Grrls, Spice Girls," *Australian Feminist Studies* 14, no. 29 (1999): 173–93; Dick Hebdige, *Subculture: The Meaning of Style* (London: Methuen, 1979); Marion Leonard, "Rebel Girl, You

168   *Isaac Gagné*

Are the Queen of my World: Feminism, 'Subculture' and Grrrl Power," in *Sexing the Groove: Popular Music and Gender*, ed. Sheila Whiteley (London: Routledge, 1997; Jessica Rosenberg and Gitana Garofalo, "Riot Grrrl: Revolutions from Within," *Signs* 23, no. 3 (1998): 809–41.

9. Ian Condry, *Hip-Hop Japan: Rap and the Paths of Cultural Globalization* (Durham, NC: Duke University Press, 2006).

10. Ikuya Sato, *Kamikaze Bikers: Parody and Anomy in Affluent Japan* (Chicago: University of Chicago Press, 1991).

11. Since the 1960s in particular a variety of youth groups, often called zoku (tribes), used this space for their youthful expression. See Henshūshitsu Across, *Sutorīto Fasshon 1945–1995: Wakamono Stairu no 50-nen Shi* [Street Fashion: Fifty Years of Youth Style] (Tokyo: Parco, 1995); Hirosuke Mizuno, "Toshi Media Ron 5: 'Toshi to Eiga' (Sono 1) Josetsu [Urban Media Theory 5: 'Cities and Movies' (Part 1) Preface]," *Saitama University College of Liberal Arts Bulletin* 46, no. 2 (2010): 205-212; Shunya Yoshimi, *Toshi no Doramaturugī: Tōkyoō Sakariba no Shakaishi* [Dramaturgy of the City: The Social History of Popular Entertainments in Modern Tokyo] (Tokyo: Kawade, 2008).

12. These included the "body-conscious girls" (bodikon gyaru), who dressed in sexy and form-fitting clothing; the "flamboyant stage girls" (otachidai gyaru) who danced on the stages at nightclubs; the "three negatives girl" (san nai gyaru), who did not have work, marriage, and children; and even the "old guy girls" (oyaji gyaru) who talked and acted like middle-aged men. See Laura Miller, "Those Naughty Teenage Girls: Japanese Kogals, Slang, and Media Assessments," *Journal of Linguistic Anthropology* 14, no. 2 (2004): 225–47, 227.

13. Kawamura, "Japanese Teens"; Kinsella, "Minstrelized Girls."

14. Miller and Bardsley, *Bad Girls.*

15. See Kinsella, "Minstrelized Girls."

16. Miller, "Those Naughty," 225.

17. Miller and Bardsley, *Bad Girls.*

18. Hiroshi Aoyagi, "Pop Idols and Gender Contestation," in *Japan at the Millennium: Joining Past and Future*, ed. David Edgington (Vancouver: University of British Columbia Press, 2004), 161.

19. R. W. Connell, *Gender and Power* (Cambridge: Polity Press, 1987).

20. Alexandra Jane Allan, "The Importance of Being a 'Lady': Hyper-femininity and Heterosexuality in the Private, Single Sex Primary School," *Gender and Education* 21, no. 2 (2009): 145–58.

21. Carrie F. Paechter, "Masculine Femininities/Feminine Masculinities: Power, Identities and Gender," *Gender and Education* 18, no. 3 (2006): 253–63.

22. Judith Butler, *Gender Trouble: Feminism and the Subversion of Identity* (New York: Routledge, 1999).

23. Paechter, "Masculine Femininities," 258–59.

24. Ibid., 255.

25. Allan, "The Importance."

26. Ibid., 147.

27. John Treat, "Yoshimoto Banana Writes Home: Shōjo Culture and the Nostalgic Subject," *Journal of Japanese Studies* 19, no. 2 (1993): 353–87, 364.

28. Karen Nakamura and Hisako Matsuo, "Female Masculinity and Fantasy Spaces: Transcending Genders in the Takarazuka Theatre and Japanese Popular Culture," in *Men and Masculinities in Contemporary Japan: Dislocating the Salaryman Doxa*, eds. James Roberson and Nobue Suzuki (New York: Routledge, 2003), 69.
29. Ibid., 67.
30. In contrast to the subjectivity of actual Lolita participants, the media images of Lolita frequently invoke tropes of inter-gender animosity and sexual perversion. See Brian Bergstrom, "Girliness Next to Godliness: Lolita Fandom as Sacred Criminality in the Novels of Takemoto Novala," *Mechademia* 6 (2011): 21-37; and Mari Kotani, "Doll Beauties and Cosplay," *Mechademia* 2 (2007): 49-62, for their analyses of these images.
31. Treat, "Yoshimoto Banana."
32. See Sabine Fruhstuck, "Then Science Took Over: Sex, Leisure, and Medicine at the Beginning of the Twentieth Century," in *Culture of Japan as Seen Through its Leisure*, eds. Sepp Linhart and Sabine Fruhstuck (Albany: State University of New York Press, 1998); Inoue, *Vicarious Language*.
33. George DeVos, *Socialization for Achievement: Essays on the Cultural Psychology of the Japanese* (Berkeley, CA: University of California Press, 1973), 161.
34. See Erich Goode and Nachman Ben-Yehuda, *Moral Panics: The Social Construction of Deviance* (Oxford: Blackwell Publishing, 2009).
35. Merry White, *The Material Child: Coming of Age in Japan and America* (New York: The Free Press, 1993).
36. Michel Foucault, *History of Sexuality, Vol. 1: An Introduction* (New York: Vintage Press, 1990).
37. Gregory Pflugfelder, *Cartographies of Desire: Male-male Sexuality in Japanese Discourse, 1600–1950* (Berkeley, CA: University of California Press, 1999), 19.
38. Ibid.; Fruhstuck, "Then Science."
39. White, *The Material Child*, 175.
40. Wim Lunsing, "LGBT Rights in Japan," *Peace Review: A Journal of Social Justice* 17 (2005): 143–48.
41. See David Leheny, *Think Global, Fear Local: Sex, Violence, and Anxiety in Contemporary Japan* (Ithaca, NY: Cornell University Press, 2006).
42. White, *The Material Child*.
43. Karen Nakamura, "The Chrysanthemum and the Queer: Ethnographic and Historical Perspectives on Sexuality in Japan," *Journal of Homosexuality* 52, no. 3/4 (2007): 267–81, 273.

Works Cited

Across Henshūshitsu. *Sutorīto Fasshon 1945–1995: Wakamono Stairu no 50-nen Shi* [Street Fashion: Fifty Years of Youth Style]. Tokyo: Parco, 1995.
Allan, Alexandra Jane. "The Importance of Being a 'Lady': Hyper-femininity and Heterosexuality in the Private, Single Sex Primary School." *Gender and Education* 21, no. 2 (2009): 145–58.
Aoyagi, Hiroshi. "Pop Idols and Gender Contestation." In *Japan at the Millennium: Joining Past and Future*, ed. David Edgington, 144–67. Vancouver: University of British Columbia Press, 2004.

Bergstrom, Brian. "Girliness Next to Godliness: Lolita Fandom as Sacred Criminality in the Novels of Takemoto Novala." *Mechademia* 6 (2011): 21–37.

Butler, Judith. *Gender Trouble: Feminism and the Subversion of Identity.* New York: Routledge, 1999.

Condry, Ian. *Hip-Hop Japan: Rap and the Paths of Cultural Globalization.* Durham, NC: Duke University Press, 2006.

Connell, R. W. *Gender and Power.* Cambridge: Polity Press, 1987.

DeVos, George. *Socialization for Achievement: Essays on the Cultural Psychology of the Japanese.* Berkeley, CA: University of California Press, 1973.

Driscoll, Catherine. "Girl Culture, Revenge, and Global Capitalism: Cybergirls, Riot Grrls, Spice Girls." *Australian Feminist Studies* 14, no. 29 (1999): 173–93.

Foucault, Michel. *History of Sexuality, Vol. 1: An Introduction.* New York: Vintage Press, 1990 [1978].

Fruhstuck, Sabine. "Then Science Took Over: Sex, Leisure, and Medicine at the Beginning of the Twentieth Century." In *Culture of Japan as Seen Through its Leisure,* eds. Sepp Linhart and Sabine Fruhstuck, 59–79. Albany, NY: State University of New York Press, 1998.

Goode, Erich and Nachman Ben-Yehuda. *Moral Panics: The Social Construction of Deviance.* Oxford: Blackwell Publishing, 2009 [1994].

Hebdige, Dick. *Subculture: The Meaning of Style.* London: Methuen, 1979.

Inoue, Miyako. *Vicarious Language: Gender and Linguistic Modernity in Japan.* Berkeley, CA: University of California Press, 2006.

Jackson, Carolyn and Penny Tinkler. "'Ladettes' and 'Modern Girls': 'Troublesome' Young Femininities." *Sociological Review* 55, no. 2 (2007): 251–72.

Kawamura, Yuniya. "Japanese Teens as Producers of Street Fashion." *Current Sociology* 54, no. 5 (2006): 784–801.

Kinsella, Sharon. "Cuties in Japan." In *Women, Media and Consumption in Japan,* eds. Brian Moeran and Lise Skov, 220–54. Honolulu: Curzon & Hawaii University Press, 1995.

———. "What's Behind the Fetishism of Japanese School Uniforms?" *Fashion Theory: The Journal of Dress, Body & Culture* 6, no. 2 (2002): 215–37.

———. "Minstrelized Girls: Male Performers of Japan's Lolita Complex." *Japan Forum* 18, no. 1 (2006): 65–87.

Kotani, Mari. "Doll Beauties and Cosplay." *Mechademia* 2 (2007): 49–62.

Leheny, David. *Think Global, Fear Local: Sex, Violence, and Anxiety in Contemporary Japan.* Ithaca, NY: Cornell University Press, 2006.

Leonard, Marion. "Rebel Girl, You Are the Queen of my World: Feminism, 'Subculture' and Grrrl Power." In *Sexing the Groove: Popular Music and Gender,* ed. Sheila Whiteley, 230–56. London: Routledge, 1997.

Lunning, Frenchy. "Under the Ruffles: Shôjo and the Morphology of Power." *Mechademia* 6 (2011): 3–19.

Lunsing, Wim. "LGBT Rights in Japan." *Peace Review: A Journal of Social Justice* 17 (2005): 143-148.

McClelland, Mark. "No Climax, No Point, No Meaning? Japanese Women's Boy-Love Sites on the Internet." *Journal of Communication Inquiry* 24, no. 3 (2000): 274–91.

Merskin, Debra. "Reviving Lolita? A Media Literacy Examination of Sexual Portrayals of Girls in Fashion Advertising." *American Behavioral Scientist* 48, no. 1 (2004): 119–29.

Miller, Laura. "Those Naughty Teenage Girls: Japanese Kogals, Slang, and Media Assessments." *Journal of Linguistic Anthropology* 14, no. 2 (2004): 225–47.

Miller, Laura and Jan Bardsley, eds. *Bad Girls of Japan.* New York: Palgrave Macmillan, 2005.

Mizuno, Hirosuke. "Toshi Media Ron 5: 'Toshi to Eiga' (Sono 1) Josetsu [Urban Media Theory 5: 'Cities and Movies' (Part 1) Preface]." *Saitama University College of Liberal Arts Bulletin* 46, no. 2 (2010): 205–12.

Nakamura, Karen. "The Chrysanthemum and the Queer: Ethnographic and Historical Perspectives on Sexuality in Japan." *Journal of Homosexuality* 52, no. 3/4 (2007): 267–81.

Nakamura, Karen and Hisako Matsuo. "Female Masculinity and Fantasy Spaces: Transcending Genders in the Takarazuka Theatre and Japanese Popular Culture." In *Men and Masculinities in Contemporary Japan: Dislocating the Salaryman Doxa,* eds. James Roberson and Nobue Suzuki, 59–76. New York: Routledge, 2003.

Paechter, Carrie F. "Masculine Femininities/Feminine Masculinities: Power, Identities and Gender." *Gender and Education* 18, no. 3 (2006): 253–63.

Pflugfelder, Gregory. *Cartographies of Desire: Male-male Sexuality in Japanese Discourse, 1600–1950.* Berkeley, CA: University of California Press, 1999.

Rosenberg, Jessica and Gitana Garofalo. "Riot Grrrl: Revolutions from Within." *Signs* 23, no. 3 (1998): 809–41.

Sato, Ikuya. *Kamikaze Bikers: Parody and Anomy in Affluent Japan.* Chicago: University of Chicago Press, 1991.

Shamoon, Deborah. "Situating the Shōjo in Shōjo Manga: Teenage Girls, Romance Comics, and Contemporary Japanese Culture." In *Japanese Visual Culture: Explorations in the World of Manga and Anime,* ed. Marc W. MacWilliams, 137–54. Armonk, NY: M.E. Sharpe, 2008.

Stansell, Christine. *City of Women: Sex and Class in New York, 1789–1860.* New York: Knopf, 1986.

Treat, John. "Yoshimoto Banana Writes Home: Shōjo Culture and the Nostalgic Subject." *Journal of Japanese Studies* 19, no. 2 (1993): 353–87.

White, Merry. *The Material Child: Coming of Age in Japan and America.* New York: The Free Press, 1993.

Winge, Theresa. "Undressing and Dressing Loli: A Search for the Identity of the Japanese Lolita." *Mechademia* 3 (2008): 47–63.

Yoshimi, Shunya. *Toshi no Doramaturugī: Tōkyoō Sakariba no Shakaishi* [Dramaturgy of the City: The Social History of Popular Entertainments in Modern Tokyo]. Tokyo: Kawade, 2008 [1987].

| 10

Favela Models: Sexual Virtue and Hopeful Narratives of Beauty in Brazil

Alvaro Jarrin

Learning to Dream

In one of Rio de Janeiro's most famous favelas, *Cidade de Deus* [City of God], teenage girls walk up and down a makeshift catwalk in the community's small basketball court for their bi-weekly lesson in the local modeling school, called *Lente dos Sonhos*, or Dream Lens. I observe them from the bleachers, sitting next to the girls' mothers and other curious passersby that have gathered to look at the girls and cheer them on. Their teacher, a model in her early twenties called Gisele who grew up in the same community, is giving the girls tips on how to sway their hips as they walk on high heels. She demonstrates how to pose twice at the end of the catwalk, looking ahead at imaginary cameras taking their pictures, before twirling around and walking back. Some girls look nervous and self-conscious, obviously uncomfortable about being the center of attention, while others carry themselves with confidence and contained excitement, taking the class very seriously and professionally.

I ask one of the girls' mothers sitting next to me why she enrolled her daughter in a modeling class, and she answers that many people had commented on her daughter's beauty and encouraged her to try out for modeling. "Who knows," she says with a gleam of hope in her eyes, "she might get lucky and get discovered, then she can make a career out of this and guarantee her future." The modeling school allows the girls to practice becoming a model and thus "produce" the beauty their mothers hope will become a real source of income in the future. In Portuguese, the verb *se produzir* [to produce oneself] is used to describe the process of embellishment through makeup, hairdo, clothing, and physical performance. Beauty, therefore, is not seen as an inherent quality of the body, but as something that can be practiced, learned, and improved. There is hopeful anticipation in every step these girls rehearse, because it means incorporating a gendered performance associated with success and upward mobility.

The girls who take classes with Gisele look up to her as a symbol of this success because she has a contract with a modeling agency, has traveled to Europe, and has appeared in local media outlets a few times. Newspaper articles have congratulated Dream Lens as "able to transform poor girls into models,"[1] showing a picture of Gisele posing in front of the Eiffel Tower in a fashionable jacket, boots, skinny jeans, and long, straight hair, as proof of this veritable "carioca fairy tale."[2] The photograph is meant to symbolize the wonder of social inclusion through beauty, which brought the "daughter of a maid and a fruit-seller" to Paris for the "career of her dreams." As another newspaper article argues, this is "fashion in the service of citizenship."[3] Ironically, it is only once Gisele is seen as having transcended her origins—by performing the mobility, cosmopolitanism, and success associated with transnational fashion—that she becomes a full citizen of the Brazilian nation.

During the class, Gisele rarely boasts about her accomplishments, but she always carries herself as a model would, having mastered all the small details that make her presentation on the catwalk convincing. When Gisele walks flawlessly down the runway, the improvised catwalk made of old rugs held down with bricks begins to fade away, yielding the spotlight to the powerful model taking the stage—her head high and her body focused on the prize. Through her perfectly tailored gestures, Gisele is able to communicate a sophisticated femininity that symbolizes a more luxurious world than the one her students know and experience every day. Learning to perform beauty like Gisele is a way of having access to that world, even if only for a fleeting moment. This almost magical transformation holds despite the fact that Gisele has in reality found it difficult to book many modeling jobs, and her material conditions have barely changed since she began modeling. She still lives in her small one-room, humble home in City of God, and dreams of one day being able to parade the catwalks of famous designers in Europe.

The magic of make-believe is not simply an imitation exercise; it is a form of beauty work that promises girls from poor communities that they can transcend their reality through the outside recognition of their beauty. As the name "Dream Lens" suggests, it is through the lens of a camera that a girl's unrealized potential is thought to be able to blossom into tangible success. The founder of Dream Lens, the local photographer Tony Barros, acknowledges that very few girls who take the modeling course will actually make a living from modeling. For him, though, teaching the girls to value their own beauty is a source of motivation and self-esteem—for themselves and for the community as a whole. Learning how to "take care of themselves" will lead to job opportunities in areas where appearance is fundamental, like the beauty industry and receptionist jobs. He tells me he believes the modeling school "rescues these girls from prostitution or from becoming pregnant at a very young age," because it gives them something to look forward to. In this way, beauty is seen to fundamentally change their lives. After working with Dreams Lens, Tony says, girls are recognized in their community as "models": an identity that is met with admiration and respect.

The Value of Beauty

In this article, I aim to explain why beauty produces hope in a context where there is little else to hope for. Following Ghassan Hage, I define hope as the longing for opportunities of self-realization. Hage argues that societies, not individuals, provide social significance to life pursuits, and thus any given society has the capacity to produce and distribute hope amongst its members. For Hage, a "decent" society ought to generate equally meaningful forms of "societal hope" for all its members.[4] In capitalist societies, however, hope is distributed in a highly unequal fashion, through two very powerful mechanisms. On the one hand, the nation-state provides hope through identification with the State project, giving citizens the opportunity to belong to something larger than themselves. On the other hand, capitalism promises individuals the possibility of upward mobility through hard work, despite the massive inequalities on which capitalism depends.[5]

Hage argues that as post-Fordist capitalism renders these hopes more fragile, by generating more precarious work conditions and undermining the role of the State as guarantor of the population's general welfare, individuals take to "magical means" that still produce hopefulness in the face of uncertainty.[6] Jean and John Comaroff have also pointed out the global rise of "occult economies" that aim to magically produce value out of nothing, in the context of the widespread insecurity produced by "millennial capitalism."[7] I want to argue here that beauty is one such form of magic in Brazil, because it is able to produce value out of the only guaranteed capital low-income women possess: their own bodies. This embodied form of value, however, depends on the recognition of another, who will "discover" the young girl's potential and "save" her from her otherwise bleak future. In fact, models who come from poor backgrounds are frequently portrayed in the Brazilian media as "Cinderellas" touched by a magic wand, transported from poverty into the idealized world of fashion after being recognized by a modeling scout.

The urgency of "rescuing" poor young girls through beauty, which Tony Barros believed would also preserve their sexuality from the dangers of sex work and unwed motherhood, is a narrative that resonates in very powerful ways within Brazilian society. Narratives of upward mobility through beauty are interwoven throughout diverse forms of media—from journalistic accounts of recently "discovered" models, to the carefully crafted storylines of soap operas and beauty pageants. In what follows, I will argue that these narratives construct an idealized image of poor young women that is sexualized and racialized in very particular ways. In the first place, virtuous sexual behavior is understood as an essential component for the eventual success of these teenage girls. Additionally, this imagined sexual purity is associated with specific physical characteristics, like lighter skin and straighter hair, in contrast to the hyper-sexual archetype of the "mulatta" ever-present in Brazilian popular culture. The recognition of beauty that is supposed to bring about social inclusion, therefore, reinforces a preference for whiteness and "appropriate" feminine behavior that excludes most poor women of color from the outset.

If beauty is so laden with hope, however, it is only because there are very limited possibilities for upward mobility and full citizenship in Brazil. Structural inequalities have historically excluded the Brazilian poor from having equal access to housing, education, and employment; this produces a precarious future for most low-income households.[8] There is a tension, therefore, between the urgencies of the political present and the hopeful future produced by beauty. The labor of beauty has the potential to politicize working-class women, by providing them an immediate way to reframe how their bodies are valued, but can simultaneously depoliticize these women by continuously deferring hope onto the future. Examining media narratives about beauty allows us to understand both their strong appeal as a form of hope, and the underlying tensions about Brazilian society they attempt to smooth over. At the end of this article, I will also look at an alternative beauty contest organized in Rio de Janeiro, which performs a working-class aesthetic that both refuses the hope of upward mobility and its emphasis on the bourgeois disciplining of the body.

Recognizing the Good Girls

Brazilian *telenovelas* [soap operas] are cultural texts of utmost importance within the national context. In the most powerful television network in Brazil, Rede Globo, they make up a large part of daily programming, with five *telenovelas* running Monday through Saturday and occupying most of the afternoon and evening schedule. Ethnographic accounts of serialized dramas, like Purnima Mankekar's work in India and Lila Abu-Lughod's research in Egypt, have pointed out the ways in which these "national texts" create archetypical images of womanhood. These hegemonic narratives, however, are not passively consumed by target audiences, but are rather actively interpreted in relation to the daily concerns of viewers.[9] Brazilian *telenovelas* also produce archetypal images of womanhood, but almost always craft these narratives as morality tales about beauty, femininity, and upward mobility. As Esther Hamburger argues, characters from *telenovelas* represent archetypes from Brazilian society about which the spectator can make moral judgments, deciding whether to root for their success or wish for their downfall. In either case, though, the spectator makes use of the national "lexicon" provided by *telenovela* narratives to make sense of his or her own immediate concerns.[10]

One of the most common narratives within Brazilian *telenovelas* is the story of a *mocinha* [good girl] whose virtue and honesty hold up in the face of a series of obstacles that prevent her from finding happiness, success, and true love, which she always finds at the end. There are generally two routes the plot takes; the *mocinha* is either from humble origins and must confront the villains who prevent her from succeeding, or she is initially wealthy and loses everything to conniving villains who steal everything from her, and from whom she must then strive to recover what is rightfully hers. The *mocinha* is usually portrayed by some of the most beautiful and talented actresses in Brazil, and these actresses' beauty becomes a central lynchpin of their characters' path out of poverty and into love and success. The *mocinha*'s beauty is equated with upward mobility because it is what provides her a new job opportunity, like a modeling career, or what makes her attractive to a wealthy *galã* [male lead]. The male lead is very much like a prince charming, who sweeps the *mocinha* off her feet and offers her a better life, going against social conventions.

The villain is usually characterized as someone who disapproves of this union and will do anything to stop it, or as a female competitor who envies the good girl and wants the male lead for herself. At least a couple of *telenovelas* (*Mulheres de Areia*, aired in 1993, and *Paraíso Tropical*, aired in 2007) featured twin sisters with opposite personalities; the "good twin," who is genuinely in love with the wealthy male lead, and the "evil twin," a gold-digger who wants to take her sister's place by manipulating her way up the social ladder. Even though in both *telenovelas* the same actress played the parts of the *mocinha* and the villain, it was relatively easy to tell them apart on screen, because the "evil twin" wore heavier makeup and dressed more sensuously than her sexually modest "good twin." Given that these plots relied frequently on one sister impersonating the other, however, it was up to the scriptwriters and the actresses to give the audience subtle clues about who was the "real" sister under the costume.

Since the moral message crafted by *telenovelas* is that female beauty is a double-edged sword—providing power and mobility to both good and bad women—the humble personality of the *mocinha* can never come into question as she pursues her dreams. Otherwise, she is likely to bear a resemblance to the overly ambitious villains. Male leads, on the other hand, are usually portrayed as having character flaws—such as falling prey to a female villain's sexual advances—that the *mocinha* must work to transform and redeem through her own virtuous example. The *mocinha*'s virtuous femininity represents a virginal Catholic ideal that men cannot fulfill within the *telenovela* genre. The beautiful and desirable *mocinha* will only have sexual relations with her "true love," and even if she falls for a villain's false love vows, her love for him is genuine and pure. The upward mobility and happiness she achieves by the end of the *telenovela* are portrayed as a fair reward for her untarnished qualities and her beauty.

The definition of beauty written into *telenovelas*, however, is very narrow and reflects the views of the upper-middle-class scriptwriters. The *mocinha* might be poor, but she is usually lighter-skinned or has lighter eyes than most of the women of her social class. She is recognized as beautiful by the male lead because, despite having a menial job, she stands out as someone who physically does not "read" as working-class. The moment of recognition of a *mocinha*'s uncommon beauty was central to the aptly titled soap opera *Belíssima* [So Beautiful], which aired between 2005 and 2006. In a flashback scene that was aired in the first episode, we see the *mocinha* Vitória as a poor white girl living on the streets, selling candy at a stoplight to the drivers passing by, with her younger brother beside her. When the handsome Pedro looks out of the window of his car, he is awestruck by her beauty, and offers to buy the whole box of candy Vitória is selling, which takes her by surprise. Their dialogue is interrupted when an unidentified man threatens to hit Vitória's younger brother, and Pedro steps out of his car to defend the boy, saving them both. The camera then focuses again on Vitória, zooming in beyond her torn clothes and dirty hands to display only her beautiful face, her light eyes hopeful and expectant as she looks back toward Pedro, who is now smiling at her.

No dialogue is necessary to explain that this is the beginning of a Cinderella fairy tale, and that Pedro will marry Vitória despite the objections from his grandmother, the powerful businesswoman Bia Falcão. The villainous grandmother makes several attempts at destroying their relationship, including an assassination attempt that by mistake kills her own grandson Pedro instead of Vitória. At the end of the *telenovela*, we discover that Vitória is actually the illegitimate child of Bia Falcão, whom she abandoned at birth. In other words, Pedro unknowingly married his own aunt, and recognized in her the beauty of the upper-middle class to which she rightly belonged all along. The *telenovela* thus constructs Vitória's whiteness as a symbol of her true social status, suggesting that a man who rescues a beautiful white woman from poverty is really rescuing one of his own. Seeing feminine beauty is therefore a form of self-recognition, reinforcing the association between the *mocinha*'s white femininity and upward mobility.

Scouting for Sameness

The fairy-tale narrative of the young *mocinha* who is recognized through her beauty has found new life in reality television, particularly beauty contests. The contest *Beleza na Favela*, or "Beauty in the Favela," was a popular segment of the morning variety show *Hoje em Dia* in Rede Record during 2007 and 2008. The premise of the contest was to send scouts to some of the poorest communities in Brazil looking for teenage girls who had the potential to become models, and then taking them "from the [urban] peripheries to the catwalk."[11] Each segment would begin in the favelas of a given Brazilian state, where the modeling scout picked one among dozens of girls who had signed up enthusiastically to compete. The show would then shift to the television studio in São Paulo, where the winner from each favela walked the catwalk, and a panel of judges decided on which girl would represent the state in the national finals.

The move from the favela to São Paulo already signified a transcendent move into modernity, as represented by the flashiness of the television studio. It was also stressed that this was the first time the girls had boarded a plane and travelled so far from home, all for the "dream of being a model so they can help their families."[12] The contestants were very careful to stress that they were looking to help not themselves, but rather their parents and their community, thus disavowing any ambitious tendencies that might be considered unseemly in a *mocinha*. These girls were represented as models of behavior for all other teenagers and not only models of beauty. As the scholarly literature on beauty pageants argues, these events build national communities by constructing femininity as a symbol of national unity, citizenship, and pluralism, even as it defines "respectable" womanhood as sexually proper and racially unmarked.[13]

In "Beauty in the Favela," the recognition of these teenage girls as beautiful on national television was meant to symbolize a form of social justice that would include the Brazilian poor in the larger national community. As one television host put it:

> Winning "Beauty in the Favela" is not simply winning a beauty contest, it is defeating prejudice, defeating the difficulties and obstacles, defeating social difference, and showing to all Brazilians, all the population, that Brazil is much more…than the neighborhoods of the South Zone of Rio de Janeiro and the South Zone of São Paulo, those that we see on television every day. Brazil is a country that has in its most impoverished communities great values, great talents that only need to be discovered. That is the Midas touch of our program, through the reporters who went forth and made their discoveries.[14]

The stated purpose of "Beauty in the Favela," then, is to conquer prejudice and social difference by revealing unknown beauties obscured by the very poverty of their surroundings. One presenter compared it to "revealing the diamond hidden in the favelas of Brasil."[15] This discovery of an unrecognized Brazilian natural resource, as it were, positions the television program as a progressive and nationalistic enterprise. Furthermore, the accomplishment of transforming these girls into models is portrayed as uplifting their entire communities, by reinstating these forgotten Brazilian peripheries into the national imaginary through the beauty of their young women.

By positioning itself as the facilitator of these "discoveries," the program becomes an arbiter of what is beautiful and who is worthy of being hopeful. This authority is enacted through the self-congratulatory "Midas touch" of its scouts, who are commended for venturing into uncharted, even dangerous territory. What was worthy beauty in the eyes of these scouts? First of all, the teenage girls who were chosen were tall and thin, since it was a prerequisite that they must be able to compete within global modeling standards. Additionally, the scouts almost always looked for the one girl that seemed out of place, because she had lighter eyes while the rest had brown eyes, or because her nose was thin and pointy while the others had larger noses. Long, straight hair was not a precondition, but seemed a very desirable quality. The girls who were chosen might be dark-skinned, but not exaggeratedly so. In short, the scouts looked for the type of beauty that is ever-present in Brazilian television and advertising, and which is valued in the wealthy South Zones of Rio de Janeiro or São Paulo that the show claimed to be transcending.

The scouts never bothered to ask what people in the communities they visited might admire as beautiful, reinforcing the idea that the periphery can only be revalued by acquiescing to the standards emanating from the metropolitan centers. The panel of judges making the decision of who would be the finalist from each Brazilian state reinforced this choice, weeding out racial difference and, perhaps unconsciously, making the contestants as uniform as possible. Brazilian beauty is thus constructed as homogeneously single, a whiteness that might be tinged with a hint of racial mixture but not overwhelmed by it. Contests like "Beauty in the Favela" claim to promote social inclusion, reassuring television viewers through hopeful narratives of upward mobility, at the same time that they reinforce the aesthetic judgments that exclude a majority of the Brazilian population from what I call "cosmetic citizenship." While the girls provide the raw capital of beauty, the judgment of their value rests on the media's standards.

At all points during the contest, however, the television presenters stressed that this recognition would merely provide the girls a small opportunity to follow their dreams as models, and they would still have to work toward that future. Their youth represents a different future to be imagined, but not yet accomplished. As Lee Edelman argues, the investment in children's futures esestablishes a political vision that is always a vision of futurity rather than one of the present.[16] The collective investment into children's and teenagers' appearance, therefore, always displaces the hope of upward mobility onto the future, seeming to always require additional labor to become a reality. Parents already see the value of their children's beauty, but in order to transform this value into capital, they require the recognition of the media's gaze, in the same way that the *mocinha*'s value only becomes recognized when she is noticed by her male lead, and in the same way that the photographic lens provides recognition to the dreams of Gisele and her students. This promise of recognition can be perpetually delayed, beckoning the labor of parents and their children without ever fulfilling the dream of truly expanding the hegemonic definition of beauty. In what follows, I will look at an alternative politics of beauty that might perhaps approximate Edelman's call to refuse hope altogether, and revel instead in the immediate *jouissance* of having no future.[17]

Short-Circuiting Hope

Since 2003, the central market in Rio de Janeiro, known as the Saara, has promoted a yearly beauty contest to elect a *Garota da Laje*, or "Concrete-Roof Girl." The *laje* is the simple flat roof made of concrete that is typical of working-class homes in Brazil, which unlike a finished roof with tiles, allows the homeowner to add another level to the structure if necessary. This common practice of slowly building and adding to one's own home, which anthropologist James Holston calls "autoconstruction," allows working-class families to continuously personalize their homes according to need, and lay claim to membership within their community through homeownership.[18] The architectural aesthetic of autoconstruction is considered "ugly" by upper-middle-class Brazilians because, by displaying the concrete and bricks that constitute the house's structure, it refuses the appearance of being a finished product that one could purchase. The *laje* [concrete roof] is a particularly important element in the architecture of an autoconstructed home because it also serves as a space of socialization during hot summer days. Given that in Rio de Janeiro most working-class neighborhoods are located far away from the beach, it has become customary among working-class women to suntan themselves on the concrete roofs of their homes.

The *Garota da Laje* contest not only recognizes this gendered beauty practice, but also gives value to the type of working-class housing that gives rise to it. The organizer of the beauty contest portrayed the aim of the event as "transforming the corny into a craze, [and] showing the beauty of the *comunidade* [fave-la/community] and the periphery."[19] The *Garota da Laje* is thus representative of feminine beauty and also of the architectural aesthetic valued by the working-class. The contestants of *Garota da Laje* are not expected to be perfectly beauti-ful or highly *produzidas* [produced/beautified]. The contestants are not very tall, thin, or young, and are of every color and hue available in Brazil. Many of them are already married and have children. As a contestant explained, the only re-quirement for contestants is "to have natural beauty, because no one here has had cosmetic treatments or plastic surgery, everybody has cellulite, everyone is natural."[20]

The visible, natural imperfections on the body of these women are held up as evidence of the authenticity of these women, like the noticeable construction materials in their autoconstructed homes. The contest thus provided a space for women to express their discontent with the idea that beauty cannot be a per-sonalized aesthetic, but should be a mass-produced, uniform product of beauty work. Another contestant who worked every day at a bakery shop exclaimed, "Brazil needs to find its true identity…The Brazilian woman is *mestiça* [racially-mixed], she needs to wake up at 4 am to work, and does not have the time to go to a beauty salon."[21] By emphasizing the racial diversity and busy working schedule of the average Brazilian woman, this contestant is pointing out how hegemonic representations and practices of beauty are largely irrelevant to them.

Additionally, the *Garota da Laje* contest celebrates beauty, but does not seek to create a narrative of upward mobility associated with beauty. The prizes are not large amounts of money or fancy modeling contracts, but rather a seven-year-old car (the winning prize), a plastic pool, and other smaller items typically available at the Saara market.[22] These are prizes associated with non-conspicuo-us consumption and with leisure, like the weekend barbeques that take place at the *laje*. Hopes for immediate and communal enjoyment replace the hopes for future success. The media, unable to fit this beauty pageant within its usual nar-rative of upward mobility, pokes fun at the event, joking that, "in the land of the *Garota de Ipanema* [Girl from Ipanema], the *Garota da Laje* has reached new heights."[23]

The organizers and contestants seem to use the banter of the media to their advantage, however, since they do not take the contest that seriously in the first place. The contest takes place at the Saara market in the center of Rio de Janei-ro during a normal weekday, attracting the attention of hundreds of workers and shoppers going about their way. The contestants parade in bikinis but they also wear leopard prints, lingerie, and similar clothing that would never be con-sidered appropriate in a traditional beauty pageant. Additionally, they do not simply walk down the makeshift runway, they dance *pagode* and *funk* (musical styles associated with the working-class), they toss their hair around dramatically, and some even crawl on their hands and knees. The mostly male audience responds to these over-the-top performances with enthusiasm, by hooting loudly and hollering sexual compliments, and the contestants flirt back.[24] In short, the contest is a celebration of unapologetic sensuality, corny clothing, and outrageous behavior that the Brazilian upper-middle class would dismiss as debasing, vulgar, and unsophisticated.

The beauty work performed by this working-class representation of femininity is radically different from that deployed by the hegemonic narratives about beauty I previously examined. The *Garota da Laje* is a parody of conventional beauty pageants, replacing the flawless image of a delicate, refined femininity with an unseemly and unruly femininity that is purposefully tasteless. Following Laura Kipnis, it is this very tastelessness that is transgressive and powerful because it upsets bourgeois mores regarding privacy, shame, and disgust, and thus serves as a reminder of the excessive, grotesque materiality of the body that can never be fully contained and disciplined.[25] I would add that this tastelessness also destabilizes the teleological timeframe that imagines beauty as a form of progress and ascension. By grounding beauty on the physicality and sensuality of the body, and celebrating the erotic exchanges between the contestants and the audience, the unruly sexuality of the *Garota da Laje* engages in a *jouissance* that refuses a longing for the future. There are no objectives to the contest other than the immediate enjoyment of the event itself, and no promises of betterment and social inclusion. The beauty they celebrate is not a form of value that can in turn generate more capital, constantly demanding more labor from them, but rather is an end in itself. This is why *Garota da Laje* resonates politically amongst women who already work hard every day and for whom beauty does not make sense unless it can be immediately enjoyed. A beauty with no future is a beauty that exists only for its own sake, not for the sake of others.

Notes

1.   "Da Cidade de Deus à Cidade Luz," *Jornal O Dia* (2007).

2.   "Conto-de-fadas Carioca," *Jornal Extra* (October 20, 2007).

3.   "Á Francesa," *Jornal O Dia* (October 2007 edition of "Revista Tudo de Bom").

4.   Ghassan Hage, *Against Paranoid Nationalism: Searching for Hope in a Shrinking Society* (London: Merlin Press, 2003), 16.

5.   Ibid., 13.

6.   Ibid., 25.

7.   Jean Comaroff and John L. Comaroff, "Millenial Capitalism: First Thoughts on a Second Coming," *Public Culture* 12, no. 2 (2000): 291–343.

8. James Holston, *Insurgent Citizenship: Disjunctions of Democracy and Modernity in Brazil* (Princeton, NJ: Princeton University Press, 2008).

9. Purnima Mankekar, "National Texts and Gendered Lives: An Ethnography of Television Viewers in a North Indian City," *American Ethnologist* 20, no. 3 (1993): 543–63; Lila Abu-Lughod, *Dramas of Nationhood: The Politics of Television in Egypt* (Chicago, IL: University of Chicago Press, 2005).

10. Esther Império Hamburger, *O Brasil Antenado: A Sociedade das Novelas*. Rio de Janeiro: Jorge Zahar Editora, 2005.

11. *Hoje em Dia*. (November 11, 2007).

12. *Hoje em Dia*. (November 19, 2007).

13. Huma Ahmed-Ghosh, "Writing the Nation on the Beauty Queen's Body: Implications for a 'Hindu' Nation," *Meridians: Feminism, Race, Transnationalism* 4, no. 1 (2003): 205–27; Sarah Banet-Weiser, "Miss America, National Identity, and the Identity Politics of Whiteness," in *"There She Is, Miss America": The Politics of Sex, Beauty and Race in America's Most Famous Pageant*, eds. Elwood Watson and Darcy Martin (New York: Palgrave Macmillan, 2004).

14. *Hoje em Dia*, (December 10, 2007).

15. *Hoje em Dia*, (December 9, 2007).

16. Lee Edelman, "The Future is Kid Stuff: Queer Theory, Disidentification and the Death Drive," *Narrative* 6, no. 1 (Jan. 1998): 18–30.

17. Ibid.

18. James Holston, "Autoconstruction in Working-Class Brazil," *Cultural Anthropology* 6, no. 4 (1991): 447–65.

19. "Concurso da 'Garota da Laje' Pára o Centro do Rio," *Jornal Hoje* (November 14, 2008).

20. *RJTV*. Program aired November 17, 2008. Rede Globo.

21. "A Garota da Laje." *Revista Trip* (October 24, 2003).

22. "Concurso Garota da Laje dá Carro Usado de 2001 de Prêmio." *O Globo* (November 12, 2008).

23. "Concurso da 'Garota."

24. *Profissão Repórter* (July 21, 2009).

25. Laura Kipnis, "(Male) Desire and (Female) Disgust: Reading Hustler," *Popular Culture: A Reader*, eds. Raiford Gins and Omayra Zaragoza Cruz (London: Sage Publications, 2005).

Works Cited

Abu-Lughod, Lila. *Dramas of Nationhood: The Politics of Television in Egypt*. Chicago: University of Chicago Press, 2005.

"Á Francesa." *Jornal O Dia*. October 2007 of "Revista Tudo de Bom."

"A Garota da Laje." *Revista Trip*. October 24, 2003.

Ahmed-Ghosh, Huma. "Writing the Nation on the Beauty Queen's Body: Implications for a 'Hindu' Nation." *Meridians: Feminism, Race, Transnationalism* 4, no. 1 (2003): 205–27.

Banet-Weiser, Sarah. "Miss America, National Identity, and the Identity Politics of Whiteness." In *"There She Is, Miss America": The Politics of Sex, Beauty and Race in America's Most Famous Pageant*, eds. Elwood Watson and Darcy Martin. New York: Palgrave Macmillan, 2004.

"Beleza na Favela." *Hoje em Dia.* Rede Record. 2011.

Belíssima. Program aired from November 7, 2005 to July 8, 2006. Rede Globo.

Comaroff, Jean and John L. Comaroff. "Millenial Capitalism: First Thoughts on a Second Coming." *Public Culture* 12, no. 2 (2000): 291—343.

"Concurso da 'Garota da Laje' Pára o Centro do Rio." *Jornal Hoje,* November 14, 2008.

"Concurso Garota da Laje dá Carro Usado de 2001 de Prêmio." *O Globo,* November 12, 2008.

"Conto-de-fadas Carioca." *Jornal Extra,* October 20, 2007.

"Da Cidade de Deus à Cidade Luz." *Jornal O Dia.* October 2007 of "O Mulher."

Edelman, Lee. "The Future is Kid Stuff: Queer Theory, Disidentification and the Death Drive." *Narrative* 6, no. 1 (Jan. 1998): 18—30.

Hage, Ghassan. *Against Paranoid Nationalism: Searching for Hope in a Shrinking Society.* London: Merlin Press, 2003.

Hamburger, Esther Império. *O Brasil Antenado: A Sociedade das Novelas.* Rio de Janeiro: Jorge Zahar Editora, 2005.

Hoje em Dia. November 11, 2007.

Hoje em Dia. November 19, 2007.

Holston, James. "Autoconstruction in Working-Class Brazil." *Cultural Anthropology* 6, no. 4 (1991): 447—65.

————. *Insurgent Citizenship: Disjunctions of Democracy and Modernity in Brazil.* Princeton: Princeton University Press, 2009.

Kipnis, Laura. "(Male) Desire and (Female) Disgust: Reading Hustler." *Popular Culture: A Reader,* eds. Raiford Gins and Omayra Zaragoza Cruz. London: Sage Publications, 2005.

Mankekar, Purnima. "National Texts and Gendered Lives: An Ethnography of Television Viewers in a North Indian City." *American Ethnologist* 20, no. 3 (1993): 543—63.

Mulheres de Areia. Program aired from February 1 to September 25, 1993. Rede Globo.

Paraíso Tropical. Program aired from March 5 to September 28, 2008. Rede Globo.

Profissão Repórter. Program aired on July 21, 2009. Rede Globo.

RJTV. Program aired November 17, 2008. Rede Globo.

"Chongas" in the Media: The Ethno-Sexual Politics of Latina Girls' Hypervisibility

Jillian Hernandez

Often described by Latin@s in South Florida as a low-class, slutty, tough, and crass young woman, the hypervisible figure disparagingly labeled as a "chonga" is practically invisible in queer theory, media studies, and feminist scholarship. Representations of chonga girls such as the widely viewed YouTube video "Chongalicious" mock young Latina women who don tight clothing, heavy lip liner, and large hoop earrings. In this chapter I examine the sexual politics of visual representations of chongas across media such as contemporary art, YouTube, and print/broadcast outlets. How do the varying forms of production, circulation, and reception that attend these media produce and reflect discourses about Latina girls' sexuality? How does the chonga come to signify and embody tropes regarding Latina girls' hypersexuality?

I take an expansive approach to selecting the images under consideration in this chapter, as I analyze visual media that mobilize the term "chonga" in addition to works that do not, yet whose subjects fit the discursive framework of the figure via sartorial style. I will conduct visual analyses of the YouTube video *Chongalicious*, artist Luis Gispert's *Cheerleaders* photographs, and images of chongas in broadcast and print media such as the Latin television network Univision. My arguments will also be based on a questionnaire regarding chongas that I administered to South Florida residents in 2008. The questionnaire responses illustrate the meanings associated with chonga identity and reflect the discursive field in which images of these young women circulate. The chonga images and questionnaire responses inform each other, as there is a recursive relationship between social discourse and visual production. This two-pronged methodology aims to provide the reader with a context for situating the chonga figure that is just emerging in scholarship.

I claim that the non-normative "sexual-aesthetic excesses" of chonga bodies signify a queer politics that undermines sexual policing and conveys indifference toward portraying an assimilated white bourgeois subjectivity. Akin to a camp Butlerian parody, the chonga girl's denaturalized visibility is a citation of gender, class, and racial/ethnic signifiers, from her faux-gold jewelry, gelled-straight hair, and synthetic nails to the imitation designer clothes she buys at the flea market. I offer sexual-aesthetic excess as a concept in order to theorize modes of dress and comportment that are often considered "too much": too ethnic, too sexy, too young, too cheap, too loud.

Excessive Presence: Latina Bodies in Visual Culture

The images of chongas and chonga-esque women I will discuss in what follows stem from the history and politics of representation of Latina bodies in the U.S. context. Filmmaker and scholar Celine Parreñas Shimizu notes the critical role visual representations play in organizing social relations in the United States in her statement, "The stakes are indeed high—the bodies of women, people of color, and sexual minorities signify reproductive futures and new morphologies of the family and American national identity."[1] Latin@ cultural and communications studies scholars also focus on visual representations due to the material ramifications of the biopolitics Shimizu identifies.[2] They demonstrate how representations of Latinas structure social relations in the United States by fashioning an exotic, "tropicalized" other in response to ongoing panic over Latina reproduction and immigration.[3] Most literature, however, analyzes images of Latina celebrities such as Celia Cruz, Jennifer Lopez, and Salma Hayek. This article advances scholarship on representations of Latina bodies in visual culture by interrogating the vernacular figure of the chonga, who is not represented by a well-known actress or music performer. The chonga figure warrants examination as it is an emerging "icon" that is producing and circulating discourses about Latina young women.[4]

Communications scholar Isabel Molina Guzman (2007) has shown how Latinas are often portrayed as "disorderly bodies" that are emotionally and sexually excessive. In "Disorderly Bodies and Discourses of Latinidad in the Elian Gonzalez Story," she describes the "visual excess" that marked the news coverage of Marisleysis Gonzalez, the aunt of Elian Gonzalez, a young Cuban boy who was at the center of a high profile immigration and custody case in 2000. Guzman notes how the "excesses" the media focused on, such as Marisleysis's public crying, long acrylic finger nails, and form-fitting clothes marked her as a brown, unlawful body that did not fit the framework of a "proper" U.S. subject.

The mobilization of Marisleysis's excessive body discursively unraveled the privileged, model minority status of Cuban Americans and helped to frame them as "bad," disorderly subjects who held impassioned demonstrations on the streets of Miami following the decision to return Elian to Cuba.

The hyperbolic, stereotypical representations of Latinas often found in visual culture are measured against an imagined (white/middle class) construct of U.S. citizenship. Latina bodies are read as out of control and used against the communities they "represent." Many efforts to counter these constructions in Latin@ communities signify the internalization of technologies of discipline that center on policing women's bodies.[5] Are Latina women hoping to embody the "normal" so that they are not confused with those "other" bodies of excess?

As Shimizu states, "To panic about being identified within perversity can too easily lead us to strive toward self-restricting normalcy or the impossible constraints of sexual purity."[6] I focus on the *sexual-aesthetic excess* that marks the over-adorned chonga body and propose that rather than critique visual representations of these young women for reproducing negative stereotypes, we read them as indexing ethnic pride, personal confidence, and non-normative or queer sexuality. Subjects who embody sexual-aesthetic excess in their style and behavior are often the targets of discipline by institutions and sexist, racist, classist individuals who are threatened by difference, radical creativity, and sexual agency. Those who dress flamboyantly and are not ashamed of being poor, queer, hyperfeminine, and pleasure seeking are often targeted for mockery, state/school intervention, and violence. Aesthetic excesses of style such as heavy makeup are often read as indicators of low-class status and bad taste. This bad taste in turn is routinely framed as indicative of sexual excess, or deviancy. Chongas and other similarly marked bodies such as African American "hoochies" are subject to the cultural dynamics of sexual-aesthetic excess. I posit that sexual-aesthetic excess can function as a cultural agitator by making sexual, gender, and class difference loud and visible in a neoliberal context that seeks docile subjects who lose themselves in the promise of equality.

Sexual-aesthetic excess is akin to Shimizu's concept of the *productive performance of perversity*. In her study *The Hypersexuality of Race: Performing Asian/ American Women on Screen and Scene*, she focuses on representations of Asian/American women in pornography, independent/mass-market films, and theater. In describing her theoretical approach Shimizu notes,

> Productive perversity involves identifying with "bad" images, or working to establish a different identity along with established sexual images so as to expand racial agendas beyond the need to establish normalcy and standardization. To engage hypersexuality as a politically productive perversity pays attention to the formulations of sexual and

racial identity that critique normative scripts for sexually and racially marginalized subjects.[7]

Like Asian/American women, Latinas have also been subject to hypersexualization in visual media from popular discourses surrounding Jennifer Lopez's ass to more dated representations of voluptuous dancers balancing fruit on their heads.[8]

In the contemporary moment young Latina bodies are being marketed by the culture industry that is driven to profit from the growing population of Latin@s. Media scholar Angharad N. Valdivia demonstrates the need to examine representations of young Latina girls when she points out, "Three elements—census data, a Latina/o cultural boom, and the gendered tweening of popular culture—coalesce to redirect our attention to the location of Latina girls in popular culture."[9] Through engaging with chonga images, I hope to demonstrate the need for a re-evaluation of urban girls' hypersexual representations in order to complicate academic work that aims to "empower" girls of color by disassociating them from harmful stereotypes to the point that their sexual agency becomes effaced and viewed as primarily dictated by males and mainstream culture. My conceptualization of agency here draws from anthropologist Laura Ahearn's definition of it as the "socioculturally mediated capacity to act."[10] Girls' sexuality cannot be divorced from social context, yet it should be recognized that they play various roles in framing the meanings associated with their sexual identities and practices.

"You Could See Me, You Could Read Me": ## YouTube and the Branding of the Chonga Body

Chola
Chusma
Chocha
Chula
Chonga

These Spanish terms, some emerging in the United States among Latin@s, index female sexuality. Roughly translated, in order, they denote a street girl ("homegirl"), loud/gossipy/lower-class woman, vagina (or "pussy"), "cute chick," and slut/thug girl. Their lexical similarities point to gender and class inscriptions that are articulated and reproduced through everyday speech in Latin communities. Such terms interpellate specifically marked bodies in primarily urban locations (Miami, New York, Los Angeles). To employ the Althusserian (1971) term, women whose dress and behavior are interpreted as sexual and low/working class, are *hailed*, literally (in everyday social interaction, e.g.,

"Oye/Hey mami!") and discursively, as representative of these marginalized or "bad" subjectivities.

Performance theorist Jose Esteban Munoz has described the chusma identity as antithetical to "standards of bourgeois comportment":

> Chusmeria is, to a large degree, linked to a stigmatized class identity. Within Cuban culture, for instance, being called *chusma* might be technique for the middle class to distance itself from the working class; it may be a barely veiled racial slur suggesting that one is too black; it sometimes connotes gender nonconformity. In the United States, the epithet *chusma* also connotes recent immigration and a general lack of "Americanness," as well as excessive nationalism—that one is somewhat over the top about her Cubanness. The sexuality of individuals described as *chusmas* is also implicated. The prototypical *chusma's* sexuality is deemed excessive and flagrant—again, subverting conventions.[11] (emphasis in original)

The chonga, a more recent term that appears to have stemmed from the Cuban-American community, is in many ways a younger version of the chusma, or the chusma-as-teenager.

The chonga finds a Chicana counterpart in the chola ("homegirl"). In her essay, "Re-Imagining Chicana Urban Identities in the Public Sphere, Cool Chuca Style," Rosa Linda Fregroso describes the absence of young women interpellated by these terms in feminist scholarship:

> Within the Chicana feminist deconstruction of Chicano familial discourse, the figure of the pachuca, chola, or homegirl is inadvertently overlooked as an agent of oppositional practices, despite her notable contribution to the politics of resistance.[12]

I am situating this essay in the critical "chusma" and "chola" theorizations of Munoz and Fregroso, in addition to Shimizu's readings of productive perversity, as they look beyond the negative connotations of racialized sexual subjectivities to uncover progressive politics.

Though no "officialized" definition of the chonga exists, she entered the realm of popular discourse in South Florida through the YouTube video *Chongalicious*, which presents a characterization that has resonated in this community. The work was posted on the site www.youtube.com on April 1, 2007 and tallied almost one million views within several months (over five million to date). *Chongalicious* parodied the 2006 song *Fergalicious* by pop music performer Fergie, which likely bolstered its rapid local circulation.

The video was created by Latina teens Mimi Davila and Laura Di Lorenzo, then drama students attending an arts magnet high school in the Aventura area of North Miami-Dade County on a night in which they were hanging out at Davila's house with a friend.[13] The girls neither anticipated nor initially worked toward garnering widespread attention. What would have just been a silly faux music video circulating among a group of friends for laughs now has the potential of entering popular culture in the era of YouTube. The viral circulation of videos from inbox to inbox and social networking site to social networking site spurs the creation of "everyday" celebrities.

In *Chongalicious* Davila and Di Lorenzo don tight outfits and vigorously move their behinds to electronic beats as they enact the sexual-aesthetic excess of the chonga script. The clothing that serves as their "costumes" consist of a basketball jersey worn as a form-fitting mini-dress, a one-piece spandex short jumper, metallic gold flip flops, and plastic mesh slippers with sequined flowers (worn with white cotton ankle socks). The girls wear large hoop earrings and dark red lipstick. Their hair is wrapped in buns worn high atop their heads and the bottom portion of their hair runs down to their shoulders in waves.

The opening shot of the video is a close-up of the girls' shaking buttocks; they then turn to face the viewer and begin to perform the *Chongalicious* song with animated hand gestures and simulated thick Latina/o accents. A school-mate recorded the performance in the interior of Davila's home and outdoors in the housing complex. The work emulates the genre of the music video through the emphasis on the girls' dancing and montage of varied scenes edited to synchronize with the song. An attempt is made to screen the domestic space, with limited success, by framing the performers against plain white walls. The majority of the shots are close-ups and capture scenes of the girls looking into mirrors while styling their hair and makeup using glue for gel and Sharpie pens for lip liner, flirting with a young man on the street, pushing each other around, and sloppily eating pizza and smearing it over their mouths. These hyperbolic, slapstick parodies serve to convey the chonga's over-indulgent nature and "excessive" or trashy application of beauty products. The performers speak in the "voice" of chongas and address the viewer/camera with a confrontational attitude throughout the work. This is a sample of the lyrics they perform in unison:

> *Chongalicious definition arch my eyebrows high*
> *They always starin' at my booty and my panty line*
> *You could see me, you could read me*
> *Cuz my name is on my earrings*
> *Girls got reasons why they hate me*
> *Cuz they boyfriends wanna date me*
> *Chongalicious*
> *But—I aint promiscuous*
> *And if you talkin' trash, I'll beat you after class*
> *I blow besos—muuuuaaah!*[14]
> *I use my Sharpie lip line*
> *And ain't no other chonga glue her hair like mine*
> *Chongalicious*

Although they claim not to be promiscuous, the lyrics nevertheless typify chongas as sexualized, antagonistic toward other girls, violent, and hypervisible ("You could see me, you could read me"). In a later segment of the video, the performers make references to the chonga's lower-class status by describing her as "ghetto" and stating that she buys her "bling" at the flea market for $2.99.[15]

Chongalicious crossed over from YouTube to traditional print, radio, and television outlets in South Florida. It was featured in a news segment by the internationally broadcast Spanish-language network Univision and the song the girls performed in the video frequently rotated on Miami's urban music station Power 96. Despite its seeming status as a media-generated "sensation," *Chongalicious* circulated virally via the Myspace and Live Journal pages of locals prior to its intensive media blitz. A host of spin-offs and parodies of the video appeared on YouTube such as *Preppylicious, Hoochielicious, No More Chongalicious!!!,* and Davila and Di Lorenzo's sequel video *I'm in Love with a Chonga* (the number of hits these videos have attained, in the hundreds of thousands, seem minimal compared with those of *Chongalicious*). The coverage on chongas, particularly in Spanish language media, has persisted since 2007. An episode of the Univision talk show *Cristina* that featured the *Chongalicious* performers aired in January 2009 and in 2011 YouTube users continue to post comments on the video on a regular basis. I will later discuss how reactions to the *Chongalicious* video and the coverage it attracted have ranged from celebration to disgust among South Florida residents.

Production value was added to the do-it-yourself aesthetic of the video in the photographs that appeared in the feature article on *Chongalicious* in Miami's alternative weekly paper *The New Times.* The front cover features Davila and Di Lorenzo wearing matching outfits and significantly more jewelry, makeup, and hair styling products than in the video. The use of a plain background signals that the girls are performing, as they are not embedded in a social context. The bright pink hue of the backdrop further indexes them as gendered and infantile. Their "fake" and "immature" personalities are depicted through exaggerated facial expressions, such as wide-open eyes, and hand gestures that accentuate their long acrylic fingernails. In another photograph, they face the camera as if looking into a mirror and apply makeup while struggling to hold the beauty products that are spilling out of their arms. In *The New Times* story, reporter Tamara Lush joins the girls during trips to the mall and media appearances where they draw attention from passers-by and receive requests for autographs from teenage fans who recognize them as parodic characters.

After receiving a flood of attention from the South Florida community Davila and Di Lorenzo aimed to capitalize on the chonga body by branding it in order to sell themselves as emerging actresses in order to crossover from

YouTube to more lucrative teen and tween venues such as MTV, Disney Channel, and Nickelodeon. In "Branding the Post-Feminist Self: Girls' Video Production and YouTube," communications scholar Sarah Banet-Weiser describes how young women's performances on YouTube often function more as promotional tools than modes of self-expression. Banet-Weiser discusses how often in girls' homemade videos brands are referenced in order to describe their identities and logos are visible in the background of their rooms. In describing the neoliberal politics that undergird girls' video production on YouTube Banet-Weiser notes, "The fact that some girls produce media—and thus ostensibly produce themselves through their self-presentation—within the context of a commercially-driven technological space is not only evidence of a kind of empowering self-work but also a way to self-brand in an increasingly ubiquitous brand culture."[16]

The performers of *Chongalicious* were not attempting to present themselves but rather to embody the chonga trope as a comedic shtick. The attention they garnered, however, prompted them to sell themselves as performers who could reach the sought after market of Latin@ youth. On the website of the talent agency Uno Entertainment there are promotional photographs of the girls, without chonga regalia, marketing them as actresses, comedians, and "YouTube starlets." The company applies the gendered language of old Hollywood, with its attendant associations of whiteness, to new media production in order to brand the girls as wholesome and potentially lucrative marketing investments. A banner on the Uno Entertaiment site reads:

> YouTube starlets, actresses, comedians, and writers Mimi Davila and Laura di Lorenzo aka Chonga Girls present their own spin on the news with Chisme News and other stuff, Enjoy!!! With a coast-to-coast fan base of over 8 million 14–24 year olds, Mimi and Laura have an insider's fluency with urban youth and Hispanic-American culture, and they celebrate and poke fun at their surroundings in a way that brings everyone together.[17]

Here the logic of marketing merges with the logic of neoliberal multiculturalism to make the mockery of urban girls Di Lorenzo and Davila emulate benign and in good taste. Mockery of the chonga body is employed to create a brand and achieve publicity.

Despite their marketing work the performers of the *Chongalicious* video have yet to achieve crossover success. I posit that this stems from the association that has been forged between the performers and everyday chonga girls. The attempts of Uno Entertainment to brand Davila and Di Lorenzo as multi-talented starlets cannot wipe away the ethnic smudge of chonga girl hypersexuality. The makeup that they used to construct the chonga mask seems more difficult to take off than they had imagined; they have been marked by ethnic hypersexuality. Although their performance as chongas received a wide audience the connection that was established between them and "real" chongas may have already positioned them as unfeasible products for the teen/tween media enterprise. Unfortunately for aspiring and talented Latina young women such as Davila and Di Lorenzo, Latina girls can only fit a narrow range of roles, ranging from the marginalized excess of chonga girls, to the dramatic dorkiness of Ugly Betty and the new normative "cool" of emerging Latina stars like Selena Gomez.

Selena Gomez is a young pop music performer and actress who rose to fame through her leading role in the Disney Channel television series *Wizards of Waverly Place*. She was named after the Chicana singer-songwriter Selena, her identity fused with the hope for Latina iconicity and crossover into the mainstream. Although Selena Gomez's character, Alex, on *Wizards of Waverly Place* is Latina she often downplays her heritage and finds it embarrassing. Her embodiment on the show and in media appearances is not ethnically marked. Her tall, thin frame often sports trendy and casual wear that is popular with other mainstream performers like the Caucasian singer/actress Miley Cyrus. Selena Gomez is the normative antithesis to the ethnically marked hypersexual embodiment of chonga girls.

In "This Tween Bridge over My Latina Back: The U.S. Mainstream Negotiates Ethnicity," Valdivia discusses the representational politics of mass-market figures and products such as Selena Gomez and Bratz dolls. In a cultural industry that is targeting the growing population of Latin@s in the U.S. with aggressive marketing tactics, the figure of the light-skinned Latina girl has emerged as a vehicle for attracting audiences and consumers. Valdivia, drawing from the pioneering work of women of color feminists such as Gloria Anzaldua, argues that light skinned Latin@s are serving as viable marketing products as they do not embody the threat of difference and political power of African Americans. She states, "The bridge metaphor remains useful in this cultural moment. In all of these sites of contemporary mainstream tween girl culture the identifiable and the ambiguous Latina serves as a bridge between whiteness and difference."[18]

The Chonga as Ethnic Spectacle

The excessive figure of the chonga is often framed as the antithesis of the respectability and class that has historically marked white and light Latina femininity. The manner in which the chonga typifies a sexualized hyperethnicity was staged on the *Cristina* talk show episode on chongas that aired on the Spanish-language network Univision in 2009, in which chongas were literally posed against whiteness. The talk show host herself, who critiqued the style of the

chonga girls she invited on the show embodied the social aspirations of normative white Latinidad with her straightened, bleached blonde hair and Chanel
inspired jacket. Each self-proclaimed chonga girl on the panel was seated next
to a light-skinned Latina in modest, contemporary trendy dress (printed feminine dresses, simple jewelry, straightened hair) that served as her opposite. The
chongas were asked questions that prompted them to defend their mode of
dress and the "normal" Latinas barraged the girls with negative comments while
they pontificated about feminine class, dress, and style. The overall aim of the
show was to laugh at the chonga girls and advise them to change their style so
that they would not look ridiculous.

A segment of the episode featured a "chonga makeover" in which queer,
light-skinned celebrity stylist Rodner Figueroa stated that he was going to transform a "pretty" woman into an "ugly" woman by turning a well-dressed audience member into a chonga. Through the makeover the homonormative Latino
stylist sustains heteronormativty and racial/ethnic hierarchies by disciplining the
bodies of chonga girls and "scaring" them into abandoning their "ugly," excessive look.[19]

In the episode a young, self-proclaimed chonga named Elizabeth who was
on the panel claimed to have been the inspiration for the *Chongalicious* video.
She wore large bright neon-colored combs in her hair, tight short shorts, a black
shirt, heavy makeup, and many bangles and necklaces. In the show she was
consistently called "vulgar" by a tall, thin Latina woman with a fashion model
physique who had light and straightened hair. Elizabeth became increasingly
agitated during the show due to the consistent negative comments directed at
her and told Cristina, the celebrity stylist, and the other women on the panel
and in the audience that she would continue to dress like a chonga no matter
what advice they had to persuade her to the contrary. When it came time for the
audience to respond to the panel Elizabeth's mother stood in front of the mi-
crophone stand and said that she wanted to defend her daughter who is an
honor roll student. Emboldened by her mother's public statement, the young
chonga girl proclaimed,

> Yo puedo salir ahora vestida asi porque yo tengo el balance academico y social que
> puedo vestirme como yo quiero. Lo que tengo acqui no me lo quita nadie.

> I can go out right now dressed like this because I have the academic and social balance
> that I can dress the way I want. What I have here (pointing to her brain) no one can
> take away from me.

Here the chonga body talks back and queers dichotomies between sexualized
self-presentation and academic performance, feminized grooming practices and
self esteem.

The chonga as a marker of racial/ethnic difference was also staged in a fol-low-up video by Davila and Di Lorenzo that was posted on YouTube in 2009 titled *Chonga Ladies, Chola Ladies*. The video pays homage to their fan base and includes a montage of videos produced by girls across the country in response to *Chongalicious*. The performers follow a similar formula as in *Chongalicious* by parodying a popular song, in this instance Beyonce's hit "Single Ladies (Put a Ring on It)." Davila and Di Lorenzo change the lyrics to tell the story of the chonga girls' rivalry with two "regular girls" who are also performed by Davila and DiLorenzo. The "regular girls" wear modest pastel-colored dresses and have no makeup on, which results in their skin looking lighter, making them appear less ethnically marked. In the video the chonga girls are upset that a light-skinned Latino boy wearing hip hop fashions is not paying attention to them but rather to the normal girls. The chongas make fun of the regular girls and call them "shones," a word that emerged in the Florida hip hop scene that signifies a whore. The joke of the video is that the chonga girls, who are framed as being the "real" skanky girls are negatively judging the normative "good girls," making them look ridiculous. The two sets of girls are juxtaposed to showcase their different and differently valued embodiments. The normative girls gain coveted male attention and the ethnically marked chongas are framed as stupid and desperate.

The spectacle of chonga embodiment has also been staged in the contem-porary art world. The works that launched the career of Cuban-American artist Luis Gispert were a series of photographs entitled *Cheerleaders* (2000–2002). The works feature a cast of multi-racial young women donning cheerleader uniforms with hair, makeup, and accessories that reference chonga style such as large gold earrings, acrylic nails, stylized ponytails, and athletic shoes. The young women enact scenes ranging from the fantastical to the mundane such as posing in lux-ury vehicles or floating in air as if in a trance. The poses of the subjects often cite canonical art historical narratives such as Mary mourning the body of Jesus. The *Cheerleaders* series was most recently on view at the Museum of Contempo-rary Art in Miami in a critically acclaimed retrospective of Gispert's work that ran from April through June 2009.

In *Untitled (Chain Mouth, a.k.a. Muse Ho)*, a work from the series, Gispert references contemporary artist Bruce Nauman's well-known photograph *Self-Portrait as Fountain* (1967–1970). Nauman's *Self-Portrait as Fountain* is a play on art historical conventions of statuesque male nudes. Often described as a reference to Marcel Duchamp's *Fountain* of 1917, Nauman playfully conflates his body with an object by capturing himself unclothed and spewing a stream of water from his mouth. Unlike Nauman, Gispert utilizes the body a young woman to execute the parodic gesture in *Untitled (Chain Mouth, a.k.a. Muse Ho)* instead of his own.

The description of the subject as a "ho" in the title and the manner in which her makeup, hair, and costume are styled situate her in the discourse of sexual-aesthetic excess attributed to chongas. It is worth noting that Gispert grew up in Cuban-American enclaves in Miami, where he likely encountered "chonga" discourse. Where Nauman emits a thin jet of water from his mouth in *Self-Portrait as Fountain*, the female figure in *Untitled* expels a long, thick, phallic gold chain. The sexual athleticism on display is reinforced by the cheerleader uniform, which symbolizes a "type" of girl that is usually framed as being, like the chonga, sexually available, immature, surrounded by men, and hostile toward other girls.

Most of the young woman's body is decked in gold. The ornamentation makes her seem otherworldly and goddess-like but the tattoos that ring her arm and belly button situate her in contemporary culture. The tattoos, coupled with the frosty blue eye shadow she wears (which is considered out of step with current conventions of taste and style), further signify her as a "trashy" subject. The uniform that clothes the figure makes the quasi-mythical scene anachronistic. The lack of a contextualizing background in the photograph leaves the eye to wander ceaselessly around her body. Enticed and guided by the ornaments, the viewer, like her, is visually arrested by the body.

The green chroma-key background that frames the performances of Gispert's cheerleaders divorces them from a social milieu and indexes them as "types" on view. *The New Times* employed a similar approach in their photographs of the *Chongalicious* performers in character, which are captured against an empty background. These images represent chongas as spectacles and stock characters.

The *Cheerleader* series, completed soon after Gispert's graduation from Yale's Master of Fine Arts program, were ripe for commodification by the art world. In *The Miami Herald* article, "Homecoming: Luis Gispert returns to his Miami roots as a major art world player" published on October 14, 2007, reporter Tom Austin introduces Gispert to the reader by recounting the unpredictable success of the *Cheerleader* series. Austin explains how "Gispert's image of an airborne cheerleader was featured in the 2002 Whitney Biennial, then bought by the Whitney and used in a Biennial advertising campaign."[20] The chonga images successfully "branded" Gispert as an up-and-coming artist from the city that typifies *Scarface* action and hip hop bling. He has since exhibited work at the Royal Academy of Art in London, PS1 Contemporary Art Center, and Guggenheim—Bilbao, among other prestigious venues. The appeal of the chonga-esque girl as a symbol of Miami facilitated the success of the artist, which the city lauds in turn through the "local success story" discourse expressed in the article in order to highlight its cultural cache.

Perhaps representations of chongas are adopted when they are consumed in the context of "ghetto-fabulous" portrayals of Miami that are successfully mobilized in mainstream culture through video games such as *Grand Theft Auto: Vice City*. The pleasure garnered from the chonga's idolized visual representation, however, does not seem to be echoed in South Floridians' descriptions of her corporeal presence in their day-to-day encounters in the city, for which she is derided.

It is not my aim to frame the images in *Chongalicious* and *Cheerleaders* as "bad" representations. I am withholding such critique due to the unreliability and unknowability of representation as described by Shimizu, who holds that visual media are limited in their capacity to fully capture subjects and social experiences as the creative process involves complex negotiations of meaning making among those involved. Among other methodologies, Shimizu illustrates this unknowability and unreliability through interviews with Asian/American actresses who play stereotypical roles in works such as *Miss Saigon*. Shimizu describes how the actresses exhibit agency through making subtle changes in the narrative via their real-time performances (gestures, cadences) and illustrates how feminist Asian/American artists explore "taboo" or "non-normative perverse" roles such as "whores" and "druggies."[21] Shimizu's work suggests that the models in Gispert's works may have had some influence in how they were portrayed, and would further recognize that perhaps the *Cheerleader* and *Chongalicious* images could be, or have been, affirming to girls who are hailed by the chonga script.

The Meaning(s) of "Chonga"

The emerging hypervisibility of the chonga body prompted me to develop a questionnaire regarding chongas and the *Chongalicious* video that I distributed through the Web via e-mail from my location in New Jersey to friends and family members who live in Miami. Respondents were instructed to submit completed questionnaire forms to me via e-mail. As in a snowball sample, my initial pool of subjects aided me in recruiting additional participants via e-mail, Facebook messages, and Myspace posts. For example, my brother, who at the time the study was conducted was an eighteen-year-old senior in a Miami-Dade County high school recruited fellow eighteen-year-old peers to participate through his Myspace account. In this way, the circulation of the survey paralleled that of the *Chongalicious* video.

The questionnaire posed questions concerning the provenance and meaning of the term *chonga* and the reception of the *Chongalicious* video. In addition to those regarding demographics (gender, race, nationality, age, and South Florida neighborhood where subjects reside) it consisted of the following questions: Have you heard the term "chonga" before? Where did you hear the term first? Do you think it is an official Spanish word? Where do you think the word came from? Who uses the term? What is a chonga?[22] Is describing someone as a chonga positive or negative? Have you ever met anyone that describes themselves as a chonga? Have you seen the *Chongalicious* video on YouTube? How did you find out about it? Did you enjoy it? Do you think the video is a realistic representation of chongas? Do you think the video was popular?

I am approaching the responses to my questionnaire as discursive texts. In some instances, I will aggregate responses in order to highlight interesting points of consensus and divergence among the participant group; I do not intend for these figures to be interpreted as statistical data. While it is not possible to present my findings as symptomatic of how most Miamians feel about chongas or the *Chongalicious* video, they provide a window into the meanings associated with the chonga with regard to sexuality, gender, class, race, and ethnicity.

I received thirty-one responses to the *Chongalicious* questionnaire. All respondents reside in Miami-Dade County with a concentration in the middle-class neighborhoods of Westchester, South Miami, and Kendall. This may present a middle-class bias in my study that excludes poor and working-class subjects who may be labeled as chongas. However, I suggest that the responses of these middle-class South Floridians can point to how the chonga identity is perceived and constructed by the dominant culture. The majority of respondents, twenty-six, were female. Twenty-one participants identified themselves as Latina/o or as a specific nationality (Colombian, Dominican, etc.); over half of these specified Cuban descent. Two respondents identified as African American. Twenty-five respondents were between the ages of eighteen to twenty-four, the eldest respondent in the sample was thirty-four years of age (eighteen years of age being the youngest).

When asked where they first heard the term, twenty respondents stated they encountered it in school, mostly in middle school/junior high. The remainder recalled learning it from friends or public discourse in Miami. The connection articulated between exposure to the word "chonga" and the middle school setting points to the negotiation of identity that often takes place in adolescence. Molding an identity can sometimes employ a negative process of defining oneself via the recognition of who one is *not*.[23] Respondents of the chonga questionnaire described how the function of the term was to identify, exclude, and deride "bad" subjects.

Most participants stated that the term is slang, not "official" Spanish. Connections to other words were proposed in response to the question regarding the provenance of "chonga," among them associations to the Chicana girls known as cholas. Links of the term to Afro-Cuban spiritual practices were also forged. One respondent posited that it could have derived from the syncretic religion Santeria. Another more specifically offered that the root of the word "chonga" might be found in *Chango*, the name of a male Yoruba deity whose Santeria icon is the Catholic Saint Barbara. These racial associations suggest the status of the chonga as an "other" Cuban-American identity that is often disavowed by elite Cubans through its connection to marginalized subjects such as Afro-Cubans and African Americans via the chonga's adoption of hip hop culture.[24]

Ten respondents offered that "everyone" uses the term, followed by six who stated that "chonga" primarily circulates in teenage circles. Other groups noted for use of the term included Cubans, Puerto Ricans, Dominicans, and people "under 40." An additional six participants suggested that "chonga" circulates among homosocial groups of women in the antagonistic mode of drawing attention to and mocking the girl identified as such ("Girls that hate on each other," "Mainly females describing other females," "Everyone who wants to offend someone else, mainly a girl"). Several respondents noted that the word is used by people who do not identify as chongas, or who were chongas prior to being "preppy." Beyond its classed Caucasian connotations, "preppy" in Miami denotes an upper-class, non-Black Latina/o that lives in an exclusive area of Miami such as Coral Gables.

Twenty-four out of thirty-one respondents stated that describing someone as a chonga is negative, with others proposing that it is context-specific. One respondent suggested that the chonga's negative connotation is due to the fact that it "melds all the bad Hispanic stereotypes into one word." For the most part, participants advanced that the detrimental quality of the word stems from its deriding and exclusionary function.

Eighteen respondents stated that they have encountered individuals who describe themselves as chongas. Several indicated that this was representative of a phase in their own life or that of a friend. In addressing the question, "Have you ever met anyone who describes themselves as a chonga?" one subject responded, "Yes, myself, in the mirror along with all of my adolescent friends." An eighteen-year-old subject wrote, "My best friend, lol, she used to be the biggest chonga till she met me and my friends."[25] The portrayal of the chonga as juvenile may stem from the view that it is an identity that is passed through and sheds with maturity and social/class mobility.

Subjects who claimed they had not encountered individuals who identified as chongas made sweeping and assertive proclamations such as "no chonga admits to being a chonga" and "no [I have not met someone who describes themselves as a chonga]…but sadly they are blinded," one even went as far as declaring "If I did [encounter a self-described chonga] I'd slap them." The majority of respondents attributed little to be desired in the chonga role. She is framed as an identity antithetical to the efforts made by second- and third-generation Latina/o youth to assimilate into American culture. Like an embarrassing cousin one is reluctant to introduce to friends, the chonga is not a figure to be associated with, as she loudly speaks her broken English and wears all the "right" commodity items (jewelry, trendy clothes) the wrong way. The deployment of the term, and the attendant laughter it induces, can enable Latina/o teens to distance themselves from her hypersexual, hyperethnic, and under-class inscription.

The question that generated the most lengthy responses was: "What is a chonga?" Twenty-nine of thirty-one participants provided vividly detailed descriptions of a young urban female's style of dress. She was described as wearing ill-fitting clothes that were either too baggy or too tight, applying an excessive amount of gel to her hair, donning large gold hoop earrings engraved with her name in cursive lettering, using heavy eye and lip liner, and gaudy amounts of jewelry. Chongas were largely described as Latinas. Several respondents proposed that there are also white chongas (a pop culture figure like Fergie could fit into this framework due to her mode of dress). Study subjects situated chongas in middle- and lower-class areas of Miami-Dade County such as Hialeah, Sweetwater, Westchester, Cutler Ridge, and Kendall. Her class status was also articulated through descriptions of where and what she consumes. Respondents stated that they eat large amounts of fast food and shop at flea markets, U.S. Tops, and D'or, establishments that sell juniors clothing at bargain prices. The hypersexuality of the chonga was indexed by references to her "skimpy" or "hoochie" style of dress and assertions that "they aren't home bodies" and "chill with a lot of guys."

She was additionally portrayed as "reffy," a term used in Miami to denote recent refugees (recall Munoz's description of the hyperethnic chusma). The chonga was framed by some as being "loud," "crass," and able to master neither English nor Spanish, thus speaking "Spanglish." Other respondents described chongas as "un-intellectual" and apathetic about gaining skills and bettering themselves through education. The characteristics attributed to chongas are tinged with failure. She fails at acculturating, not being able to speak English "correctly" or without an accent. Her flaunting visibility is perceived as foolish, as "they are not aware of how ridiculous they look in public." She also falls short of convincingly projecting a hip hop-inspired attitude of toughness, as one respondent stated, she is a "girl that's fake and acts like she's from the ghetto" or a "wannabe ghetto Hispanic chick" who "tries to talk like they're from New York but never quite achieves the tone." Davila and Di Lorezno articulate the chonga's aspirations for thugdom in the *Chongalicious* lyric, "g-to the h-to the-e-t-t-o girl you ghetto."

The recurring characteristics of the chonga as un-intellectual, hypersexual, and of lower class stems from stereotypical views regarding urban girls of color that have been circulating in the dominant culture and elite circles of Latinas/os for decades.[26] *The New Times* story on the *Chongalicious* video has reinforced this view. Reporter Tamara Lush makes efforts to articulate to the reader how *unlike* chongas Davila and Di Lorenzo *really* are. Lush notes,

> In character, they are brash, sexy, bold creatures. They seem self-assured rather than the moody, curious girls they really are…They have noticed that guys like them better as chongas, a fact that makes them more than a little depressed. Both girls get plenty of looks from guys as they walk down the street in their chonga wear—but not, for example, when they are sitting in their AP English class, wearing sweatshirts, jeans, and glasses.[27]

Lush continually makes references to the fact that the girls reside in Aventura in her report, an area of Miami-Dade County replete with "luxury" high-rise condominium developments and a large mall with exclusive stores and boutiques. When describing how the girls came up with the idea for the video she recounts the story of how they conversed about the "chonga-like" outfits worn by girls in the school cafeteria and secures this admission from Davila, "We were kinda making fun of them."[28] In Lush's framework, the roles of chonga and intelligent young woman are mutually exclusive. Davila and Di Lorenzo are applauded for their clever parody and are protected from the negative ramifications of embodying the sexual-aesthetic excess of the chonga role through allusions to their intelligence, modest form of dress, and upper-class lifestyle.

Twenty-four respondents reported they viewed *Chongalicious* on YouTube. Ten noted that they heard about it from friends. The remainder learned of it through the radio (with some specifying the Power 96 radio station), TV, and the Web, particularly Myspace comments and Live Journal entries. When asked if they enjoyed their viewing twenty subjects stated that they had, overwhelmingly, because it made them laugh. Those who did not enjoy the video found it "annoying," "stupid," and a "waste of time." Fourteen subjects suggested that the video was a realistic depiction of chongas, the remaining participants stated that it was "exaggerated." Most participants (twenty-two) proposed that the video was popular. The most recurrent reasons provided for its positive reception were its accuracy of representation and reflection of Miami culture. One subject explained that the girls were glorified "as the true embodiment of the Female Miami Image."

The New Times reporter's attempts to normalize the creators of *Chongalicious* did not hinder the circulation of negative responses to the story. In a thread on the *New Times Chongalicious* article on the blog site *Miaminights*, a user by the name of "Laura" posted a comment on June 15, 2007 that read,

> I grew up with females like this and it's gross…how can people admire this shit? This makes me want to move away from here so bad. They're your stereotypical ghetto His-panics who cause uproar for attention. They call themselves "Chongas", I call them ig-norant.[29]

The blogger's intense reaction points to the chonga's intimate connection to Miami as place, as she describes how the sensation generated by *Chongalicious* makes her want to relocate. If the chonga is to be so disavowed, why did many other South Floridians celebrate and enjoy their performance? In "Exploring Dora: Re-embodied Latinidad on the Web," a study on the discourse surround-ing the image of the Latina Nickelodeon cartoon character Dora the Explorer, communications scholars Susan J. Harewood and Angharad N. Valdivia state:

> We argue that, despite the rhetoric of "disembodiedness" that often accompanies the Web, its representations, and its participants, the body follows the narrative, repeatedly reinserting itself as a way of enforcing and policing boundaries about ethnicity and mainstream culture. Dora reminds us of the impossibility of leaving the body behind in any kind of form of popular culture because people are always bringing the body back into discussion and embodying the representational, which itself embodies dominant tropes of ethnicity.[30]

Drawing from this understanding, I posit that the video generated pleasure in viewers through the *recognition* enabled by Davila and Di Lorenzo's perfor-mance. Viewers were reminded of the embodied young women they encounter in their everyday lives and by extension, Miami as place. The chonga exemplifies Miami the way that "booty" music by acts like 2 Live Crew typified the city in the 1990s. Like chongas, the controversial group did not project normative bourgeois roles. The hedonistic nature of their music spoke to the materialistic identity of the city as a tropical playground for the rich and famous that has been celebrated by popular performers such as Pit Bull, Will Smith, and P. Did-dy. However, where 2 Live Crew provided a cultural space for men and women to openly engage in sexual discourse, the chonga's sexuality is framed as imma-ture and humorous. She succeeds only in arousing laughter.

Conclusion

What does the laughter toward the chonga girl perform? I suggest that the mockery of the chonga girl body aims to manage, contain, and police her flam-boyant difference from norms of race, ethnicity, class, gender, and "proper" sexual behavior for girls, making her a queering figure that embodies and performs sexual-aesthetic excess. It is often assumed that girls who dress in sexy clothing and wear heavy makeup have low self-esteem and are in search of male attention, however, I would argue that although many girls experiment with chonga-esque styles as they view themselves through an increasingly sexualized lens in adolescence, the style has more to do with ethnicity and girl culture than boys or sex. As sociologist Julie Bettie observes in her ethnographic study of Mexican American girls in a California high school who employed the "chola" style in middle school before adopting a less stylized, yet still ethnically and sexually marked mode of dress,

> Las chicas' [a term the girls used as self-referents] gender performance and girl culture worked, whether by intent or not, as a strategy to reject the prep version of schooling but, despite appearances, were not necessarily designed to culminate in a heterosexual relationship. Some of the girls whose feminine performance appeared the most sexualized were actually the least interested in heterosexual relations, marriage, or children. Despite what appeared to be an obsession with heterosexual romance, a "men are dogs" theme was prevalent among them. They knew men could not be counted on to support them and any children they might have, and they desired economic independence. And so their girl culture was less often about boys at all than about sharing in rituals of traditional femininity as a kind of friendship bonding among girls.[31]

I am concerned with how the arguments in scholarship on girls of color such as the *Urban Girls* anthologies place emphasis on how they *resist* stereotypes. My position does not hold that these girls are indeed just like the harmful negative typologies that circulate about them. Yet I am loathe to stress their subversion and resistance as if they should be ashamed of being loud, sexual, aggressive, and lower/working class, if that is how they view themselves. I have used works like the *Urban Girls* anthologies as resources and recognize that they address issues that the predominant girls' studies discourses on white, middle-class subjects do not. However, girls' scholars should consider the question of who becomes excluded in frameworks regarding healthy girlhood and stereotype resistance.

I have observed that most popular/academic books on "troubled" girls usually have images of sexualized, sullen, or angry white young women on their covers.[32] Contrastingly, yet equally problematic, the covers of the *Urban Girls* anthologies present images of girls that have literally been "white-washed." The cover of the first anthology edited by Bonnie J. Ross Leadbeater and Niobe Way in 1998 features a young African American girl dressed in white and smiling as she is bathed in sunlight. In *Urban Girls Revisited*, edited by Ross Leadbeater and Way in 2007, a group of girls of color wearing white shirts pose together and smile. The design of the cover has altered the photograph so that it is tinged with a grainy light lavender color. These images reinforce notions of "good" and "bad" girls. White girls are framed as needing a "rescue" that will return them to normalized bourgeois subjectivity as they are starting to engage in sexual and aggressive behavior due to the "toxic" gendered representations found in popular culture. Girls of color, who have been historically character- ized as hypersexual in the dominant culture, are framed as being in need of an image makeover in order to be perceived as "good" subjects who are unlike stereotypes. Would a book on girls' empowerment be marketable if it had a pic- ture of a chonga-esque girl on its cover? Or would her image work best in sell- ing books on "troubled" girls? What is the message we send to girls who do not conform to normative bourgeois conventions of dress and behavior? Shimizu's project calls on feminist and critical race scholars to complicate approaches to stereotype analysis as many critiques of sexual representations of women can "unconsciously get caught up in an agenda of moralism and propriety."[33] I call for a shift away from stereotype critiques of girls' representations that generate moral panics toward reflexive critical analysis that is framed by the sexual poli- tics of queer theory and examines how embodiment and representation affect girls' lives on the ground.

This chapter is dedicated to Paola Cordoba, a chonga girl whose makeshift memorial I pass regularly as I walk through the parking lot of the Museum of Contemporary Art where I work as a youth educator. She was killed in a fight with another young woman outside of a bar in North Miami, Florida that is in close proximity to the museum. Real chonga girls live real lives...Latin@ existence.

Notes

1. Celine Parrenas Shimizu, *The Hypersexuality of Race: Performing Asian/American Women on Screen and Scene* (Durham, NC and London: Duke University Press, 2007), 13.
2. Michel Foucault, *The History of Sexuality: An Introduction* (New York: Vintage, 1978); Laura Briggs, *Reproducing Empire: Race, Sex, Science, and U.S. Imperialism in Puerto Rico* (Berkeley, CA and London: University of California Press, 2002); Bernadette Marie Calafell and Fernando P. Delgado, "Reading Latina/o Images: Interrogating *Americanos*," *Critical Studies in Media Communication* 21, no. 1 (2004): 1–21.
3. Frances R. Aparicio and Susana Chavez-Silverman, *Tropicalizations: Transcultural Representa- tions of Latinidad* (Hanover, NH: Dartmouth College and University Press of New England, 1997); Myra Mendible, ed., *From Bananas to Buttocks: The Latina Body in Popular Film and Cul- ture* (Austin, TX: University of Texas Press, 2007).
4. Isabel Molina Guzman and Angharad N. Valdivia, "Brain, Brow, and Booty: Latina Iconici- ty in U.S. Popular Culture," *The Communication Review* 7 (2004): 205–21.
5. Michel Foucault, *Discipline and Punish: The Birth of the Prison* (New York: Vintage, 1977).
6. Shimizu, *The Hypersexuality*, 5.
7. Ibid., 21.

8. Magdalena Barrera, "Hottentot 2000: Jennifer Lopez and Her Butt," in *Sexualities in History: A Reader*, eds. Kim M. Phillips and Barry Reay (New York and London: Routledge, 2002); Mendible, *From Bananas*, 2007.

9. Angharad N. Valdivia, "This Tween Bridge over My Latina Back: The U.S. Mainstream Negotiaties Ethnicity," in *Mediated Girlhoods: Explorations of Girls' Media Culture*, ed. Mary Celeste Kearney (New York: Peter Lang, 2011), 94.

10. Laura M. Ahearn, "Language and Agency," *Annual Review of Anthropology* 30 (2001): 109–37, 112.

11. Jose Esteban Munoz, *Disidentifications: Queers of Color and the Performance of Politics* (Minneapolis and London: University of Minnesota Press, 1999), 182.

12. Rosa Linda Fregoso, "Re-Imagining Chicana Urban Identities in the Public Sphere, *Cool Chuca Style*," in *Between Woman and Nation: Nationalisms, Transnational Feminisms, and the State*, eds. Caren Kaplan, Norma Alarcon, and Minoo Moallem (Durham, NC and London: Duke University Press, 1999), 78.

13. The *Miami New Times* reported that Davila is of Cuban-Bulgarian heritage and Laura Di Lorenzo of Venezuelan-Italian descent. Tamara Lush, "Chongas! Two Aventura Girls' YouTube Sensation is Only the Beginning," *Miami New Times* 22, no. 22 (June 14–20, 2007), 22.

14. "Besos" is Spanish for kisses.

15. "Bling" is a hip hop term for jewelry.

16. Sarah Banet-Weiser, "Branding the Post-Feminist Self: Girls' Video Production and YouTube," in *Mediated Girlhoods: New Explorations of Girls' Media Culture*, ed. Mary Celeste Kearney (New York Peter Lang, 2011), 284.

17. http://www.unoentertainment.com.

18. Valdiva, "This Tween Bridge," 106.

19. Lisa Duggan, *The Twilight of Equality?: Neoliberalism, Cultural Politics and the Attack on Democracy* (Boston: Beacon Press, 2003).

20. "Homecoming: Luis Gispert Returns to His Miami Roots as a Major Art World Player," *The Miami Herald* (October 14, 2007).

21. Ibid., 21.

22. I did not want to present my subjects with the assumption that a chonga is a person in this question.

23. Julie Bettie, *Women Without Class: Girls, Race, and Identity* (Berkley and London: University of California Press, 2003); C. J. Pascoe, *Dude You're a Fag: Masculinity and Sexuality in High School* (Berkeley, CA and London: University of California Press, 2007).

24. Miguel A. De La Torre, "Ochun: (N)either the (M)other of All Cubans (n)orthe Bleached Virgin," *Journal of the American Academy of Religion* 69, no. 4 (2001): 837–61.

25. "Lol" is an acronym for "laugh out loud" used in internet chat applications.

26. Jill McLean Taylor, Carmen N. Veloria, and Martina C. Verba, "Latina Girl: 'We're Like Sisters—Most Times!" in *Urban Girls Revisited: Building Strenths*, eds. Bonnie J. Ross Leadbeater and Niobe Way (New York and London: New York University Press, 2007).

27. Ibid., 30–1.

28. Ibid., 24.

29. http://www.miaminights.com/miami-new-times-dissects-the-chonga-trend-4242.phtml

208

Jillian Hernandez

30. Susan J. Harewood and Angharad N. Valdivia, "Exploring Dora: Re-embodied Latinidad on the Web," in *Girl Wide Web: Girls, the Internet, and the Negotiation of Identity*, ed. Sharon R. Mazzarella (New York: Peter Lang Publishing, 2005), 86.
31. Bettie, *Women without Class*, 64.
32. Examples include Sharon Lamb and Lyn Mikel Brown, *Packaging Girlhood* (New York: St. Martin's Press, 2006); Rachel Simmons, *Odd Girl Out: The Hidden Culture of Aggression in Girls* (Orlando: Harcourt, 2003); James Garbarino, *See Jane Hit: Why Girls are Growing More Violent and What We Can Do About It* (New York: Penguin Press, 2006); and eds. Martha Putallaz and Karen L. Beirman, *Aggression, Antisocial Behavior, and Violence among Girls* (New York: Guilford Press, 2004).
33. Shimizu, *The Hypersexuality*, 18.

Works Cited

Ahearn, Laura M. "Language and Agency." *Annual Review of Anthropology* 30 (2001): 109–37.
Althusser, Louis. "Ideology and Ideological State Apparatuses (Notes Towards an Investigation)." In *Lenin and Philosophy*. London: Verso, 1971.
Aparicio, Frances R. and Susana Chavez-Silverman. *Tropicalizations: Transcultural Representations of Latinidad*. Hanover, NH: Dartmouth College and University Press of New England, 1997.
Banet-Weiser, Sarah. "Branding the Post-Feminist Self: Girls' Video Production and YouTube." In *Mediated Girlhoods: New Explorations of Girls' Media Culture*, ed. Mary Celeste Kearney, 277–93. New York: Peter Lang, 2011.
Barrera, Magdalena. "Hottentot 2000: Jennifer Lopez and Her Butt." In *Sexualities in History: A Reader*, eds. Kim M. Phillips and Barry Reay, 407–18. New York and London: Routledge, 2002.
Beltran, Mary C. "The Hollywood Latina Body as Site of Social Struggle: Media Constructions of Stardom and Jennifer Lopez's 'Cross-over Butt.'" *Quarterly Review of Film and Video* 19 (2002): 71–86.
Bettie, Julie. *Women Without Class: Girls, Race, and Identity*. Berkeley, CA and London: University of California Press, 2003.
Briggs, Laura. *Reproducing Empire: Race, Sex, Science, and U.S. Imperialism in Puerto Rico*. Berkeley, CA and London: University of California Press, 2002.
Butler, Judith. *Gender Trouble: Feminism and the Subversion of Identity*. New York and London: Routledge, 1990.
Calafell, Bernadette Marie and Fernando P. Delgado. "Reading Latina/o Images: Interrogating *Americanos*." *Critical Studies in Media Communication* 21, no. 1 (2004): 1–21.
De La Torre, Miguel A. "Ochun: (N)either the (M)other of All Cubans (n)orthe Bleached Virgin." *Journal of the American Academy of Religion* 69, no. 4 (2001): 837–61.
Duggan, Lisa. *The Twilight of Equality?: Neoliberalism, Cultural Politics and the Attack on Democracy*. Boston: Beacon Press, 2003.
Foucault, Michel. *Discipline and Punish: The Birth of the Prison*. New York: Vintage, 1977.
———. *The History of Sexuality: An Introduction (Volume 1)*. New York: Vintage, 1978.
Fregoso, Rosa Linda. "Re-Imagining Chicana Urban Identities in the Public Sphere, *Cool Chuca Style*." In *Between Woman and Nation: Nationalisms, Transnational Feminisms, and the State*, eds.

Caren Kaplan, Norma Alarcon, and Minoo Moallem, 72–91. Durham, NC and London: Duke University Press, 1999.

Garbarino, James. *See Jane Hit: Why Girls are Growing More Violent and What We Can Do About It.* New York: Penguin Press, 2006.

Guzman, Isabel Molina. "Disorderly Bodies and Discourses of Latinidad in the Elian Gonzalez Story." In *From Bananas to Buttocks: The Latina Body in Popular Film and Culture*, ed. Myra Mendible. Austin, TX: University of Texas Press, 2007.

Guzman, Isabel Molina and Angharad N. Valdivia. "Brain, Brow, and Booty: Latina Iconicity in U.S. Popular Culture." *The Communication Review* 7 (2004): 205–21.

Harewood, Susan J. and Angharad N. Valdivia. "Exploring Dora: Re-Embodied Latinidad on the Web." In *Girl Wide Web: Girls, the Internet, and the Negotiation of Identity*, ed. Sharon R. Mazzarella. New York: Peter Lang Publishing, 2005.

"Homecoming: Luis Gispert Returns to His Miami Roots as a Major Art World Player." *The Miami Herald.* October 14, 2007.

Kearney, Mary Celeste. *Mediated Girlhoods: New Explorations of Girls' Media Culture.* New York: Peter Lang, 2011.

Lamb, Sharon and Lyn Mikel Brown. *Packaging Girlhood.* New York: St. Martin's Press, 2006.

Lush, "Chongas! Two Aventura Girls' YouTube Sensation is Only the Beginning,." *Miami New Times* 22, no. 22. June 14–20, 2007.

Mendible, Myra, ed. *From Bananas to Buttocks: The Latina Body in Popular Film and Culture.* Austin, TX: University of Texas Press, 2007.

Munoz, Jose Esteban. *Disidentifications: Queers of Color and the Performance of Politics.* Minneapolis and London: University of Minnesota Press, 1999.

Pascoe, C.J. *Dude You're a Fag: Masculinity and Sexuality in High School.* Berkeley, CA and London: University of California Press, 2007.

Putallaz, Martha and Karen L. Beirman, eds. *Aggression, Antisocial Behavior, and Violence among Girls.* New York: Guilford Press, 2004.

Rodriguez, Juana Maria. *Queer Latinidad: Identity Practices, Discursive Spaces.* New York: New York University Press, 2003.

Shimizu, Celine Parrenas. *The Hypersexuality of Race: Performing Asian/American Women on Screen and Scene.* Durham, NC and London: Duke University Press, 2007.

Simmons, Rachel. *Odd Girl Out: The Hidden Culture of Aggression in Girls.* Orlando, FL: Harcourt, 2003.

Sontag, Susan. "Notes on Camp." In *Against Interpretation and Other Essays.* New York: Farrar Straus Giroux, 1986.

Taylor, Jill McLean, Carmen N. Veloria, and Martina C. Verba. "Latina Girl: 'We're Like Sisters— Most Times!" In *Urban Girls Revisited: Building Strenths,* eds. Bonnie J. Ross Leadbeater and Niobe Way, 157–76. New York and London: New York University Press, 2007.

Valdivia, Angharad N. "This Tween Bridge Over My Latina Back: The U.S. Mainstream Negotiaties Ethnicity." In *Mediated Girlhoods: Explorations of Girls' Media Culture,* ed. Mary Celeste Kearney, 93–109. New York: Peter Lang, 2011.

| 12

Heteroflexibility: Female Performance and Pleasure

Jennifer Apple

In 2003, Madonna performed at the annual MTV Video Music Awards. Sporting a revealing tux with tails and donning a top hat at a jaunty angle, she played the role of the experienced groom to her two blushing brides: Britney Spears and Christina Aguilera. At the end of a flirty rendition of "Like a Virgin," Madonna played the role of the groom to its predictable conclusion, bestowing a slow kiss on each pop princess bride. The on-air kisses propelled media frenzy, but the image of heterosexual identified women enacting a more fluid (and generally public) sexuality has become increasingly common. Featured in popular episodes of hit television series such as *Sex and the City*, *The OC*, *Desperate Housewives*, and *Gossip Girl* expressions of female same-sex exploration have given rise to the coining of a new term—heteroflexibility.

The concept of heteroflexibility is nicely summarized in the lyrics of singer Katy Perry's 2008 smash hit "I Kissed a Girl." In the chorus of the song, Perry sings enthusiastically, "I kissed a girl and I liked it/the taste of her cherry chap stick/*I kissed a girl just to try it/I hope my boyfriend don't mind it*" (emphasis mine). Perry's lyrics succinctly explicate the basic concept of heteroflexibility: an experiment in female same-sex sexuality that acknowledges some same-sex desire/attraction without explicitly challenging a "mostly" heterosexual self-identification. Lest we think that being heteroflexible is purely a media construction, a recent study on sexual behavior and identity development found that approximately twenty percent of the female college students surveyed identified as heteroflexible or "mostly straight."[1]

The existence of heteroflexibility in the two distinct (if interrelated) realms of popular culture and embodied lived experience demands an analysis that acknowledges and accounts for the distinct nature of personal experience and meaning making in contrast to the constructed images present in the media. It is the different meanings, possibilities, interpretations, and intentions of these acts within the two distinct contexts that is the concern of this study. Is this trend a symbol of growing recognition of sexual identities beyond the tired hetero/homo dichotomy? Or do these explicit displays of sexual expression, framed as fluidity and freedom, reify women's sexual subordination and compulsory heterosexuality? Is heteroflexibility a potentially subversive act that provides radical opportunities for breaking out of the heterosexual/homosexual binary and exploring explicitly female forms of sexual pleasure? After examining both media images in popular culture and the lived experiences of heteroflexible participants I argue that embodied heteroflexible experience represents an act/identity that has subversive possibilities, complicating the binary of either subversion, or reification, of heteronormative scripts.

Methods

This project is an exploratory study in which I utilize grounded theory to explore how heteroflexibility is perceived, enacted, and reflected upon by respondents who have participated in heteroflexible activities.[2] In addition, I contrast these experiences with a close reading of media depictions of heteroflexibility in an effort to explore the potential of heteroflexibility as a site for feminist theorizing on embodied female sexuality and sexual pleasure in a contemporary context.[3]

Literature Review

The concept of heteroflexibility as an act, a performance, or an identity fits within a growing scope of research on female same-sex sexuality. Feminist analyses of heteroflexibility generally condemn it as hopelessly apolitical, male-directed, and always fitting within a postfeminist framework. These scholars posit that heteroflexible images and acts function primarily to essentialize sexuality, obscure compulsory heterosexuality, depoliticize sex, and co-opt women's sexuality for male arousal.[4] Studies utilizing quantitative surveys function to make sharp distinctions between sexual behaviors, fantasies, and attraction to pin down what identifying as heteroflexible entails.[5] These studies complicate the relationship between reported identities and actual attractions/behaviors, while also implicitly troubling the hetero/homo dichotomy as an insufficient binary that cannot speak to lived experience. Other studies focus on sexual identification over extended periods of time, or during a certain period of the life cycle, emphasizing the instability or fluidity of sexual categorization and pointing to the possibility of a fissure in heteronormativity and compulsory heterosexuality.[6] Finally, both qualitative and quantitative studies focus on women's greater erotic plasticity or sexual fluidity in comparison to men, positing fluidity as a normative element of female sexual development.[7] Although research on heteroflexibility is growing, there remains a paucity of scholarly work that includes, but moves beyond, pop culture spectacle and examines the meaning making occurring among young women. This comparative study provides a critical feminist analysis that acknowledges the theoretical "messiness" of heteroflexible sexuality *without* foreclosing its political potential by framing it solely as female exploitation for male arousal.

Analysis

Media: Heteroflexibility as Performative

Media depictions of female same-sex sexuality in mainstream film and television have become increasingly common. Indeed their ubiquity in sitcoms has become a clichéd symbol of an attempt at boosting ratings. These depictions often follow a stereotypical format that generally includes three key elements: first, the overt construction of female same-sex sexuality as a visual spectacle; second, the lack of a discourse of female sexual desire or pleasure; and third, a reification of the hetero/homo dichotomy, disallowing the possibility of sexual fluidity or even bisexuality.[8]

The 2003 performance of Madonna, Britney Spears, and Christina Aguilera referenced earlier provides an emblematic example that includes all three of the elements of the stereotypical media portrayal of female heteroflexibility. The performance carefully utilizes an iconic set (the giant wedding cake originally seen during Madonna's first MTV performance of "Like a Virgin"), a nod to the star persona of Madonna, and the titillating presentation of scantily clad pop princesses Britney and Christina, receiving the pop star torch from Madonna herself. These meticulously crafted elements of the performance create a highly visual spectacle of the climactic moment—the staged kisses.

As the curtain rises on this performance, two things occur simultaneously; the iconic three-tiered wedding cake is visible and the familiar beat of "Like a Virgin" fills the air. At an MTV event, these two elements signal instant recognition of pop icon Madonna and the promise of yet another lavish, sexualized, and theatrical performance. The presence of Britney Spears and Christina Aguilera emphasizes their position as up-and-coming pop sensations, plays with the media panic of the time over the sexualization of teen female pop stars, and underscores the absence of Madonna from the stage—an absence which serves to make her central to the performance and builds anticipation for her grand entrance. When Madonna appears atop the giant wedding cake, her costume of a skin-tight tuxedo with tails and top hat positions her as the central piece of the narrative around which the wedding imagery and virginal brides turn. Her masculine-coded position and costuming reference the star persona of Madonna as a highly sexual, gender-bending icon with an ever-evolving identity that always aims to shock and arouse. She takes her place between Britney and Christina and the three perform Madonna's new single, "Hollywood," while performing a sensual routine in which the "groom" caresses and dances with each bride. Madonna's ambiguously sexual and overly theatrical interaction with each pop princess aids in building anticipation for the climax of the performance. The anticipation and the sexual ambiguity of the performance is reiterated by interspersed camera shots of the audience, specifically repeated shots of Britney's ex-boyfriend Justin Timberlake and the famous "Fab Five" of the television show *Queer Eye for the Straight Guy*. These repeated camera shots heighten the sexual nature of the performance by both reminding the audience at home of Britney's heterosexual orientation (and thus increasing the titillation of her sexually ambiguous interaction with Madonna) and clearly associating openly gay men (the "Fab Five") with Madonna as a gay icon and thus subtly acknowledging the possibility of "non-normative" sexual meanings or acts on stage.

In the final moments leading up to the kisses, Madonna kneels at Christina's feet and slowly removes Christina's garter while Britney coyly looks on, mouth agape, as if she is shocked at the display. Madonna then turns to Britney, leans in and kisses her, to the squeals of the audience. At the end of their kiss the camera abruptly turns to capture Justin Timberlake's reaction and then quickly shifts back to show Madonna leaning in and kissing Christina. These final moments are particularly relevant to the heteroflexibility as spectacle trope.

First, during the removal of the garter and during the kisses, the bodies of Madonna, Britney, and Christina are positioned frontally to provide maximum visibility for the audience. By positioning their bodies frontally and twisting their necks to touch mouths, the kisses are perfectly staged for filming. Their bodies do not touch, they do not embrace, each woman's arms are slightly lifted away from her torso, so that the line of each woman's body is clearly visible to the audience in addition to the perfect profile of their lips touching, mouths slightly open, hinting at the possibility of tongue.

Second, immediately after Madonna and Britney's kiss the camera cuts to Justin Timberlake in the audience to reveal a reaction shot. This reinforces the kiss as a spectacle, particularly for a male voyeur, insinuating the notion of female same-sex sexuality as performative for male arousal and simultaneously reminds the audience (again) of the heterosexual availability of Britney Spears.[9]

Third, it is important to note that the Christina Aguilera–Madonna kiss immediately follows the kiss with Britney and thus the cut to Justin Timberlake necessarily flubs an ideal shot of the kiss with Christina—which emphasizes the focus on a male voyeuristic gaze and a heterosexualizing of the participants over the opportunity to present another perfectly staged female–female kiss. This cut to Timberlake underscores the acts on stage as performative, highlighting the importance of audience reaction over the actual kisses. The focus on Timberlake (and audience reaction more generally) points to another of the stereotypical elements of media depictions of heteroflexibility: the absence of a recognizable discourse of female pleasure and desire. The kisses between Madonna and Britney and Christina are not being conceptualized as a representation of Madonna's desire for the pop princesses, nor the mutual pleasure experienced during the kiss; they are framed purely as an intentionally "shocking" performance that plays on male desire and arousal and the pleasure experienced by the audience "gazing" at the on-stage performance.

The media frenzy that ensued after this performance also reinforces the interpretation of performative visual spectacle, and subsequent interviews provide evidence of the disavowal (particularly by Spears) of any sexually fluid interpretations that could disrupt the archaic heterosexual/homosexual binary *or* the possibility of an interpretation that might frame Spears as a desiring female sexual subject. Author Lisa Diamond aptly notes Spears' reiteration of her heterosexual identity and avoidance of any acknowledgment of pleasure she experienced during the kiss in the comments she made following the performance. Spears explained she "probably wouldn't kiss a woman again" and emphasized that she "didn't know it [the kiss] was going to be that long and everything."[10] Indeed, Diamond uses this evidence to assert that this immediate reframing of the kiss in a politically "neutralized" manner ultimately erases the potential of the act to challenge the homo/hetero dichotomy. I would argue that it also erases the potential of acknowledging Britney (and Christina) as an actively desiring subject and only perpetuates the far less politically progressive notion of adolescent girls as being sexy without being sexual.

The Madonna, Britney, Christina performance has become an iconic representation of female heteroflexibility; however, other iconic depictions maintain the same format that generally obscures a sexually progressive reading. The well-known heteroflexible scene in the film *Wild Things* with Neve Campbell and Denise Richards clearly conforms to the same tropes. Campbell and Richards engage in a lengthy sexual interaction in a pool, during which they kiss and caress one another and ultimately become topless. The camera repeatedly pans over each of their bodies, arguably mimicking a male gaze. However, if the camera fails to clearly represent a male voyeur, Kevin Bacon appears on screen briefly, hiding in the nearby bushes watching *and* filming the two women in the pool. Immediately following their encounter in the water, Richards and Campbell engage in a threesome with Matt Dillon, the chosen erotic object of both female characters in the film. Therefore, the heteroflexible behavior of Richards and Campbell is constructed for and channeled through a male voyeur, obscuring female pleasure and desire. Further, the immediate threesome with Matt Dillon following their heteroflexibility effectively reiterates the primarily heterosexual orientation of both women, enabling an interpretation of them as *still* available to the (male) heterosexual viewer.

The increasingly commonplace nature of female heteroflexibility is clear when the variety of media in which it appears are acknowledged. Heteroflexible acts appear in a broad spectrum of media from family-friendly *Friends* and teen-focused *Glee* and *Gossip Girl* to the more sexually explicit or adult-themed *Sex in the City* and *Desperate Housewives*. The cultural ubiquity becomes obvious when we consider commentary on the practice itself, which appears in the family-friendly and critically-acclaimed television show *Gilmore Girls*. In *Gilmore Girls*, main characters Paris (Liza Weil) and Rory (Alexis Bledel) are on spring break from college, relaxing beachside. In a particularly poignant scene, Bledel and Weil are discussing the "do's and don'ts" of spring break with "experts" Madeline (Shelly Cole) and Louise (Teal Redmann). In addition to advising Weil and Bledel on the importance of finding the "hot" night club and sleeping away the afternoon to enable all-night partying, they also advise that a key way to get into clubs that might card (all characters are under twenty-one) is to "make out!" Bledel asks, "With who?" to which Redmann responds, "each other!" In addition to helping the underage girls get into night clubs, Redmann and Cole explain that "we've found that if we kiss each other we can get anything we want from guys," including, "drinks, food, t-shirts, boat rides, Frisbees [and] sea-doos" ("Girls in Bikinis, Boys Doin' The Twist"). While there is no visible heteroflexibility occurring, the discussion of it acknowledges its characteristic male-directedness and possible "utility" with tongue placed firmly in cheek.

Later, in this same episode, set in a "hot" night club, Weil and Bledel begin to fret that as notorious bookworms they are not performing the normative spring break persona effectively and thus not enjoying spring break as much as their free-wheeling counterparts. In an attempt to enact the spring break persona she sees around her, Weil impulsively grabs Bledel and awkwardly kisses her. In contrast to the previously analyzed heteroflexible kisses, this one is decidedly (and intentionally) "un-sexy" as Bledel squirms away from Weil and blurts out, "what are you doing?" After explaining that she has no desire to be "like" their heteroflexible friends, Bledel begins to make her way out of the night club. On her way out she is confronted by a guy who asks if he can accompany her outside. As Bledel is hesitantly accepting the guy interrupts, stating in an exaggeratedly conspiratorial tone, "maybe your girlfriend wants to come along" ("Girls in Bikinis, Boys Doin' The Twist"). Bledel responds with a confused, "my girlfriend?" and the guy exclaims, "I gotta tell you, that was some kiss!" grinning expectantly. Bledel frowns and lets out an exasperated, "oh my god," and exits the bar, leaving the nameless male voyeur in her wake.

The *Gilmore Girls* heteroflexible episode functions as the exception that proves the rule. The first scene provides a comedic acknowledgment of heteroflexibility as a performance utilized to gain things (drinks, t-shirts, or ratings), while the latter scene presents the male voyeur as over-eager and absurdly aroused by a superficial interaction void of pleasure or desire. The episode serves as a meta-commentary on the practice within media by exposing the cynical treatment of heteroflexibility by participants and portraying the male spectator as boorish and utterly unappealing to the main character. The sarcastic treatment of heteroflexibility is only effective and readable within *Gilmore Girls* because of the lack of diversity in heteroflexible media depictions more generally. The audience is encouraged to groan, roll their eyes, and laugh as the episode exposes and pokes fun at the ubiquity of superficial heteroflexible acts in the media.

Media depictions of female same-sex sexuality generally do not invite a sexually progressive reading. The consistency with which these depictions conform to apolitical spectacle-driven cultural tropes results in an elision of the subversive potential of heteroflexibility as an act or identity that *could* challenge binary sexuality and compulsory heterosexuality, or even provide a more complex representation of women as desiring subjects. However, the simplistic nature of media depictions of heteroflexibility does not preclude the possibility of greater complexity, or subversive potential, of the lived experience of heteroflexibility. The ubiquity of heteroflexible media depictions and the presence of a "knowing" analysis, or reaction to, heteroflexibility as a male-centered practice treated cynically by participants are important to keep in mind as we turn to exploring the lived experiences of women participating in heteroflexibility outside of the media spotlight. The omnipresent nature of heteroflexibility in various media leads to a more complex examination of heteroflexibility in lived experience because young women are acutely aware of the notion of heteroflexibility as a spectacle for a male audience. While the media presents heteroflexibility as a relatively uncomplicated one-dimensional performance, participants often grapple with issues that the media's simple portrayals obscure.

Interviews: Public Performance and Private Pleasures

After transcribing and analyzing interviews with my participants, a variety of themes emerged. The recurring themes in the data fit into several distinct but interrelated categories that always reflected the broader framework of female same-sex sexual experimentation as a complicated interplay between public performance and private pleasures. How participants experienced, reflected upon, and explained their same-sex sexual experiences fit into the following three discrete but interconnected categories: The public vs. private distinction, performance vs. "authentic" attraction, and disrupting heteronormative scripts.

Public vs. Private Distinction:

All of the participants made an explicit distinction between sexual experiences that took place in public vs. private spaces. The potential meaning of the acts was understood to be dependent upon the environment in which they occurred. As Margot stated, "you can kiss a girl for fun at a party, you can kiss a guy for fun at a party and it won't go anywhere. But if you're one-on-one with someone, it's a more intimate experience with different potential." All participants were careful to explicate the context in which the experience took place. The language used to explain the distinction was informative with regard to how participants conceptualized the acts.

Generally, the acts that took place in public settings (usually parties or bars) were framed as purely frivolous fun and lacking any substantial meaning. Margot explained, "The last time I [interacted sexually with a woman] was at a party with my friend, and I don't know, once I've had a couple beers I just start kissing girls. I kiss girls at parties pretty regularly." Margot acknowledges the public nature of her same-sex experimentation and links it with the consumption of alcohol and ultimately frames it as normative behavior ("pretty regularly") and thus does not attribute significance to the event. Indeed, with regard to the motivation of the experience, Margot further explains, "we were playing a game of beer pong and we just started kissing a little bit. We were trying to distract the members of the other team." The potential of the public act is implicitly categorized as "just fun" or possibly a tool that can be utilized to win a party game, rather than an expression of sexual attraction or an opportunity to experiment.

In contrast to the public acts, the acts that took place in private were often framed as "escaping" a male gaze and inherently different than public acts. Indeed, most participants described instances in which they were in public spaces and sought out private spaces to engage in sexual activity. As Belinda explains, "One night we had both done a bit of drinking and I just didn't really care [that it was public] and then of course I got very awkward because I look over my shoulder and there is a huge crowd of guys around and I was like, 'okay I am not into *this* right now.'" This explanation of feeling "awkward" due to a very literal male gaze provided the foundation for Belinda's description of other sexual experiences with women. Upon meeting a woman in a crowded bar, Belinda stated, "I found this one girl really attractive and so we went to the bathroom and locked ourselves in a stall and were just kissing and petting in there, away from the bar crowd."

The potential for the acts to have greater meaning was often linked to whether or not they occurred in private. As Elissa explained, "I think [the private experience] was more meaningful, compared to just making out with a girl when I'm drunk in a bar or something." Jane added, "I've done some experimentation in public, but it has never really gone as far as the others [in private]." The participants that expanded upon their choice to make an experience private vs. public generally acknowledged the role of a male voyeur in public spaces, and recognized a greater potential for the meaning and the level of intimacy pursued in private.

In addition to making a distinction between public and private acts, some of the participants expressed strong feelings with regard to what they perceived as the "common" occurrence of girl-on-girl "action" in public settings. In an effort to explicate the cliché nature of public sexual acts between women, Belinda stated sarcastically, "I mean really, the whole chicks making out at a party thing. Okay, God, I mean really!?" In a similar tone, Jane explained, "I kind of resent when girls just get drunk and make out in front of people just to get other people's attention." Although all of the respondents admitted to participating in sexual activity with women in public settings, they generally attempted to make a distinction between the "immaturity" of the public display "for attention" (often as something they participated in when they were younger) and the private, more "mature" experimentation.

Performance vs. "Authentic" Attraction

When expanding upon the motivation behind their heteroflexibility, participants began to further explore the public/private dichotomy by bringing two key concepts to the fore: performance and "authentic" attraction. Reflecting upon her motivation for heteroflexible acts, Belinda stated, "When I was with her privately, it wasn't just a show thing, because I really did feel attracted." In this statement, Belinda recognizes the "show" or performative aspect of engaging sexually with a woman in public that she perceives as (at least partially) erasing her sexual agency. In private she can acknowledge her attraction for her female partner because the act no longer includes an active audience. Belinda explains further:

> With her privately, it felt more mature. When you are doing the show thing, you're not doing it really for yourself or for the woman, in a way you're doing it for male sexual attraction, male appeal. So, for me, I never really like to be out in a public atmosphere because then I feel like it's performance, whereas when you're on your own it's really about your sexual experience and her sexual experience. It's taking the male out of it.

Belinda is not only acknowledging the previously elaborated distinction between public and private acts, but also the ways in which the public act is necessarily more performative. Additionally, she implicitly conceptualized the private act as more "authentic" by reiterating the way privacy shifts the emphasis from the act as "spectacle" to an intimate experience in which the women are focusing on their own pleasure.

Although the participants generally described public acts of heteroflexibility as being more overtly performative and less about "authentic" sexual attraction and connection, some participants insinuated that the "authentic" attraction may still be present during public acts, even while often overshadowed by the performance. While Margot's public heteroflexibility was framed as frivolous fun that she used to "distract" an opposing team in a game of beer pong, she ultimately added that part of her motivation for kissing her friend was that, "she had really nice lips," indicating a level of sexual attraction/desire even within the larger context of performance. While describing public heteroflexibility as a "way of getting guys' attention," Jane added, "but secretly, I think it's more just exploration or curiosity." The appearance of sexual desire in these performative instances begins to trouble the public/private dichotomy, possibly acknowledging the ways in which women explore their own sexual wishes under the comfortable guise of male approval and voyeurism.

Disrupting Heteronormative Scripts

All the participants in the study described heteroflexibility as a space that disrupted "accepted" heteronormative scripts with regard to sexual activity. Each participant expressed important distinctions between being with men vs. being with women that implicitly and explicitly confronted simplistic, goal-oriented heteronormative constructions of "sex." Overwhelmingly, the women interviewed identified heterosexual interactions as following an accepted and expected script that progressed in predictable ways, which differed sharply from their experiences with other women. Margot explained, "With my roommate it just wasn't as hurried as it is with men. With her it was more ambiguous, like okay, what do we want to do now? What is going on here?" Similarly, Elissa explained, "there was less pressure on me, [because] there wasn't this ultimate goal in mind." All of the participants framed sexual experiences with women as less scripted, less "hurried," and more open to variety with regard to exploring bodily pleasure. By conceptualizing their experiences as lacking a penetrative "goal," all participants framed heteroflexibility as allowing for more exploration and flexibility with regard to defining what constitutes "having sex."

Discussion

Participants' reflections on the context in which heteroflexible acts occur, and the subsequent meanings of or potential for such acts, provides a site to examine a variety of aspects of heteroflexibility. The public, and often performative, aspect of heteroflexibility necessarily leads to an examination of who is doing the "gazing" and who is being "gazed" upon and how we can interpret the power of each position. Unsurprisingly, heteroflexibility is primarily a female performance and thus creates a predictable script in which women perform and men watch the performance. However, participants' reflection upon their motivation for engaging in heteroflexibility begins the necessary work of troubling the problematic performance/private dichotomy. This dichotomy, as represented in prior work on public heteroflexibility, generally categorizes performance as always only pleasurable for the audience, negating the possibility of receiving pleasure through performance, and relegating "authentic" pleasure seeking behavior as purely private. It is imperative that feminist analyses allow for an acknowledgment of the experience of erotic pleasure to be found in the performative elements of sexuality.

Equally relevant in this examination of public performance are the ways, as indicated by participants, women may exploit male desire for and approval of public female–female sexuality to experiment sexually, satisfy curiosity, or claim a sexual agency generally denied them. Similarly, the possible exploitation of male fantasy in the service of female desire and agency is, in part, a tactic made legible for young women due to its consistent presence in the media. Additionally, it seems possible to conceptualize public heteroflexibility as "queering" public environments, as possibly invading heteronormative spaces in ways that could challenge the dominant heteronormative culture.

In contrast to the always public media images, the existence of heteroflexible practices occurring "behind closed doors" is clearly an aspect of heteroflexibility explored by participants that deserves further examination. As a space in which participants described exploring bodily pleasures in ways that disrupted "accepted" scripts for female sexuality and heterosexual sexual "normalcy," it is important to explore the way heteroflexibility provides a space for a distinctly female pleasure that is often overlooked. In an era of soaring Viagra sales and a resurgence of "research" on the notorious G-spot, heteroflexibility may disrupt archaic notions of "real" sex, the focus on penile penetration, and the search for the elusive vaginal orgasm. Private heteroflexibility occurs beyond the male gaze and seems to represent a shift in the classic "men act, women appear" script to one in which women act and men disappear.

Conclusions

While media imagery most often frames female same-sex sexuality as a visual spectacle for male voyeurs, elides a discourse of female pleasure, and reifies the hetero/homo binary, female participants revealed heteroflexibility to be an act, performance, or identity that both explicitly and implicitly grapples with the simplistic and regressive sexual tropes of the media. Respondents reflected upon heteroflexibility in a way that often disrupted female–female sexuality as male-directed, inflected acts with actively desiring female voices and questioned the hetero/homo dichotomy. By beginning with the meaning making occurring by real women, heteroflexibility can represent more than an either/or binary of subversion or reification of compulsory heterosexuality. Conducting a close reading of media images of heteroflexibility and utilizing qualitative interviewing and grounded theory, I explored the seemingly contradictory possibilities of heteroflexibility as a contemporary representation of women's sexuality for male voyeuristic pleasure *and* an act that queers heteronormative scripts and notions of female sexuality and sexual pleasure. By exploring the meanings constructed by participants of heteroflexible acts who are fully aware of the media construction of heteroflexibility as male-directed, it seems that heteroflexibility may not purely reinforce essentialist notions of sexuality, but simultaneously disrupts and reifies heteronormative scripts while providing an avenue for queering heteronormative spaces and allowing for alternative conceptions of female sexual subjectivity and pleasures. Even regressive and apolitical media images may in fact provide a foundation upon which subversive action is possible. Ultimately, embodied heteroflexibility may create productive fissures in "accepted" conceptions of female sexuality that encourage increasingly critical analyses to better comprehend the underlying complexities of how female sexuality is constructed, enacted, and represented.

Notes

1.   E.M. Morgan and E.M. Thompson, "Young Women's Sexual Experiences Within Same Sex Friendships: Discovering and Defining Bisexual and Bi-Curious Identity," *Journal of Bisexuality* 6, no. 3 (2006): 7–34, 16.

2.   Anselm Strauss and Julie Corbin, *Basics of Qualitative Research: Techniques and Procedures for Developing Grounded Theory* (Thousand Oaks, CA: Sage, 1998).

3.   Fred Pfeil, *White Guys: Studies in Postmodern Domination and Difference* (New York: Verso, 1995), xiii–xiv.

4.   Lisa M. Diamond, "I'm Straight, But I Kissed a Girl: The Trouble with American Media Representations of Female–Female Sexuality," *Feminism and Psychology* 15, no. 1 (2005): 104–10; Breanne Fahs, "Compulsory Bisexuality? The Challenges of Modern Sexual Fluidity,"

Journal of Bisexuality 9, no. 3 (2009): 431–49; Sue Wilkinson, "Bisexuality 'A la Mode,'" *Women's studies International Forum* 19, no. 3 (1996): 293–301.

5. E.M. Thompson and E.M. Morgan, "'Mostly Straight' Young Women: Variations in Sexual Behavior and Identity Development," *Developmental Psychology* 44, no. 1 (2008): 15–21; Robin Hoburg, Julie Konik, Michelle Williams, and Mary Crawford, "Bisexuality Among Self-Identified Heterosexual College Students," *Journal of Bisexuality* 4, no. 1/2 (2004): 25–36.

6. Thompson and Morgan, "'Mostly Straight," 2006; Lisa M. Diamond, "Having a Girlfriend without Knowing It," *Journal of Lesbian Studies* 6, no. 1 (2002): 5–16; Diamond, "I'm Straight," 2005.

7. Lisa M. Diamond, *Sexual Fluidity: Understanding Women's Love and Desire* (Cambridge, MA: Harvard University Press, 2008); Roy F. Baumeister, "Gender Differences in Erotic Plasticity: The Female Sex Drive as Socially Flexible and Responsive," *Psychological Bulletin* 126, no. 3 (2000): 347–74.

8. Diamond, "I'm Straight," 2005.

9. Ibid.

10. Ibid., 107.

Works Cited

Baumeister, Roy F. "Gender Differences in Erotic Plasticity: The Female Sex Drive as Socially Flexible and Responsive." *Psychological Bulletin* 126, no. 3 (2000): 347—74.

Diamond, Lisa M. "Having a Girlfriend without Knowing It." *Journal of Lesbian Studies* 6, no. 1 (2002): 5—16.

———. ."A New View of Lesbian Subtypes: Stable versus Fluid identity Trajectories over an 8-Year Period." *Psychology of Women Quarterly* 29 (2005a): 119—28.

———. "I'm Straight, But I Kissed a Girl: The trouble with American Media Representations of Female—Female Sexuality." *Feminism and Psychology* 15, no. 1 (2005b): 104—10.

———. *Sexual Fluidity: Understanding Women's Love and Desire.* Cambridge, MA: Harvard University Press, 2008.

Fahs, Breanne. "Compulsory Bisexuality?: The Challenges of Modern Sexual Fluidity." *Journal of Bisexuality* 9, no. 3 (2009): 431—49.

Garnets, Linda D. and Letitia Anne Peplau. "A New Paradigm for Understanding Women's Sexuality and Sexual Orientation." *Journal of Social Issues* 56, no. 2 (2000): 329—50.

Hoburg, Robin, Julie Konik, Michelle Williams, and Mary Crawford. "Bisexuality Among Self-Identified Heterosexual College Students." *Journal of Bisexuality* 4, no. 1/2 (2004): 25—36.

Morgan, E. M. and E. M. Thompson. "Young Women's Sexual Experiences Within Same Sex Friendships: Discovering and Defining Bisexual and Bi-Curious Identity." *Journal of Bisexuality* 6, no. 3 (2006): 7—34.

Pfeil, Fred. *White Guys: Studies in Postmodern Domination and Difference.* New York: Verso, 1995.

Strauss, Anselm C. and Julie M. Corbin. *Basics of Qualitative Research: Techniques and Procedures for Developing Grounded Theory* (2nd ed.) Thousand Oaks, CA: Sage, 1998.

Thompson, E.M and E.M. Morgan. "'Mostly Straight' Young Women: Variations in Sexual Behavior and Identity Development." *Developmental Psychology* 44, no. 1 (2008): 15—21.

Wilkinson, Sue. "Bisexuality 'A la Mode.'" *Women's Studies International Forum* 19, no. 3 (1996): 293—301.

PART THREE

MEDIA CAMPAIGNS AND LITERACY PROJECTS

"Hey Media, Back Off and Get Off My Body": SPARK is Taking Sexy Back

Deborah L. Tolman, Lyn Mikel Brown, and Christin P. Bowman

The usual images: A video of little girls dressed in fishnets, revealing outfits, and high heels—performing "All the Single Ladies" with all of Beyonce's moves. An ad for jeans depicting a young woman flashing her breasts at a surveillance camera with the caption: "Smart may have the brains, but stupid has the balls. Be stupid." A t-shirt that reads "Who needs brains when you have these?" Heavily made-up, carefully coifed five-year-olds prancing down a runway in pitch perfect impersonation of adult models on any episode of the runaway hit television show *Toddlers and Tiaras*. Costume stores jammed with Halloween attire for school-aged girls: French maids, sexy witches, and barely-there cheerleader outfits.

Alternative images: A video of girls saying what sexy means to them: "Women's bodies are not marketing tools!" An ad from a popular tween brand that girls have recaptioned: "I am more than eye candy...Why can't Candies treat me that way?" A group of girls wearing white t-shirts with "Being sexy is not a look, it's a feeling!" and "Use your imagination INSTEAD OF ME to sell cars, clothes, airfare, cologne, burgers, or booze!" projected onto them. An Intervene in Halloween costume fashion show won by a girl dressed cleverly as hipster candy—Eminem the M&M. An auditorium jammed with girls and young women proclaiming with feeling: "We're taking sexy back!"

SPARKing History

In May 2010, a convening of thirty people, representing large and community-based organizations that work with girls, scholars, young feminist activists, policy think tanks, media organizations and funders, made a commitment to raise awareness about the sexualization of girls in the media. Two profound problems quickly became clear. The first, that sexualization is a secret in plain sight, was hardly a secret really, but so pervasive as to appear impossibly entrenched, as well as "the way things are," a "natural" evolution and the persuasive narrative in the wake of growing sexual freedoms for women, trickling down to girls. The second, that parents, educators, health professionals, community, religious leaders, and media talking heads are comfortable doing a lot of judging and pessimistic hand wringing, but offer little concerted effort to push back against the gargantuan tide of increasing objectification, commodification, and sexualization of girls. What began as an idea to host a one-day summit on the sexualization of girls transmogrified into a plan to launch a movement to name this emerging reality as unacceptable, and to challenge it, *while strengthening our commitments to supporting girls' and young women's right to the development of their sexuality and overall wellbeing.* This positioning and set of goals recognizes and redresses the profound lack of and need for "enabling conditions"[1] that require the end of or at least a substantive challenge to sexualization, the constant and monolithic press in the media to be a "good sexual object" rather than an embodied (sexual) subject.[2]

The spark that ignited this convening, summit, and movement began with a conversation between two feminist psychologists who have been friends and colleagues since graduate school, where they had been part of the Harvard Project on the Psychology of Women and the Development of Girls. Deborah Tolman had gone on to study adolescent girls' sexuality and sexual agency development as a relational process (i.e., Tolman, 2002), while Lyn Mikel Brown studied girls' resistance to idealized femininity (Brown, 1998, 2003) and developed feminist strength-based approaches to working with girls (Brown, 2008). Tolman, a member of the 2007 American Psychological Association Task Force on the Sexualization of Girls, had been in discussion with the Women's Foundation of California and the Ms. Foundation about holding a national summit in response to the Task Force Report's call for raising awareness and grassroots mobilizing around the clear and present danger that sexualization poses to girls and young women. Lyn Mikel Brown had been working with the girl-serving nonprofit she co-founded a decade ago, Hardy Girls Healthy Women (HGHW), to pull together an alliance of feminist grassroots girl-serving organizations under the umbrella "Powered By Girl" to address media sexism and sexualization. Reframing the summit as the launch of a movement generated the need and possibility of joining these efforts into a previously unimagined whole that would be greater than its parts. The symbiosis and energy of bringing together these initiatives—research and activism, summit and public awareness—resulted in a movement, ultimately an ongoing collective effort to "connect the dots" of research, policy, funding, and the collective power of small, nimble local groups to form a heftier force and to build a wider platform than any singular effort could offer.

We named the summit "SPARK," an acronym for Sexualization Protest: Action, Resistance, Knowledge, and it continues to be an engagingly apropos moniker for the movement. Our original plan was to coordinate a collaboration of organizations rather than to form a new one, with an expanded leadership team that could support the growing demands of the Summit and subsequent movement, consisting of Hardy Girls Healthy Women and Tolman's start up intiative at Hunter College at the City University of New York to bridge academia and activism; Women's Media Center, an organization started by Gloria Steinem, Jane Fonda, and Robin Morgan and founding director Carol Jenkins to raise progressive women's voices in the media; the Ms. Foundation, serving as funding partner; ISIS (Internet Sexuality Information Services), an organization leading efforts to integrate media into sexual health initiatives; TrueChild, a nonprofit repackaging of GenderPac started by Riki Wilchins and Gina Reiss-Wilchins dedicated to eradicating gender stereotypes in society; and Hunter College, which generously provided location and logistical support for the summit, as well as endorsement from the school's President and Provost and leadership from students in the Women and Gender Studies program.

Sowing the Seeds of a Movement: SPARK Summit

A movement needs more conceptual infrastructure than a daylong event, and so we articulated principles and commitments that we believed would enable impact. First and foremost, rather than simply talking to girls about sexualization, we were determined that SPARK should be girl/youth-focused and driven, to engage girls to become social change agents of and by media—a part of the solution rather than victims of the problem who are in need of protection. Therefore, we committed to being an intergenerational movement, to develop a platform where some of the nagging fissures between older and younger feminists might be mended, as well as where adults who care about young people can support youth efforts and learn from them as well. We also made a commitment to promoting healthy sexuality—not an easy task when challenging sexualization, which at first glance could be interpreted as "frumpy feminists" being anti-sex. This commitment is further complicated, because media and marketing have effectively sold sexualization and self-objectification to girls and young women as empowerment, control, choice, and fun.[3] Ensuring diversity of all kinds went without saying—sexualization may impact all women and girls but not in the same ways, and recognizing and understanding those differences was essential to our success.

Every dimension of the summit was part of our strategy for seeding the movement. What seemed like an action-packed, high-energy day (and it was indeed that and more!) was also groundwork for our larger goal. Inviting male allies to be part of SPARK from the beginning reflected our understanding that boys and men are producers and consumers of all media, that sexualization of girls is bad for boys and men as well,[4] and also that a real and effective challenge to the sexualization of girls would only be possible with boys' and men's commitments. At the same time, the need and desire for SPARK to be a girl-dominated space was primary, so our male allies were present but not in front-row seats.

We know that media literacy is necessary for change and that it more often than not ends with the ability to "see" what is problematic—which is a critical first step and not always easy or obvious until the proverbial "aha!" moment. This strategy was inspired by PBG and the effectiveness of other alliances of small, grassroots girls' organizations' engaging and innovative ways of giving girls strategies to vent and talk back to media's sexualization of them and also to creatively produce both fun and scathing alternatives. We wanted the summit to be a dynamic context for girls to experience the symbiosis and energy of working together in the same space.

In this way, the movement provided the means for small grassroots organizations doing transformative youth-driven media activism an alternative to scaling up, what we are calling "scaling out," that is, utilizing the platform that SPARK creates to showcase and disseminate their work with the support of over sixty partner organizations at the summit and growing as part of the movement. As organizations are under increased pressure to scale up, we recognized that it is not feasible for all small organizations to expand, and also that it is not productive for those doing effective and outstanding local work to do so. "Scaling out" enables more impact without having to grow larger or be subject to more funding pressures and thus ensures viability in the current strained economic situation. As we will describe below, through being part of the SPARK movement, such organizations can report to their funders that their impact is even greater and moves beyond the outskirts of their communities while enabling them to stay focused and on the ground.

Our choice of date was yet another strategic decision. We were tired of receiving what had become predictable media calls just prior to Halloween as "expert commentators" on the growing concern about sexualized costumes for young girls and few alternatives for teens and young women. These calls had persisted for several years, underscoring for us that nothing was changing.

Knowing that we had the mainstream media's attention, both on the issue and for our own voices in a particularly visible way for Halloween, we decided that the summit had to be held just prior to Halloween. This timing provided us with the chance to reframe public discourse about sexualization from the "woe is me" party line to what girls and adults could do to begin to push back and demand change. We selected October 22, 2010, right before the news cycle on this topic would begin. As a movement, SPARK will continue to claim Halloween as a moment when we can garner attention and provide strategies for taking action to challenge sexualization.

We recognized that taking on sexualization was in some sense a risky proposition. One ostensible response to focusing on the issue is the impulse to protect and/or contain girls, putting their sexuality further under wraps. Since we had claimed to be a movement to support girls' healthy sexuality and its development, we were confronted with the quandary of how to be against sexualization and for sexuality. We resolved this dilemma by claiming the motto, "We're taking sexy back!" This rallying cry has been very useful in formulating the problem—that marketers and media have defined a narrow vision of "sexy" and have rewritten sexy as a look—while we simultaneously seek solutions such as reclaiming "sexy" as an embodied feeling that girls and women can and should define for themselves. Rather than jettison the concept of sexy, SPARK chose to embrace it and "wrest" it back from its limiting function in current public discourse to redeploy it as a discursive site for redefinition and reclamation.[5]

To be true to our commitment to a girl-focused and driven summit and movement, we were mindful about meeting girls where they are to engage them as actors, inviting in and utilizing as tools the things they are usually asked to set aside when gathered in an auditorium. Girls were encouraged to use their cell phones to text their friends and access their social media venues to report on what was happening at SPARK. We distributed "mingle stix," a kind of flash drive device that, when pointed at another such device, automatically exchanged contact information, driving network building. These mini hard drives also contained materials from participating organizations that could be accessed by summit participants at a later time. The summit was chaotic, raucous, a constant din of chatter and discussion, of movement, of doing, of connecting and communicating. Sometimes soberly silent listening to the "The Numbers Don't Lie" panel (organized by another APA Task Force member, well-known media researcher Dr. L. Monique Ward) of research findings, reports from researchers on negative impacts of sexualization on girls' cognitive performance and school achievement, career aspirations and self-esteem, sometimes dashing down the hall to try out street performing or podcasting or hip hop that refuses rather than replicates sexualization or trying Pilates, eating, munching, yelling, hugging—all of these embodied ways of being were an active part of SPARK.

To be girl-centered and girl-focused, the summit was organized quite differently from the usual fare. Headed by Hardy Girls Healthy Women, a collection of grassroots girl-serving organizations served as a planning committee for the action focus of the day, each with access to groups of girls to give us input on all elements of the summit to ensure our plan passed muster with them. Organizations were chosen deliberately, based on diversity with respect to geography, girls served in their local programming, and approaches to media activism: Hardy Girls Healthy Women (Waterville, Maryland); About-Face (San Francisco, California); Girls for Gender Equity and viBe Theater Experience (Brooklyn, New York); The Blacklight Project (New Brunswick, New Jersey); Girls for a Change (Phoenix, Arizona); Project Girl (Madison, Wisconsin); and Women, Action and the Media/WAM! (Boston, Massachusetts).

Another key decision was to reach out to girls who were already "media literate"—that is, girls and young women who did not have to be "convinced" that sexualization is persistent or problematic but arrived with this level of understanding in hand in order to take that awareness into activism. We initiated a SPARKTeam of twenty (now thirty) young women, nominated by community-based organizations, to be trained to blog about sexualization and to be a nascent savvy girl media force. The SPARKTeam continues to blog (300+ blogs to date and counting!), to grow (thirty-six girls strong, with over 100 applying to join in 2012), to engage in online and on the ground activism, and to be an absolutely essential part of SPARK's ongoing and growing public voice, as well as enabling girl-driven debates about these complicated issues.

The summit was suffused with media. It was live streamed and accessed by over 3,000 individuals on our SPARK YouTube channel, which now hosts multiple videos from the summit that are being used to drive movement building. Slideshows providing examples of sexualized media as well as research findings about the impact of sexualization ran throughout, and the summit ended with a slideshow of the resistance and media creations that the participants had produced throughout the day. Keynotes featured both young women, such as Yanique Richards, an active blogger who had just started college, and established and well-known figures, like Geena Davis, who started the Geena Davis Institute on Gender and the Media. Most of the girls had never heard of *Thelma and Louise* but its iconic portrayal shown in clips at the summit once again proved inspirational. Plenary panels included teen activists and adult women activists who had successfully pushed back against sexualization through online campaigns, script writing, on-campus activism, and established grassroots organizations such as Hollaback!, which provides women, young and old, with the chance to resist street harassment in real time through a cell phone app.

The heart of the summit was a series of hands-on workshops on everything from creating zines, to writing and performing theater, hip hop, and spoken word, to culture jamming media and organizing change campaigns. In addition, a large room accommodated 13 different hands-on "Action Spots," introducing girls to a range of media activism and offering the chance to make their own media. Examples included Project Girl's Commercial Land collages, in which girls developed pieces of original art and then made uploadable videos explaining their "take back" of media images into positive conceptions of themselves; a male allies station co-sponsored by Men Can Stop Rape and "manned" by male peer educators from Planned Parenthood of New York City; the CUNY chapter of the Campus Coalition for Sexual Literacy and high school students, at which girls were invited to ask boys any question and receive a sincere, honest answer; and a Woman, Action and the Media (WAM!) petition booth, where summit-goers were invited to talk back to *Glee* stars about their exquisitely timed sexualized *GQ* spread. The summit also provided introductions to mind-body movement practices, including yoga, Pilates, and flamenco dancing. The day ended with an Intervene in Halloween costume show, where girls attending the conference joined those who had submitted photos online to showcase fun, creative costumes they want to see in stores.

We cannot underestimate the impact and importance of social media in giving the summit lift, visibility, broader engagement and impact, an instant track record, and evidence of how the desire to do something about the sexualization of girls is profoundly ready to ignite. Encouraging participants to text, post and tweet yielded tremendous internet presence. Well-known young feminist bloggers, including Shelby Knox and Deborah Siegel, blogged in real time. On the day of the summit, we had over 3 million impressions on Twitter that catapulted us to a top-ten trending topic in New York, almost 2,500 visits to our website, and just as many Facebook visitors. Social media on all fronts remains one of the most potent tools in SPARK's arsenal, with a constantly updated Twitter feed on our website, multiple postings on our Facebook page daily, and plans afoot to enhance traffic and "likes" to our page. Our SPARK YouTube channel continues to be accessed, with over 65,000 views to date. These strategies are efforts to enlarge the SPARK community so that it can be mobilized for campaigns and easily alerted to new resources that SPARK and our partners are generating.

We also utilized the summit itself as a chance to muscle in to mainstream media, and very quickly SPARK became the go-to for public comment on sexualization. For instance, Tolman and Brown published an op-ed in *The Huffing-*

ton Post and were interviewed for radio programs at the time of the summit. In line with the launch of a movement, as of August, 2011, SPARK has been persistently tapped for input, commentary, and quotes in media ranging from documentaries to talk shows to articles for mainstream venues such as *Good Housekeeping, The Daily Beast, USA Today, Toronto Star,* and *The New York Times.* Finally, SPARK won a policy victory in announcing a new relationship with Common Sense Media to integrate attention to sexualization into their materials. Success continues apace and quickly (check our website, www.sparksummit .com, for the latest campaigns and actions).

Deep Background: Motivation for SPARKing a (Media) Movement

Why focus on the media? Sexualization is certainly an element of sexism in a plethora of contexts such as harassment in schools, evaluation of girls and women in malls and on walkways through college campuses, as well as a component of dating violence, sexual abuse, and commercial sexual exploitation. However, the critical mass and unequivocal social acceptance of the sexualization of girls in the media provides a constant and consuming context of sexualization within which girls' relational and psychosocial development now takes place. Moreover, reflecting the pervasiveness of media in our lives, there is now a convincing body of research on the impact of media sexualization on girls and young women.

Media formats such as television, magazines, and the internet continue to impose age-inappropriate sexual characteristics upon girls and young women. Nearly thirty percent of web-based advertisements for girls' clothing are explicitly sexual,[6] and almost ninety percent of music videos, crossing all genres, incorporate objectifying images of women, often portraying women as prostitutes and servants.[7] Magazines aimed at girls, adolescents, and young women encourage women to think of themselves as sexual objects who should strive constantly for male attention and connection.[8] Even cartoons feature sexualized images of girls and women,[9] with female characters wearing sexy costumes that do not match their roles in films like *Ella Enchanted.*[10]

More and more evidence points to the damaging effects of the sexualization of girls on those girls themselves, on adult women, on boys and men, and ultimately on society as a whole.[11] Girls who are exposed to sexualizing or objectifying media are more likely to experience body dissatisfaction, eating disorders, low self-esteem, and depression.[12] Because girls are constantly exposed to images of sexual objectification in the media and in their lives, they internalize this objectifying perspective and learn to look at themselves as sexual objects, harboring a "male gaze" in their own psyches. This self-objectification involves constantly assessing one's own body in order to evaluate how successfully one is conforming to cultural standards of attractiveness.[13] Among the most devastating consequences of self-objectification is the impairment of cognitive and physical functioning. Self-objectification has been shown to affect girls' math performance[14] and logical reasoning and spatial skills,[15] diminish girls' career aspirations,[16] and their ability to throw a ball.[17]

By setting an unachievable standard for what it means to be female in terms of narrow beauty ideals and appearance-focused sexuality, and saturating the visual, aural, and interactive landscapes with sexualized imagery, the media has severely constrained the psychological imagination of girls and women and narrowed their perceptions of healthy relationships. Future possibilities appear limited for girls as they learn to value themselves based on painfully narrow standards of beauty and sexuality and to discount their competence and achievements outside of the "beauty myth."[18] Professional ambitions emphasizing appearance and sexuality, such as 'glamour model,' are slowly replacing career ambitions that focus on intelligence and ability, such as 'doctor' or 'teacher.'[19]

Leveraging Research: Building a Bridge From Academia to Activism

Academic research regarding girls and women has the tendency to circulate within the academy, rarely reaching those girls and women to whom it is most pertinent. SPARK embodies a departure from the entrenched ivory tower goals and focus of academia, utilizing this research as a springboard for preparing girls to be agents of change, incorporating systematic empirical evidence as necessary to public persuasion as well as intellectual debate. From the beginning, a key SPARK principle has been to scaffold girls' engagement with peer-reviewed research. The SPARK Summit included a plenary session entitled "Numbers Don't Lie," which reviewed current research on the impact of media sexualization on girls and women.

As the summit came to a close, the SPARK leadership team sought a way to keep the girls and young women engaged with current relevant research. We wholeheartedly believed that girls could consume complex academic research if it was presented to them in a format that was accessible, convenient, and engaging to them. Having had considerable success with our SPARK team bloggers and in order to keep the flow of the latest and most exciting research on sexualization integral to the movement, we launched a research blog as a regular feature on the website. Written by Bowman, a graduate student in psychology, who is training others in this strategy for knowledge dissemination, the blog has a playful and witty voice to make current research accessible and to bring it to life for SPARK readers. Rather than the jargon-filled, statistic-laden academic writing that is the usual delivery mechanism for research, the SPARK research blog cuts through the insider-speak, "translating" into plain language explanations of difficult concepts like "self-objectification" and "sexualization." The blog often includes interviews with the researchers about their findings or how they conceived their questions. By rendering dense material more widely comprehensibly, the blog explains how research is relevant to girls' lived experiences while also providing a model for how to communicate this information in mainstream venues.

Each blog tackles a new piece of research, explaining in simple terms the research question, methods, and results. The blogs conclude with a discussion of the implications of the research for girls and young women who want to be critical of their environments. Presented from a first-person perspective by "twenty-something" women who, like us all, are constantly bombarded by sexualization and look to research to make sense of and develop strategies to resist it, the blogs invite the reader in as both subjected and resistant to sexualization. Throughout the discussion of the research, the blogger maintains her playful, critical voice, usually concluding with a call to action. For example, in a blog discussing the true meaning of "sexual empowerment" in advertising (reporting on Halliwell et al., 2011), Bowman writes:

> These so-called "empowering" images of women turn out to be just the opposite. They're a lie, a Venus flytrap. They lure us in with sweet promises of empowerment, and then SNAP! They gobble us up in the same old sexualized rhetoric. Well I'm not falling for it. Real sexual empowerment isn't about what you look like. It doesn't require stick-thinness or exhibitionism. Real sexual empowerment is about how women feel in their bodies. It's about knowing what you want (and don't want) and not being afraid to let your partner know. It's about sexual pleasure. It's about having fun in your body and loving your body and really feeling your body. When the media can figure out how to show us this kind of healthy female sexuality, I'll be glad to call it sexual empowerment too.

Communicating her own subjectivity through phrases like, "Well I'm not falling for it," Bowman models for girls how to be critical of the media. Far from simple critique, however, the blog ends with suggestions for how to resist media oppression and "take sexy back" by envisioning and emphasizing one of SPARK's key messages, that sexy is not simply a *look*, but most essentially, a sexy *feeling* in our bodies to which we are all entitled.

SPARK: The Movement

Girls' experiences of and responses to sexualization and objectification sit within existing contexts of power that constrain and restrict the kinds of choices and range of options available to them. Sexualization is ironically frequently framed and misnamed in media as female empowerment—a fun choice in a "postfeminist" world. This discourse often provides a compelling cover for sexual double standards and unequal power relations and does so in a glitzy, inviting way, such that girls and young women choose to embody the very conditions that serve to constrain, restrict, and subordinate them. A truly freely chosen, embodied, healthy sexuality, Correa and Petchesky suggest, requires the presence of "enabling conditions" that are both "material and infrastructural" and "cultural and political."[20] We approached SPARK as a way to lay bare this contradiction and to reveal how this experience of "choice" is in fact much more fraught than it appears to be—in part, how media serves commodification and thus itself while cloaking its disservice to girls in well-disguised contradictions.

Two specific SPARK activities provide space for girls, along with women and their male allies, to think about and express how sexualization makes them feel, and how it limits and undermines their felt sense of freedom to move through the world. The SPARKTeam, a collection of girl blogger/activists from across the country, and the SPARKits, a series of online free downloadable media literacy and activism projects inspired by the summit action spots, create public spaces for critical perspectives on sexualized media and enable a push back to a media-saturated environment that "crowds out" or "overwrites" possibilities for young women's sexuality, sense of self and being in relationship.

The SPARKTeam

From the beginning, the SPARK leadership group was determined to bring girls and young women into the summit planning process and to join with them to develop the shape and trajectory of the movement. As the primary targets of media and marketers, girls have grown up in a culture saturated with messages about what it means to be a "successful girl" and how "being sexy" is central in that accomplishment, and have spent their lives negotiating a relationship with media. We knew any progress around this set of issues required the experiences, insight, wit, and activist spirit of girls and young women. With this in mind, SPARK circulated an August 2010 call for nominations in search of a diverse group of girls between the ages of fourteen and twenty-two from across the country to make up a SPARKTeam of bloggers. The call invited girls to help SPARK launch an intergenerational movement to support and stand with girls against sexualized media, engage girls to be part of the solution rather than to protect them from the problem, challenge the belief that the current media landscape is "just the way things are," and then articulate and demonstrate what the alternatives can be. We sought a SPARKTeam of girls and young women who were interested in "challenging the sexualization and objectification of women and girls and/or promoting girls' sexual rights and healthy sexuality" to be bloggers for the SPARK Summit and movement. The initial twenty girl bloggers chosen ranged in age from fifteen to twenty-one; half of the young women self-identified as white; half self-identified as of color.

The SPARK bloggers came to us with varied experience interacting with mainstream media and with movement building. The younger bloggers had taken a high school class in feminism or had been actively involved with what Jessica Taft terms "transformative" girl serving organizations—those organizations, such as Hardy Girls Healthy Women and Girls for Gender Equity, that encourage "girls to think systematically about the conditions of their lives and their communities and the intersecting forces of racism, sexism, classism and ageism (among others)"—but had little experience as bloggers or activists, whereas some of the college-aged bloggers came to us with majors in Women's, Gender, and Sexuality Studies and experience leading actions or blogging for other established activist organizations.[21] Carmen Rios, nineteen, for example, was editor and blogger for THE LINE Campaign and founded an educational campaign, *(con)sensual*, on her college campus. Melissa Campbell, twenty-one, an established Tumblr blogger, had developed and led public actions for the community-based organization About-Face in San Francisco.

The girls participated in an online training with activist and blogger Shelby Knox and the day before the summit participated in a two-hour Progressive Girls' Voices training with Jamia Wilson of the Women's Media Center. The bloggers now iChat twice monthly on the Powered By Girl Ning site (an invitation-only safe online space that allows multiple users to participate in real-time conversations), generating blog and activism ideas, commenting on one another's drafts, and planning online and on the ground actions; in addition, they communicate daily on their Facebook group page. Blogging advice and feedback is offered by former SPARK blogger, Melissa Campbell, who is now on staff. Financial support comes from SPARK, ensuring that each girl gets paid for her blogs and other SPARK actions on a monthly basis.

The SPARKTeam bloggers write about the realities and impact of sexualization, as well as promote and define possible alternatives, including an agentic healthy embodied sexuality. The SPARK Summit rallying cry, "We're taking sexy back!" resonated with the bloggers, and they have grappled with what sexy should and could be, demanding more positive and realistic images of girls, and considering what conditions are necessary for healthy sexuality.

"We want control over our sexuality," Juliana writes, expressing a dominant thread running through the SPARKTeam blogs. Through their blogs the girls have developed language and created space for this control. Blogging gives each individual girl some measure of agency, power to determine the significance of media messages, and a means to talk back, but their collective public effort, scaffolded by the SPARK network of sixty partner organizations, website and social media, creates a broader platform to advocate both for resistance to sexualization and for support of healthy sexuality. Together the girl bloggers offer their readers a critical vocabulary, public dialogue, and a set of resistance strategies. Brown describes how the bloggers contribute to the creation of enabling conditions for healthy sexuality by opening up more space for a diversity of options and complexity of what it means to be sexual;[22] publicly interrupting and disrupting an increasingly normalized set of discourses and imagery; and widening options for participation in social and political action in response to increased sexualization, objectification, and what has been called "pornification" of girls' media.[23]

The girls promote one another's blogs on Facebook and Tumblr and, in this way, create a steady stream of thoughtful critique about their experiences as both consumers and producers of media. When they invite media activism, it is usually a mix of playful, satiric, and pointed criticism that catches the attention of their peers and adults alike. For example, when Maya, sixteen, heard that Candies (a brand of tween clothing and shoes) had announced a contest to design a new clothing ad, she called them out on their disingenuous invitation:

> When I went on the Candies website, there wasn't a place to make any sort of ad I wanted to see. There wasn't a place I could upload my own pictures or even a variety of pictures to choose from. Instead what I saw was a cookie cutter mold for sexist ads. There were about 10 pictures of Vanessa Hudgens, the current "Candies Girl," in various sexualized positions and states of undress…The site gives the appearance of freedom and creativity…but in reality any advertisement I made would be pretty much the same. Not to mention that in order to submit the ad I'd have to upload a Candies logo…

On behalf of the SPARKTeam, Maya invited readers to "take their sexist ad contest and throw it right back at them. So go ahead, log on and make an ad for them, but make it satiric. Use the functions they supply, like text boxes and a drawing pen and *question* the sexist ads they're selling…Be sure to take a screen shot and post on our SPARK Facebook page."

When thirteen-year-old Julia Bluhm successfully petitioned *Seventeen Magazine* to include digitally unaltered images of girls in their pages, she and her SPARKTeammates staged a mock photoshoot in front of the magazine's Manhattan headquarters, playfully grabbing media attention with satiric slogans and hand-made signs. The Team's strength is the creative mix of critique and humor they bring to every action.

The SPARKTeam works together to create sites of resistance, making visible creative forms of agency in response to sexualized media that promise freedom but deliver a set of narrow choices and constraining options. But SPARK is also about engaging adults and offering girl-serving community-based organizations much needed media literacy and activism tools and resources they can use to participate actively in the growing movement.

The SPARKits

Designed in collaboration with Hardy Girls Healthy Women and Powered By Girl, the SPARK Summit "Action Spots" were chosen on the basis of their potential to seed the movement. Developed in collaboration with SPARK partner organizations, they became the inspiration for a series of free downloadable interactive SPARKits. An important feature of this initiative is to enable those organizations offering SPARKits to share their work with other girls across the country and internationally via SPARK's social media and website. SPARKits are strategically named to convey simultaneously that they are a kit by which girls and others can "do" SPARK work and, in so doing, they will "spark it"— ignite the SPARK movement—in their group and community.

Each co-branded interactive SPARKit enables girls, community-based organizations, parents, families, schools, and communities to engage with the SPARK movement; in turn, the growing coalition of partners supports the use of the Kits, and extends the movement worldwide via social media. As we mentioned earlier, this allows the smallest grassroots SPARK partners, many of which have some of the most creative media literacy projects and actions, to extend their reach. This also allows marginalized or economically stressed schools, organizations, and communities free access to some of the most creative and fun media literacy and activism materials available.

The first SPARKit was developed in collaboration with Project Girl, a grassroots media activism-through-the-arts organization in Madison, Wisconsin. Run by visual artist Kelly Parks Snider and videographer Jane Bartell, Project Girl had a small but ardent following as a result of their traveling art exhibit, art activism workshops, creative online gallery of girl art, and progressive curricular materials. Project Girl developed a Summit Action Spot based on their Commercial Land Collage. They invited girls and young women to use art to develop critical commentary on the media targeting them and videotaped their art talks. Their SPARKit offers free downloadable collage-making instructions and invites girls to upload their art and commentary into Project Girl's online SPARKit gallery for others to see and appreciate (see the SPARK Commercial Land Collages and listen to the girls art talks).[24]

After their SPARKit was announced, Project Girl's Facebook page numbers doubled, and they received offers from coast to coast to do workshops with girls. In fall 2012, they spoke at the National Women's Studies Association annual conference about their Kit and their work with girls.

Twelve SPARKits developed from the original action spots at the summit have been assembled into an integrated curriculum for teen girls called *SPARK-*

ing Change, Encouraging Activism.[25] The curriculum includes extensive guidelines and instructions for using the kits to teach and enable media literacy and activism, as well as a list of SPARKTeam blogs to engage girls in discussion.

SPARKing the Future

SPARK has the distinction of being both a highly planned summit and movement and a context that feeds and fuels innovation with the best of unintended consequences. As a movement dedicated to resisting the onslaught of sexualization of girls while promoting girls' right to develop healthy sexuality, it is tantamount that we grow. As more partners join SPARK, they continue to transform and improve the movement, enabling us to draw attention to and protest sexualization, as well as offer alternatives to it.

SPARK is also in the process of becoming a formalized entity. We have hired a director, Dr. Dana Edell, founder and former executive director of viBe Theater Experience. Dana was instrumental in organizing the action spots at the summit and now brings her considerable skills to realizing SPARK's strategic plan. We have launched successful actions and campaigns to secure LEGO's engagement on reworking their line for girls, and convinced *Seventeen* magazine's editor to take a public pledge in her August 2012 letter to readers that the magazine will never alter images of girls' faces or bodies. We have collaborated with partners on national awareness and protest campaigns, including the #Keep-ItReal campaign with Miss Representation and #Proud2BMe campaign with the National Eating Disorders Association. We will be developing a college campus initiative through collaboration with women's studies programs and women's centers. We have already expanded the SPARKteam and are hard at work instituting reposts of their blogs on websites beyond our immediate focus. We have plans to expand internationally, beginning with a Canadian Women's Foundation-initiated SPARKit contest for girl-serving organizations across Canada, designed as a template for future work with other countries. We have no shortage of ideas for how to grow the SPARK movement to create what SPARK leadership team member Jamia Wilson of the Women's Media Center, utilizing Malcom Gladwell's concept (2002), has termed "a cultural tipping point where sexualization of girls is no longer acceptable, tolerable or profitable." Some might say we are overreaching, but we know, based on historical shifts to intolerance around racism and sexism, meeting such a goal requires only our imagination, our commitment, and our passion for raising awareness of the injustice that sexualization brings and the possibilities that media activism holds.

Notes

1. Sonya Correa and Rosalind Petchesky, "Reproductive and Sexual Rights: A Feminist Perspective," in *Feminist Theory Reader: Local and Global Perspectives*, eds. Carole R. McCann and Seung-kyung Kim (New York: Routledge, 2009).
2. Niva Piran et al., "On Girls' Disembodiment: The Complex Tyranny of the 'Ideal Girl,'" in *Women, Health, and Education: CASWE 6th Bi-Annual International Institute Proceeding*, eds. Diana L. Gustafson and L. Goodyear (St. John's, NL: Memorial University, 2006); Deborah Tolman, "Object Lessons: Romance, Violation, and Female Adolescent Sexual Desire," *Journal of Sex Education and Therapy* 25, no. 10 (2000): 70; Deborah Tolman, *Dilemmas of Desire: Teenage Girls Talk about Sexuality* (Cambridge, Massachusetts: Harvard University Press, 2002).
3. Sharon Lamb and Lyn Mikel Brown, *Packaging Girlhood: Rescuing Our Daughters From Marketers' Schemes* (New York: St. Martin's Press, 2006); Angela McRobbie, *The Aftermath of Feminism: Gender, Culture and Social Change* (London: Sage, 2009).
4. Michael Kimmel, *Guyland: The Perilous World where Boys Become Men* (New York: Harper Collins, 2009); Deborah Tolman, "Object Lessons," 70.
5. Michel Foucault, *The History of Sexuality: Volume 1* (New York: Random House, 1979).
6. Goodin et al., "Putting On Sexiness: A Content Analysis Of The Presence Of Sexualizing
6. Goodin et al., "Putting On Sexiness: A Content Analysis Of The Presence Of Sexualizing Characteristics In Girls' Clothing," *Sex Roles* 65 (2011): 1–12.
7. Julie Andsager and Kimberly Row, "'What's Your Definition of Dirty, Baby?' Sex in Music Videos," *Sexuality and Culture* 7 (2003): 79–97.
8. McRobbie, *The Aftermath*, 2009.
9. Stacy Smith, *Changing the Status Quo: Industry Leaders' Perceptions of Gender in Family Films* (Geena Davis Institute on Gender and the Media: Los Angeles, CA, 2011).
10. Lamb and Brown, *Packaging Girlhood*, 2006.
11. Deborah Tolman, "It's Bad for Everyone: Impact of Sexualization of Girls on Boys, Men and Women," in *Sexualization of Girls and Girlhood*, eds. Eileen Zurbriggen and Tomi-Ann Roberts (Oxford University Press, 2012); eds. Eileen Zurbriggen and Tami-Ann Roberts, *Sexualization of Girls and Girlhood* (Oxford University Press, 2012).
12. APA, "Task Force on the Sexualization of Girls," *Report of the APA Task Force on the Sexualization of Girls*, 2007.
13. Barbara L. Fredrickson and Tami-Ann Roberts, "Objectification Theory: Toward Understanding Women's Lived Experiences And Mental Health Risks," *Psychology of Women Quarterly* 21 (1997): 173–206.
14. Barbara L. Fredrickson et al., "That Swimsuit Becomes You: Sex Differences In Self-Objectification, Restrained Eating, And Math Performance," *Journal of Personality and Social Psychology* 75 (1998): 269–84.
15. Rebecca Bigler and Sarah McKenney, *Conceptualizing and Testing the Consequences of Internalized Sexualization for Girls: Developmental Outcomes* (New York: October 2010); Kathrine Gapinski, Kelly Brownell, and Marianne LaFrance, "Body Objectification And 'Fat Talk': Effects On Emotion, Motivation, And Cognitive Performance," *Sex Roles* 48 (2003): 377–88.

16.   Aurora Sherman and Eileen Zurbriggen, *"'I can be…' anything?: Playing with Barbie Reduces Girls' Career Aspirations"* (New York: October 2010).

17.   Fredrickson and Harrison, 2005.

18.   Anita Harris, *All About the Girl: Culture, Power, and Identity* (New York: Routledge, 2004); Naomi Wolf, *The Beauty Myth: How Images of Beauty are Used Against Women* (New York: Perennial, 1991).

19.   Maddy Coy, "Milkshakes, Lady Lumps and Growing Up to Want Boobies: How the Sexualisation of Popular Culture Limits Girls' Horizons," *Child Abuse Review* 18 (2009): 372–83.

20.   Correa and Petchesky, "Reproductive and Sexual Rights," 92.

21.   Jessica Taft, "Girlhood in Action: Contemporary U.S. Girls' Organizations and the Public Sphere," *Girlhood Studies: An Interdisciplinary Journal* 3, no. 2 (2010): 11–29, 23.

22.   Lyn Mikel Brown, "We're Taking Back Sexy: Girl Bloggers SPARKing a Movement," *Girlhood Studies* 4 (2011): 47–69.

23.   Gail Dines, *Porn Land: How Porn Has Hijacked Our Sexuality* (Boston, MA: Beacon Press, 2011).

24.   http://www.projectgirl.org/girl-artists-gallery/project-girl-workshops-collage.php

25.   Lyn Mikel Brown and Amy Castro, *SPARKing Change, Encouraging Activism* (Waterville, ME: Hardy Girls Healthy Women, 2012).

Works Cited

American Psychological Association. "Task Force on the Sexualization of Girls." *Report of the APA Task Force on the Sexualization of Girls*, 2007.

Andsager, Julie and Kimberly Row. "'What's Your Definition of Dirty, Baby?' Sex in Music Videos." *Sexuality and Culture* 7 (2003): 79–97.

Bigler, Rebecca and Sarah McKenney. *Conceptualizing and Testing the Consequences of Internalized Sexualization for Girls: Developmental Outcomes*. Presented at the SPARK Summit, NY, October 2010.

Brown, Lyn M. *Raising their Voices: The Politics of Girls' Anger*. Cambridge, MA: Harvard University Press, 1998.

———. *Girlfighting: Betrayal and Rejection Among Girls*. New York: New York University Press, 2003.

———. "The 'Girls' in Girls' Studies." *Girlhood Studies: An Interdisciplinary Journal* 1 (2008): 1–12.

———. "We're Taking Back Sexy: Girl Bloggers SPARKing a Movement." *Girlhood Studies* 4 (2011): 47–69.

Brown, L.M. and A. Castro. *SPARKing Change, Encouraging Activism*. Waterville, ME: Hardy Girls Healthy Women, 2012.

Correa, Sonya and Rosalind Petchesky. "Reproductive and Sexual Rights: A Feminist Perspective." In *Feminist Theory Reader: Local and Global Perspectives*, eds. Carole R. McCann and Seung-kyung Kim, 119–32. New York: Routledge, 2009.

Coy, Maddy. "Milkshakes, Lady Lumps and Growing Up to Want Boobies: How the Sexualisation of Popular Culture Limits Girls' Horizons." *Child Abuse Review* 18 (2009): 372–83.

Dines, Gail. *Porn Land: How Porn Has Hijacked Our Sexuality*. Boston, Mass: Beacon Press, 2011.

Foucault, Michel. *The History of Sexuality: Volume 1*. New York: Random House, 1979.

Fredrickson, Barbara L. and Tami-Ann Roberts. "Objectification Theory: Toward Understanding Women's Lived Experiences And Mental Health Risks." *Psychology of Women Quarterly* 21 (1997): 173–206.

Fredrickson, Barbara L., Tami-Ann Roberts, Stephanie Noll, Diane Quinn, and Jean Twenge. "That Swimsuit Becomes You: Sex Differences In Self-Objectification, Restrained Eating, And Math Performance." *Journal of Personality and Social Psychology* 75 (1998): 269–84.

Gapinski, Kathrine, Kelly Brownell, and Marianne LaFrance. "Body Objectification And 'Fat Talk': Effects On Emotion, Motivation, And Cognitive Performance." *Sex Roles* 48 (2003): 377–88.

Goodin, Samantha M., Alyssa Van Denburg, Sarah K. Murnen, and Linda Smolak. "Putting On Sexiness: A Conten Analysis Of The Presence Of Sexualizing Characteristics In Girls' Clothing." *Sex Roles* 65 (2011): 1–12.

Harris, Anita. *All About the Girl: Culture, Power, and Identity*. New York: Routledge, 2004.

Kimmel, Michael. *Guyland: The Perilous World where Boys Become Men*. New York: Harper Collins, 2008.

Lamb, Sharon and Lyn M. Brown. *Packaging Girlhood: Rescuing Our Daughters From Marketers' Schemes*. New York: St. Martin's Press, 2006.

McRobbie, Angela. *The Aftermath of Feminism: Gender, Culture and Social Change*. London: Sage, 2009.

Piran, Niva, M. Antoniou, R. Legge, N. McCance, J. Mizevich, E. Peasley, and E. Ross. "On Girls' Disembodiment: The Complex Tyranny of the 'Ideal Girl'." In *Women, Health, and Education: CASWE 6th Bi-annual International Institute Proceedings*, eds. Diana L. Gustafson and L. Goodyear, 224–29. St. John's, NL: Memorial University, 2006.

Sherman, Aurora and Eileen Zurbriggen. "'I can be…' anything?: Playing with Barbie Reduces Girls' Career Aspirations." Presented at the SPARK Summit, New York: October 2010.

Smith, S. *Changing the Status Quo: Industry Leaders' Perceptions of Gender in Family Films*. Geena Davis Institute on Gender and the Media: Los Angeles, CA, 2011.

Taft, Jessica. "Girlhood in Action: Contemporary U.S. Girls' Organizations and the Public Sphere." *Girlhood Studies: An Interdisciplinary Journal* 3, no. 2 (2010): 11–29.

Tolman, Deborah. "Object Lessons: Romance, Violation, and Female Adolescent Sexual Desire." *Journal of Sex Education and Therapy* 25, no. 10 (2000): 70.

———. *Dilemmas of Desire: Teenage Girls Talk about Sexuality*. Cambridge, MA: Harvard University Press, 2002.

———. "It's Bad for Everyone: Impact of Sexualization of Girls on Boys, Men and Women." In *Sexualization of Girls and Girlhood*, eds. Eileen Zurbriggen and Tami-Ann Roberts. Oxford: Oxford University Press, 2012.

Wolf, Naomi. *The Beauty Myth: How Images of Beauty are Used Against Women*. New York: Perennial, 1991.

Zurbriggen, Eileen and Tami-Ann Roberts, eds. *Sexualization of Girls and Girlhood*. Oxford: Oxford University Press, 2012.

| 14

From Media Propaganda to De-Stigmatizing Sex: Exploring a Teen Magazine By, For, and About Girls

Linda Charmaraman and Brittany Low

The sexualization of adolescent girls in television, movies, magazines, music videos and lyrics, the internet, and advertising is widespread. At a time when adolescent girls feel more self-conscious about their developing bodies, media images of perfection almost exclusively feature achieving a physically thin ideal to become popular with peers. Several research studies have linked the hyper-sexualization of girls to mental health problems like depression, eating disorders, and low self-esteem.[1] Self-objectification has been associated with lack of sexual assertiveness and decreased condom use among adolescent girls.[2] Frequent exposure to sexualized media affects how girls view femininity and sexuality, leading them to endorse stereotypes of females as sexual objects and to value physical attractiveness over all other characteristics.[3]

The American Psychological Association convened the *Task Force on the Sexualization of Girls*, defining self-motivated sexual exploration and age-appropriate exposure to sexual information as a part of healthy sexual development, while *sexualization* entails one or more of the following: a) valuing sexual appeal or behavior at the exclusion of other characteristics, b) narrowly defining physical attractiveness as being sexy, c) sexually objectifying others, and/or d) inappropriately imposing sexuality on others, particularly on children.[4] Few studies have documented the contents and messages of non-mainstream/alternative media, particularly those created by youth for youth consumption. The current study is a media content analysis of a magazine created by teen girls augmented by an interview study of the same teen girl participants in order to document their opinions about the mainstream media's portrayals of sexualization and how they combat these depictions by generating their own alternative media content.

Literature Review

Media Sexualization of Women and Girls

Many studies have investigated how the mainstream media depicts sexuality and sexualization.[5] Generally studies analyzing television, movies, and music videos have demonstrated a lack of sexual health information, a glorification of sexual innuendo, and a depiction of sexually subservient women. In television, sexual content is typically found in verbal innuendos and visual depictions of less explicit physical acts, and television rarely provides discussion of the potential risks and consequences of sexual behaviors.[6] In movies, studies have noted a higher frequency of displays of non-marital sex than of marital sex and extremely limited references to using protection methods.[7] In terms of gender role-playing, researchers conducted a content analysis by analyzing MTV music videos which showed women behaving more sexually subservient and men more sexually dominant and aggressive.[8]

Sexual Content in Teen Girl Magazines

In 2000, the Magazine Publishers of America reported that over 200 magazines are targeted toward adolescent girls.[9] Women's magazines are read by over sixty percent of college-aged women[10] and seventy-five percent of teenage girls.[11] In a study from the Kaiser Family Foundation, Roberts, Foehr, and Rideout found that on average eight- to eighteen-year-olds read magazines approximately fourteen minutes per day, signaling that this media format is still popular and may have a powerful socialization influence on adolescent girls.[12] Much of what is depicted in these mainstream magazines upholds traditional femininity ideologies and heterosexual sexual scripts.[13] According to media dependency theory, audiences construct social realities and dependencies on media resources.[14] Media dependency is determined by one's desire for information, interest in the subject, and ability to obtain the information elsewhere. The degree of dependence on media information is key in understanding when and why media messages can affect beliefs or behaviors. To place this general media theory in the context of sexualization, objectification theory describes how we exist in a cultural milieu that objectifies the female body.[15] Girls, in particular, constantly assess their bodies in order to conform to society's standards of attractiveness, thereby evaluating themselves in terms of sexual desirability to others (rather than in terms of their own desires or wellness).

The majority of studies on the sexual content of magazines have focused on analyzing girls' and women's magazines.[16] Specifically, in magazines targeted toward adolescent girls, a review of sexual content analysis research by Ward (2003) has revealed the following common themes: a) encouragement of women to be sexually desirable to attract male attention and achieving heterosexual success, b) relationships are exclusively the domain of women, c) contradictory depictions of female sexuality, d) support of traditional sexual roles, and e) lack of diverse female sexuality information and discussion. Even though content analyses show that magazines may be perpetuating unrealistic and stereotyped norms, most studies do not explore how magazine content impacts teenage girls' sexual attitudes, though there are many studies involving college-aged young adults. There is also research that explores racial/ethnic differences in how media consumption affects young people. In one study, television, movies, music, and magazine content was associated with an acceleration of white adolescents' engagement in sexual activity and increases the likelihood of early sexual intercourse. However, black adolescents did not follow the same trend; instead, their understanding of their parents' expectations and friends' sexual behavior had more influence.[17]

Resisting Sexualization Through Alternative Media Programs

Mainstream media content is predominantly written and produced by adults even though the intended audience is young adolescents. The Task Force on the Sexualization of Girls (2010) recommended that girls become activists empowered with their unique voices to develop media alternatives, through writing for zines, producing their own blogs, books, webpages, and feminist magazines.[18] For instance, in a content analysis of thirty-three girl-produced zines, Schilt demonstrated that zines offered girls an outlet for consumer-based empowerment strategies (e.g., buying t-shirts with prefabricated feminist slogans) and were forums for girls to express their opinions and become cultural critics.[19]

For many youth media programs, it is crucial to develop media literacy skills and youth voice to counteract the misrepresentation of young people in mainstream media.[20] Media literacy—equipping students with the analytical tools that promote independent thinking and critical understanding of the media—typically entails educating consumers about implicit messages from media images and challenging their realism.[21] Rather than offering "positive, age-appropriate" media created for teen girl consumption by adults, a few girls empowerment groups increase opportunities for girls to create their *own* media, such as making their own films/videos, e.g., imMEDIAte Justice, Beyondmedia Education, Girls Making Media, Reel Grrls, and TVbyGIRLS.

In comparison to video/film programs and music programs for adolescent girls, there are only a handful of organizations that focus on girls' magazine production, for instance, *New Moon, Latinitas,* and *Teen Voices*.[22] The current study focuses on *Teen Voices*, which was founded in 1988 in Cambridge, Massachusetts. Through its programs, teen girls create *Teen Voices* and *Teen Voices Online*, two internationally distributed print and online social justice magazines reaching 50,000 readers and receiving 7.6 million hits annually from ninety-eight countries (www.teenvoices.org). According to their mission statement, *Teen Voices* supports and educates teen girls to "amplify their voices and create social change through media." *Teen Voices* magazine is published in print twice a year, though *Teen Voices Online* is produced more frequently. In the fall, spring, and summer, a group of "teen editors" work in small groups with college-aged mentors to write articles for publication. The current study focuses on the six-week summer session where teen editors work about twenty-five hours per week. One week is dedicated to teaching media literacy, working in groups to create non-exploitative commercials, and inviting guest speakers (e.g., local radio show host) to share alternative media perspectives.

Current Study

Stemming from a larger ethnographic case study on adolescent identity development within youth programs, this article focuses on the content analysis of *Teen Voices* magazines published between 2005 and 2011 and showcases the perspectives of a subset of teen participants within this youth program. Though there are numerous content studies of mainstream teen magazines that are written by adults for teen consumption, in-depth studies of programs that are designed to empower teen girls to publish their own written ideas and opinions are rare (APA, 2010). We explore the following research questions:

From 2005–2011, how much of *Teen Voices'* content was devoted to sexuality? What sexual and sexualization topics did the teens focus on and what were the underlying messages to readers? (Source of data: article content analysis)

What do these teen editors believe about mainstream media and how it depicts girls and sexuality? (Source of data: interviews)

Methods

Participants. The participants of the larger study about identity and youth development programs included twenty-five ninth through twelfth grade students attending an intensive six-week summer session at *Teen Voices*. Students came from seventeen different schools (mainly public) across metro Boston. As reported by the students, average parental level of education was between that of a high school graduate and attending some college. In terms of racial composition, forty-eight percent were black, twenty-eight percent multiracial, sixteen percent Latina, and eight percent identified as "other." The average age was sixteen (range of thirteen to eighteen). Half of the teens reported reading teen magazines such as *Teen Vogue, Seventeen, Cosmo Girl, Teen People.*

Materials and Procedures. All teens enrolled in the 2008 summer program returned signed parental consent forms and gave assent to being in the study. Participants were observed within the program daily to twice per week between four to seven hours at a time. Individual interviews were conducted with the twenty-five teens participating in the program, lasting thirty minutes on average. The interview protocol broadly probed about media depictions, identity, and reflections on program involvement. All magazine issues from fall of 2005 to spring of 2011 were used in the content analysis (n = 12 magazines). Articles and content, driven by the teen editors participating in the Teen Voices youth program as well as by letters submitted to the teen editor or to the teen advice columnist, were included in the analyses. Thus, the excluded items were either creative pieces submitted by the readers (e.g., fiction, poetry, reviews of popular culture), or programmatic reflections from the staff of Teen Voices. The total sample for the content analysis was 143 articles.

Data analysis. We drew from ethnographic content analysis to analyze the articles by using a constant comparative approach to discover emergent patterns and major themes of media messages as well as to understand the process of how they were presented to the reader.[23] Although it is similar to grounded theory, ECA does not aim to generate testable hypotheses as a foundation for theory, but rather the goal is discovery of meaning, both manifest and latent content. We documented our analysis according to the five stages of ECA by a) creating parameters around which documents to review, b) developing the protocol and data collection, c) coding and organization, d) data analysis, and e) reporting.

Transcripts of the digitally recorded interviews were analyzed for the interview component of the data, focusing on the interviews of the participants who had written an article about sexuality. For both the content analysis of articles and the interviews, the first author conducted the initial round of coding and separate codebooks of themes and patterns were developed for the media content analysis and the interviews. After repeated review of the materials and identification of the major categories and themes, the codebook was discussed with a second coder who subsequently coded all the articles and interviews independently. Coding categories were not mutually exclusive such that each article could be coded with more than one theme. Final codes were confirmed by reviewing whether there was agreement between both raters on each article and discussing disagreements until consensus. The percentage of topics devoted to each category was established by dividing the number of articles that pertain to the category by the total number of articles possible.

Results: Content Analysis of *Teen Voices* magazine

Anti-sexualization topics. Over half of the 143 articles (fifty-five percent) contained messages related to sexuality and/or critiquing sexualization, demonstrating the salience of this construct for teen girls (see Figure 14.1).[24] Out of the pieces that explored a sexual topic (n = 78), the most frequent type of article (forty percent) was critiquing sexual advertisement propaganda or encouraging media activism to fight against this sexualization. For instance, when teen editors deconstructed advertisements, from mainstream women's magazines (e.g., *Vanity Fair, Harper's Bazaar),* they wrote about their anger and distrust of media producers and industry executives who allow girls to be exploited to sell products. The teen editors wrote about how these magazines photographed women in sexually degrading positions, using images akin to pornography to enhance sales. Commentating on Dove's ad campaign for Real Beauty, the teen editors of "Are curves in or is the media still selling thin?" observed that although they appreciate the joy and confidence of the Dove models who are curvy and not overly seductive-looking, there is a mixed message from Dove since they are still trying to sell a skin firming lotion to look thinner. One article raised awareness of the controversy of TV networks such as FOX and CBS who pulled commercials which depicted men who don't use condoms as pigs— commercials that were broadcast by other networks such as MTV, Comedy Central, and the Cartoon Network. The teen editors debated whether the ads encouraged promiscuous sex outside of serious relationships or the responsibility of both men and women to use condoms and attain sexual equality.

To encourage media activism to combat sexualization, teen editors provided several suggestions for prosocial action on the article topic, such as writing to the CEOs of companies who allow hypersexualization of girls in their advertisements. A template letter was offered to readers to send to editors of magazines such as *Seventeen, Teen Vogue,* and *Vogue,* stemming from an article about the effect of airbrushing on teen readers:

> Dear Editor, We think you should try to send out a more positive message. For one, try putting realistic people in your magazine—flaws and all—because we're able to relate to them more. Second, if you're going to try to relate to an audience of teens, try asking them what they would want to see and stop assuming they want to see "perfect" images. Last, we encourage you to embrace different ideals of beauty—because we know that we're beautiful, no matter what our shape or size.

A large volume of the articles (thirty-eight percent) highlighted the negative impact of unrealistic media standards of beauty, providing negative media role models to girls who consume those images. In one such article, the teen editors wrote about how rare it is to find naked men selling products compared to women and how these ads "disempower" girls. Other articles invited readers to reflect on the impact of reality shows about plastic surgery, which "reinforces the false ideal of beauty and encourage Barbie doll perfection."

Instead of focusing only on the negative socialization of unrealistic role models, the contributions of positive media role models was a theme in twenty-two percent of the articles, ranging from a story about the musician Alicia Keyes, who has a reputation for not selling sex and aims to raise awareness about AIDS, to the Indigo Girls who sing messages about female empowerment and sexual acceptance.

Sexuality and sexual health topics. In addition to topics about sexualization, teen editors focused on sexual health promotion (e.g., birth control, pregnancy, STIs) in thirty-one percent of the articles. These articles have discussed such topics as how to talk to gynecologists about obtaining birth control. In one such article entitled "Debunked! Separating birth control fact and fiction," the teen editors interviewed a Planned Parenthood community health educator and a nurse practitioner at the Boston Public Health Commission who named and gave biological explanations for the five most common myths about birth control, e.g., not being able to get pregnant if it's the first time.

In twenty-two percent of the articles, the teen editors attempted to de-stigmatize teen sexuality. These articles highlighted the reality of unintended teen pregnancies and the normal, healthy sexual desires of teens. For instance, in "Let's talk about sex: It's your decision," the teen editors emphasized that sexual decision making is complex and encouraged readers to explore individual values, feelings, and needs, referring readers to the website www.sexetc.org, a teen-generated sexual information online source. In "Teens and miscarriage: Loss, healing, and strength," the teen editors discussed symptoms of miscarriage and profiled a support website for teen moms, a stigmatized segment of the community. In their advice column *Dear D*, readers wrote to the magazine about the dilemma of losing one's virginity and the fear of being a "whore." In response, the teen editors discussed the sexual revolution where sex has the potential to be a positive and an equally enjoyable experience, particularly for the woman.

Relationships, communication, and the gender divide. A large number of articles focused on dating relationships and how to manage healthy communication and decision-making (twenty-eight percent). Typical articles in this category discussed such topics as the dangers of boyfriends who are over-controlling about their girlfriends' internet whereabouts, or how to talk to your partner about his/her sexual history. In the advice column *Dear D*, in an entry entitled "Ready to rumble or keeping a cool head," the teen editors responded to readers who wanted to convince their mothers that they are mature enough to have relationships. In this feature, the teen editors also offered a quiz to their readers, which helped them assess whether they are an "aggressive, assertive, or passive communicator."

Highlighting the unjust sexual double standards in mainstream media were topics in twenty-one percent of articles. In an advice column dedicated to whether to have sex or not with one's boyfriend, the teen editors wrote about how to deal with sexual pressure and gender differences in readiness for sex. In an article entitled "Tarnished stars? Who's making Hollywood bad girls bad?" the teen editors discussed the double standard of women being scrutinized more than men as public figures. For instance, "Miley Cyrus had to apologize for photos in *Vanity Fair* that were described as 'provocative' and 'racy' even though they were meant to be artsy." They remarked on the intense pressure on women to be perfect role models whereas if men display themselves in provocative ways, it's not a big deal.

Sexual violence was a theme in twenty-one percent of the articles, ranging from sex trafficking to date rape. In an article called "Don't be a silent victim: Finding your voice after an assault," the teen editors showcased letters from teen readers who have dealt with being sexually assaulted and provided tips on the healing process. In another article about the fine line between sexual harassment and "hollering," the teen editors reflected on how they are offended by unwanted sexual attention and sexual name-calling, such as "hey sexy!" or "lesbian" from men and boys on the streets.

Fewer articles addressed topics related to internet safety, e.g., sexting and social networking sites (eight percent), and LGBT issues (four percent), although if articles that mentioned LGBT issues in a minor way are counted, this group would constitute fifteen percent of all sexuality-related articles.

Behind the Scenes: Reflections From the Teen Editors

To better understand the motivations of the contributors, we had the opportunity to interview all of the teen editors during the summer of 2008 and invited them to discuss the process of producing an article for public consumption.[25] The thematic analysis of the teen interviews of those who incorporated sexuality in their articles yielded broad themes that transcended the topic of sexuality but focused on media literacy development and combating media stereotypes through media activism. Two teen editors reflected about their personal journey in learning about the media and how they had been bombarded with multiple messages and images without critically analyzing them in the past.

> When I watch videos, some of the times you don't really pay attention to what's going on. So when you pick a topic and you learn about it you're like, Oh my gosh, last month I didn't even know about that.—Tessa

> American Apparel ads…this is like soft pornography. What is going on here, people? I
> don't think I've seen those before and I think now I'm happy I haven't. I mean some
> of the stuff that is out there is crazy… pretty much the entire purpose of this program
> anyway—to see the different types of things that are portrayed in the media and you
> care about it and you find out ways to inform other people that it shouldn't be this way.
> And you can do something about it.—Karina

Even though she did not personally work on the article about American Apparel ads, Karina, an eighteen-year-old working on her 2nd *Teen Voices* issue, learned about sexy advertisement propaganda during the editorial "workshopping" process. She identified with its social message as a fellow *Teen Voices* editor and acknowledged that this was one of the core goals of the *Teen Voices* program.

The impact of advertisements on girls and their sense of identity and self was a theme in several interviews. For instance, fifteen-year-old Sabrina talked about how "money" was the root cause of these magazine's editorial decisions such as which advertisements to run, pointing out that *Teen Voices* is highly selective of the ads that get published regardless of the production costs. Nadine, a first-time fifteen-year-old editor, was particularly proud of this policy: "The ads that are in *Teen Voices* aren't going to tell you to buy some facial cream to look beautiful."

Still others moved beyond their own personal transformation to being motivated by the possibility of spreading the word, sending their proactive media message to other teen readers, encouraging them to take action and/or to become more aware of media stereotypes and the damaging effects on girls' sense of self. Shanonda, a fifteen-year-old editor working on her third *Teen Voices* issue (and her third article about sexuality), noted what makes this alternative magazine so unique: "One, we don't use makeup (on our covers). We don't have people who fix our eyebrows or our eyes to make it look like the 'it' girl." The teen editors typically critiqued unrealistic and hypersexualized depictions in mainstream ads, such as an ad with Gwen Stefani where she is "busting" out of her perfume box, commenting that:

> Drenched in her perfume, she seems to be being sold along with her product. Stefani
> fits the media's image of what women should look like: slender, tall, white, blonde, and
> possessing flawless skin. Furthermore, she is half-naked, wearing really short shorts, no
> bra, and a see-through wet white top. Her facial expression looks as though she is en-
> joying sexual pleasures, and the quote next to her mouth says, 'I want you all over
> me…'

During Shanonda's interview, she described the process of constructing the article "Porn Sells???" (co-edited by Nadine) which began with researching the topic by reviewing a compilation of ads featuring photos of women pretending to have intercourse with men, of women sitting on top of men suggestively (the fashion company Sisley), or of a woman sucking a lollipop with her legs spread

open (Lee Jeans). One of the ads was by Tom Ford where a large cologne bottle
is placed between a woman's breasts. They commented:

> The ad suggests that if a man buys this product, the cologne will be replaced by his pe-
> nis. The woman has her mouth open, as if she is enjoying something, and she is not
> wearing any clothes. This suggests that men will not only use the cologne, but will also
> use the woman. The woman is reduced to a sex object because her face is not shown…

During the interview, Shanonda talked about her role in typing up the interview,
writing, and editing the commentary conclusions with her co-editors, which
included revealing the e-mail addresses of each of the companies to encourage
teens to voice their opinions of these advertisements. The article concludes by
sharing some internet resources with their teen readers (e.g., www.GenderAds.
com and www.sexinadvertising.com).

When asked to reflect on her potential impact on the media landscape,
Shanonda was cautious about her efforts toward prosocial media actions:

> I am just one little girl. People might not really listen, but I think that when we connect
> and unite together, we empower and we have a voice to stand out. It is about what we
> say because we have a voice and we tell them the things that we want to change. We
> want to make a difference in our world instead of livin' the same day.

In the quote above, Shanonda imparted a realization of a collective mission of
being a part of something greater than herself. By being part of a socially proactive media forum, she understood that it took more than a single voice to be
heard in order to make a difference in the broader media landscape.

Discussion and Implications

The lack of healthy sexuality and anti-sexualization messages explored in
magazines for girls and women has been noted in prior research.[26] Prior content
analyses revealed that about half of all articles in mainstream teen magazines
(e.g., *Seventeen, Teen, YM,* and *Sassy*) pertained to physical beauty, body image,
fashion, sex or romance.[27] Comparable to other teen magazines in volume of
topics that relate to sexuality or romance (fifty-five percent), the current content
analysis of *Teen Voices* revealed that they focus more on promoting *anti-*
sexualization and media activism, rather than a romanticized, hyperfeminine
notion of girlhood. Other teen magazines have been found either to have a contradictory message encouraging sexually provocative appearances and behaviors
yet discouraging sexual activity[28] or to focus on sexual victimization, equating
sex with risk.[29] In contrast, *Teen Voices* promotes sexual health, de-stigmatizing
sexuality, and encouraging healthy relationships (both heterosexual and homo-
sexual). Rather than focusing on the health hazards of sex, *Teen Voices* promotes
the notion of teen agency in their sexual health by encouraging a balanced per-

spective that is appropriate for teen girls who have yet to explore their sexuality; it also discusses safe sexual practices for those who are already sexually active. In contrast to mainstream magazines that focus on maintaining heterosexual relationships and perpetuating gender stereotypes, the articles in *Teen Voices* emphasize more empowering relationship dynamics by focusing on topics such as healthy communication, recognizing the dangers of not talking to one's partner about STDs, how to relate to one's parents regarding sexual decision making, or how to deal with homophobia.

The *Teen Voices* program helped girls engage in pervasive and oppressive stereotypes that challenged girls to reflect on their multiple intersecting identities. Not only does the program increase attention to gender identity by critiquing sexual double standards, it empowers girls to be an authentic version of their female selves that is not based on unrealistic and hypersexualized celebrity images. Through articles ranging from how African American and Latina celebrities are depicted in the media to limited access to affordable sexual healthcare to homophobia, *Teen Voices* also raises awareness about the non-mainstream issues of concern for racial/ethnic minorities, teens from households with limited income or resources, and the LGBT population.

Finally, interviews with teen editors demonstrated their developing understanding of media literacy, in particular sexual media literacy, and how girls' images are manipulated to sell products and for companies to make money. When the teens had opportunities to reflect on media depictions of women, they felt fortunate to have a discussion forum within the program to debate about the hidden meanings behind the media hype, including how these depictions convey a prototype of the typical female as being white, slender, heterosexual, and able to afford many products to attract the opposite sex. The interviews showed that they were motivated to create positive messages for consumption, almost acting as a media-based "superpeer" mentor to an unseen teen readership.[30] Overall, the teen editors strove to portray prosocial and educational messages that downplayed negative stereotypes while at the same time focused on a positive, realistic, not-over-sexualized depiction of girlhood. Through the empowering concept of their collective voice at *Teen Voices*, these adolescents often felt that they made a difference in their own ways to combat the negative, sexually explicit, and derogatory depictions of them in mainstream media.

Future Directions

Though there are studies that examine the impact of media literacy programs on body image,[31] alcohol use,[32] and television violence,[33] to date there have been no studies that have focused on media literacy training's impact on sexualization of girls (APA, 2010). Evaluators of media literacy training programs and other related curricula (e.g., sex education, health, social studies) might assess the effectiveness of raising awareness of the sexualization of women. Studies could explore the impact on both girls who consume sexualized media and boys who are exposed to these images and may treat girls in a manner influenced by the media.

The following are recommended practice and policy avenues to combat the proliferating sexualization of girls in the media through the home, school, community, and the internet: a) encouraging parent–child conversations during TV watching about sexualization and participation in youth programs that target these issues; b) developing school- and community-based media literacy training programs; c) implementing media literacy components within existing health and sex education curricula; d) increasing federal, state, and local funding for girl empowerment groups and educational internet sites that specifically counteract sexualization in the media.

Notes

1. Steven Thomsen, Michelle Weber, & Lora Brown, "The relationship between reading beauty and fashion magazines and the use of pathogenic dieting methods among adolescent females," *Adolescence* 37 (2002): 1–18; Monique Ward, "Wading through the Stereotypes: Positive and Negative Associations between Media Use and Black Adolescents' Conceptions of Self," *Developmental Psychology* 40 (2004): 284–94.

2. Emily Impett, Deborah Schooler, and Deborah L. Tolman, "To Be Seen and Not Heard: Femininity Ideology and Adolescent Girls' Sexual Health," *Archives of Sexual Behavior* 35, no. 2 (2006): 129–42.

3. Monique Ward and Rocio Rivadeneyra, "Contributions of Entertainment Television to Adolescents' Sexual Attitudes and Expectations: The Role of Viewing Amount Versus Viewer Involvement," *Journal of Sex Research* 36 (1999): 237–49; Eileen Zurbriggen and Elizabeth Morgan, "Who Wants to Marry a Millionaire? Reality Dating Television Programs, Attitudes Toward Sex, and Sexual Behaviors," *Sex Roles* 54 (2006): 1–17.

4. American Psychological Association, Task Force on the Sexualization of Girls. 2010. *"Report of the APA Task Force on the Sexualization of Girls."*

5. Laura M. Carpenter, "From Girls into Women: Scripts for Sexuality and Romance in Seventeen Magazine, 1974–1994," *Journal of Sex Research* 35 (1998): 158–68; Meenakshi G. Durham, "Dilemmas of Desire: Representations of Adolescent Sexuality in Two Teen Magazines," *Youth and Society* 29 (1998): 369–89; Ellis Evans et al., "Content Analysis of Contemporary Teen Magazines for Adolescent Females," *Youth and Society* 23 (1991): 99–120; Joe Gow, "Reconsidering Gender Roles on MTV: Depictions in the Most Popular Music Videos of the Early 1990s," *Communication Reports* 9 (1996): 151–61; Nicole Krassas, Joanne Blauwkamp, and Peggy Wesselink, "*Boxing Helena* and Corseting Eunice: Sexual Rhetoric in Cosmopolitan and Playboy Magazines," *Sex Roles* 44 (2001): 751–71; Debra Merskin, "Reviving Lolita? A Media Literacy Examination of Sexual Portrayals of Girls in Fashion Advertising," *American Behavioral Scientist* 48, no. 1 (2004): 119–29; Scott Plous and Dominique Neptune, "Racial and Gender Biases in Magazine Advertising: A Content Analytic Study," *Psychology of Women Quarterly* 21 (1997): 627–44; Monique Ward, "Talking about

Sex: Common Themes about Sexuality in the Prime-Time Television Programs Children and Adolescents View Most," *Journal of Youth & Adolescence* 24 (1995): 595–615.

6.   Dale Kunkel, Kirstie Cope, and Erica Biely, "Sexual Messages on Television: Comparing Findings From Three Studies," *Journal of Sex Research* 36 (1999): 230–36; Monique Ward, "Understanding the Role of Entertainment Media in the Sexual Socialization of American Youth: A Review of Empirical Research," *Developmental Review* 23 (2003): 347–88.

7.   Ward, "Understanding the Role," 2003.

8.   Rita Sommers-Flanagan, John Sommers-Flanagan, and Britta Davis, "What's Happening on Music Television? A Gender Role Content Analysis," *Sex Roles* 28 (1993): 745–53.

9.   Laura S. Stepp, "Today's Real Girls," *The Washington Post*, May 25, 2000.

10.   Thomsen, McCoy, Gustafson, and Williams, 2002.

11.   Klein et al., "Adolescents' Risky Behavior and Mass Media Use," *Pediatrics* 92, no. 1 (1993): 24–31.

12.   Donald F. Roberts, Ulla G. Foehr, and Victoria Rideout, *Generation M: Media in the Lives of 8-18 Year Olds* (Menlo Park, CA: Kaiser Family Foundation, 2005).

13.   Angela McRobbie, *Feminism and Youth Culture* (New York: Routledge, 2000).

14.   Melvin L. DeFleur and Sandra J. Ball-Rokeach, *Theories of Mass Communication* (New York: Longman, 1982).

15.   Barbara L. Frederickson and Tomi-Ann Roberts, "Objectification theory: Toward Understanding Women's Lived Experience and Mental Health Risks," *Psychology of Women Quarterly* 21 (1997): 173–206; Nita M. McKinley and Janet S. Hyde, "The Objectified Body Consciousness Scale," *Psychology of Women Quarterly* 20 (1996): 181–215.

16.   See Robert L. Duran and Diane T. Prusank, "Relational Themes in Men's and Women's Popular Magazine Articles," *Journal of Social and Personal Relationships* 14 (1997): 165–89; Durham, "Dilemmas of Desire," 1998; Evans et al., "Content Anlysis," 1991; Ana Garner, Helen Sterk, and Shawn Adams, "Narrative Analysis of Sexual Etiquette in Teenage Magazines." *Journal of Communication* 48 (1998): 59–78; Ward, "Understanding the Role," 2003.

17.   Jane D. Brown, Kelly L. L'Engle, Carol J. Pardun, Guang Guo, Kristin Kenneavy, and Christine Jackson, "Sexy Media Matter: Exposure to Sexual Content in Music, Movies, Television, and Magazines Predicts Black and White Adolescents' Sexual Behavior," *Pediatrics* 117 (2006): 1018–1027.

18.   See Carla E. Stokes, "Representin' in Cyberspace: Sexual Scripts, Self-Definition, and Hip Hop Culture in African American Adolescent Girls' Home Pages," *Culture, Health, & Sexuality* 9 (2007): 169–84.

19.   Kristin Schilt, "'I'll Resist with Every Inch and Every Breath': Girls and Zine Making as a Form of Resistance," *Youth and Society* 35 (2003): 71–97.

20.   Patricia B. Campbell, Lesli Hoey, and Lesley K. Perlman, "Sticking With My Dreams: Defining and Refining Youth Media in the 21st Century" (2001); Linda Charmaraman, "Media Gangs of Social Resistance: Urban Adolescents Take Back Their Images and Their Streets Through Media Production," *Afterschool Matters* 7 (2008): 27–37; Linda Charmaraman, "The Importance of Audience and Agency to Re-present: Urban Youth Media Producers in the Bay Area," *Sociological Studies of Children and Youth* 13 (2010): 207–33.

21.   Renee Hobbs, "The Seven Great Debates in the Media Literacy Movement" (1996); James W. Potter, "Argument for the Need for a Cognitive Theory of Media Literacy," *American Behavioral Scientist* 48 (2004): 266–72.

22.   Katherine Bayerl, "Mags, Zines, and gURLs: The Exploding World of Girls' Publications."
      Women's Studies Quarterly 28 (2000): 287–92; Sharon Lamb and Lyn M. Brown, *Packaging
      Girlhood: Rescuing our Daughters from Marketers' Schemes* (New York: St. Martin's Press, 2006).

23.   David L. Altheide, "Ethnographic Content Analysis," *Qualitative Sociology* 10, no. 1 (1987):
      65–77.

24.   Other non-sexuality articles were about such topics as celebration of diversity, environmen-
      talism, depression, career aspirations, etc.

25.   All names are pseudonyms to protect privacy.

26.   See Stacey J. Hust, Jane D. Brown, and Kelly L. L'Engle, "Boys will be Boys and Girls
      Better Be Prepared: An Analysis of the Rare Sexual Health Messages in Young Adoles-
      cents' Media," *Mass Communication & Society* 11 (2008): 3–23.

27.   Dawn H. Currie, *Girl Talk: Adolescent Magazines and Their Readers* (Toronto, Canada: Univer-
      sity of Toronto Press, 1999); Deanna Davalos, Ruth Davalos, and Heidi Layton, "Content
      Analysis of Magazine Headlines: Changes Over Three Decades?" *Feminism & Psychology* 17,
      no. 2 (2007): 250–58; Kate Peirce, "A Feminist Theoretical Perspective on the Socialization
      of Girls Through *Seventeen* Magazine," *Sex Roles* 23 (1990): 491–500.

28.   Durham, "Dilemmas of Desire," 1998; Garner et al., "Narrative Analysis," 1998.

29.   Carpenter, "From Girls," 1998.

30.   Jane D. Brown, Carolyn T. Halpern, and Kelly L. L'Engle, "Mass Media as a Sexual Super
      Peer for Early Maturing Girls," *Journal of Adolescent Health* 36 (2005): 420–27.

31.   E.g. Lori M. Irving and Susan R. Berel, "Comparison of Media-Literacy Programs to
      Strengthen College Women's Resistance to Media Images." *Psychology of Women Quarterly* 5
      (2001): 103–12.

32.   E.g. Erika W. Austin, Kristine Austin, and Kay Johnson. "Effects of General and Alcohol-
      Specific Media Literacy Training on Children's Decision Making About Alcohol," *Journal of
      Health Communication* 2 (1997): 17–42.

33.   E.g. Marcel W. Voojis and H.A. Van der Voort, "Learning About Television Violence: The
      Impact of a Critical Viewing Curriculum on Children's Attitudinal Judgments About Crime
      Series," *Journal of Research and Development in Education* 26 (1993): 133–42.

Figures

Figure 14.1. Number of articles which had major and minor topics related to sexuality (n = 78)

Works Cited

Altheide, David L. "Ethnographic Content Analysis." *Qualitative Sociology* 10, no. 1 (1987): 65–77.

American Psychological Association, Task Force on the Sexualization of Girls. "*Report of the APA Task Force on the Sexualization of Girls.*" 2010. http://www.apa.org/pi/women/programs/girls/report-full.pdf

Austin, Erica W., Kristine Austin, and Kay Johnson. "Effects of General and Alcohol-Specific Media Literacy Training on Children's Decision Making About Alcohol." *Journal of Health Communication* 2 (1997): 17–42.

Bayerl, Katherine. "Mags, Zines, and gURLs: The Exploding World of Girls' Publications." *Women's Studies Quarterly* 28 (2000): 287–92.

Brown, Jane D., Carolyn T. Halpern, and Kelly L. L'Engle. "Mass Media as a Sexual Super Peer for Early Maturing Girls." *Journal of Adolescent Health* 36 (2005): 420–27.

Brown, Jane D., Kelly L. L'Engle, Carol J. Pardun, Guang Guo, Kristin Kenneavy, and Christine Jackson. "Sexy Media Matter: Exposure to Sexual Content in Music, Movies, Television, and Magazines Predicts Black and White Adolescents' Sexual Behavior." *Pediatrics* 117 (2006): 1018-27.

Campbell, Patricia. B., Lesli Hoey, and Lesley K. Perlman. "Sticking with my Dreams: Defining and Refining Youth Media in the 21st Century." 2001.http://www.campbell-kibler.com/youth_media.html

Carpenter, Laura M. "From Girls into Women: Scripts for Sexuality and Romance in Seventeen Magazine, 1974–1994." *Journal of Sex Research* 35 (1998): 158–68.

Charmaraman, Linda. "Media Gangs of Social Resistance: Urban Adolescents Take Back Their Images and Their Streets through Media Production." *Afterschool Matters* 7 (2008): 27-37.

———. "The Importance of Audience and Agency to Re-Present: Urban Youth Media Producers in the Bay Area." *Sociological Studies of Children and Youth* 13 (2010): 207–33.

Currie, Dawn H. *Girl Talk: Adolescent Magazines and Their Readers.* Toronto, Canada: University of Toronto Press, 1999.

Davalos, Deana B., Ruth A. Davalos, and Heidi S. Layton. "Content Analysis of Magazine Headlines: Changes Over Three Decades?" *Feminism & Psychology* 17, no. 2 (2007): 250–58.

DeFleur, Melvin L. and Sandra J. Ball-Rokeach. *Theories of Mass Communication.* New York: Longman, 1982.

Duran, Robert L. and Diane T. Prusank. "Relational Themes in Men's and Women's Popular Magazine Articles." *Journal of Social and Personal Relationships* 14 (1997): 165–89.

Durham, Meenakshi G. "Dilemmas of Desire: Representations of Adolescent Sexuality in Two Teen Magazines." *Youth and Society* 29 (1998): 369–89.

Evans, Ellis D., Rutberg, J., Sather, C., and Turner, C. "Content Analysis of Contemporary Teen Magazines for Adolescent Females." *Youth and Society* 23 (1991): 99–120.

Frederickson, Barbara L. and Tomi-Ann Roberts. "Objectification Theory: Toward Understanding Women's Lived Experience and Mental Health Risks." *Psychology of Women Quarterly* 21 (1997): 173–206.

Garner, Ana, Helen M. Sterk, and Shawn Adams. "Narrative Analysis of Sexual Etiquette in Teenage Magazines." *Journal of Communication* 48 (1998): 59–78.

Gow, Joe. "Reconsidering Gender Roles on MTV: Depictions in the Most Popular Music Videos of the Early 1990s." *Communication Reports* 9 (1996): 151–61.

Hobbs, Renee. "The Seven Great Debates in the Media Literacy Movement." 1996.http://www.medialit.org/ReadingRoom/keyarticles/sevengreat.htm

Hust, Stacey J. T., Jane D. Brown, and Kelly L. L'Engle. "Boys Will be Boys and Girls Better be Prepared: An Analysis of the Rare Sexual Health Messages in Young Adolescents' Media." *Mass Communication & Society* 11 (2008): 3–23.

Impett, Emily A., Deborah Schooler, and Deborah L. Tolman. "To be Seen and Not Heard: Femininity Ideology and Adolescent Girls' Sexual Health." *Archives of Sexual Behavior* 35, no. 2 (2006): 129–42.

Irving, Lori M., and Susan R. Berel. "Comparison of Media-Literacy Programs to Strengthen College Women's Resistance to Media Images." *Psychology of Women Quarterly* 5 (2001): 103–12.

Klein, Jonathan D., Jane D. Brown, Carol Dykers, Kim Walsh Childers, Janice Oliveri, and Carol Porter. "Adolescents' Risky Behavior and Mass Media Use." *Pediatrics* 92, no. 1 (1993): 24–31.

Krassas, Nicole R., Joan M. Blauwkamp, and Peggy Wesselink. "*Boxing Helena* and Corseting Eunice: Sexual Rhetoric in *Cosmopolitan* and *Playboy* Magazines." *Sex Roles* 44 (2001): 751–71.

Kunkel, Dale, Kirstie M. Cope, and Erica Biely. "Sexual Messages on Television: Comparing Findings from Three Studies." *Journal of Sex Research* 36 (1999): 230–36.

Lamb, Sharon, and Lyn M. Brown. *Packaging Girlhood: Rescuing our Daughters from Marketers' Schemes.* New York: St. Martin's Press, 2006.

McKinley, Nita M., and Janet S. Hyde. "The Objectified Body Consciousness Scale." *Psychology of Women Quarterly* 20 (1996): 181–215.

McRobbie, Angela. *Feminism and Youth Culture*. New York: Routledge, 2000.

Merskin, Debra. "Reviving Lolita? A Media Literacy Examination of Sexual Portrayals of Girls in Fashion Advertising." *American Behavioral Scientist* 48, no. 1 (2004): 119–29.

Peirce, Kate. "A Feminist Theoretical Perspective on the Socialization of Girls through *Seventeen* Magazine." *Sex Roles* 23 (1990): 491–500.

Plous, Scott and Dominique Neptune. "Racial and Gender Biases in Magazine Advertising: A Content Analytic Study." *Psychology of Women Quarterly* 21 (1997): 627–44.

Potter, W. James. "Argument for the Need for a Cognitive Theory of Media Literacy." *American Behavioral Scientist* 48 (2004): 266-272.

Roberts, Donald F., Ulla G. Foehr, and Victoria Rideout. *Generation M: Media in the Lives of 8–18 Year Olds*. Menlo Park, CA: Kaiser Family Foundation, 2005.

Schilt, Kristen. "'I'll Resist with Every Inch and Every Breath': Girls and Zine Making as a Form of Resistance." *Youth and Society* 35 (2003): 71–97.

Sommers-Flanagan, Rita, John Sommers-Flanagan, and Britta Davis. "What's Happening on Music Television? A Gender Role Content Analysis." *Sex Roles* 28 (1993): 745–53.

Stepp, Laura S. "Today's Real Girls." *The Washington Post*, 4. May 25, 2000.

Stokes, Carla E. "Representin' in Cyberspace: Sexual Scripts, Self-Definition, and Hip Hop Culture in African American Adolescent Girls' Home Pages." *Culture, Health, & Sexuality* 9 (2007): 169–84.

Thomsen, Steven R., Michelle M. Weber, and Lora B. Brown. "The Relationship Between Reading Beauty and Fashion Magazines and the Use of Pathogenic Dieting Methods Among Adolescent Females." *Adolescence* 37 (2002): 1–18.

Voojis, Marcel W., and H.A. Tom. "Learning about Television Violence: The Impact of a Critical Viewing Curriculum on Children's Attitudinal Judgments about Crime Series." *Journal of Research and Development in Education* 26 (1993): 133–42.

Ward, L. Monique. "Talking about Sex: Common Themes about Sexuality in the Prime-Time Television Programs Children and Adolescents View Most." *Journal of Youth & Adolescence* 24 (1995): 595–615.

———. "Understanding the Role of Entertainment Media in the Sexual Socialization of American Youth: A Review of Empirical Research." *Developmental Review* 23 (2003): 347–88.

———. "Wading Through the Stereotypes: Positive and Negative Associations between Media Use and Black Adolescents' Conceptions of Self." *Developmental Psychology* 40 (2004): 284–94.

Ward, L. Monique and Rocio Rivadeneyra. "Contributions of Entertainment Television to Adolescents' Sexual Attitudes and Expectations: The Role of Viewing Amount Versus Viewer Involvement." *Journal of Sex Research* 36 (1999): 237–49.

Zurbriggen, Eileen L. and Elizabeth M. Morgan. "Who Wants to Marry a Millionaire? Reality Dating Television Programs, Attitudes Toward Sex, and Sexual Behaviors." *Sex Roles* 54 (2006): 1–17.

"We're All Straight Here": Using Girls' Groups and Critical Media Literacy to Explore Identity with Middle School Girls

Amy Rutstein-Riley, Jenn Walker, Alice Diamond,
Bonnie Bryant, and Marie LaFlamme[1]

Girlhood, Identity, and Girl Culture, a girls' studies course with an imbedded focus on body image, media literacy, and identity development is researching what happens when twenty college women and twenty-five urban middle school girls engage in weekly girls' groups to examine and discuss girlhood and critical media literacy. Entering our fourth year of the *Girlhood Project,* urban youth come to Lesley University in Cambridge, Massachusetts to participate in a seven-week girls' group as part of a service-learning course, where college students develop, implement, and facilitate girls' groups for middle school girls. Using principles of feminist pedagogy and feminist group process, college students engage with the youth to build relationships that collaboratively examine the meanings and experience of being a girl in a culture where numerous social institutions, including the media, bombard girls with messages about how they should be, act, look, and feel about themselves.

A central part of the *Girlhood Project* is the examination of what happens between the college students and middle school girls, and how issues of identity, body image, relationships and especially sexuality, surface from the girls' group sessions. In this chapter, we explore these important issues that emerged and how identity is negotiated, in the context of the girls' groups. Using data collected from reflections of the forty college student facilitators, as well as from the arts-based projects created by the forty-three middle school girls, such as their own identity magazine covers, body image collages, body maps, and discussion of music videos, we explore how issues of sexuality emerge as a topic of conversation between the college women and girls, how both of these populations attempt to discuss and dissect gender stereotypes in the media (print, video, music, internet), and how these media images contribute to developing identities and visions of self as girls and young women in contemporary Western culture.

Our analysis shows that throughout the various activities utilized during the girls' group sessions, the middle school girls initiated conversation about sex, sexuality, and relationships with the college student facilitators. Even in the first week of the girls' groups, the middle school girls expressed interest in talking about these issues, with one student asking what sexual orientation meant and another middle school girl replying that it didn't matter because, "we're all straight here." We also examine how race, ethnicity, and heteronormativity influence the exchanges and ideas expressed about sexuality and relationships between the young college women and middle school students.

Finally, we will consider the role of girls' groups and critical media literacy as tools for examining, deconstructing, and reconstructing media images as a way to harness girls' strength and resilience in the face of social pressures to conform to gender-based stereotypes consistently communicated by the media. The importance of relationship between college women and middle school girls and the application of feminist group process and feminist pedagogy enhances the meaning made of critical media literacy skill development.

Introduction

Girls and young adult women live and develop in media saturated environments in which they consume a range of diverse forms of media that communicates a hypersexualized and heteronormative gender ideal. Media texts (TV, music, print, internet, advertising) convey to girls and women increasingly narrow and rigid representations of how they should perform and display gender. "…[M]edia portrayals generally provide little information about sexual health and tend to promote sexual stereotypes."[2] The ubiquitous presence of sexualized media messages pose direct implications for girls and young women as they work to construct healthy identities. Girlhood, Identity, and Girl Culture is a curriculum and girls' group created for middle school girls and college students to come together to explore and challenge the ways in which media socially construct girlhood and womanhood in contemporary culture.

Bre, a college student in this course states,

Soon after Meghan mentioned talking about sexual orientation, a voice on the other end (I'm not sure who) said something along the lines of 'well, we're all straight here' to which someone else replied, 'I sure hope so'. During the third exercise when the girls were sharing topics that they wanted to go over in future groups Meghan suggested that we talk about sexual orientation. After we discussed the meaning of sexual orientation a few of the girls made some homophobic remarks. This was surprising to me because I am not used to hearing reactions like that. I didn't know how to respond to the comments in the moment but hopefully in the future we can discuss this topic more with the group.[3]

Bre's comment is a metaphor for other hegemonic assumptions regarding sexuality, gender, race, and class that we interrogate in this project.

Why a Focus on the Media?

I thought a lot about how media was important when I was a kid, but now I think it's just, like, expanded so much, in so many different ways, especially about, like, sexualization of girls and a place for girls in the world. (Dana, 2010)

In our course, Girlhood, Identity & Girl Culture, we explore the role of media as a social institution in shaping girlhood, as well as specific forms of media including print, video, music, and social media. Together, we consider the ways in which consumption of such forms of media influence and contribute to the social production of body image, self-esteem as related to one's body image, social relationships, and a gendered identity.[4] Reviewing the impact of media literacy programs on body image, self-esteem, eating behaviors and weight concerns, social comparison, teasing, and mental health for girl only or gender-mixed groups reveals varied outcomes including increased understandings of media literacy, decreased internalization of the thin ideal, increased feelings of self-acceptance and self-efficacy, and a greater sense of critical awareness of media and its messages regarding gender, sex, and sexuality.[5]

Critiquing the production of print media and music videos makes salient the ways in which images of idealized hegemonic norms of beauty are created and maintained. Viewing Jean Kilbourne's *Killing Us Softly 4* and studying techniques of critical media literacy offers the college students a strategy for deconstructing and understanding the role and impact of media in girls' and women's lives.[6] It makes possible a new way of reading, challenging, and responding to the media. Examining one's own media use and the social structures that contribute to the ways it is used can make visible previously held assumptions about such media. This process of seeing enables a critical lens to be developed and practiced. Assigning the college students with the task of creating a girls' group to explore the intersections of body image, identity, and critical media literacy continues to challenge their own previously held beliefs about the relationship between body image, identity, and the media. Since media and its representations of girls' and women's identities is the central topic organizing the girls' groups, one of the research questions we consider is how group discussions affect the way girls see and make meaning of media, and in turn, themselves.

A similar research question explored by Durham found that the most important sociocultural norm in girls' lives is heterosexuality.[7] Girls use femininity to adapt to the heterosexuality norm, and mass media contributes to their constructions of their femininity and thus, their heterosexuality. In our girls' groups media is used as a tool to deconstruct cultural messages of femininity, the beauty ideal, race/ethnicity, and sexuality. The girls and college students discuss various forms of media, and the explicit and implicit messages in these media through discussion and activities. Though the simple act of creating collages to represent their own beauty ideals, narrowly defined representations of girlhood in the media becomes apparent. Dialogue in-group creates opportunity to challenge these representations, the implicit messages about gender, race, and class, and the meanings the girls make of this media.

Teitelman, Bohinski, and Boente examine the different avenues through which girls develop their sexual identities, finding family, peers, school, and the media to be the most common sources for learning about sex, sexuality, and sexual health.[8] Few middle school girls in our groups express comfort talking with a teacher or parent about sex, and recognize information from their friends and the media is rarely accurate. For a number of our middle school girls, talk of sexuality is silenced in their homes, making our program a safe space for exploring this central developing aspect of the girls' identities. Teitelman et al. suggests that those who work with girls promote a multidimensional view of sexual health, incorporating emotional, physical, and developmental sexual health and sexuality.[9] Egan and Hawkes argue that girls' sexuality should not be overlooked, and when sexualization is taken out of the picture entirely, girls are seen as passive recipients of sexualization, with no autonomy for their own sexuality.[10] Sexuality is a central task of development and an issue frequently raised by the girls in our groups.[11]

The APA Report on the Sexualization of Girls (2010) acknowledges the dearth of research on girls' sexuality despite the cultural current of hypersexualized media targeting young female audiences. What is known about girls is largely derived from research on women.[12] Depending on sociocultural factors, girls' sexual scripts are dictated as virgins, promiscuous, or a Lolita-esque combination of both. The sexuality of girls is marketed and exploited by advertisers and the media.[13] This necessitates creating opportunities for girls to engage with these scripts, to deconstruct them, so they may re-author them.

In the girls' groups, the middle school girls and college students work together in cohesive, productive, and mutually engaged relationships.[14] It can be challenging to negotiate the boundaries of these relationships, and for the college students to define their roles: are they mentors, role models, peers, or teachers? Brown discusses similar challenges to these, theorizing mentoring through the lens of borderlands: places where two or more cultures, races, or socio-economic statuses meet and their differences lessen as intimacy grows.[15] These borderlands can create barriers through ineffective mentoring, or allow girls and mentors to strengthen their bond by seeing each other's unique strengths and challenges. Brown suggests that the most empowering mentoring connections were formed through inclusiveness and the embracement of diversity. While all girls face gender oppression, girls of color face racism and gender oppression. Girls who are of lower socio-economic status have another -ism that they must navigate. An intersectional lens is a central component of our feminist girls' group process.[16]

"Girls are major consumers of media and receive and engage with these messages every day."[17] The effects of dominant representations of femininity, especially those that sexualize and objectify girls and women, are powerful and include body image dissatisfaction, negative self-esteem, eating disorders, and depression.[18] One strategy to challenge these outcomes is media literacy. Feminist media scholars assert the significance of girls not simply consuming and critiquing media but to authoring and producing it as well.[19] In our girls' groups, the college students facilitate activities with the middle school girls where they deconstruct different forms of media, analyze their messages, and reconstruct these messages anew in their own voices. We think it is imperative for girls to create media that represent their lived experiences, rather than the false reality of girls' lives portrayed by the media.

Girlhood, Identity, and Girl Culture

…being able to work with girls just opened my eyes to a lot, to, yeah our differences but our similarities as well. So, I don't feel, you know, as intimidated by it anymore. (Janie, 2010)

Girlhood, Identity, and Girl Culture is an advanced-level sociology/service-learning course, where students are exposed to the discipline of girls' studies while participating in a seven-week service project with middle school girls from Cambridge, Massachusetts. Service-learning is a pedagogical approach that actively engages learners within their communities as a "means to learn about others, as well about how to be deliberate actors working to improve one's community."[20] A feminist approach to service-learning is attuned to diminishing power differences between faculty and student. Instead, the faculty is a facilitator and mentor, partnering with the college students as they research, design, implement, reflect, and revise the seven weeks of the service project. "Learning through engagement," in relationship with the middle school girls, co-constructing an experience with the girls, diminishes power differences between the college students and middle school girls.[21] Feminist pedagogy,[22] feminist group process,[23] individual and group reflective practice,[24] and learning in connection and relationship[25] guide the classroom instruction, the approach to service-learning, and the research arm of this project.

Our community partner, Tutoring Plus of Cambridge, has been an active participant in the evolution of the project as we have refined the course and as we attend to the desires of the middle school girls who participate with the college students in the project. Tutoring Plus is a nonprofit organization providing after school tutoring and academic enrichment to students living in Cambridge Massachusetts, serving students who live in the Area IV neighborhood, which has the lowest income and is the third most densely populated of all of Cambridge's neighborhoods. Area IV is home to the largest percentage of children under eighteen years of age (twenty-three percent vs. thirteen percent on average for the rest of Cambridge), and over half of all Area IV family households are headed by a single parent. Sixty percent of Area IV residents self-identify as minorities (City of Cambridge 2000). Tutoring Plus students come from a variety of racial and ethnic backgrounds: African American, Cape Verdean, Ethiopian, Haitian, Jamaican, Portuguese, Spanish, and Trinidadian.

In Girlhood, Identity, and Girl Culture, we examine the theoretical foundation of girls' studies, and explore what it means to be a girl in contemporary U.S. society. We view girlhood through a feminist, sociocultural, historical, developmental, and intersectional frame. We explore our own lived experiences of girlhood, and interrogate our individual and collective experiences through discussion, writing assignments, reflections, and activities such as mapping girlhood, body maps, collaging, and deconstructing and reconstructing print media. What initially began as a project tightly focused on body image and media literacy, has refocused to explore body image and its related elements of identity development, relationships (friendships, romantic relationships, and relational health), and sexuality, while also maintaining a focus on critical media literacy skill development, self expression, and creating a safe space for all voices to be heard and supported.

To contextualize our understandings of the girls we work with, the community partner and colleagues from the fields of social work and psychology join our discussion to address issues of group process, talk and disclosure, confidentiality, relationship building, and creating a safe space. Our community partner shares demographic data regarding the girls, as we prepare to initiate the girls' groups. It is the expectation that the college students will develop the girls' groups and the weekly content and programming in collaboration with each other and in relationship with the middle school girls. Support from the faculty and team of teaching and research assistants scaffold the experience. In this course college students are empowered to be highly responsive in a reflexive way to the needs and interests of the girls. Each year each girls' group is different, with its own unique personality, agenda, process, approach, and outcomes. However, within the groups and cohorts, there are some central commonalities including a focus on body image, self-esteem, and an examination of those factors, which contribute to the construction of body image, including the media.

The girls' groups run for a total of seven weeks during the course sessions of Girlhood, Identity, and Girl Culture. The middle school girls arrive on campus for each of these weeks for ninety-minute sessions. A typical session begins with the college students welcoming the girls, followed by icebreakers, check-in, and a shared dinner. This time is meaningful in terms of bonding, building relationships, and girl talk, and provides an important part of the group experience in which checking-in, individual and group reflection, and agenda co-construction occurs. After dinner, teams of college students serve as leaders/facilitators for the evening. They guide the agenda, incorporating adjustments suggested by the girls. Activities range from defining girlhood, exploring relationships, critiquing music lyrics and music videos, critiquing TV advertisements, deconstructing print advertising, collaging, creating "I" magazine covers, and body mapping exercises. Each activity is conducted in both large and small group to foster open dialogue, exploration, and to create the opportunity for new insights on the topic of inquiry.

Project Participants

A total of forty college students from 2010 and 2011 consented to have academic work used for analysis. A total of forty-three middle school girls from the Cambridge community also participated. Both parental consent and assents from the students were obtained for participation in the groups as well as the research activities of the project. Demographic data pertaining to the middle school girls is discussed in an earlier section of this chapter. The college student participants in the 2010 cohort are between the ages of eighteen to twenty-four, self-identify as Caucasian, and eighteen of twenty self-identify as heterosexual. Seventeen students in the 2011 cohort are between the ages of eighteen to twenty-four, two between twenty-five and thirty, and one student is fifty; seventeen self-identify as Caucasian, two as Asian, and one as Haitian. A slightly broader range of sexual identities is expressed in the 2011 group, seventeen self-identify as heterosexual, two as bi-sexual, and one as "not identifying with any category."

Data Collection

For the last two years we have collected multiple data points to address the central research question, *What happens when college women and middle school age girls collaborate in girls' groups to examine body image, media literacy, and identity?* Sub research questions explore: (1) the impact of the girls' groups on self-identity; 2) perception of media and its relationship to self-identity and body image; 3) media literacy skill development and body image self concept for middle school girls and college-age women; and 4) role and value of relational engagement among middle school girls and college women on these issues. Reflection data was collected for each of the college students through the use of Critical Incident Questionnaires (CIQs) adapted for this project.[26] The CIQ is a tool which asks individuals to reflect in the moment on an experience, in this case the events of the girls' group in a particular week, in order to gain access to the students' emotional experiences of and to one's own learning.[27] Each college student submits one CIQ following each girls' group session and an additional reflection one week later after having time to "percolate" on the experience of the session and make further, perhaps deeper, connections to their own experiences, to reading and research of the course, and to reflections and memories of their own girlhoods. In addition, a final reflection is submitted at the completion of the girls' group experiences. Focus groups with the middle school girls conducted by the college students, and focus groups with the college students, conducted by faculty, collected data on various aspects of the project. Follow-up interviews with college students have been completed for the 2010 cohort and are in progress with the 2011 cohort. Finally, each of the seven weeks of the girls' groups have been video- and audio-recorded and fully transcribed.

Data Analysis

For the study of this paper the authors have reviewed seven weeks of CIQs from the 2010 and 2011 cohort of college students, n = 43 college students in total. In addition, weekly reflection papers and final reflection papers from these students have been included. Follow-up interviews with students from the 2010 cohort (n = 10) provide opportunity for further exploration of experience from the perspectives of the college students. Artifacts relevant to the themes emerging from the data have been pulled and reviewed, and discussions among members of the research team provide context for understanding themes in the data.

After multiple readings of the CIQs by members of the research team, initial codes were created, refined, revised, expanded, and contracted through the constant comparative method.[28] Themes reflecting the experiences and meanings of the participants were built, and then used for the readings of reflection papers. Interviews with a sub-set of the college students also deepened understanding of themes and concepts constructed. The data analysis process was fluid and iterative, moving back and forth across the CIQs, interview data, and reflections. The development of codes, categories, and themes is derived from the CIQ data and further elaborated upon by interview and reflection data. During the process of data analysis research memos were written and analysis discussed by members of the research team.

Findings

Using the interviews and secondary data analysis, we explore three thematic areas that emerged from the data: 1) how participants addressed emerging discussions regarding sex and sexuality, 2) how race and sexuality developed from conversations intended to explore body image and 3) how "cultural difference" was understood and shape differences of opinion on topics such as domestic violence.

"To be honest, I'm not sure it was our place to do so anyways:" Talking about Sex and Sexuality in the Girls' Groups

The groups often started with all participants sharing a meal. During this time, there was casual conversation that ranged from discussions about food, what the girls did in school that day, and talking about boys. One student reported that, while eating in the college cafeteria with other college students one of the girls,

> made me laugh so hard, especially when she was waving at the [college] boys and getting them to wave back.

The girls seemed interested in talking with the college students about relationships and boys but didn't necessarily say so forthrightly.

> One girl had said boys and a few others were giggling and laughing. I stood up and said "who wants to talk about boys during your time here?" They all want to talk about it but no one wanted to stand up and say it. (Kelly, 2011)

In both cohorts, the college students intended to discuss relationships, including romantic relationships with the girls. College students first reported interest in talking about boys from the middle school girls when they were soliciting topics for the groups,

> When the girl's were asked what they wanted to talk about over the next few weeks the overwhelming topic was "girls stuff." When we asked what this meant to them, they couldn't quite explain but boys was certainly a subcategory of this girls' stuff. I feel that

dissecting this and what it means to be a girl through their eyes will be extremely important over the next few weeks. (Liza, 2011)

Another student noted that when the college students asked the middle school girls what they wanted to discuss that, "They ended up coming up with some really great topics. Some were vague such as 'girl issues' and some were right to the point like 'boys.' I was really glad that one girl said that she wanted to talk about sexual orientation." While there may have been giggling and shyness, the middle school girls clearly indicated an interest in talking about boys, relationships and sexuality.

The college students planned to discuss these issues throughout the girls' groups. To initiate conversation with the girls, the college students' different activities, such as body mapping, collaging and analyzing music videos were utilized. Watching music videos was particularly effective in encouraging conversation about gender and sexuality.

> Today we had a great discussion after watching some music videos of songs the girls said they liked. They all objectified women. The girls opened up about what boys say in school, what they think about the girls in the video, how boys see them, and the impressions the videos make on them. One girl, Meghan, was simply poetic. She talked in depth about the objectification of women, how boys see those girls in the music videos, therefore that's what the boys think they want and then that's how our girls feel they have to dress and be in order to please them. Other girls talked about how some girls at school say mean things to them and spread rumors about them. They spoke about how they feel self-conscious about their bodies and what they should do if a boy only cares about how they look. (Janie, 2011)

Some of the videos that were shown include "Beautiful" by Christina Aguilera, "Perfect" by Pink, "Unpretty" by TLC, and "Pon de Floor" by Major Lazer. With the exception of Christina Aguilera's video, which featured one gay couple, all of the videos portray heterosexual relationships. Even though sexual orientation was something that the college women planned on discussing, heteronormative and homophobic commentary, in response to conversation and activity, dominated much of the conversations in both cohorts.

In the 2010 cohort, one student in particular seemed to initiate conversation about sexual orientation. One college student mentioned that she "was excited when Meghan (a middle school girl) mentioned that she was curious about talking about sexual orientation. She went on to ask, why is a gay guy called 'fruity'?" Other students also reflected on this student bringing up questions about sexual orientation and the reaction from others in the girls' group. Another student reported,

> Many of the girls did not even know what sexual orientation meant. But as soon as we gave it a definition they all had something to say. The clique of girls from the bigger

school started making comments such as "I only go straight," or "I sure hope everyone here is straight" and giggled while making other snide remarks. I felt that Meghan had a lot of courage to put herself out in the open like that and request recognition and acceptance from her peers on this topic. I would imagine that she would probably be ridiculed at school on a regular basis simply for even considering bringing up this topic. (Emma, 2010)

In the second cohort, a similar instance occurred, where a girl provoked discussion about sexual orientation by sharing that her brother was gay. A college student reported that, "one of the girls told that her brother was gay and her friend did not even know it. Her friend thought it was a joke, but it wasn't but [the friend] apologized and felt bad." This college student went on to say that "the most confusing part is how to deal with [this particular] situation." Talking about sex and sexuality was confusing for the college students as they tried to walk a fine line between being responsive to the questions and needs of the girls and respectful of the community partner's wishes to not provide explicit sexual education for the girls. In the 2011 cohort, one college student shared,

> At one point, it was just Carla, Regina (a middle school girl) and I at the table. Regina said something along the lines of, "I am going to ask you guys a personal question." Then proceeded to ask Carla and I if we were still virgins. Although people had warned us this question might come up I didn't think it actually would. I couldn't really respond because I got super nervous and just kept looking to Carla to save us. Regina immediately read our reactions and said never mind, you don't have to answer.

This college student went on to say that she was, "disappointed that [she] was not prepared for the question and couldn't come up with an appropriate response in the midst of [her] anxiety." Another college student reported that the middle school girls asked the college women if they were "good girls" when they were in school and the student reported not knowing how to respond since she "was absolutely not a good kid in school" but she felt "really uncomfortable with lying to the girls in any capacity."

In a follow-up interview, a college student from the 2010 cohort shared an example of the girls' homophobic remarks that came up while watching a music video:

> Interviewee: We were talking, um, about images and music videos and one of the music videos we brought up was the Christina Aguilera "Beautiful" video and in it there's a transgender man who is, uh, is dressing in, you know, you know, feminine, quote-unquote feminine clothing, and then I think there's this scene where two gay men are kissing? And um their reactions to that were sort of like "Ew! That's gross! Ew!" And then, um, so we didn't address it immediately, cause we didn't know how to, but then in our next session with the girls we sort of sat them down and said "Hey! Why did you say 'ew'? Why was that gross?" And they were like, "Well, boys don't kiss."

When the college student was asked how the group felt about hearing the girl's response, she stated,

> We talked briefly after the session, with the (middle school) girls, and we were like, "Wow, we did not expect that response. And what should we do going forward, and…" Because we did not know how to address it in the moment and we wanted to take some time to think about it, so we talked about it and then we sort of said, "Alright, well, we're having a sit down with them in the next week anyways, so why don't we just put it out there and see why they felt that way and then just talk about it."

There is a clear struggle for the college students who facilitated the girls' groups; while remaining open to the needs and questions of the middle schools girls with whom they are working, they must balance the desire of the community partner to not engage in formal sex education, learn to articulate the limits of their willingness to disclose information to the girls, and help the girls develop a critical perspective without telling them how they should feel about issues related to sex and sexuality as they emerge. As the following sections show, this struggle permeated many other issues that arose in the girls' groups.

"I didn't know if we should say something or just ignore it": Body Talk as Bonding, Difference, and Sexuality

Instances where bodies and body image are discussed between the participants reveal notable tensions. While discussions were intended to provoke conversations about body image, these conversations also highlighted the racial differences between the college students and middle school girls and also allowed the middle school girls to comment on each other's bodies in a sexual way. In one particular class, the college students showed a video of the Tyra Banks show where black women talk about their hair. According to one student, "The clip was about African American hair and how women are insecure about it." This prompted a discussion between the college women and middle school girls about hair,

> A discussion that surfaced in today's group was the discussion of weave versus extensions. It was interesting to see how the girls reacted to this and how most of them viewed weave as a black girl thing and extensions as a white girl thing. One of the girls tried to argue that essentially they were the same that culturally the names were just different. However, most of the girls definitely viewed hair for black girls and white girls to be different. (Shauna, 2011)

> The younger girls were saying that they use hair weaves, which are the same as hair extensions. It was brought up that although they are the same thing, women of color are more apt to call them hair weaves while Caucasians, like myself, usually use the term hair extensions. Some girls were able to identify that the difference was not in product, but a difference in cultural terms and preferences. (Nicole, 2011)

One college student seemed dissatisfied with their conversation noting that her question about "drawing a line between weaves and extensions" was not answered and that "kind of bugged [her]" but another college student shared that she felt most engaged because "[her] mother judged her because [she] had a lot of body hair" and reported that "the (middle school) girls seemed very interested in the experience."

The body mapping activity, where the college students traced the outline of a middle school girls' body also provoked further discussion about the body, particularly in a sexualized way. A student reported:

> During the body map there came a point to trace between the legs. I was able to sense that the girl being traced did not want to widen her legs to create a space in between. Unfortunately, an older girl didn't read the body language in time and provoked her to move her legs apart in order to trace more thoroughly. This gave one of the other young girls the opportunity to make a vulgar comment like "you always have your legs open." (Wyn, 2010)

Another student shared that, "[W]hen Kit was being traced ... one of the other girls said she should "bend over" alluding to a sexual position. It was awkward not only because it was inappropriate but also because I don't think any of us knew if we should say something or just ignore it." These moments were clearly challenges for the college students to navigate and it appears that they didn't anticipate these exercises designed to initiate conversation on body and body image would also provoke comments regarding sexual activity.

"They are taught to fight back no matter what...": Negotiating Race, Class, and Culture in Discussions on Sexuality and Relationships

A particularly impactful moment for many college students came when the college students showed a clip of an interview with Rihanna, a singer involved in a high profile domestic abuse incident with her then-boyfriend, singer Chris Brown. The college students wanted to talk about relationship violence and decided to show the girls an interview where Rihanna "breaks her silence" about the event with *Good Morning America* host, Dianne Sawyer. Overwhelmingly the college students reported that the girls were critical of Rihanna, suggesting that she deserved or provoked an attack from Brown and that violence between men and women in romantic relationships was to be expected.

After watching the clip of the interview that Rihanna did where she talked about the abuse that occurred between her and Chris, we were able to have a really intense discussion about abuse and what it means to be abused...[It] was shocking to hear a lot of what the girls thought was just normal in regards to being hit by a man... (Molly, 2011)

Other college students reported,

For the first time in the girls group I was really surprised at the responses the younger (middle school) girls were stating. Some of the girls had mothers who had been in abusive relationships and were taught to hit back. A lot of the girls shared similar opinions about abuse and how the abuser is at fault. When we discussed the Rihanna video, in which she talked less about her side of the story and more about dating abuse awareness the girls seemingly cared more about their opinions stating who's side they were on. (Lianna, 2011)

The (middle school) girls were adamant that Rihanna deserved what she got and that Chris Brown was a victim as well because the media wanted to make him look bad. It was interesting because when we brought up the topic of domestic violence and gave the girls scenarios if their friends had an abusive boyfriend or family member, their ideas on the subject changed. They said that it would NOT be OK. We pointed out the difference to the girls and while some maintained their position that it's OK to hit in some situations some of the girls…started to take the position that it is never OK for anyone to hit, which was encouraging. (Julie, 2011)

The college students were surprised that the middle school girls shared these reactions and they struggled both to respond in a way that felt appropriate and to understand the context of their views. One student shared that the conflict between the middle school students and college students was difficult to manage and required the facilitation assistance of a teaching assistant,

I thought it was really helpful when Deb made a comment during our big discussion with the (middle school) girls. The conversation was about physical abuse being acceptable or unacceptable. A lot of the girls felt that it was acceptable, and the majority of the college students felt that it was unacceptable. A college student made a statement, "No kind of abuse, whether its physical, verbal, or emotional is acceptable." This made the girls a little standoffish and Deb sensed that and made a comment to the group, "So there seems to be some sort of a disagreement between some people. Some say that it was partly Rihanna's fault…why do you say that?" She redirected the conversation so it was less "WE ARE TELLING YOU THIS IS RIGHT" and instead asked the girls that believed it was Rihanna's fault to explain why they felt that way. (Ana, 2011)

Another college student indicated a struggle to express her view that abuse and violence are never okay while respecting the middle school girls' rights to have their own opinions by writing,

At first I was worried about these (middle school) girls and their future romantic relationships and I so desperately wanted to change their opinions on the matter but then I realized their opinion was equally important and I shouldn't try and change their feelings if it really is that important to them, but at least we got a good discussion and had them thinking about alternatives. (Bobbie, 2011)

The way in which the college students explained the reaction of the middle school girls was, by and large, attributed to a "cultural difference" between the white college students and the racially diverse middle school girls. One student wrote,

> It was also brought to our attention that some of the (middle school) girls' ideas about this is very cultural. In their culture, they are taught to fight back no matter what and to defend themselves physically, this greatly differs from the ideas of most of the college age girls ideals and opinions on the subject.

Another student echoed those sentiments saying,

> What surprised me the most was the culturalistic [sic] differences…In terms of abuse I was never taught to hit back or stay in an abusive relationship. I was also saddened but not surprised that many (middle school) girls blamed the "abused" in terms of justifying abuse due to something he/she must have said or done to deserve it.

One student blamed the media for the middle school girls' reactions which she felt was more heavily in favor of Chris Brown,

> After seeing articles and websites written about the Rihanna/Chris Brown incident and the way the girls responded to it, we see how much the media affects us. I think that if there was more information in Rihanna's favor on the web, we may have seen a big difference in how the girls reacted. (Liza, 2011)

Discussion

Girlhood, Identity, and Girl Culture is both an experiential and experimental course. The experiences of the college students and middle school girls suggest that girls' groups that explore the intersections of media, body image, and identity have the potential to make possible discussion of a wide range of issues relevant to girls and young women. Using feminist group process and diverse group activities to examine the role of media in pre- and adolescent girls' lives provides a "hook" for girl-to-girl discussion of a variety of important issues from basic questions about sex and sexualities, sexual orientation, sexual behavior and relationships, to relationship violence. Discussion about the intersections of sex and gender with race and ethnicity were also possible through the deconstruction of media texts. Pairing media literacy activities such as media collaging, creating "I" magazine covers, analyzing favorite lyrics, and watching music videos with discussion about the ways in which girls and women of diverse racial and ethnic backgrounds are presented, made visible stereotypical representations which could then be unpacked and explored through a feminist and intersectional lens. The act of deconstructing sexualized and racialized representation of the beauty ideal provided the middle school girls and college students with tools and language for thinking about and resisting gender, racial, ethnic, and sexual stereotypes in the media.

Our data suggests that sex and sexuality/ies is a complicated topic for the college women and middle school girls to discuss. Poignant moments of middle school girls posing questions and comments to the college students reveal the tensions and paradox in these discussions. Why do the college students who seek to be authentic and fully present with the girls hold back and silence themselves in these important exchanges? Perhaps a structural tension in the curriculum design in part creates a barrier for the college women. Our community partner is tentative about the boundaries of what we can/cannot discuss with the middle school girls about sex and sexuality/ies. Parental permission drives girls' participation in the groups, and our community partner must accommodate their preferences. Collaboratively we must be more proactive and share with community members the important benefits of a girls' group that authentically addresses the interests and needs of the girls we serve. This question is in part an unintended consequence of service-learning and this course in particular. In addition, the college students are in process of forming their own identities as emerging adult women, actively doing their own gender, sexuality/ies, and racial identity work. While some college students may be confident in their beliefs and perspectives, others are very much in active formation, and perhaps less able to voice and assert confident responses to the middle school girls' questions and probes.

Creating activities to explore how girls and women are represented in the media opens a gate to the exploration of sex and sexuality/ies. Empowering the college students to delve deeply into topics interconnected with media literacy, namely sexuality, is essential for the success of the girls' groups. Deepening course content to support the college students in how to talk authentically with middle school girls about sex and sexuality/ies may lessen the moments of not knowing and anxiety experienced by the college students. Examination of the media is growth fostering for the middle school girls and for the college students alike.

The middle school girls ask the college students personal questions about their sex lives and some of the college students feel uncomfortable answering. Some of the middle school girls are sexually active, and want to discuss their questions about sex. Some of the girls have questions about sexual orientation, and they are sometimes dismissed by other girls in the group through heteronormative and homophobic comments. Creating a girls' group relational space that invites and encourages girls to co-construct with the college students an experience that ulitmaltey allows them to explore their identities, developing sexualities, and feelings about themselves as girls and women is a lofty goal. It requires establishment of rapport, a sense of belonging and safety to voice their comments and questions. This goal is complicated by the boundaries and borderlands the girls and college students must negotiate together in the girls' groups.[29]

The college students are primarily white women and the middle school girls primarily girls of color. Class, language, and differences in ethnic and religious background make these borderlands vibrant and tension-filled. Negotiating the boundaries of race/ethnicity, class, and gender for some of the college students is challenging and an entirely new experience; critical discussions about the media and what it provokes makes perceived and real differences and similarities visible. Readings of the data reveal the significant opportunities we have for crossing borders with the middle school girls, and paying deep attention to multiple aspects of identity that are present in the girls' group experiences. The college students actively grappled with the stereotypes about race, ethnicity, social class, and gender in different ways. Some struggled to challenge the sterereotypes while others were able to do so. This is most obvious when the middle school girls collectively assumed heteronormativity, and the college students were surprised and challenged by that, first responding in the moment and reporting feeling ill at ease at how they navigated this topic. However, through reflection and active discussion in the girls' groups they were able to subsequently open up discussion about the meaning of heteronormativity in their lives. By creating moments to examine the media's representations of girls and women, talking about our bodies and body images, we can create spaces to share our thoughts, beliefs, and perhaps the questions and comments about our identities that we might otherwise be afraid to share. Our girls' groups are creating moments of opportunity to foster girls' resiliencies through relationships that empower girls and women.

Notes

1. Acknowledgement: Jennifer O'Neil, M.S.W., for technical and editorial support.
2. Pinkleton et al., "Effects of a Peer-Led Media Literacy Curriculum on Adolescents' Knowledge and Attitudes Toward Sexual Behavior and Media Portrayals of Sex," *Health Communication* 23, no. 5 (2008): 462–72, 463.
3. All interview excerpts and reflection statements presented were gathered from student-research participants with permission. Names used are pseudonyms.
4. Dina L. Borzekowski and Angela M. Bayer, "Body Image and Media Use Among Adolescents," *Adolescent Medicine Clinics* 16, no. 2 (2005): 289–313; Linda Duits, "The Importance of Popular Media in Everyday Girl Culture," *European Journal of Communication* 25, no. 3 (2010): 243-257; Michael P. Levine, "Mass Media and Body Image: A Brief Review of the Research," *Healthy Weight Journal* 14, no. 6 (2000): 84–5; Charlotte N. Markey, "Invited Commentary: Why Body Image Is Important to Adolescent Development," *Journal of Youth and Adolescence* 39, no. 12 (2010): 1387–91; Monique L. Ward and Kristin Harrison, "The Impact of Media Use on Girls' Beliefs About Gender Roles, Their Bodies, and Sexual Relationships: A Research Synthesis," in *Featuring Females: Feminist Analyses of Media*, eds. Ellen Cole and Jessica H. Daniel (Washington, DC: American Psychological Association, 2005).

5.   Lori Irving and Susan Berel, "Comparison of Media Literacy Programs to Strengthen College Women's Resistance to Media Images," *Psychology of Women Quarterly* 25 (2001): 103–11; Pinkleton et al., "Effects," 2008; Niva Piran, Michael P. Levine, and Lori Irving, "Go GIRLS! Media Literacy, Activism, and Advocacy Project," *Healthy Weight Journal* 14, no. 6 (2000): 89–90.

6.   *Killing Us Softly 4: Advertising's Image of Women*, produced by Jean Kilbourne (2010; Northampton: Media Education Foundation), DVD.

7.   Meenashki Durham, "Girls, Media, and the Negotiation of Sexuality: A Study of Race, Class, and Gender in Adolescent Peer Groups," *Journalism and Mass Communication Quarterly* 76, no. 2 (1999): 193–216.

8.   Anne M. Teitelman, Julia M. Bohinski, and Alyssa Boente, "The Social Context of Sexual Health and Sexual Risk of Urban Adolescent Girls in the United States," *Issues in Mental Health Nursing* 30, no. 7 (2009): 460–69.

9.   Ibid.

10. Danielle R. Egan and Gail L. Hawkes, "Endangered Girls and Incendiary Objects: Unpacking the Discourse on Sexualization," *Sexuality and Culture* 12, no. 29 (2008): 291–311.

11. American Psychological Association, Task Force on the Sexualization of Girls, *Report of the APA Task Force on the Sexualization of Girls*, 2010.

12. Ibid., 3.

13. Sharon Lamb and Lynn Mikel Brown, *Packaging Girlhood. Rescuing Our Daughters From Marketers' Schemes* (New York: St. Martin's Press, 2006); Diane Levin and Jean Kilbourne, *So Sexy So Soon: The New Sexualized Childhood And What Parents Can Do To Protect Their Kids* (New York: Ballantine Books, 2008).

14. Jill Denner, Beth Meyer, and Steven Bean, "Young Women's Leadership Alliances: Youth-Adult Partnerships in an All-Female After School Program," *Journal of Community Psychology* 33, no. 1 (2005): 87–100; Nicolina Fedele and Elizabeth Harrington, "Women's Groups: How Connections Heal," *Jean Baker Miller Training Institute Work In Progress* 47 (1990): 1–12; Carolyn K. West, "The Map Of Relational-Cultural Theory," *Women & Therapy* 28, no. 3/4 (2005): 93–110.

15. Ruth N. Brown, "Mentoring on the Borderlands: Creating Empowering Connections Between Adolescent Girls and Young Women Volunteers," *Human Architecture: Journal of the Sociology of Self-Knowledge* 4, no. 3 (2006): 4105–121.

16. Patricia Hill Collins, *Black Feminist Theory: Knowledge, Consciousness, and the Politics of Empowerment* (Boston: Unwin Hyman, 1990); Crenshaw et al., *Critical Race Theory: The Key Writings That Formed The Movement* (New York: New Press, 1996); Stephanie A. Shields, "Gender: An Intersectionality Perspective," *Sex Roles* 59, no. 5/6 (2008): 301–11; Lynn Weber, *Understanding Race, Class, Gender, And Sexuality: A Conceptual Framework* (New York: Oxford University Press, 2010).

17. ASA Task Force, *Report*, 4.

18. Ibid., 23–4.

19. Rebecca R. Bullen, "The Power and Impact of Gender-Specific Media Literacy." *Youth Media Reporter* 3 (2009): 149–52; Mary C. Kearney, *Girls Make Media* (New York: Routledge, 2006); Sharon Mazzarella, ed., *Girl Wide Web 2.0. Revisiting Girls, the Internet, and the Negotiation of Identity* (New York: Peter Lang, 2010).

20. Becky Ropers-Huilman and Betsy Palmer, "Feminist And Civic Education: Bridging Parallel Approaches To Teaching And Learning," in *Most College Students are Women. Implications for Teaching, Learning, and Policy*, eds. Jeanne Allen, Susan Dean and Diane Bracken (Sterling: Stylus, 2008), 17.
21. Ibid., 16.
22. Belenky et al., *Women's Ways of Knowing: The Development of Self, Voice, and Mind* (New York: Basic Books, 1997); Francis A. Maher and Mary K. Tetreault, *The Feminist Classroom* (New York, Basic Books, 1994).
23. Jean S. Bolen, *Millionth Circle; How to Change Ourselves in the World. Essential Guides to Women's Circles* (York, ME: Conari Press, 2003); Fedele and Harrington, "Women's Groups," 1990.
24. David Boud, "Using Journal Writing to Enhance Reflective Practice," *New Directions in Adult and Continuing Education* 90, no. 1 (2001): 9–17; Stephen Brookfield, "Experiential Pedagogy: Grounding Teaching in Students' Learning," *The Journal of Experiential Education* 19, no. 2 (1996): 62–8.
25. Allen, Dean, and Bracken, "Women Learners," 2008; Comstock et al., "Relational-Cultural Theory: A Framework For Bridging Relational, Multicultural, And Social Justice Competencies," *Journal of Counseling & Development* 86, no. 3 (2008): 279–87; West, "The Map," 2005.
26. Brookfield, "Experiential Pedagogy," 1996.
27. Ibid.
28. Julie Corbin and Anselm Strauss, *Basics of Qualitative Research* (Los Angeles: Sage Publications, 2008).
29. Brown, "Mentoring," 2006.

Works Cited

Allen, Jeanne K., Susan Dean, and Diane Bracken. "Women Learners On Campus." In *Most College Students Are Women. Implications For Teaching, Learning, And Policy*, eds. Jeanne Allen, Susan Dean, and Diane Bracken, 1–10. Sterling: Stylus, 2008.
American Psychological Association, Task Force on the Sexualization of Girls. *Report of the APA Task Force on the Sexualization of Girls.* 2010. http://www.apa.org/pi/ women/programs/ girls/report-full.pdf
Belenky, Mary F., Blythe Clinchy, Nancy Goldberger, and Jill Tarule. *Women's Ways of Knowing: The Development of Self, Voice, and Mind.* 10th Anniversary Edition. New York: Basic Books, 1997. [1986]
Bolen, Jean S. *Millionth Circle; How to Change Ourselves in the World. Essential Guides to Women's Circles.* York, ME: Conari Press, 2003.
Borzekowski, Dina L. and Angela M. Bayer. "Body Image and Media Use Among Adolescents." *Adolescent Medicine Clinics* 16, no. 2 (2005): 289–313.
Boud, David. "Using Journal Writing to Enhance Reflective Practice." *New Directions in Adult and Continuing Education* 90, no. 1 (2001): 9–17.
Brookfield, Stephen. "Experiential Pedagogy: Grounding Teaching in Students' Learning." *The Journal of Experiential Education* 19, no. 2 (1996): 62–8.

Brown, Ruth N. "Mentoring on the Borderlands: Creating Empowering Connections Between Adolescent Girls and Young Women Volunteers." *Human Architecture: Journal of the Sociology of Self-Knowledge* 4, no. 3 (2006): 4105–4121.

Bullen, Rebecca R. "The Power and Impact of Gender-Specific Media Literacy." *Youth Media Reporter* 3 (2009): 149-152.

City of Cambridge, MA Census 2000 Demographic Atlas. http://gis.cambridgema.gov/census 2000/index.html

Collins, Patricia H. *Black Feminist Theory: Knowledge, Consciousness, and the Politics of Empowerment.* Boston: Unwin Hyman, 1990.

Comstock, Dana L., Tonya R. Hammer, Julie Strentzsch, Kristi Cannon, Jacqueline Parsons, and Gustavo Salazar. "Relational-Cultural Theory: A Framework For Bridging Relational, Multicultural, And Social Justice Competencies." *Journal of Counseling & Development* 86, no. 3 (2008): 279–87.

Corbin, Julie and Anselm Strauss. *Basics of Qualitative Research.* 3rd Ed. Los Angeles: Sage Publications, 2008.

Crenshaw, Kimberle, Neil Gotanda, Gary Peller, and Kendall Thomas. *Critical Race Theory: The Key Writings That Formed The Movement.* New York: New Press, 1995.

Denner, Jill, Beth Meyer, and Steven Bean. "Young Women's Leadership Alliances: Youth–Adult Partnerships in an All-Female After School Program." *Journal of Community Psychology* 33, no. 1 (2005): 87–100.

Duits, Linda. "The Importance of Popular Media in Everyday Girl Culture." *European Journal of Communication* 25, no. 3 (2010): 243–57.

Durham, Meenakshi. "Girls, Media, and the Negotiation of Sexuality: A Study of Race, Class, and Gender in Adolescent Peer Groups." *Journalism and Mass Communication Quarterly* 76, no. 2 (1999): 193–216.

Egan, R. Danielle and Gail L. Hawkes. "Endangered Girls and Incendiary Objects: Unpacking the Discourse on Sexualization." *Sexuality and Culture* 12, no. 29 (2008): 291-311.

Fedele, Nicolina M. and Elizabeth A Harrington. "Women's Groups: How Connections Heal." *Jean Baker Miller Training Institute Work In Progress* 47 (1990): 1–12.

Irving, Lori M. and Susan Berel. "Comparison of Media Literacy Programs to Strengthen College Women's Resistance to Media Images." *Psychology of Women Quarterly* 25 (2001): 103–11.

Kearney, Mary C. *Girls Make Media.* New York: Routledge, 2006.

Killing Us Softly 4: Advertising's Image of Women. Produced by Jean Kilbourne. 2010. Northampton: Media Education Foundation. DVD.

Lamb, Sharon and Lynn Mikel Brown. *Packaging Girlhood. Rescuing Our Daughters From Marketers' Schemes.* New York: St. Martin's Press, 2006.

LeCroy, Craig. "Evaluation Of An Empowerment Program For Early Adolescent Girls." *Adolescence* 39, no. 155 (2004): 427–41.

Levin, Diane and Jean Kilbourne. *So Sexy So Soon: The New Sexualized Childhood And What Parents Can Do To Protect Their Kids.* New York: Ballantine Books, 2008.

Levine, Michael P. "Mass Media and Body Image: A Brief Review of the Research." *Healthy Weight Journal* 14, no. 6 (2000): 84–5.

Maher, Francis A. and Mary K. Tetreault. *The Feminist Classroom.* New York, Basic Books, 1994.

Markey, Charlotte N. "Invited Commentary: Why Body Image Is Important to Adolescent Development." *Journal of Youth and Adolescence* 39, no. 12 (2010): 1387–91.

Mazzarella, Sharon, ed. *Girl Wide Web 2.0. Revisiting Girls, the Internet, and the Negotiation of Identity.* New York: Peter Lang, 2010.

Novek, Eleanor. "Service-Learning Is a Feminist Issue: Transforming Communication Pedagogy." *Women Studies in Communication* 22, no. 2 (2003): 230–40.

Pinkleton, Bruce E., Erica W. Austin, Marilyn Cohen, Yi-Chun Y. Chen, and Erin Fitzgerald. "Effects of a Peer-Led Media Literacy Curriculum on Adolescents' Knowledge and Attitudes Toward Sexual Behavior and Media Portrayals of Sex." *Health Communication* 23, no. 5 (2008): 462–72.

Piran, Niva, Michael P. Levine, and Lori M. Irving. "Go GIRLS! Media Literacy, Activism, and Advocacy Project." *Healthy Weight Journal* 14, no. 6 (2000): 89–90.

Ropers-Huilman, Becky and Betsy Palmer. "Feminist And Civic Education: Bridging Parallel Approaches To Teaching And Learning." In *Most College Students are Women. Implications for Teaching, Learning, and Policy*, eds. Jeanne Allen, Susan Dean, and Diane Bracken, 11–28. Sterling: Stylus, 2008.

Shields, Stephanie A. "Gender: An Intersectionality Perspective." *Sex Roles* 59, no. 5/6 (2008): 301–11.

Teitelman, Anne M., Julia M. Bohinski, and Alyssa Boente. "The Social Context of Sexual Health and Sexual Risk of Urban Adolescent Girls in the United States." *Issues in Mental Health Nursing* 30, no. 7 (2009): 460–69.

Ward, Monique L. and Kristen Harrison. "The Impact of Media Use on Girls' Beliefs About Gender Roles, Their Bodies, and Sexual Relationships: A Research Synthesis." In *Featuring Females: Feminist Analyses of Media*, eds. Ellen Cole and Jessica H. Daniel, 3–23. Washington, DC: American Psychological Association, 2005.

Weber, Lynn. *Understanding Race, Class, Gender, and Sexuality: A Conceptual Framework.* New York: Oxford University Press, 2010.

West, Carolyn K. "The Map Of Relational-Cultural Theory." *Women & Therapy* 28, no. 3/4 (2005): 93–110.

Contributors

Jennifer Apple earned her master's degree in Women's Studies from The Ohio State University in 2009. Her research focused on how sexuality is constructed, enacted, and represented. She is currently a corps member for Teach for America, teaching secondary English.

Christin P. Bowman is a doctoral student in Social-Personality Psychology at the Graduate Center, CUNY. She is broadly interested in the ways hegemonic and patriarchal structures limit how women and girls live their lives and make meaning of their experiences. She is proud to be an active member of the ASAP Initiative (Analyzing Sexuality for Action and Policy). She writes the research blog for the SPARK website.

Lyn Mikel Brown, Ed.D., is Professor of Education at Colby College and co-creator of the nonprofit Hardy Girls Healthy Women (www.hghw.org), where she works with communities to support girls' healthy development and with girls to challenge media stereotypes online at Powered By Girl (www.poweredbygirl.org). She is the author of five books, including *Meeting at the Crossroads: Women's Psychology and Girls' Development* (with Carol Gilligan) and *Packaging Girlhood: Rescuing Our Daughters From Marketer's Schemes* (with Sharon Lamb). Dr. Brown is a co-founder (with Deborah Tolman) of the Sexualization Protest Action Resistance Knowledge (SPARK) movement, a growing coalition of partners and thought leaders united in their determination to challenge the sexualization of girls and work collectively to demand girls' rights to embodiment and healthy sexuality.

Bonnie Bryant earned her BA in Human Services at Lesley University.

Kellie Burns is a lecturer in the Faculty of Education and Social Work at The University of Sydney, Australia. Her doctoral thesis is entitled *Blood, Sweat and Queers: (Re)Imagining Global Queer Citizenship* at the Sydney 2002 Gay Games. Her current work focuses on the relationships between discourses of health, sexuality, gender, and citizenship. Her work is published in journals and edited collections, most recently in *Discourse: The Cultural Politics of Education, The Journal of Lesbian Studies,* and *Sexualities.*

Linda Charmaraman is a research scientist at the Wellesley Centers for Women at Wellesley College, the National Institute on Out of School Time, and a former National Institute of Health Child Health and Human Development (NICHD) postdoctoral scholar. Her research interests include youth media, adolescent sexuality and identity development, and positive urban youth development. Her dissertation focused on how youth media production increases agency, sense of community, and activism. Linda has conducted evaluation research for Planned Parenthood's *Get Real* sex education curriculum and has published articles regarding early adolescent sexuality in *Journal of Adolescent Health* and *Sexuality Research and Social Policy.* She has also conducted CDC-funded research pertaining to middle school bullying and sexual violence collaborating with the University of Illinois, Urbana–Champaign. She recently partnered with *Teen Voices* on a multi-media strategy to promote public awareness of the educational road for girls of color. She received her Ph.D. in Human Development and Education from University of California, Berkeley.

Cristyn Davies is a Research Associate at The University of Sydney. Her areas of expertise include gendered and sexual subjectivities and citizenship; constructions of childhood and youth; sex education, health, and wellbeing; neoliberalism and governmentality; cultural policy and law; regulation and moral panic; innovative pedagogies and educational practice; and narrative and (heritage and new) media. She has collaborated with academics, writers, performance artists, and digital and new media artists on a range of projects. Cristyn's research is published in *Sexualities, Cultural Studies, Cultural Studies Review, The Journal of Lesbian Studies,* and *Sexuality and Culture,* amongst other journals. She has co-edited several special editions of journals, and the following books: *Rethinking School Violence: Theory, Gender and Context* (2012), and *Queer and Subjugated Knowledges: Generating Subversive Imaginaries* (2012).

Alice Diamond, M.S., is the Associate Dean for Career and Community Service at Lesley University.

Catherine Driscoll is Associate Professor of Gender and Cultural Studies at the University of Sydney. Her research focuses on youth and girls studies, media and popular culture, rural cultural studies, and cultural theory. Her books include *Girls: Feminine Adolescence in Popular Culture and Cultural Theory* (Columbia, 2002), *Modernist Cultural Studies* (Florida, 2009/2012), *Teen Film: A Critical Introduction* (Berg, 2010), and *The Australian Country Girl: Image, History, Experience* (Ashgate, 2013). She has also published many essays and articles. Her current research includes a multidisciplinary team project on cultural sustainability in Australian country towns (funded by the Australian Research Council) and a new project on classification systems. She is also a founding member of the International Girls Studies Association.

Elena Frank is a doctoral candidate in Gender Studies at Arizona State University. Her research interests include gender, sexual subjectivity, agency, pleasure, health, and embodiment. Her dissertation work examines the silence around women and masturbation (and its disruptions) and the way(s) that female masturbation has been given individual and social meaning in order to develop an understanding of the way(s) that gender, power, and pleasure converge to influence women's lives.

Isaac Gagné is a Ph.D. candidate in cultural anthropology at Yale University. His research covers issues of morality, ethics, religion, and youth culture in contemporary Japan. He is the author of "Urban Princesses: Performance and 'Women's Language' in Japan's Gothic/Lolita Subculture" in *Journal of Linguistic Anthropology* 18(1), 2008. He has also written on new religions, social networks, and the transformations of family in Japan.

Kate Harper earned her Ph.D. in Gender Studies at Arizona State University. She has published work in *The Girlhood Studies Journal* on the contradictory messages of female adolescence in the *Nancy Drew* mystery series, and her dissertation explores the discursive construction of the ideal girl and her non-ideal counterparts in popular girls' series through the twentieth century. More broadly, her research interests include histories of girlhood and intersecting representations of sexuality, race, and class in literature and popular culture.

Jennifer Helgren is assistant professor of history at the University of the Pacific in Stockton California where she has taught since 2006. She edited *Girlhood: A Global History* (Rutgers, 2010) with Colleen Vasconcellos and is the author of several articles on U.S. girls' cultures. Helgren earned her doctorate in U.S. and women's history at Claremont Graduate University. She is currently research-ing internationalism and youth culture following World War II.

Jillian Hernandez is a Ph.D. candidate in the Women's and Gender Studies department at Rutgers University and an independent curator. Her research interests include contemporary art, new media, sexualities, and girls' studies. She is currently conducting dissertation research on girls' embodiment and sexuality in Miami, where she directs the Women on the Rise! art outreach program for teenage girls at the Museum of Contemporary Art. Her work has been pub-lished in peer reviewed and edited publications and she has presented research at conferences organized by the College Art Association, Cultural Studies Asso-ciation, and National Women's Studies Association, among others.

Alvaro Jarrin is currently a visiting assistant professor at Union College, New York. He received his B.A. from Williams College in 2003 and his Ph.D. in Cultural Anthropology from Duke University in 2010. Alvaro has received gen-erous support from several institutions in order to advance his research and complete his dissertation, including but not limited to the Wenner-Gren Foun-dation, the Program in Women's Studies at Duke University and the Mellon/ACLS Early Career Fellowship Program. His research focuses on the biopolitics of beauty, the development of new biotechnologies, and the imbrica-tions of gender, racial, and class difference in Brazil.

Yasmina Katsulis, Ph.D. graduated with a degree in Anthropology from Yale University in 2003, and is currently an Associate Professor of Women and Gender Studies at Arizona State University. A former NIMH Postdoctoral Fel-low with the Center for Interdisciplinary Research on AIDS, Dr. Katsulis spe-cializes in gender, sexuality, and health. Her first book, *Sex Work and the City: The Social Geography of Health and Safety in Tijuana, Mexico*, is the first major ethno-graphic publication on contemporary prostitution in Tijuana, providing a de-tailed analysis of how work settings shape occupational health outcomes, including violence, drug use, mental health, and sexually transmitted infections. Her current research focuses on gender, parenting, housing security, and home-lessness. Dr. Katsulis has received funding from the National Science Founda-tion and the National Institutes of Health.

Michael Kimmel is Distinguished Professor of Sociology at SUNY Stony Brook. Among his books are *The Gendered Society*, *Manhood in America*, and *Guy-land*.

Marie LaFlamme holds an M.A. in School Counseling from Lesley University.

Vera Lopez is an Associate Professor in Justice & Social Inquiry at Arizona State University. She received her Ph.D. in Educational Psychology from the University of Texas at Austin. She completed a one-year clinical internship at the Institute for Juvenile Research at the University of Illinois–Chicago and a two-year NIMH-funded post-doctoral research fellowship at ASU's Prevention Research Center. Dr. Lopez's interests include adolescent girls' delinquency, substance use, sexual risk taking, and prevention research. She recently completed an NIMH-funded pilot study on HIV and substance prevention needs among high-risk Latina adolescents. Dr. Lopez has published in a number of outlets including *Journal of Family Issues, Journal of Youth and Adolescence, Violence Against Women, Family Relations, Feminist Criminology, Criminal Justice & Behavior,* and *Journal of Early Adolescence.*

Brittany Low graduated from Wellesley College in 2010 with a bachelor's in Women's and Gender Studies. During college, she worked as an intern at *Teen Voices*, where she collaborated with staff to plan and execute a summer youth program and mentored a group of teenage girls as they wrote an article on sex trafficking published in *Teen Voices* magazine. Also, in her senior year, she began working as a research assistant for Linda Charmaraman at the Wellesley Centers for Women. Currently, she is a Data Analyst at a media research firm based in Boston, Massachusetts.

Amanda Rossie is a Ph.D. candidate and Distinguished University Fellow in the Department of Women's, Gender, & Sexuality Studies at The Ohio State University. Her dissertation project argues that the production of hegemonic femininities in U.S. popular culture has become explicitly linked to the maternal in and through a new and increasing range of technologized practices across genre and medium. Her other research interests include representations of girlhood in American culture, popular culture digital media studies, and the intersections of neoliberalism and postfeminism. She has an M.A. in Journalism from the University of Southern California (2009) and a B.A. in English from Presbyterian College (2007).

Amy Rutstein-Riley, Ph.D., M.P.H., is a Sociologist at Lesley University in Cambridge Massachusetts. She holds a joint appointment in the College of Liberal Arts & Professional Studies and the Graduate School of Education where she directs the Adult Learning & Development Specialization in the Ph.D. Program in Educational Studies. Amy teaches courses in medical sociology, women's studies, girls' studies, family studies, and adult learning and development. She is the principle investigator of Girlhood, Identity, and Girl Culture and has received the American Association of University Women's Community Action Grant (2-years) and a grant from the Reebok Foundation to fund the project and research activities. Amy serves as co-chair of the Lesley University Women's Studies Steering Committee and co-directs the Women's Center. Amy recently completed a two-year appointment as a Visiting Scholar in the Women's Studies Research Center at Brandeis University where she conducted research on emerging adult women's health.

Georganne Scheiner Gillis is Faculty Head for the Women and Gender Studies Program at Arizona State University. Her research interests include girlhood and adolescence, and women in popular culture. She is the author of *Signifying Female Adolescence: Film Representations and Fans 1920–1950* (Praeger, 2000). She has also published articles on such topics as Sandra Dee, fan clubs, and the 1950s TV show, *Queen for a Day*. Scheiner Gillis is currently at work on a book-length manuscript, *Haven for Hopefuls: The Hollywood Studio Club and Women in the Film Industry*.

Deborah L. Tolman is Professor of Social Welfare and Psychology at the Hunter College School of Social Work and the Graduate Center, CUNY. She has been doing research on girls' sexuality and gender ideologies for twenty years. She founded and directed the Center for Research on Gender and Sexuality at San Francisco State University and of the ASAP Initiative at Hunter/CUNY, which analyzes sexuality for action and policy. An author of the American Psychological Association's *Task Force on the Sexualization of Girls*, she is also a co-founder of SPARK, a movement to challenge the sexualization of girls.

Jenn Walker earned her Masters in Applied Sociology at University of Massachusetts, Boston.

Suzan Walters is currently pursuing a Ph.D. in Sociology at SUNY—Stony Brook. Her research interests include gender, sexuality, and inequality.

Index

A

abortion, 110, 114–115, 118, 124, 127-128, 131–132
abstinence, 115, 129–130
activism, 49
  linked with research, 235–236
adolescence, 32, 144, 158, 160
  changing conceptions of, 32–33, 100, 164, 205
  definitions of, 97
advertising, 114, 143–145, 148, 180, 198
aestheticization, 157–159, 166
agency
  conditional, 115, 125, 132
  exercise of, 132, 133, 142, 145, 199
  sexual, 70, 87, 90, 102, 113, 123, 124–126, 142, 189, 190, 221
Alexander, Ruth M., 18, 73
alternative media, 139, 147–148, 193, 246–247, 252
  created by youth, 246
  zines, blogs, 247
"altporn", 7
Andy Hardy, 11–12, 29
anime; *manga,* 157–159
APA Task Force on the Sexualization of Girls, 5–6, 228, 245, 267
Apple, Jennifer, 14, 16, 211, 285

appropriation, 158
aristocratic, 78, 85, 160
attraction, 86, 87, 167, 211–212, 218–220
Attwood, Feona, 6, 7, 135
audience, 31, 39, 64, 114, 177, 183, 195, 196, 214–215, 217, 219, 221
authenticity, 125, 182, 218–221
autonomy, 32, 129–130, 164

B

Bae, Michelle, 3, 20
Bailey, Beth, 20, 32, 57
Bazalgette, Cary, 8
belonging, 160
birth control pill, 127–129, 131, 133
bisexuality
  see also homosexuality, queer, sexuality
bodies, 50, 80, 117, 118, 131–133, 140–143
  body image, 176, 266, 274
  body mapping, 275
  disorderly bodies, 71, 111, 140, 188–191, 196, 202
Bowman, Christine, 17, 227, 285
boys, 62–63, 78, 104, 143–144, 205
  girls' relationships with, 130, 272
  representations of, 35–38, 68
Brazil, 14–15, 173

beauty pageants in, 15, 173
"Favela" models, 15, 173
standards of beauty in, 15, 173
Brown, Lyn Mikel, 17, 208, 227, 285
Bryant, Bonnie, 263, 285
Burns, Kellie, 11, 14, 139, 286
Butler, Judith, 19, 97, 150, 162, 188

C

Camp Fire Girls, 12, 45, 47, 53
capitalism, 117, 175
Charmaraman, Linda, 17, 245, 286
Chongas, 16, 187
Christianity, 110, 119, 129
church, 88, 110, 130
cinema (*see* film)
citizenship, 93, 111, 140–142, 149, 174,
176, 189
cosmetic citizenship, 180–181
fetal citizenship, 114, 117–118
Civil Rights Movement, 47, 49–50
class (*see* socio-economic status)
upward mobility, 47, 181–183
working class, 124, 176, 181–183,
191, 200
collective investment, 181
Collins, Patricia Hill, 20
commodification, 158, 198
compulsory heterosexuality, 212–213, 217,
222
condoms, 129, 147
consumerism, 3, 6, 64, 89, 139–142, 147–
149
consumption, 100, 125, 159–160, 182, 202
contraception (*see* condoms, birth control
pill), 115, 120, 139
cultural capital, 160

D

dating, 29–30, 32–33, 99, 163
interracial, 47, 49, 66
patterns in *Harry Potter*, 66, 68
"rating and dating" system, 33, 36, 38
violence, 111, 113, 276

Davies, Cristyn, 11, 14, 139, 286
Deleuze and Guattari, 103
delinquency, 34, 46, 95
depoliticization, 176, 212
desire, 29–30, 35, 62–63, 79, 81–81, 100,
125, 133, 142, 143, 213, 215–217
deviance, 116, 164, 165
Diamond, Alice, 263, 286
Diamond, Lisa, 215
discipline; disciplining the body, 133, 176,
183, 189
discourse, 46, 49, 64, 72, 103, 111, 114,
125, 127, 139, 157, 187, 190, 198–
200
Disney princesses, 7
dominant femininity, 46–47
Doring, Nicola, 8
Douglas, Susan, 18
Dracula, 78, 89
Driscoll, Catherine, xi, 93, 150, 167, 287
Durbin, Deanna, 30
Durham, M. Gigi, 19

E

education (*see* sexual education), 100, 104,
113, 145, 160, 176, 202
Egan, R. Danielle, 5, 21
Eklund, Lina, 8
embodiment, 79, 133, 158, 161, 175, 189,
194–197, 204–205, 212
disembodiment, 113–114
emulation, 158
emphasized femininity
appropriate, 35, 71, 72, 176
cuteness, 89, 162
good girls, 46, 99, 143, 176–179, 206
hyperfemininity, 157, 161–164, 189
intellectual, 71
modesty, 79, 157, 177
passive, 71, 133
purity, 79, 157, 176
respect, respectability, 47, 50, 88, 89,
99, 162–163, 179

whiteness, 79, 116–118, 176, 179, 180
ladylike, 159, 161–163
morality, 111, 148, 165, 177
virtue, 47, 79, 99, 173, 177
empowerment, 2, 8–9, 124–125, 139, 142, 206
ethnicity (*see* girlhood, girls, identity, race)
ethnography, 176, 205
ethnographic content analysis, 249

F
fashion, 80–81, 158–168, 174, 176, 196
Fass, Paula, 18, 46
female empowerment, 120
critique of, 125, 139, 142, 206, 237
femininity (*see* dominant femininity, emphasized femininity, neoliberal femininity, transgressive femininity
feminism, 147, 194–195, 212–213
feminist group process, 268
feminist pedagogy, 268
see also postfeminism
femme fatale, 36
Fields, Jessica, 135
film
adolescent, 29, 93, 213, 215
American Pie, 99, 103
The Bachelor and the Bobby-Soxer, 94, 97
Cruel Intentions, 96, 99
Gidget, 98–99
flapper films, 94
Harry Potter and the Deathly Hallows, 61
Harry Potter and the Goblet of Fire, 74
Harry Potter and the Half-Blood Prince, 62, 65
Harry Potter and the Order of the Phoenix, 70, 74
Juno, 109
Kiss and Tell, 94
Little Darlings, 96–97, 99
Mean Girls, 82
Not Another Teen Movie, 94
Porky's, 99

Saved!, 98
She's All That, 94, 96, 99–100
Sixteen Candles, 100–101
Twilight, 13, 77
Where the Boys Are, 99
The Plastic Age, 94, 99
The Wild Party, 94
Wild Things, 215–216
Fine, Michelle, 19, 134, 135
Forman-Brunell, Miriam, 18, 46
Foucault, Michel, 98, 103, 136, 149, 169, 206
Frank, Elena, 11, 123, 287
Freedman, Estelle, 20, 33, 46
Freud, Sigmund, 97–98, 166

G
Gagné, Isaac, 14–15, 157, 287
gaze, 74, 90, 94, 181, 215–216, 218
gender
equality, 189
norms/normative, 125, 126, 132, 140, 205
roles, 64, 118, 163, 166, 264–265
socialization, 165, 166
stereotypes, 62, 78, 131, 146, 190, 246, 264–265
Gill, Rosalind, 2, 4, 9, 125–126, 151
Girlhood Project, 263
curriculum—Girlhood, Identity, and Girl Culture, 265, 268
Girl Scouts, 12, 47, 55
girls
and ethnicity, 47, 65, 70, 143, 196, 204–205
and gender, 68, 70
and identity, 62, 72, 97, 125, 142, 145, 190, 200–202, 212, 217
and nationality, 4, 10, 14–15, 174, 188
and race, 4, 7–8, 17, 47, 64–65, 70, 116, 205–206
and religion, 117, 130, 201

and sexuality, 10, 33–34, 110–111, 123, 187, 211–213, 217
and socioeconomic status, 4, 118, 187
material conditions
   in the 1930s, 33–34
   in the 1950s, 47–48
Girls' Studies, 1–2
glamourization, 162
grounded theory, 136, 212

H
Harper, Kate, 11, 12, 61, 287
Harris, Anita, 24, 150
Harry Potter, 12, 61
hegemony/hegemonic, 72, 126, 132
Helgren, Jennifer, 11, 12, 45, 287
Hernandez, Jillian, 14, 16, 187, 288
hetero-feminine, 162
heteroflexibility, 16, 211–222
heteronormativity, 71, 125, 132–134, 143, 147, 196, 272, 273
heterosexual/homosexual binary, 212, 215
heterosexuality, 35, 62, 97–98, 163, 205
   see also sexuality
high school, 31–33, 81–83, 86, 160
Hobbs, Renee, 8, 22
homogeneity, 180
homophobia, 72, 97, 273
homosexuality, 61, 102, 163
   see also girls, lesbian, queer, sexuality
Howe, Cymene, 7
HPV vaccination, 14, 139
Hunter, Jane, 18
hypersexualization, 80, 87, 116, 187, 189–190, 195, 202–203, 206, 245

I
ideal/idealized, 45, 48, 52, 99–100, 143, 158, 176, 178
identity, 158–161, 175, 182
   development, 266
impoverishment, 180
independence, 95

infantalization, 36, 112, 164
Inness, Sherrie, 19
innocence (*see* sexuality), 133, 158, 164
intersectionality, 62, 65, 116, 267, 275
intimacy, 69, 71
Irvine, Janice M., 20

J
Jackson, Sue, 2, 7, 9, 19, 135
Japan, 14, 15, 157
   adolescent girls in, 15, 157
   linguistic practices, 15
   "Lolita" subculture, 15, 157
Jarrin, Alvaro, 14, 15, 173, 288
"just say me", 123, 130–132

K
Katsulis, Yasmina, 1, 288
Kearney, Mary Celeste, 18, 207
Kimmel, Michael, 11, 13, 77, 288
kissing, 34, 36–37, 68, 71, 211, 214–215, 218

L
LaFlemme, Marie, 263, 289
Lamb, Sharon, 2, 3, 19, 208
Latinas (*see* girls, ethnicity, identity), 188–190, 196, 202
Lazar, Michelle M., 125, 135
Lerum, Kari and Dworkin, Shari, 5, 6, 21
lesbian, 96, 97
   see also homosexuality, queer, sexuality
LGBT issues, 61, 124
life cycle, 213
liminality/liminal, 100, 104
Lolita, 158–167
love, 78, 80, 83, 87–88, 177–178
   see also romance
love potions, 66–68, 70–71
Low, Brittany, 17, 245, 289

M
Madonna, 79, 211, 213–215

Magazines, 2, 17, 51, 158, 246–247
  American Magazine, 51
  American Girl, 55
  New York Times, 49, 51
  Parents Magazine, 51, 54
  Teen Voices, 17, 248, 250–252
  Time Magazine, 51
mainstream media, 46–48, 50, 54, 81, 163,
  199, 204, 213
male allies, 230
male-focused, 133, 190, 197, 215–219
manga; anime, 157–159
marriage, 35, 39, 46, 105, 111, 128, 129,
  147, 205
masculinity, 35, 52, 83, 85, 118
  hegemonic, 11, 66, 75
  romantic, 72, 83
  see also gender
masturbation, 127
  female, 129–130, 132–133
  male, 129
May, Elaine Tyler, 46
Mayer, Louis B., 31, 40
Mazzarella, Sharon R., 19, 208
McRobbie, Angela, 151
media activism, 250
  youth driven, 229–230
media dependency theory, 246
media literacy, 8–9, 18, 167, 248
  interventions, 9
  programs, 8, 18, 26
  projects, 17
media reception/use, 6–8, 187
media representation, 29, 124, 139, 157,
  187, 211, 246
  see also film, magazines,
  representations, television
mentoring, 267
Milkie, Melissa, 9, 21
misogynistic messages
moral panic, 4, 6, 61, 62–63, 158, 166, 206
Moran, Jeffrey P., 20

N
Nash, Ilana, 18, 73
national imaginary, 176–180
nationality, 89, 191
  see also ethnicity, girls, identity
Native Americans, 83, 85
Nerve, 7
neoliberal femininity, 143, 147, 149, 163
neoliberal multiculturalism, 194
neoliberalism, 139, 141–144, 189, 194
new media, 6

O
Odem, Mary E., 18, 57, 73
objectification, 47, 70, 87, 89, 125
  objectification theory, 246
  self-objectification, 235, 245

P
parental supervision, 32–33, 56, 100, 101,
  128, 129
Pascoe, C.J., 6, 21, 207
Pecora, Norma, 19
performance, 125, 132–133, 158–159, 174,
  183, 192, 194–199, 204–205, 211,
  213–217, 221
periphery, 180, 182
physical thin ideal, 245
pleasure, 77, 125, 129–133, 199, 211, 217–
  218, 221
policing, 188–189, 204
pornification, 4
pornography, 7, 86, 125, 190
postfeminism, 125, 126
power, 65, 83, 96, 124, 126, 129, 132, 140–
  143, 178, 197, 221
pregnancy, pregnant, 46, 109, 111–118,
  124, 127–129, 131, 175
princess, 158, 161, 163, 166, 211, 213–215
procreation, 129, 133
prostitution, 102, 176
public vs. private, 48–49, 95, 109, 115–116,
  130, 132, 166, 218–221

Q

queer

 see also homosexuality, lesbian,
 sexuality

queer film, 97–98

queer politics, 188, 197, 206

R

race (*see* girls, identity)

racial violence, 45, 46–47, 51

rebellion, 100, 165

reification, 212–213, 222

religion (*see also* Christianity, church), 64,
 130, 178, 201

representations, 1–2, 4, 6, 11, 189–190

 class stereotypes, 66, 117, 183, 205

 gender role stereotypes, 66, 78, 146

 popular media, 157–159, 163

 racial stereotypes, 66, 111, 116, 117

 sexual health and behavior, 123

reproductive choice, 111, 113–115, 117,
 118, 131

rescue, 175, 179, 206

resistance; resisters, 55, 72, 165, 191, 205

right to choose, 115, 128, 131

Roberts, Dorothy, 20

role model, 31, 82

romance, 70, 205

 see also love

Rossie, Amanda, 11, 13, 109, 289

Rowling, J.K., 61

Rutstein-Riley, Amy, 18, 263, 289

S

Scheiner Gillis, Georganne, 1, 11–12, 29,
 290

Schrum, Kelly, 18, 31

Secret Life of the American Teenager, 14, 123

Seitz, George, 30

self-concept, 54, 83, 194

self-confidence, 203

self-objectification (*see* objectification)

self-realization, 157, 175, 197

self-regulation, 110, 126, 139, 142

service learning, 268

sex

 as a rite of passage, 95

 partner, 144

 safe sex, 124, 129, 132

sexual consent, 93, 102, 124

sex crimes, 12, 46

 pathologizing victims and
 perpetrators, 46, 48

 stranger danger, 51–52

 vulnerability, 45, 176

sexual desire, 3, 12, 13, 63–64, 98, 110, 125,
 132–133, 142–143, 213, 216

 missing discourse of, 63

sexual double standard, 41, 130, 132

sexual education, 104, 110, 125, 132–133,
 144

 abstinence only until marriage, 111,
 113

sexual empowerment, 123, 125

sexual experimentation, 205, 218–219

sexual harassment, 183

sexual health, 14, 124–125, 132, 142–148

sexual fluidity, 213

sexual orientation, 265, 272–273

sexual pleasure, 3, 5, 16, 118

 girls' entitlement to, 123, 131

sexual risk, 133, 142–149

 prevention, 142–149

sexual scripts, 213, 218, 220, 222, 267

 representations of, 72

sexual subjectivity, 2, 3, 125, 133, 222

sexuality, 271

 as citizenship, 93, 95, 102

 dangerous, 46, 78, 164, 189,

 female, 110, 111, 123

 healthy, 231, 123, 143

sexualization, 3–6, 8, 78, 246, 252

 challenging, 231, 256

 desexualization, 77, 80, 83

 discourses of, 4, 30

 effects on girls, 62–63, 235

 grassroots efforts to combat, 230,
 233, 240

media activism, 228, 232, 237–238
    raising awareness of, 228
    social movements against, 228
sexualized images, 80
sexually transmitted infections (STI) 115,
    144, 147, 148
"smart smut", 7
snogging, 68–69, 71
    see also kissing
social inclusion/social currency, 36, 117,
    134, 176, 179, 183
social media, 232, 237–238
    see also media, representations
socio-economic status, 47–48, 51–52, 159–
    160, 166, 189–191, 196, 200–203
    see also girls, identity
SPARK, 17
    history, 228
    motivation, 234
    research blog, 236, 237–239
    SPARKits, 240
spectacle, 196–198, 213–215, 220, 222
Stokes, Carla, 7–8
Strauss, Anselm and Julie Corbin, 73, 114
subculture; subcultural, 116, 157–161, 166
suburbia, 47–48
subversive readings, 69, 72, 212, 217
Suicide Girls, 7
surveillance, 55, 126

T

teen magazines (*see* magazines)
teen pregnancy (*see* pregnancy)
television, 124, 126, 144–146, 179–181,
    187, 195, 211, 216
    16 and Pregnant, 13, 109
Tolman, Deborah, 3, 17, 125, 227, 290
transgressive femininity
    bad girls, 34, 164, 190, 201
    excess, excessive, 69, 183, 188, 189,
    196, 202
    ghetto (e.g., ghetto fabulous), 193,
        199, 203, 204
    hedonistic, 110, 157, 204
    hyperethnic, hyperethnicity, 196, 202

hypersexual, hypersexuality, 70, 87,
    116, 132, 176, 187–190, 195,
    206
sexual-aesthetic excess, 188, 189, 192,
    198, 203, 205
unsophisticated, 183, 202, 203
vulgar, 161, 166, 183, 196
"white trash," 117

V

virginity, 78–79, 88–89, 95, 178
    loss of, 96, 124, 133

W

Walker, Jenn, 263, 290
Walters, Suzan, 11, 13, 77, 290
"We're taking sexy back," 231
Westrup, Elizabeth, 2, 7, 135
whiteness, 176, 179–180, 194–196
    see also ethnicity, girls, identity, race
Wilson, Cary, 30
Wolhwend, Karen, 7
    "productive consumption," 7
Wouters, Cas, 3, 20

mediated youth

Sharon R. Mazzarella
General Editor

Grounded in cultural studies, books in this series will study the cultures, artifacts, and media of children, tweens, teens, and college-aged youth. Whether studying television, popular music, fashion, sports, toys, the Internet, self-publishing, leisure, clubs, school, cultures/activities, film, dance, language, tie-in merchandising, concerts, subcultures, or other forms of popular culture, books in this series go beyond the dominant paradigm of traditional scholarship on the effects of media/culture on youth. Instead, authors endeavor to understand the complex relationship between youth and popular culture. Relevant studies would include, but are not limited to studies of how youth negotiate their way through the maze of corporately-produced mass culture; how they themselves have become cultural producers; how youth create "safe spaces" for themselves within the broader culture; the political economy of youth culture industries; the representational politics inherent in mediated coverage and portrayals of youth; and so on. Books that provide a forum for the "voices" of the young are particularly encouraged. The source of such voices can range from in-depth interviews and other ethnographic studies to textual analyses of cultural artifacts created by youth.

For further information about the series and submitting manuscripts, please contact:

SHARON R. MAZZARELLA
School of Communication Studies
James Madison University
Harrisonburg, VA 22807

To order other books in this series, please contact our Customer Service Department at:

(800) 770-LANG (within the U.S.)
(212) 647-7706 (outside the U.S.)
(212) 647-7707 FAX

Or browse online by series at WWW.PETERLANG.COM